# Dreams Deferred

A Concise Guide to the Israeli–Palestinian
Conflict & the Movement to Boycott Israel

Cary Nelson

Copublished by

MLA MEMBERS
for SCHOLARS' RIGHTS

&

INDIANA UNIVERSITY PRESS

This book is a copublication of

MLA Members for Scholars' Rights
Chicago and New York

and

Indiana University Press
Office of Scholarly Publishing
Herman B Wells Library 350
1320 East 10th Street
Bloomington, Indiana 47405 USA

iupress.indiana.edu

Manufactured in the United States of America

Library of Congress Control Number: 2016939560

ISBN 978-0-253-02516-6 (cloth)
ISBN 978-0-253-02517-3 (pbk.)
ISBN 978-0-253-02518-0 (ebk.)

1 2 3 4 5 21 20 19 18 17 16

# ADVANCED PRAISE FOR
## *DREAMS DEFERRED*

*Dreams Deferred arrives as debates about the future of the Middle East and the Israeli-Palestinian conflict intensify under the extraordinary pressure of a region in chaos. The book empowers readers to be informed participants in conversations and debates about developments that increasingly touch all of our lives. Its sixty concise but detailed essays give facts and arguments to assist all who seek justice for both Israelis and Palestinians and who believe the two-state solution can yet be realized. Inspired both by the vision of a democratic Jewish state and by the need for Palestinian political self-determination, the book addresses the long history of the Israeli-Palestinian conflict and its current status. It demonstrates that the division and suspicion promoted by the Boycott, Sanctions, and Divestment (BDS) movement will only undermine the cause of peace.*

---

"For all of us who hope for a decent peace between Israelis and Palestinians, who oppose the occupation and the BDS movement, who defend, against all odds, the two state solution, this book is powerful intellectual armor and an intellectual sword."
   —**MICHAEL WALZER**, Institute for Advanced Study,
      author of *Just and Unjust Wars, Thinking Politically, The Paradox of Liberation*, and other books

"This book is aptly titled, particularly for Americans, who have our own continuing struggle with the unmet dreams and hopes of people in this land. The overwhelming temptation of parties outside the conflict in the Holy Land—i.e., those who do not live and move and have their being on that soil—is to take sides, judging one more or less just than another. The result is often exported and proxy conflict (in the US and elsewhere). The shalom and salaam that we call a just peace will come only when the parties involved sit down together to eat and share their deferred dreams. Proxies cannot do that vulnerable work of suffering, forgiveness, and growth. There are signs of hope in that work, but it is too often overshadowed by those who engage for their own, often unwitting, ends, rather than the good of all."
   —**BISHOP KATHARINE JEFFERTS SCHORI**, 2006-2015
      Presiding Bishop of the Episcopal Church of the United States

"A rare blast of cogent analysis, reliable information, and just good sense about an issue desperately in need of all three."
   —**ERIC ALTERMAN**, CUNY Distinguished Professor of English and Journalism, Brooklyn College; Media Columnist, *The Nation*

"This critical dictionary of anti-Israeli mendacities will be a sword in the hands of anybody who wants to cut through the dogmas and the intimidations of the BDS movement. It restores the disputation to first principles and first facts. It documents a foul intellectual bankruptcy. Slanders are refuted and clichés are shattered on its every page. *Dreams Deferred* is an important intervention in an important battle of ideas. I hope it finds many readers, especially on campus. Israel is not perfect, but enough is enough."
   —LEON WIESELTIER

"Attempts to boycott the State of Israel and its academic institutions, in particular, have taken place since the establishment of the State, that is to say—for 68 years. Monitoring and understanding this phenomenon is a difficult task for both policy makers and researchers. *Dreams Deferred: A Concise Guide to the Israeli-Palestinian Conflict and the Movement to Boycott Israel* diligently provides a thorough analysis of boycotts, their origins, and their various parallel manifestations alongside a historical reckoning of the social and economic periods in which they took place. Cary Nelson is the foremost researcher on the boycott phenomenon, and his work is mandatory reading for those who want to understand and draw conclusions about the boycott movement from both a scholarly and practical viewpoint."
   —MENAHEM BEN-SASSON, President,
      Hebrew University of Jerusalem

"In the miasma of the campus campaigns to boycott Israel and to reinvent the Israeli-Palestinian conflict, *Dreams Deferred* offers the reader powerful, timely, and lucid accounts of the debates and controversies, providing essential information, provocative analysis, and an accessible guide."
   —MARK YUDOF, 2008-2013 president of the
      University of California

"*Dreams Deferred* illuminates our contemporary conflict-ridden moment through its mixture of cogent analysis, careful history, and thoughtful discussion. Its accounts of the tangled relationships of Israeli Jews and Palestinian Arabs and its lucid explication of the Boycott, Divestment and Sanctions movement make it an invaluable resource for anyone seeking to understand the current crises on campus."
   —DEBORAH DASH MOORE, University of Michigan

# CONTENTS

# INTRODUCTION

What happens to a dream deferred?
        Does it dry up
        like a raisin in the sun?
        Or fester like a sore—
        And then run? . . .
        *Or does it explode?*

The epigraph above is taken from Langston Hughes' 1951 book-length poem sequence *Montage of a Dream Deferred* and to its oft-quoted poem "Harlem." With Hughes' characteristic directness and concision he opens "Harlem" with a question—"What happens to a dream deferred?"—and he answers it with a rejoinder in the form of a series of follow-up questions. To adapt Hughes' phrase and his dream of equality for the title of this book, I have made the noun plural—"Dreams"—to evoke the politically, culturally, and geographically intertwined dreams of two peoples in Palestine. While Jews worldwide saw their long-deferred dream for the renewal of their ancient homeland realized in 1948, their dream of living there in peace remains deferred still. And the failure so far to make the two-state solution a reality means that the Palestinian people simultaneously suffer the deferral of their dream of political self-determination. The use of Hughes' lines for the title of this book reflects my quarter century of archival research and scholarly writing about Hughes, but it also alludes to a subject outside the reach of this book—the possibility that poetry is especially effective in capturing both peoples' aspirations.

After several years of intensified international debate and political struggle over the Israeli-Palestinian conflict and the Boycott, Divestment, and Sanctions (BDS) campaign, there is need for a concise, accessible guide to the key terms and issues at stake. MLA Members for Scholars' Rights has published a substantial volume of essays—*The Case Against Academic Boycotts of Israel* (2015), which I coedited with Gabriel Noah Brahm—that has been widely reviewed (http://www.cary-nelson.org/nelson/Boycotts/against-boycott-reviews.html) and which is helping to educate and empower thousands of readers. But reading 550 pages of long scholarly essays requires a level of commitment that not everyone is ready to make. Moreover, even those who have read the book need a quick reference with reasonably concise entries that they can use to master the fundamentals of a subject and draw on and share in both campus and community discussions and debates. *Dreams Deferred* is intended to be that book.

To maximize the book's usefulness, I alphabetize the list of entries. But I am not seeking the kind of neutrality expected from an encyclopedia. *Dreams Deferred* aims to present basic definitions and substantial factual information objectively, but it also embraces commentary and critical analysis. Rather than aiming for a colorless encyclopedic style, contributors write in their own voices. The book's contributors are unequivocally opposed to the effort to boycott and eliminate the state of Israel, and it supports a two-state solution to the Israeli-Palestinian conflict. After years without serious negotiations toward a solution to the conflict, some who support Israel's existence have been drawn to limited boycott campaigns to express their frustration, but such projects are unlikely to have any meaningful effect on the policies of the parties involved. More productive strategies need to be proposed and pursued. Even if a comprehensive solution is unachievable in the near term, there are steps toward a two-state solution and steps to improve the lives of Palestinians and defuse tensions that can be taken now. Appropriate actions on both sides could reduce the violence that both peoples routinely face.

Some efforts to mount limited boycotts or divestment campaigns, such as those in mainline Protestant churches, try to distance themselves from actual opposition to Israel's existence, but they are typically publicized by and absorbed within the international Boycott, Sanctions, and Divestment (BDS) movement's more aggressive agenda whether or not advocates wish that to happen. All of the BDS movement's nationally prominent spokespersons make it clear they believe Israel has no legitimacy as a state and no right to exist. As BDS founder Omar Barghouti has argued, "accepting Israel as a 'Jewish state' on our land is impossible" (Cattori). California State University political scientist As'ad AbuKhalil, among many other BDS leaders, echoes those sentiments: "Justice and freedom for the Palestinians are incompatible with the existence of the state of Israel." In *The Battle for Justice in Palestine* Ali Abunimah, the Chicago-based cofounder of *The Electronic Intifada*, confidently concludes that "Israel's 'right to exist as a Jewish state' is one with no proper legal or moral remedy and one whose enforcement necessitates perpetuating terrible wrongs. Therefore it is no right at all" (44). Bay Area BDS activist Laura Kiswani, executive director of the Arab Resource and Organizing Center, offered a still more hyperbolic plea at a November 2014 Berkeley panel: "Bringing down Israel will really benefit everyone in the world and everyone in society, particularly workers." As I detail in an extended essay on her work, Berkeley literary theorist Judith Butler aims to have Israelis abandon their commitment to a Jewish state and a homeland of their own. In 2010 Palestinian-American activist and author Ahmed Moor wrote that BDS has one ultimate aim: "Ending the occupation doesn't mean anything if it doesn't mean upending the Jewish state itself" (Moor). Although the rhetoric employed in each of these examples varies, the end result, as Barghouti has put it, is the same: "euthanasia" for the Jewish state. This book considers this position to be fundamentally mistaken and in need of rebuttal.

That said, *Dreams Deferred* does not aim for political conformity. There are many areas over which the authors of these mini-essays do not agree, and the spectrum of opinion here ranges from right of center to left of center. The intent is both to detail the factual situation where it can be adjudicated and to put forward a number of arguments about it. The entries aim for concision, substance, and opportunities for debate.

The individual entries in *Dreams Deferred* are designed to stand alone and thus to satisfy the need for easy access to basic information. At the same time, the cross-references at the end of each entry identify related topics. People can thus, for example, read a cluster of entries about the BDS movement or about Zionism to gain a further level of knowledge. Many of these topics could then be researched online and in books and essays at still greater length; the aim is to help readers master the fundamentals of each topic and to empower them in debate and discussion about this most vexed of contemporary subjects. The list of sources guides those who wish to read more widely still. The essays avoid duplication except when it seems clearly necessary. In compensation, major discussions of a topic are listed in **boldface** in the index, so readers can quickly access a more thorough discussion of a subject mentioned only briefly in a given essay.

The book also encourages people to rethink the nature of the language and concepts that shape understanding of the conflict. Though many of the topics listed in the table of contents are straightforward, others are not. An entry on "The Yom Kippur War" or "Iron Dome" offers largely self-evident subject matter, but some will have to read the entry on "Holocaust Inversion" to find out what it refers to and has to offer. The section on "The Vindictive One-State Movement," which is part of the One-State Solution entry, qualifies a standard subject with a modifier, "vindictive," that identifies an aggressive motivation behind some one-state advocacy. "Teaching Arabs and Jews in Israel" is a title that runs counter to much anti-Israel bias, but many readers will also be able to anticipate the entry's feminist content.

Although most of the book is new, its deliberately unconventional set of topics would not have been imaginable without the resource of *The Case Against Academic Boycotts of Israel* and the other publications excerpted from and adapted to create these pieces. I have been able to use full-length essays in that book and elsewhere as the basis for passages here that highlight key issues and give fresh approaches to and insights into this long-running crisis. Other entries, including those I solicited or wrote, are altogether new to this publication. And many entries have both new and excerpted material. Some adapt passages from only one earlier book or essay, whereas others combine material from several sources and thus effectively create a new essay with multiple authors. In no case, however, does the book aim to produce condensed versions of earlier essays in their entirety. When the credits say "adapted from" an earlier essay that means the language from the earlier piece may be revised and updated to incorporate recent events. My role has encompassed that of author, coauthor, and editor.

*Dreams Deferred* does not, however, provide separate entries on countries in the region or on the key governmental and nongovernmental actors; a preliminary list made it clear that would require an entire additional book. Throughout the book, in cases where authors have intellectual or political reasons for using a particular spelling, as with anti-Semitism versus antisemitism, I have not imposed a single style.

Even the two books described here, however, do not meet all the needs generated by this war conducted by other means in communities throughout the world. We have thus also created a website to accommodate a third set of materials: action fliers and Q&As to distribute during debates and discussions, packets of readings enabling people to pursue some topics at length, a large international library of syllabi representing courses on Jewish and Israeli history and culture and on the Israeli-Palestinian conflict. The URL is www.israelandtheacademy.org.

The list of sources at the end of the book includes the key books and essays consulted for all the entries. The entries themselves provide short internal references for direct quotations; if there is only one book or essay listed for a given author, then the reference will include only the author's name and a page number, as in "(Shapira 96)." In cases where the internal reference is to a title only, as with "Boycott of Jewish Businesses," the full source citation will be alphabetized under that title. The list of sources also gives full bibliographic details for previously published essays excerpted here.

Readers should also consult the index, both for additional coverage of topics given their own entries and for coverage of topics not listed in the table of contents. A good example of the latter is 2014's Operation Protective Edge, a particularly relevant piece of recent history because there is no guarantee it is the last conflict to be set in Gaza. There is no separate entry for Operation Protective Edge because, as the index reveals, its treatment is divided between three entries: GAZA, HAMAS, and IRON DOME. Similarly, there is no entry for "intersectionality," but the concept is discussed under ACADEMIC BOYCOTTS and FROM FERGUSON TO PALESTINE.

A note about definition: in what follows, "Palestine" refers to the area currently encompassed by Gaza, Israel, and the West Bank.

The four maps that follow the introduction were designed by Migiwa Orino according to my specifications.

Whatever virtues *Deferred Dreams* may have, they have certainly been enhanced by the detailed and thoughtful general or targeted readings the manuscript received. I want particularly to thank Martin Bresler, Max Chamovitz, Peter Eisenstadt, Phillip Ernstmeyer, Ethan Felson, Jay Geller, David Greenberg, Robert Jennings, Amy-Jill Levine, Jeffry Mallow, Jonathan Marks, Sharon Ann Musher, Geri Palast, Nigel Paneth, Martin Raffel, Brent Sasley, Kenneth S. Stern, Paula A. Treichler, Kenneth Waltzer, and Avi Weinryb for their expertise and their dedication to the purposes this book is designed to serve. This does not, of course, mean that all these people agree with everything in the book.

In order to keep the cost of the book low and maximize the potential for wide distribution, neither I nor any of the other writers receive honoraria or royalty payments for our contributions. Finally, I want to thank the Israel Action Network for its support in the publication of this book.

—CN

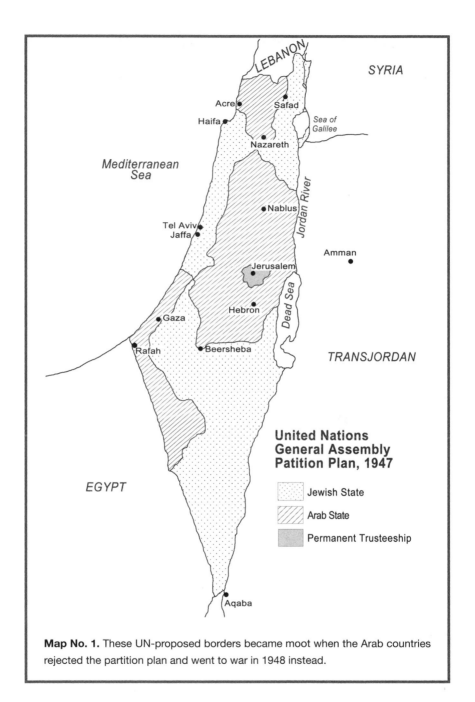

**Map No. 1.** These UN-proposed borders became moot when the Arab countries rejected the partition plan and went to war in 1948 instead.

**Israeli Borders and Armistice Lines, 1949**

- Territory of Israel
- Area under Jordanian Control
- Area under Egyptian Control
- Demilitarized Zone

**Map No. 2.** UN-negotiated armistice agreements were signed separately with Egypt and Jordan in 1949, creating what have been effectively regarded since as Israel's recognized borders.

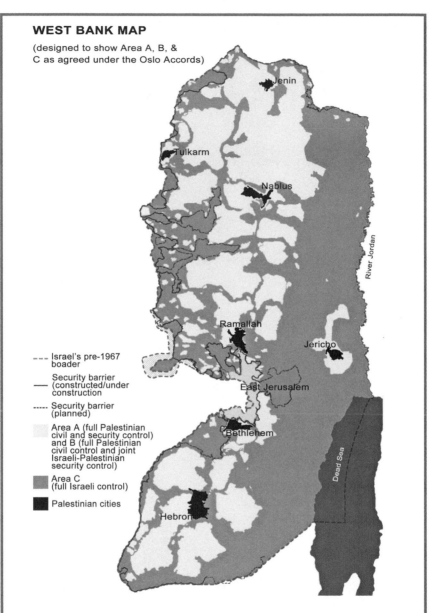

**WEST BANK MAP**

(designed to show Area A, B, & C as agreed under the Oslo Accords)

- - - Israel's pre-1967 boader

—— Security barrier (constructed/under construction

..... Security barrier (planned)

Area A (full Palestinian civil and security control) and B (full Palestinian civil control and joint Israeli-Palestinian security control)

Area C (full Israeli control)

Palestinian cities

**Map No. 3.** Except for Palestinian cities, this map excludes the distinction between Areas A & B as created under the Oslo Accords. It displays the fragmented character of the areas under Palestinian civil control, though there would be further barriers if roads and checkpoints were added.

**WEST BANK MAP**

(designed to show major
settlement blocs and cities only)
Jenin, Tulkarm, Nablus,
Ramallah, Jericho, Bethlehem,
and Hebron are Palestinian
cities. Ariel is an Israeli
settlement/city.

• Jenin

• Tulkarm

• Nablus

Ariel

• Ramallah

• Jericho

Jerusalem

• Bethlehem

• Hebron

**Map No. 4.** Limited to major settlement blocs. A map of this size including 100 additional small Israeli settlements and outposts would be too crowded to be comprehensible. Moreover, such maps are misleading because they crowd out the much larger areas with no settlements. The UN and Peace Now have large-scale maps that give greater detail.

# ACADEMIC BOYCOTTS

Academic boycotts range from calls to sever some or all relationships with a single university to wholesale efforts to boycott all the universities of a given country. Such boycotts may encompass refusing to participate in any and all activities at the target universities; refusing to write letters of recommendation for students seeking to study there; closing down joint degree programs or research projects with the boycotted universities; refusing to provide external evaluations for faculty or student projects at the targeted schools; refusing to publish articles by students and faculty at boycotted schools; blocking boycotted universities from access to resources from disciplinary organizations like announcements of academic positions or fellowship opportunities; removing faculty from editorial boards; and blacklisting and shunning of faculty. Such boycotts interrupt the free flow of ideas and block the pursuit of knowledge, a principle underpinning the very essence of academic freedom; and the argument raised by some that boycotts focused on institutions will not affect individual scholars and students is completely specious. Boycotts generate norms that isolate individual faculty, effectively creating blacklists. Several of BDS's recommendations take advantage of the power dynamic between students and faculty to the detriment of the former.

—CN

RUSSELL BERMAN, ROBERT FINE,
DAVID HIRSH, & CARY NELSON

# INTRODUCTION

There is one and only one country—Israel—that is the target of an international movement to boycott its universities. The movement is opposed by many academic leaders: more than 450 college and university presidents signed a statement opposing academic boycotts in 2007 as a result of an organized drive to gather signatures; more than 250 issued their own anti-boycott statements in 2014, this time spontaneously; and, although a number of academic organizations have endorsed boycotts, every major *multi*disciplinary academic organization that has addressed the issue opposes them as well. Yet faculty members in some humanities and social science disciplines continue to approve them as a political strategy, while those in agriculture, computer science, engineering, medicine, and the sciences show little or no interest in them. Proposals to boycott Israeli universities continue to gain limited faculty support, publicity in the press has grown, and there is a long-term potential for impact on public opinion and national policy (Debra Cohen).

In April 2013, the Association for Asian American Studies became the first US academic disciplinary association to vote for a boycott of Israeli universities and academic institutions. Rendered by a small organization, the decision received relatively little press attention. But in December 2013, 66 percent of the 1,252 members of the American Studies Association who voted (out of a total organizational membership of 5,000) voted as well to boycott Israeli academia, and that decision was widely noted and condemned. That same month the council of the small Native American and Indigenous Studies Association voted unanimously to join the boycott effort. Six months later, in July 2014, two more small academic groups—the African Literature Association and the Critical Ethnic Studies Association—added their names to the roster of boycotters. Yet another association, the National Association for Chicana and Chicano Studies, voted for the boycott of Israeli universities in April 2015. A number of boycott advocates in these groups belong to several academic organizations and have leadership roles in more than one disciplinary boycott effort.

In November 2015 the National Women's Studies Association (NWSA) endorsed a broader boycott resolution condemning not only discrimination but also the "military siege and apartheid imposed by Israel on its own Palestinian citizens" and calling not only for a boycott of Israeli universities but also for the "boycott, divestment and sanctions (BDS) of economic, military, and cultural entities and projects sponsored by the state of Israel." In an effort to connect with the NWSA's core commitments, the group condemned the "sexual and gender-based violence, perpetrated [by Israel] against Palestinians and other Arabs in the West Bank, Gaza Strip, within Israel and in the Golan Heights," thereby not only creating a fictional claim about the only Middle Eastern country with relatively full gender equality, roughly comparable to that of the US except for some cultural practices in conservative religious communities, but also ignoring the real violence against women and repression of women's rights throughout much of the Arab world. Embracing an ahistorical "intersectional" perspective, the NWSA argues that all oppression is "interconnected," but apparently some examples of oppression are more interconnected than others. Over a period of years, NWSA has marginalized itself with its single-minded radical politics; 88.4 percent of those voting endorsed the BDS resolution. Far more serious—both because of the size of the organization and the centrality of the discipline—is the academic boycott resolution overwhelmingly endorsed at the business meeting of the American Anthropological Association. It has gone to the AAA's 10,000 members for an association-wide vote in spring 2016.

None of these boycott resolutions is likely to have any impact on Israeli policy. What they will do is signal the increasingly partisan political profile of a number of humanities and interpretive social science disciplines. For the second year in a row, historians at the January 2016 business meeting of the American Historical Association (AHA) wisely rejected their own anti-Israel resolution (Rosenberg), but its sponsors will no doubt return, and meanwhile the 30,000-member Modern Language Association will be debating an anti-Israel resolution in 2016 and 2017. If the traditional core disciplines like English and history should join the BDS movement they will have compromised their reputations—one can even say discredited themselves—as places for open discussion and debate. Already too many faculty consider themselves to be communicating a fact, not expressing an opinion, when they tell their students Israel is a settler-colonialist state, or, worse still, a genocidal one. The humanities—which have been significantly defunded over a period of decades, and which now resort increasingly to hiring contingent faculty who are not eligible for tenure—will as a whole suffer a continued loss of public and institutional respect if they make BDS the public face of their disciplines. Who will want to fund propaganda machines posing as academic pursuits? Although the most passionate BDS advocates have persuaded themselves they have their hands on the levers of history and can reshape Middle East politics, it is really their own professional futures that are in the balance. Even though they are unlikely to have a significant impact on Israel's behavior, however, these efforts can over time shape the climate of opinion, and in the short term they can impose very real injustices.

Recognition that adopting a polarizing anti-Israel resolution will simultaneously divide an organization's membership and compromise its public profile has helped defeat a number of such proposals in addition to those presented at the AHA. In its October 2013 meeting in Boston, members of the American Public Health Association's Executive Council rejected a resolution condemning Israel's medical practices toward Palestinians by a vote of 74 to 36. The American Library Association's Council has also turned down BDS initiatives by wide margins. In both cases, concern about the organization taking political stands and interest in the adjudicable facts about Israel were mixed with outreach efforts to win the day. It is notable, however, that interest in the facts varies, even among academics, and some organizations are more open to considering factual evidence than others. Some are more powerfully swayed by emotion. There is typically, moreover, a core of activists who are actually eager to polarize their disciplines, as they see pro-Israel colleagues as the enemy within, and they consider it a priority to alienate, exile, and cast them out.

Graduate students in fields like anthropology, history, literature, and Middle East studies now frequently avoid specializing in Israel studies—even if it is their first choice of fields—for concern, justifiably, that it will cost them their careers, denying them jobs, publication opportunities, and fellowships. BDS has succeeded in intimidating graduate students and young faculty to the level where wariness of anti-Israel forces shapes their lifelong career choices. At professional meetings one commonly meets graduate students and young faculty who are afraid even to attend sessions devoted to BDS for fear they will be seen there and people they know will then ask them where they stand. This deeply damaging but largely unpublicized trend is at least as serious as the campus anti-Semitism frequently reported by undergraduates.

# ACADEMIC BOYCOTTS VIOLATE ACADEMIC FREEDOM

Because it imposes a political constraint on academic activity—prohibiting cooperation with the Israeli academic world based on a set of political judgments and litmus tests—a boycott would interrupt the free flow of ideas within the international scholarly community. That would block the unencumbered pursuit of knowledge, a principle that defines both academic freedom and the academy as a whole. Disciplinary organizations that advocate a boycott of universities have therefore broken faith with the scholarly community and betrayed deeply held academic values. Scholars should be free to pursue their research free from mandates of political correctness. To endorse that principle, however, means that academic boycotts must be renounced.

Some defenders of the boycott contend that they can call for fellow scholars to boycott Israeli universities without in any way undermining academic freedom, infringing on academic culture, or impeding the free flow of ideas. They argue that their ends—ameliorating the conditions of Palestinian life—justify their means: restricting others' academic freedom. This is an illusion: the boycott movement is poisoning debate in Britain, Canada, the US, and a number of European countries. It aspires to eliminate connections between Israeli universities and those in the West, thus having a chilling effect on and compromising the world of ideas. By trying to limit what individual scholars do, what conferences they attend, and with whom they collaborate, the supporters of the boycott restrict academic freedom. By trying to eliminate study abroad in Israel rooted in ties with Israeli institutions, they also restrict the academic freedom of students. These will be the real effects of the boycott, which is designed to dissuade scholars from activities in Israel or cooperation with Israeli institutions. It is remarkable and disconcerting that scholars who vote for the boycott are so prepared to endanger the foundational principles of scholarly work in the interest of pursuing a political agenda.

Some boycott proponents disingenuously deny such effects, claiming that the boycott does not restrict academic freedom because—and this remains the crux of their defense—it is directed exclusively against institutions and not against individuals: it prohibits cooperation with Israeli academic institutions, not with individual Israelis. This purported focus on institutions enables advocates to insist boycotts are ethical. Yet this differentiation between institutions and individuals is untenable. Effective scholarship always depends on institutional support for individual scholars; individual scholars can thrive only because of their institutional contexts and the resources and sponsorships that institutions make available: colleagues, students, classrooms, libraries, laboratories, and of course financial support, including salary and research funding. Strip away the institution, and the individual scholar barely survives. Yet boycotts are premised on the illusion that one can strip away the infrastructure without harming the individual scholar at all. Given that the individual necessarily depends on the institution, however, the distinction between the two, which is central to the argument that the boycott does not infringe on any individual scholar's academic freedom, melts away. A boycott of academic institutions is necessarily an attack on individual academics, no matter how much the boycott apologists implausibly assert the contrary. To pretend to welcome collaboration with Israeli scholars, while insisting that no funding come from Israeli institutions, is dishonest.

The argument is put forward that Palestinian civil society has called for a blanket boycott of Israeli academic institutions. There is an empirical question concerning how true this is—to the chagrin of BDS leaders, the call for a boycott of Israeli products and institutions is rejected by Mahmoud Abbas (1935-) and the Palestinian Authority of which he is president. But the more fundamental problem is the idea that Palestinian civil society is one homogenous bloc with one opinion. To work on this assumption is to diminish the subjectivity of Palestinians, to deny plurality within the Palestinian people, to attribute to Palestinians a single voice that is in fact an echo of that of BDS advocates. An academic boycott blocks our ears to points of view we don't want to hear, or don't want to admit might exist, or indeed to anything that questions our own self-certainty. It grants us license to invent what we assume others think, in this case Israeli academics, rather than hear what they actually say. The principle of academic freedom does not license any and all behavior but it is nonetheless fundamental. It contains norms of openness, understanding, inquiry, criticism, self-criticism, and dialogue, which we abandon at our peril.

Academic institutions in Israel proper as anywhere else, are fundamentally communities of scholars. They protect scholars. They make it possible for scholars to research and to teach. They defend the academic freedom of scholars. The premise of the "institutional boycott" is that in Israel, universities are bad but scholars are (possibly, exceptionally) good. The premise is that universities are organs of the state while individual scholars are employees who may (possibly, exceptionally) be not guilty of supporting Israeli "apartheid" or some similar formulation. But academic institutions are a necessary part of the structure of academic freedom. If there were no universities, scholars would band together and invent them to create frameworks within which they could function as professional researchers and teachers, and within which they could collectively defend their academic freedom.

Israeli academic institutions are not materially different from academic institutions in other free countries. They are not segregated by race, religion, or gender; they have relative autonomy from the state; they defend academic freedom and freedom of criticism, not least against government and political pressures. There are of course threats to academic freedom in Israel, as there are in the US and elsewhere, but the record of Israeli institutions is a good one in defending scholars from political interference. As in the US and other democratic countries, wartime hysteria and the unreflective patriotism that accompanies it means dissenting Israeli academics can be subject to verbal attacks; the issue in that context is whether faculty in Israel or elsewhere are formally sanctioned, not whether they suffer public criticism. Israel's record in these matters is not perfect, but it is comparable to that of the US—which is to say that it is on the whole quite free. There is little or no academic freedom in many Arab countries.

# TARGETING INDIVIDUAL STUDENTS & FACULTY—THE BDS GUIDELINES

The international BDS movement sometimes characterizes itself as the Western action arm of PACBI, the Palestinian Campaign for the Academic & Cultural Boycott of Israel, but it is more accurate to describe PACBI as a subset of the broader BDS movement. BDS now makes it very clear how aggressively its guidelines target individuals. The BDS/PACBI guidelines for academic boycotts—revised and expanded in July 2014 (http://www.pacbi. org/etemplate.php?id=1108)—now make much more explicit that individual faculty and students, not just institutions, will and should be targeted. The guidelines irrefutably betray the claim that BDS doesn't target individuals. Indeed, they expose that claim to be is the core deception in at the heart of almost every BDS resolution, past or present.

The recourse to the language of "institutions" is an understandable rhetorical move. Students and faculty in the US and Europe do not want to feel that they are signing on to a movement that boycotts individuals. Therefore a typical BDS resolution includes both the pious assertion that it doesn't target individuals and a list of ways individuals will be targeted. Consider the following piece of Orwellian double-speak from the 2014 guidelines: "While an individual's academic freedom should be fully and consistently respected in the context of academic boycotts, an individual academic, Israeli or otherwise, cannot be exempt from being subject to 'common sense' boycotts." Whatever "common sense boycotts" may mean is apparently up to groups and individuals to decide; the phrase is not defined. But a "common sense" reading of this sentence makes plain that for all the high-mindedness, individuals are actually not spared.

The guidelines specify how individuals will be damaged or sanctioned. They demand that all academic and economic "projects with all Israeli academic institutions should come to an end." This demand eviscerates an essential freedom that faculty and students have long had: to make their own decisions about what collaborative projects to undertake. It also does direct harm to those Palestinians engaged in collaborative projects with Israeli faculty and institutions. BDS urges all faculty and students not to publish in Israeli journals. It also insists faculty elsewhere refuse to reprint articles first published in such places, thus initiating an extraordinary blacklisting of publications and their authors. All these penalties and restrictions would apply equally to Palestinian citizens of Israel, a consequence that BDS dismisses as inconsequential collateral damage. On the other hand, if Palestinians were to be exempted, BDS would be reinforcing its discriminatory impulse, selecting individuals to be boycotted on the basis of ethnicity. Either way it is a fundamental assault on academic freedom and the free exchange of ideas that is its core principle.

BDS urges faculty not to "write recommendations for students hoping to pursue studies in Israel," once again sabotaging standard faculty rights and harming the students involved. It strains credulity to suggest students refused a letter of recommendation will not take it personally. Student programs housed at Israeli universities are characterized as "schemes" that should be boycotted and closed down. Jewish students of course are the main target of efforts to close down study abroad programs in Israel and joint American/Israeli degree programs. Jewish students are also the main recipients of scholarships or fellowships from pro-Israel organizations that BDS targets for closure or boycotting. It is disingenuous to pretend this is not a form of religious discrimination.

BDS guidelines prohibit visits to Israeli universities if they include any professional or financial link with the institution visited. But Israeli academic institutions provide academic credit for study abroad in Israel. Violators once again could be subjected to blacklisting. In a blatantly discriminatory gesture, the guidelines advise that, "If conducting research at Israeli facilities such as archives does not entail official affiliation with those facilities (e.g. in the form of a visiting position), then the activity is not subject to boycott." Israeli faculty, they generously advise, should not be automatically boycotted; they should simply be treated like all other potential "offenders." BDS says its guidelines establish a "picket line" barring all the activities it lists, including visits to Palestinian universities by faculty who have earlier visited Israeli universities and therefore "contribute to the false perception of symmetry." By what right does BDS establish such a symbolic picket line? What reasoning justifies the BDS assumption that asymmetries of power trump every other human component of the conflict and override all individual rights? Once again the academic freedom of individuals is curtailed, and the potential for interchanges promoting mutual understanding and peaceful resolution of the conflict is undermined. Meanwhile, the BDS endorsement of "common sense boycotts" strengthens what is already guaranteed: that academic, cultural, and economic boycotts will be inconsistently implemented and that malicious individual boycott initiatives will multiply.

"The logic of such boycotts was taken to its cruel conclusion when a retired Cambridge academic refused to help an Israeli girl with her school project 'until there is peace in Palestine'" (Williams). The thirteen-year-old girl, Shachar Rabinovitz, had written from a kibbutz to Dr. Marsha Levine. an expert on horse domestication, to request help on a school assignment on that topic. "You might be a child, but if you are old enough to write to me, you are old enough to learn about Israeli history and how it has impacted the lives of Palestinian people," BDS supporter Levine wrote (Ex-Cambridge).

Controversies over whether Israeli faculty members should be allowed to attend conferences in the United States have produced several absurd proposals. The American literary theorist Judith Butler argues that Israeli faculty should be permitted to attend US events so long as they pay their way themselves, instead of having their universities cover their travel costs. Although academic freedom gives faculty the right to seek research and travel support, Butler nonetheless claims her self-funding proposal preserves academic freedom. In this case, Butler is going beyond BDS's formal demands, merely one of the many instances in which individual faculty have done so. Indeed a boycott inevitably puts pressure on individual faculty to honor its imperative and decide how to conduct their own personal boycott. The resulting choices often constitute considerably more than the symbolic actions to which some BDS advocates claim the movement limits itself. By institutionalizing opposition to Israel, moreover, a boycott resolution also stigmatizes those who oppose the resolution and will not honor it.

Some boycott advocates are honest enough to admit that a boycott will compromise academic freedom. They typically add that human rights transcend academic freedom as a value. But these two principles are not in conflict. They should both be honored. Either we commit ourselves to opposition to all academic boycotts or one after another university in country after country will be boycotted, and academic freedom will have no principled standing. ■

*Adapted in part from Cary Nelson, "Introduction," Russell Berman, "The Boycott as an Infringement on Academic Culture," Robert Fine, "Speaking in Opposition," and David Hirsh, "The American Studies Association Boycott Resolution, Academic Freedom, and the Myth of the Institutional Boycott," with additional material added.*

Also see BDS: A BRIEF HISTORY, BDS AND THE AMERICAN ANTHROPOLOGICAL ASSOCIATION, BDS AND THE AMERICAN STUDIES ASSOCIATION, BDS RESOLUTIONS ON CAMPUS: THEIR LONG-TERM GOAL, CULTURAL BOYCOTTS, DIVESTMENT CAMPAIGNS, and ECONOMIC BOYCOTTS.

# ANTI-IMPERIALISM

The concept of imperialism gained currency in the late 19th century as a way either to celebrate or criticize the effort by nations to expand their territory or resources by gaining power over other countries, their peoples, or their land areas. For anti-imperialists, or imperialism's opponents, it was associated with capitalist greed, racism, and a lack of respect for other peoples' right to political self-determination. As western countries were compelled to give up political control over their colonies, they nonetheless continued to exploit their labor and natural resources. Anti-imperialism thus continues to carry historical, economic, political, and moral connotations in the post-colonial age. Not all who oppose imperialism are opposed to the Jewish state, but the concept is now widely employed by anti-Zionist political and religious movements to give their aims political legitimacy by associating Zionism, which in reality is an indigenous movement of the Jewish people for national self-determination in their historic homeland, with the historical ambitions of and abuses by the Western powers. Anti-Zionism on the left is now increasingly seen as the most important form of anti-imperialism and as a virtual litmus test for admission to the progressive community. It has come to signify rejection of the racism, colonialism, and nationalism that accompany imperialism.

—*CN*

## ALAN JOHNSON

For many decades, anti-imperialism was only "one value amongst a whole set —democracy, equality, sexual freedom, anti-totalitarianism." On much of the Left from the late 1960s on, however, it was raised to an altogether higher status: "the central value, prior to and above all others." The world was divided into two "camps": imperialism versus anti-imperialism. This dichotomy is integral to a mind-set that we might call *reactionary anti-imperialism*. Soon enough, and rapidly after the 1967 war and the occupation of the West Bank and Gaza, Israel was reframed as "a key site of the imperialist system." Since 1989 and the collapse of Communism, this has remained the dominant intellectual framework for many parts of the global Left. Reducing the complexity of the post-cold-war world to a single Great Contest—"Imperialism" against "the resistance," or "Empire" against "the multitude"—many on the Left today became gripped by the same Manichean world-view and habits of mind that dominated during the Stalinist era; from apologia to denial, from cynicism to grossly simplifying tendencies of thought, from the belief that "my enemy's enemy is my friend" to the abandonment of all who get on the wrong side of the "anti-imperialists." For example, by defining Radical Islamism as part of the anti-imperialist "resistance" to imperialism, parts of the left *redefined itself* as (not very) thoughtfully or analytically sympathetic to Radical Islamism. Anti-Zionist theorist Judith Butler, for example, insisted the eliminationist antisemites of Hamas and Hezbollah were "social movements that are progressive, that are on the Left, that are part of a global Left."

Pascal Bruckner's essay *The Tyranny of Guilt* traces the rise of this mentality ("the whole world hates us and we deserve it") and its post-communist politics (a "Third Worldism of introspection") in which guilt-ridden intellectuals, even as they enjoy and take advantage of all that Western liberal democratic society has to offer, retain a deep personal need to feel wholly oppositional to a "fallen culture." So they *turn in on the West itself*, which must now be as bad as the East was once good. Now we "hate ourselves much more than we love others." Look around, says Bruckner: "one applauds a religious revolution, another goes into ecstasies over the beauty of terrorist acts, or supports a guerrilla movement because it challenges our imperialist project." Israel, in this world-view, is part of the imperialist West. This camp-follower style framing shapes how the conflict is perceived: we end up "pursuing our own mythologies in a foreign theater." Bruckner again: "People who support the Palestinians are not hoping to aid flesh-and-blood human beings but pure ideas ... not so such engaged in inquiring into a specific antagonism—a

real estate dispute involving two equally legitimate owners, as ⌐
it—as in settling accounts with Western culture" (6, 13, 2, 60-⌐

While 19th century universalism and assimilationism gave ⌐om⌐
of the socialist left a predisposition to be hostile to the Jews as a people,
the 20th century accretion of reactionary anti-imperialism, identity politics,
and Orientalism added a predisposition to view Israel as a state beyond the
pale and to see the Palestinians as the embodiment of victimhood. And this
dichotomy is absolutely central to anti-Zionism. It underpins the radical
decontextualization of history, the discounting of Israel's security fears and
their reframing as Zionist frauds, the infantilization of the Palestinians as a
people without responsibility and beyond judgment, and the evasion of all
the evidence of Arab and Palestinian antisemitism. In toto, these tendencies
of thought treat opposition to Israel as a precondition for any analysis of the
Israeli-Palestinian conflict. ■

*Adapted from Alan Johnson, "Intellectual Incitement: The Anti-Zionist Ideology and the Anti-Zionist Subject."*

Also see JIHAD, ORIENTALISM AND THE ATTACK ON ENLIGHTENMENT VALUES, THE ONE-STATE SOLUTION, and THE SOCIAL JUSTICE MANDATE IN HIGHER EDUCATION.

# ANTI-JEWISH BOYCOTTS
# IN HISTORY

I n Western Europe, anti-Jewish boycotts started in the late 18th century as a reaction to the Enlightenment, later acquiring the "boycott" designation, and, later still, were employed by the Nazis in the 1930s and 40s to inaugurate their genocidal assault on the Jewish people. Arab boycotts against Jews were organized during the period of the British Mandate over Palestine (1920-1948), and, after 1948, were directed against the State of Israel. Some relaxation of Arab boycott at the state level has taken place as a result of peace treaties and diplomatic agreements. However, since the 2001 Durban Conference, there has been an expanded NGO thrust, primarily through the BDS movement, which uses boycotts and divestment as the main tools in its anti-Israel campaign.

In the last few years support outside the BDS movement has also grown for limited boycotts, especially against products produced in West Bank settlements, among people who support the existence of a Jewish state and who are not motivated by anti-Semitism but rather by a commitment to ending the occupation of the West Bank. Those efforts are not covered in this entry.

—CN

KENNETH L. MARCUS & ILAN TROEN

# INTRODUCTION

Anti-Jewish boycotts emerged as a reaction against the Enlightenment, in resistance to the legal equality that Jews received in France following the French revolution of 1789–1799, and then spread throughout Western Europe. Jewish emancipation, or legal equality for European Jews, carried with it a notion of acceptance and normalization: Jews would no longer be subjected to special legal disabilities or enjoy special legal protections (Arendt 21–25). Yet this emancipation placed Jewry in a double-bind. Those Europeans who embraced modernity, such as Voltaire, often disdained the Jews, seeing them as zealous and parochial, and thus a potential enemy of mankind. Other Europeans, especially in Germany and Austria-Hungary, resisted Jewish emancipation, despising the Jews as a visible, alien, and inassimilable group, seeing them as an emblem of modernization, and opposing their normalization (Laqueur 71-89). The latter responses ultimately led to anti-Jewish riots, physical attacks, exclusionary political movements, and then calls to boycott Jewish businesses in various parts of Europe during the late nineteenth century and into the early twentieth century. As Theodor Herzl observed, equality before the law became meaningless when Europeans started pursuing "attempts to thrust [Jews] out of business" by urging "Don't buy from Jews!"

Boycotts of Jews and of Israel are not new to the Arab/Israel conflict either. They first occurred in 1921, 27 years before Israel's formal establishment. At that time, the League of Nations issued the British Mandate for Palestine. It included a legal basis for the right of the Jewish people to establish a homeland in Palestine and the recognized right of Zionist institutions to become the official instrument for Jewish settlement. These first Arab boycotts targeted Jewish merchants in Jerusalem as well as Arab businesses that engaged in commerce with Jews. This ineffective gesture became a precedent during the countrywide Arab uprising in 1929 against the British Mandate and the developing Jewish presence in Palestine. During the 1930s, further sporadic attempts to boycott Jewish establishments were made. These too were ineffective since Jewish physicians, hospitals, and businesses were essential to the functioning of the country and served both Arab and Jewish communities.

# BOYCOTTS UNDER THE NAZIS

Meanwhile sporadic efforts in Europe were formalized and systematized in Germany. On April 1, 1933, two months after coming to power in Germany, the Nazis set the pattern for future anti-Jewish boycotts when they conducted, as their first nationwide action against Jews, a temporary boycott against Jewish businesses and professionals ("Boycott of Jewish Businesses"). As Lucy S. Dawidowicz has observed, Adolf Hitler's contribution was to formalize, rationalize, and channel the impulses behind hooligan attacks on stores owned by German Jews into "meaningful' political action" (52). It is important to recall that the Nazis did not justify the Nazi boycott on Jewish racial or religious issues, any more than their successors did. Rather, they explained the boycott, in the rhetoric of their era, as a response to the anti-German propaganda that Jewish people, as well as foreign journalists, were allegedly spreading in the international press. For this reason, German soldiers insisted they were defending Germans from Jewish aggression, rather than attacking Jews for racial reasons, which is why the Stormtroopers' battle-cry was, "Germans! Defend yourselves! Do not buy from Jews!" (Brackman). This ushered in the Nazis' nationwide campaign against the entire German Jewish population. Just a week later, for example, the Nazis passed a law barring civil service employment to non-"Aryans" ("Boycott of Jewish Businesses"). Like the yellow star that Jews were later forced to wear, the Nazi boycott was a systematic national socialist mechanism to strip Jews of the "normalization" that had come with emancipation. Soon after, in the Nuremberg laws, Germany de-emancipated its Jews, making them into subject aliens. During the same decade, Poland also passed and adopted a number of measures to exclude Jews from various trades and professions and established a mass boycott of Jewish shops from 1936 to 1939 (Laqueur 128–129). The culmination of European anti-Jewish campaigns was the Nazi program of systematic extermination.

From 1933 to 1945, Nazi propagandists transmitted anti-Semitic propaganda to Arabs and Muslims in the Middle East and North Africa. This included Arabic language shortwave radio programs broadcast seven days per week, as well as millions of printed items (Herf). This propaganda combined selective readings of the Koran, Nazi critiques of Western imperialism, and anti-Jewish themes in Islam. Evidently, Nazi officials considered anti-Semitism and anti-Zionism to be the best means of entering into Arab and Muslim hearts and minds (Herf 13). Nazi ideology would continue to influence both Arab nationalists and religious extremists throughout the Middle East, including among Palestinian leaders, for many decades afterwards (Rubin and Schwanitz).

# THE ARAB LEAGUE BOYCOTTS

In 1945, the 22-nation Council of the Arab League, founded the previous year, called for an economic boycott of Jewish goods and services in the British-controlled mandate territory of Palestine: "Jewish products and manufactured goods shall be considered undesirable to the Arab countries" (Bard). All Arab "institutions, organizations, merchants, commission agents and individuals" were called upon "to refuse to deal in, distribute, or consume Zionist products or manufactured goods" (Bard). At the time, the League was filled with ex-Axis collaborators (Rubin and Schwanitz 246). Three years later, following the war establishing Israel's independence, the League formalized its boycott against the state of Israel by broadening it to include non-Israelis who maintained economic relations with Israel or who were perceived to support it (Martin Weiss). During this period, admiration for Hitler's National Socialism among some in the Arab world continued unabated (Mallmann and Cüppers 211).

Although formally a boycott of the State of Israel, the Arab League boycott has been, during at least some periods, also a more general boycott of Jews. Indeed, Bernard Lewis has remarked that "the way in which the boycott of Israel, operated by all member states of the Arab League, was put into effect" is "[p]erhaps the clearest indication of the way in which the war against Israel was generalized to be a war against the Jews" (223–224). This can be seen, for example, in various examples in which Arab states canceled cultural events or rejected ambassadorial credentials based on Jewish rather than Israeli or Zionist connections, or made it clear that Jews need not apply for certain fellowships (Lewis, 224–226). Some Arab League member states and entities have formally withdrawn from the boycott, or at least some aspects of it, either through peace treaties, or other diplomatic agreements, or as a result of diplomatic relations, *e.g.*, Egypt (1979), the Palestinian Authority (1993), and Jordan (1994) (Martin Weiss 3). Today, except for Syria, most Arab states no longer enforce the secondary or tertiary boycotts. Syria, Lebanon, and Iran, the latter not being an Arab state, enforce the old primary boycott. That said, Arab trade with Israel remains limited, and the boycott still counts as political symbolism. A primary boycott prohibits direct trade between Israel, a secondary boycott is directed at companies that do business with Israel, and a tertiary boycott blacklists firms that trade with other companies that do business with Israel.

# BOYCOTTS IN THE NEW MILLENIUM

The anti-Jewish boycott movement was reinvigorated at the turn of the new millennium, as failed hopes in the Oslo Accords helped to fuel a Second Intifada and global animus against Israel. The World Conference Against Racism, Racial Discrimination, Xenophobia and Related Intolerance, held in Durban, South Africa, in late 2001 (Durban I) helped to re-launch the boycott movement on a new ideological basis. The main platform to criticize Israel and the US was the NGO Forum, held in Kingsmead Stadium in Durban, and attended by 8,000 representatives from as many as 3,900 NGOs. The Durban Conference's NGO "Meeting in Solidarity with the Palestinian People" yielded an NGO plan of action that called for "complete and total isolation of Israel as an apartheid state as in the case of South Africa which means the imposition of mandatory and comprehensive sanctions and embargoes, the full cessation of all links (diplomatic, economic, social, aid, military cooperation and training) between all states and Israel" (Baker and Shay).

This was followed by numerous calls to boycott or divest from Israel, including Palestinian boycott calls in 2002, 2003, and 2004 (Brackman 9). By October 2002, more than 50 campuses were circulating divestment petitions (Bard and Dawson 16). On July 9, 2005, over 100 Palestinian organizations issued the "Palestinian Civil Society Calls for Boycott, Divestment and Sanctions against Israel Until it Complies with International Law and Universal Principles of Human Rights." Its three explicit objectives were to end Israel's "occupation and colonization" of "all Arab lands" (presumably including all pre-1967 lands, although BDS leadership has equivocated on this), recognizing the equal fundamental rights of Israel's Arab-Palestinian citizens, and promoting a proposed Palestinian right of return to their former homes and properties in Israel itself.

The Durban I and Palestinian Call formalized, systematized, and attempted to justify the sporadic individual boycotts and anti-Jewish attacks that preceded them. The primary strategy of BDS leadership is to reject Israel's "normalization," defined as the treatment of Israel as a "normal" state with which business as usual can be conducted. Just as modern anti-Semites once opposed the normalization of Jewish "beings," today's activists oppose the normalization of the being of the Jewish state. PACBI's (the Palestinian Campaign for the Academic & Cultural Boycott of Israel) leadership openly insists they do so on political rather than racial grounds. Indeed, their public statements speak of resistance to putative Palestinian oppression, rather than of any essentially malevolent characteristics of the Jewish people. Nevertheless, their effort echoes prior anti-Jewish boycotts. It also provides a dark rejoinder to the early Zionist thinkers, who had argued that a Jewish state could solve the problem of anti-Semitism by giving the Jewish people, who had been haunted by statelessness, a sense of normalcy.

In the end, BDS's anti-normalization agenda rejects any sustaining relationship with a Jewish state; at that point, the rights of millions of Jewish citizens of Israel to any form of political self-determination in their ancestral homeland have been abrogated, and we have moved from an anti-Israel to an anti-Jewish campaign. ■

*Adapted from Kenneth L. Marcus, "Is the Boycott, Divestment and Sanctions Movement Anti-Semitic?" and Ilan Troen, "The Campaign to Boycott Israeli Universities: Historical and Ideological Sources," with additional material added.*

Also see APARTHEID, ANTI-NORMALIZATION, ACADEMIC BOYCOTTS, CULTURAL BOYCOTTS, DIVESTMENT CAMPAIGNS, ECONOMIC BOYCOTTS, and JEWISH ANTI-ZIONISM: THREE VIEWS.

# ANTI-NORMALIZATION

## CARY NELSON

ormalization is the process through which ideas, actions, and social and political arrangements come to be accepted and perceived as normal. This includes the process of normalizing building empathy and collaborative relationships between Jews and Palestinians. Anti-normalization thus refers to efforts to resist and combat that process. As applied by the Palestinian Campaign for the Academic and Cultural Boycott of Israel (PACBI) and the Boycott, Divestment, and Sanctions (BDS) movement, anti-normalization takes on a number of specific ideological aims and meanings. As PACBI put it in 2011, anti-normalization categorically rejects "the treatment of Israel as a 'normal' state with which business as usual can be conducted." PACBI goes on to detail the political convictions underlying this stand: "It is helpful to think of normalization as a 'colonization of the mind,' whereby the oppressed subject comes to believe that the oppressor's reality is the only 'normal' reality that must be subscribed to, and that the oppression is a fact of life that must be coped with. Those who engage in normalization either ignore this oppression, or accept it as the status quo that can be lived with. In an attempt to whitewash its violations of international law and human rights, Israel attempts to re-brand itself, or present itself as normal—even 'enlightened'—through an intricate array of relations and activities encompassing hi-tech, cultural, legal, LGBT and other realms" ("Israel's Exceptionalism"). In rejecting all efforts at mutual understanding, BDS puts itself at odds with the ethical principles guiding all First World countries. In dismissing all positive cultural developments in Israel as mere propaganda, BDS denies the right to judge individual and collective work on its own terms. It is not enough, however, to decry BDS's effort to substitute mutual antagonism for empathy. It is necessary both to understand and to resist the way the anti-normalization agenda undermines all efforts to seek a negotiated resolution to the Israeli-Palestinian conflict. Anti-normalization amounts to war by other means. It validates one people's national aspirations and dismisses the other's. Those who seek peace must build respect for each peoples' core narratives and establish relationships that will promote political self-realization for both Israelis and Palestinians. Negotiation requires building trust, not insisting on hostility as the basis of all interaction.

Despite the BDS movement's relentless campaign against normalization, many of those working in the area consider it unqualifiedly harmful. Ghaith al-Omari is a senior fellow at the Washington Institute and a former official in the Palestinian Authority. Joel Braunold is Executive Director of the Alliance for Middle East Peace. Huda Abu Arquob is active in a number of Palestinian organizations; she is co-founder of the Center for Transformative Education and a former educational consultant to the Palestinian Authority:

> The increasingly direct and sometimes violent methods of anti-normalization activists are aimed at preventing Palestinians from relating to Israelis. They also discourage healthy debate. This movement ignores the Palestinians' unique and rich history of political diversity and instead seeks to impose the kind of uniformity that has traditionally plagued other Arab societies. Anti-normalization activists have a right to hold their own views, but they should not be able to prevent other Palestinians from dissenting or exercising their right to engage in joint activities with Israelis. Preventing Palestinians and Israelis from interacting directly would deprive the Palestinians—individually and collectively—of the opportunity to gain a deeper, more textured, and ultimately more accurate understanding of Israel.

> —Ghaith al-Omari

In their effort to delegitimize coexistence programming, anti-normalization activists lampoon people-to-people activities as Israelis and Palestinians coming together to eat hummus, then go home. This is an utterly false representation of the people-to-people movement today. Look at the thousands engaged by Parents Circle or Combatants for Peace, the farmers whose crops have not been wasted thanks to Olive Oil Without Borders or the communities receiving fresh water owing to the work of EcoPeace. These are just a sample of thousands of people whose lives have been changed through joint programs.

—Joel Braunold & Huda Abu Arquob

After Al Quds University faculty member Mohammed Dajani Daoudi took 27 Palestinian students on a March 2014 trip to the Auschwitz death camps, he faced more than an ordinary backlash. He was vilified as a traitor, there were Palestinian demands that he be fired, his car was burned, and in the end he felt he had to resign. He has said he hoped the university would refuse his resignation, but instead it was promptly accepted. The response can be understood not only as evidence of Palestinian anger at perceived Israeli indifference to what they see as their own historical tragedy—the Nakba, the 1948 flight and expulsion of 700,000 Arabs from the new state of Israel—but also as a sign of the growing movement to castigate all efforts to "normalize" relations between Israelis and Palestinians. A few months later, in July 2014, PACBI consolidated its opposition to all efforts at Palestinian-Israeli dialogue and cooperation in a revised set of Guidelines for the International Academic Boycott of Israel. The Boycott, Divestment, and Sanctions Movement (BDS) cosponsored the statement (http://www.pacbi.org/etemplate.php?id=1108):

Academic activities and projects involving Palestinians and/or other Arabs on one side and Israelis on the other (whether bi- or multi-lateral) that are based on the false premise of symmetry/parity between the oppressors and the oppressed or that claim that both colonizers and colonized are equally responsible for the "conflict" are intellectually dishonest and morally reprehensible forms of normalization that ought to be boycotted. Far from challenging the unjust status quo, such projects contribute to its endurance. Examples include events, projects, or publications that are designed explicitly to bring together Palestinians/Arabs and Israelis so they can present their respective narratives or perspectives, or to work toward reconciliation without addressing the root causes of injustice and the requirements of justice.

Joint projects were exempt, they added, if "the project/activity is one of 'co-resistance' rather than co-existence." This anti-normalization campaign was immediately applied to all cultural and political activities, not just those taking place in higher education. The logic of BDS's position is fundamentally at odds with liberal-democratic notions of individual responsibility.

In one form or another, the campaign has been in existence for over a decade, but it has significantly intensified since 2014. The underlying logic is that joint Israeli- Palestinian activities provide legitimacy for the State of Israel while the occupation of Palestine continues, but it is unclear how eliminating dialogue will facilitate the peace process or make the establishment of a Palestinian state more likely. Indeed curtailment of Israeli-Palestinian interaction seems more likely to have the opposite effect. As one anthropologist has written, "The BDS anti-normalization project is specifically designed to eliminate all cooperation with centers of progress and reform in Israel" (https://anthrodialogue.wordpress.com/2015/10/28/isaiah-silver-and-the-strange-crimes-of-israeli-anthropologists/). Anti-normalization tactics have repeatedly crossed the line into blatant intimidation. After the Indian classical dance group Kathak performed in Tel Aviv, anti-normalization activists interrupted its 2014 West Bank performance in Ramallah (MAP 3) and tried to force its closure.

Projects to promote mutual empathy and understanding have been in progress for decades. Those focusing on Palestinian and Israeli children have reached many hundreds over that time. Some of the graduates are now young adults who represent a core of people well prepared to facilitate and promote a two-state solution should the opportunity come to pass.

The campaign against normalization has had a special impact on American higher education, where dialogue and communication are central to the very definition of the academy. Thus many local Students for Justice in Palestine (SJP) chapters have declined as a matter of principle to talk with other groups focused on the Israeli-Palestinian conflict. The SJP chapter at the University of California at San Diego rejected dialogue with J Street U as "counterproductive to the Palestinian fight for human rights," thereby rejecting interaction with a progressive group highly critical of Israel's West Bank policies.

A March 2015 statement by Scholars for Israel and Palestine (SIP) and the Alliance for Academic Freedom (AAF) points out that the anti-normalization campaign

> **Separates** Palestinians and their supporters from those Israeli and Diaspora Jews who themselves seek to end Israeli occupation of Palestinian lands;
> **Deprives** Palestinians of channels to highlight, to Israelis, the injuries and injustices of their lives under Israeli military rule;
> **Prevents** Palestinians from building common cause with those who share their views and aspirations;
> **Provokes** recriminations within Palestinian society, where political leaders and community activists accuse each other of acts of treason merely for advocating the Palestinian cause to Israelis and supporters of Israel and seeking allies among them;

**Undermines** the forces in Israeli society and among supporters of Israel seeking an end to the occupation and the establishment of an independent state of Palestine;

**Discourages** cooperation with organizations and activities working to build up the kinds of mutual recognition, awareness, and understanding necessary for achieving genuine peace;

**Promotes** elements of ideological rigidity and exclusion in the movement for Palestinian rights that work against freedoms of thought and expression dear to democrats of all persuasions; and

**Threatens** the principles of academic freedom and open intellectual exchange, stigmatizes and excludes groups of students on unfair and divisive grounds, and undercuts the process of learning and scholarship in colleges and universities (http://thirdnarrative.org/israel-palestine-articles/anti-normalization-prevents-peace-sustains-the-occupation-undermines-academic-freedom-and-harms-students/).

It is extraordinary that anti-normalization actually limits opportunities for Palestinians to present their case for redress of their grievances to Israelis in the kind of humane and empathic interactions that might succeed. The cumulative result is corrosive for both societies, but Palestinians themselves pay the higher price for the imposition of an anti-normalizing ideology. Perhaps the most telling example of that is the BDS castigation of the gleaming hilltop Palestinian city of Rawabi under construction north of Ramallah. Funded substantially by Qatar, it will emphasize high-tech industries and give 30,000 Palestinians not only a coordinated role in the industries of the future but also an extraordinarily beautiful place to live. It offers clear evidence of one way an independent Palestinian state could flourish economically, but BDS nonetheless condemns it as a "normalization" project with Israel (Schwartz). The goal of anti-normalization is to maximize the polarization of the Israeli-Palestinian conflict. Is the issue of human rights on the West Bank best addressed by undermining the very foundations of liberal education? ■

Also see ACADEMIC BOYCOTTS, APARTHEID, BDS: A BRIEF HISTORY, BDS AND THE AMERICAN ANTHROPOLOGICAL ASSOCIATION, CULTURAL BOYCOTTS, and PALESTINIAN THEOLOGY OF LIBERATION.

# ANTI-ZIONISM
# AS ANTI-SEMITISM

Classical antisemitism denies the rights of Jews as citizens within society. Anti-Zionism denies the equal rights of the Jewish people to its lawful sovereignty within the community of nations . . . . All that has happened is that the discriminatory principle has been transferred from the realm of individual rights to the domain of collective identity.

—Abba Eban

Antisemitism . . . is not, or not primarily, a pathological disposition or function of the individual mind, but rather a type of *social* or *cultural* pathology: a self-replicating structure of temptations and apparently explanatory delusions embodied, independently of the individual mind, in a multitude of enduring written and quasi-proverbial forms, that stands permanently ready to introduce itself, like the scrap of self-replicating genetic material that constitutes a virus, into the minds of people struggling to define their relationship to society, and of society to them, in moments of political crisis.

—Bernard Harrison (Uniqueness 318)

I would argue that anti-Zionism crosses the line [into anti-Semitism] in the following instances:
1.  when it questions the legitimacy of the Jewish state, but no other state, and the legitimacy of Jewish nationalism, but no other nationalism, either in the Middle East or elsewhere.
2.  when it denies to the Jewish state, but no other state, the right to express the character of the majority of its citizens (that is, to be Jewish as France is French);

**3.** when it demonizes the Jewish state, turning the Arab-Israeli conflict into a morality play, a problem that Jews, and Jews alone, created and for which Jews and Jews alone, are responsible;

**4.** when it expresses an obsessive, exclusive, and disproportionate concern with the shortcomings of the Israelis and the suffering of the Palestinians—to the point that a conflict between two small peoples is transformed into a cosmic, Manichean struggle between the forces of good and evil.

When criticism of Israel crosses any of these lines and begins to traffic in the fantasies, obsessions, fears, and irrationalities that are the stock-in-trade of full-blown antisemitism, it becomes nearly indistinguishable from that which it claims not to be.

—Todd M. Endelman (71)

For a number of years a debate has been ongoing about whether anti-Zionism is equivalent to anti-Semitism. Zionism is a belief that Jews have a right to political self-determination in a land of their own. Anti-Zionism opposes that right and rejects the existence of the Jewish state, thereby denying six million Israeli Jews any right to political self-determination. That is an anti-Semitic agenda and goal, whether or not its advocates understand that. It reflects a form of structural anti-Semitism, similar to structural racism, in which one does not have to be personally anti-Semitic in order to inadvertently perpetuate anti-Semitic memes, tropes, and structures. Those rhetorical devices have survived through the decades and centuries in which anti-Semitism has evolved and mutated. After the Enlightenment, religious-based anti-Semitism was supplemented by an ethic-based anti-Semitism. In our time an anti-Zionist anti-Semitism has emerged with ferocity. Some act as if Zionism is a belief that a Jewish state should encompass all of Palestine, from the Mediterranean Sea to the Jordan River, and argue against it on those grounds. Belief in such a Greater Israel, however, embodies a very particular Zionist political or religious ideology; it should not be confused with the fundamental Zionist principle that Jews have a right to a homeland in Palestine. Efforts to conflate a minority political agenda with the fundamental meaning of Zionism are often driven by ignorance, but they also reflect a deeper strain of anti-Semitism. When anti-Zionism becomes obsessional, its advocates may discount the tragedy for both Jews and Palestinians that would unfold if Israel's existence as a Jewish state were really in jeopardy.

—CN

## RUSSELL BERMAN

Criticism of Israeli policies or of Zionism is not necessarily anti-Semitic. However, it also holds, obviously, that the mere fact that one has anti-Zionist views does not prove that one is not anti-Semitic. It is a logical fallacy to assert that the presence of anti-Zionism proves the absence of anti-Semitism. That should not be difficult to understand. On the contrary, it would hardly be surprising to discover that individuals with pronounced anti-Semitic sentiments might be hostile to Israel and Israelis, and an empirical study has demonstrated just such positive correlations between accepting anti-Semitic stereotypes and anti-Zionist positions. In particular in the Middle East and the public sphere of the Arab press, anti-Zionist politics often go hand in hand with anti-Semitic caricatures. Nonetheless, some boycott defenders would prefer to suppress discussions of anti-Semitism in their own ranks by complaining implausibly that they constantly face insinuations of anti-Semitism—when it is probably a whole lot less than "constantly." Their refusals to face anti-Semitism amount to an attempt to silence the Jewish community in the face of racism and adversity. What adversity? Leave aside the fantastic discourses in the Middle East, such as when 2013-2014 President of Egypt Adly Mansour was imagined by his opponents to be Jewish in order to attack him. We can stay closer to home: In the *Electronic Intifada* in late 2013 Rania Khalek counts the Jews—not the Zionists, but the Jews—at *The Nation* and decides there are too many. With that, the progressive camp has come around to Jew-counting with hardly a peep of protest, certainly not from the American Studies Association or any more distinguished humanities association. Not all anti-Zionists fit this paradigm, but when boycott proponents automatically reject claims of anti-Semitism *a priori*, they undermine their own anti-racist credibility.

## MITCHELL COHEN

Nothing exemplifies the return of old junk more than the "new" anti-Semitism and the bad faith that often finds expression in the statement: "I am anti-Zionist but not anti-Semitic." The fixation on Israel/Palestine within parts of the left, often to the exclusion of all other suffering on the globe, ought to leave any balanced observer wondering: What is going on here? This fixation needs demystification.

In theoretical terms, anti-Zionism and anti-Semitism are pretty easy to distinguish. Anti-Semitism is a form of race or national prejudice that crystallized in the nineteenth century. In part, it displaced or reinvented anti-Jewish religious prejudice (although centuries of religious prejudice easily wafted into racial and national bigotry). Its target was clearly Jews, not simply "Semites." It also, for some, mixed matters up further by identifying Jews with capitalism. Sadly, this became a steady feature within parts of the left that would later, habitually, conflate Jews, capitalism, and Zionism. Oddly enough, that is also what Jewish neoconservatives have tried to do in recent decades, though for them these associations are positive.

Anti-Zionism means, theoretically, opposition to the project of a Jewish state in response to the rise of anti-Semitism. Let's be blunt: there have been anti-Zionists who are not anti-Semites. But the crucial question is prejudicial overlap, not intellectual niceties . . . . To what extent does much anti-Zionism replicate the mental patterns of anti-Semitism? And to what extent do demagogic articulations of anti-Zionism enhance anti-Semitism? A few years ago I sought to outline commonalities between anti-Semitic and anti-Zionist discourses in a scholarly journal. It is worth reproducing. Here are major motifs that inform classical anti-Semitism:

1. **Insinuations**: Jews do not and cannot fit properly into our society. There is something foreign, not to mention sinister, about them.
2. **Complaints**: They are so particularistic, those Jews, so preoccupied with their "own." Why are they so clannish and anachronistic when we need a world of solidarity and love? Really, they make themselves into a "problem." If the so-called "Jewish problem" is singular in some way, it is their own doing and usually covered up by special pleading.
3. **Remonstrations**: Those Jews, they always carp that they are victims. In fact, they have vast power, especially financial power. Their power is everywhere, even if it is not very visible. They exercise it

manipulatively, behind the scenes. (But look, there are even a few of them, guilty-hearted perhaps, who will admit all this to you.)

4. **Recriminations**: Look at their misdeeds, all done while they cry that they are victims. These ranged through the ages from the murder of God to the ritual slaughter of children to selling military secrets to the enemy to war-profiteering, to being capitalists or middlemen or landlords or moneylenders exploiting the poor. And they always, oh-so-cleverly, mislead you.

Alter a few phrases, a word here and there, and we find motifs of anti-Zionism that are popular these days in parts of the left and parts of the Muslim and Arab worlds:

1. **Insinuations**: The Zionists are alien implants in the Mideast. They can never fit there. Western imperialism created the Zionist state.
2. **Complaints**: A Jewish state can never be democratic. Zionism is exclusivist. The very idea of a Jewish state is an anachronism.
3. **Remonstrations**: The Zionists carp that they are victims but in reality they have enormous power, especially financial. Their power is everywhere, but they make sure not to let it be too visible. They exercise it manipulatively, behind people's backs, behind the scenes—why, just look at Zionist influence in Washington. Or rather, dominance of Washington. (And look, there are even a few Jews, guilty-hearted perhaps, who admit it.)
4. **Recriminations**: Zionists are responsible for astonishing, endless dastardly deeds. And they cover them up with deceptions. These range from the imperialist aggression of 1967 to Ehud Barak's claim that he offered a compromise to Palestinians back in 2000 to the Jenin "massacre" during the Second Intifada.

## KENNETH L. MARCUS

In the last analysis, the BDS campaign is anti-Semitic, as its predecessors were, because some of its proponents act out of conscious hostility to the Jewish people; others act from unconscious or tacit disdain for Jews; and still others operate out of a climate of opinion that contains elements that are hostile to Jews and serve as the conduits through whom anti-Jewish tropes and memes are communicated; while all of them work to sustain a movement that attacks the commitment to Israel that is central to the identity of the overwhelming majority of Jewish people. This does not imply that all or even most of BDS' proponents are anti-Semites. That is a different question. Based on the best available empirical research, it appears that some of Israel's critics are not motivated by prejudice. Rather, they oppose Israel's actions for legitimately non-discriminatory reasons. Their reasons may be good or bad, convincing or unconvincing, logical or illogical. But they are not anti-Semitic.

Nevertheless, it ought to give them pause to realize that, for whatever reasons, they are participating in a boycott that has deeply unsavory roots and ramifications. It is not coincidental that the world's only Jewish state is subjected to greater scrutiny and pressure than most of the world's other nations. Nor is it coincidental that current efforts to boycott the Jewish State resemble in nearly all ways the constant efforts that have been made to boycott Jewish businesses since well before Israel's establishment. The historical record is clear that many and perhaps all of these efforts have been based, in no small part, on the basest forms of human bigotry. Some BDS advocates may be ignorant of this history, but this only makes them unwitting agents in a process by which hatred articulates itself across time.

# CARY NELSON

In the end, one of the key cultural and historical traditions that makes it possible to isolate Israel conceptually and politically from all other nations is anti-Semitism. It is the long and abiding international history of anti-Semitism that makes Israel not only available to be singled out but also always already singled out—*othered*, set apart. Anti-Semitism is a fundamental condition enabling the possibility of unqualified opposition to the Israeli state. It is certainly not the only impulse underlying opposition to Israel, but it helps make such opposition culturally, psychologically, and politically available. Some feel betrayed by conditions on the West Bank because they long championed Israel as an example of liberal democracy. But opposition to Israel also provides anti-Semitism with its contemporary intellectual and moral credibility. Anti-Zionism is thus anti-Semitism's moral salvation, its perfect disguise, its route to legitimation. Absolute opposition to Israel's *existence* increases anti-Semitism's cultural and political reach and impact. Arguments about whether a given opponent is or is not anti-Semitic are thus necessarily at least in part irrelevant. If you augment and empower anti-Semitism unwittingly, it may not matter what is in your heart. In that light, denial of anti-Semitism among those who reject Israel's right to exist—as opposed to those who oppose only the occupation of the West Bank—counts only as affirmation. Thus Barbara Harlow's seemingly idiotic answer "Why not?"—delivered at the 2014 Modern Language Association in response to the question "Why Boycott Israel?"—actually speaks to the existential reality. Why not single out the country that already stands alone in our minds? Indeed it stands alone in the minds of Jews and non-Jews alike.

Anti-Semitism, it is critical to realize, is the inescapable enabling precondition that makes it possible to castigate Israel when its national practices are the same, similar to, or better than those of other countries, not categorically different from them. Judgments about Israel indeed are often not based on factual comparisons with other countries at all, but rather on the programmatic invocation of cultural and political categories: Israel is a settler colonialist state; Israel discriminates against segments of those peoples under its control; Israel is a religious state, and we object to religious states on principle; Israel's warrant to exist as a nation state is based on power dynamics, not on an international consensus; other populations believe they have equal or greater right to the land; Israel's borders have not remained the same since its founding, so nothing about its existence can be certified; the country is a kind of affront in flux; Israel's human rights record in areas over which it exercises control is imperfect. All these concerns are less applicable to Israel than to more than a score of other countries in the Middle East and elsewhere, yet BDS advocates consider Israel alone a pariah among nations. It is no surprise, moreover, that BDS advocates discount both past and future violence against Israel and that anti-Semitism makes it possible to do so. Everything that might be done to a group of Jews has already been done, has already happened. Violence against Jews is a time-honored tradition. Such violence is not just a risk or a theoretical possibility; it is a historical given.

Everyone interested in ameliorating and solving the Israeli-Palestinian and Arab-Israeli conflicts has special reason for concern about the degree to which anti-Zionism and Anti-Semitism overlap, intersect, or become indistinguishable in the Middle East. Derek Penslar makes an important distinction between the forms of Arab anti-Semitism "that wax and wane in response to developments in Arab-Israeli relations" and "the Manicheanism of extremist Muslim fundamentalists who, no less than the Nazis, imagine Jews as literally the handmaids of Satan and call for their eradication from the face of the globe. It is essential to draw a clear distinction between these two different forms of anti-Semitism, one of which may be malleable, subject to change in a dynamic and constructive political environment, while the other kind is incurable and must be confronted with unequivocal condemnation, isolation, and, when necessary, forceful suppression" ("Anti-Semites" 28). Many throughout the world conflate these forms of Arab anti-Semitism. On the Right, both in Israel and throughout the world, Arab anti-Semitism is often seen as irredeemably Manichean, whereas as the left often optimistically attributes it to malleable sentiment based on current political conditions. Neither exclusivist position is fair to the complexity of real world conditions.

# DAVID HIRSH

Today's anti-semitism is difficult to pin down. It doesn't come in a Nazi uniform. The most threatening anti-Semitism in Britain today is carried by people who believe they are opponents of all racism. Today's anti-Semitism thinks Israel is a key evil on the planet and Israelis need to be excluded from the global community. It thinks Israel murders Palestinian children out of evil and that Israel is a false nation, founded to steal and occupy other people's land. Today's anti-Semitism thinks Israel is powerful and controls opinion and governments around the world.

These opinions constitute part of the natural "common sense" of people who believe themselves to be good and progressive in today's Britain. Many believe that those who do hate Jews, who march in London with anti-Semitic banners or who shoot Jews in Paris supermarkets or in Brussels museums are simply over-reacting to Israeli provocation.

But there is something else. Today's anti-Semitism comes with in-built protection against accusations of anti-Semitism. When good people today hear an accusation of it, they have learnt to recognize the accusation, not the anti-Semitism, as the dirty trick; an attack made by right-wingers and "Zionists" to smear and silence people who criticize Israel. Today's anti-Semitism incorporates the notion that those who complain about anti-Semitism are the racists. Opponents of anti-Semitism, not anti-Semites, it says, are the cynical ones; opponents of anti-Semitism, not anti-Semites, it says, are the powerful ones.

People who hold anti-Semitic views may not be aware they hold them, and so there is nothing to exclude Jews from feeling part of this community of the good and the progressive. In fact, a small minority of Jews play an important role in legitimizing, for example, the campaign to boycott Israel, as being not anti-Semitic. There is nothing to prevent Jews from participating in contemporary anti-Semitism.

## GABRIEL NOAH BRAHM & ASAF ROMIROWSKY

When today's "new" anti-Semitism (as it's called) distinguishes itself qualitatively from just more of the same "old" kind, it does so largely on the basis of attacks against not only Jews but the Jewish state, some of which even go so far as advocating an end to Israel as a Jewish state. For this is the *sine qua non* of peace, freedom, and justice in the world. So, is not the very proposition of boycotts with the intent of helping to eventually wipe Israel from the map anti-Semitic by definition, even if many BDS followers do not understand that? While those in the academic boycotts movement (in this not unlike most Jew-haters around the world today) have disdain for the discredited, moldy old label, "anti-Semite" (even members of Hamas and its supporters reject the accusation), they proudly emblazon the term "anti-Zionist" upon their escutcheons (again, in line with virtually all kinds of resurgent anti-Semitism today). So there is a question here too. Has the world really forgotten what this reviled thing *Zionism*—which it is assumed to be so respectable to declare oneself openly "anti-"—really was and is? Namely, the movement for the self-preservation (only partly successful) and autonomy of a people no less beleaguered by oppression than any in history.

We believe BDS to be, in actuality, a movement that is anti-Semitic, first and foremost, *in intent*—if indeed, hopefully not, as it appears from the gutted 2014 Modern Language Association resolution's meaningless wording, in effect, with apologies to Lawrence Summers for our inversion of his well-known formula. Stalwart BDSers, who know better, often seek to evade the "anti-Semitic" (because anti-Zionist) label, by resorting to ignoring or covering up what Palestinians say *in Arabic* about their political demands; the definition of their national identity; and widespread attitudes toward Israelis. The movement for academic and cultural shunning of Israel—the anti-Israel boycott lobby, understood as an outgrowth and organ of the "new anti-Zionist anti-Semitism"—is a movement against the Jews as a distinctive thread in the tapestry of humanity. It is a racist—anti-Semitism is a form of racism—movement. Anti-Zionism—anti-Zionism is a form of anti-Semitism—is immoral and, indeed, in its current guise as a campaign that proposes embargoing scholarship as a "place to start" since "why not," another self-inflicted wound to the reputation of today's university in crisis, or what one might term a "crime against the humanities." For it is no secret that anti-Zionism is the sort of prejudice that would see a Jewish state selectively excised from the map no less surely than the "old" anti-Semitism would like to have seen the Jewish people erased from the face of the earth.

# ALAN JOHNSON

When faced with Arab antisemitism, anti-Zionist ideology tends to minimize it, rationalizing, bracketing, and rendering it, or just plain falsifying it. For example, in Ilan Pappé's *The Idea of Israel*, one would never know that the Palestinian leader Haj Amin Al-Husseini was so supportive of the Nazis that he formed a Muslim SS Unit. Pappé presents this as just "an episode" in the "complex" life of a nationalist; a "foolish flirtation" that should only be of interest to the reader because it has been exploited by Zionists to "demonize" the Palestinians and "made it easy for Israeli historiography" (175–176). Al-Husseini, you see, was "forced" into the alliance with Hitler because the British had expelled him from Palestine after the Revolt of 1937. Similarly, the antisemitism of the Al-Qassam brigades is lawyered away by Pappé and the antisemitic British foreign secretary Ernest Bevin is retouched as a "pragmatic and sensible" figure. More seriously, Pappé flirts with the notion of Jewish responsibility for antisemitism. Discussing the 17th century pogroms against the Jews in Eastern Europe, Pappé invokes the "heresy" of Israel Shahak in order to argue that Jews must acknowledge "some degree of Jewish responsibility" for those pogroms; it was the "lack of empathy or identification with the oppressed peasants" on the part of the Jews that led to their targeting. Pappé urges the reader to ignore those Zionist textbooks that say Jews were attacked "because of who they were and not because of anything they did." Pappé then tells us that the "same explanation"—antisemitism is, at least in part, about what Jews do—can be applied "to the hatred and aggression of the Arabs or Palestinians against Israelis" (74–75).

Pappé also claims that the exodus and expulsion of Jews from the Arab lands after 1948 had no anti-Semitic component. After all, the Jews of the Arab lands were enjoying "organic cohabitation ... in Arab and Islamic societies ... a life of integration and coexistence" until Zionism "reintroduced this schism in modern times" (188-89). Similarly, for Ariella Azoulay and Adi Ophir, the "long positive history of coexistence shared by Jews and Arabs in various countries, including Palestine until the end of the British Mandate," is "played down" by "the Zionists," while "shows of anti-Semitism are magnified out of all proportion" (256).

And when Jacqueline Rose erases the distinction between the Palestinian suicide bomber and his Israeli civilian victim, *uncritically* passing on to the reader the view of the Hamas leader Abdul Aziz al-Ratansi ("If he wants to sacrifice his soul in order to defeat the enemy and for God's sake—well, then he's a martyr"), are we not reminded of Moshe Postone's observation about the "Orientalist reification of the Arabs and/or Muslims as the Other, whereby the Other, this time, is affirmed."? ■

*Adapted from Russell Berman, "The Boycott as an Infringement on Academic Freedom," Kenneth L. Marcus, "Is BDS Anti-Semitic?," Cary Nelson, "The Problem With Judith Butler," Gabriel Brahm & Asaf Romirowsky, "In Intent, If Not in Effect: The Failure of BDS," Mitchell Cohen, "Anti-Semitism and the Left That Doesn't Learn," and David Hirsh, "Antisemitism, not the accusation of antisemitism, is the dirty trick," with additional material added.*

---

Also see APARTHEID, BDS: A BRIEF HISTORY, HOLOCAUST INVERSION, JEWISH ANTI-SEMITISM: THREE VIEWS, ZIONISM: ITS EARLY HISTORY, and ZIONISM AS PHILOSOPHY AND PRACTICE.

# APARTHEID

In 2012, scholars were waiting for a panel to begin at the South African Sociological Association Conference. A leading sociologist appeared: "Which one is the Israeli?" he asked. The Israeli made himself known. He was then challenged to denounce Israel as an apartheid state. When he declined to do so, the other participants in the session left the room and carried on their panel in another place. The Israeli was left to give his paper to nobody. This way of weaponizing the apartheid analogy is far removed from the methods of comparative study, of reason, of giving evidence, of relating to the work rather than to the person.

—David Hirsh (Conference presentation, 2016)

Comparisons between Israel's treatment of Palestinians and South Africa's treatment of its majority non-white population during its apartheid period have gradually achieved visibility since the 1967 war when Israel gained military authority over the West Bank and its resident Palestinian population. The comparison gained credibility from the title of former president Jimmy Carter's 2006 book *Palestine: Peace Not Apartheid*. Some, including Israelis, have warned that conditions on the West Bank constitute a form of latent apartheid and that unless Israel rids itself of the bulk of the West Bank the economic and political conditions that prevail there will evolve into actual apartheid. Others, including many in the Boycott, Divestment, and Sanctions (BDS) movement, maintain that military checkpoints, separate villages and roads, travel restraints, the security barrier (MAP 3), the I.D. system, and inequities in resources and legal treatment on the West Bank already amount to a form of apartheid. Peter Beinart distinguishes between "democratic and undemocratic Israel," which is an objective characterization, unlike the apartheid accusation. Certainly there is ethnically based separation on the West Bank, with Jewish settlers being legally, politically, and economically privileged over Palestinians. The population is ethnically divided between citizens and non-citizens, a division that does not apply to Jews and Arabs in Israel proper, since both groups there are citizens. There are separate towns, separate roads, and areas to which West Bank Palestinians are forbidden access. The autonomy the Palestinian Authority has on the West Bank is easily abrogated in periods of crisis. Some extend this accusation to Israel proper in a hostile effort to stigmatize and delegitimize Israel as a whole, although Arab citizens in Israel enjoy full democratic rights and participate in the wide range of integrated Israeli institutions, from hospitals to universities to the courts. Some Israeli Arabs face discrimination in housing and other areas, much as African Americans historically did in the US, but these disadvantages are correctible through funding and legislation. They are not a basis for international sanctions. The Israeli government has committed itself to a substantial increase in spending on Arab education and infrastructure over the next five years; that will help improve the situation. Palestinians on the West Bank, moreover, seek their own political self-realization, not citizenship in a Jewish State. The BDS movement's references to Israel as an apartheid state are not designed as a warning and a wake-up call; they do not herald a reform agenda. Rather they are designed, by analogy with South Africa, to urge that the Jewish state be dismantled. Apartheid is a term that has effectively been weaponized for use in the Israeli-Palestinian conflict. It is designed to override any and all differences between Israel and apartheid South Africa.

—CN

# BENJAMIN POGRUND

The Arabs of Israel are full citizens. Admittedly, these Palestinian citizens of Israel do suffer discrimination, starting with severe restrictions on land use. Their generally poorer school results mean lower rates of entry into higher education, which has an impact on jobs and income levels.

Yet, they have the vote, and Israeli Arabs sit in parliament. An Arab judge sits on the country's highest court; an Arab is chief surgeon at a leading hospital; an Arab commands a brigade of the Israeli army; others head university departments. Arab and Jewish babies are born in the same delivery rooms, attended by the same doctors and nurses, and mothers recover in adjoining beds. Jews and Arabs travel on the same trains, taxis, and—yes—buses. Universities, theatres, cinemas, beaches, and restaurants are open to all.

So why is the apartheid accusation pushed so relentlessly, especially by the Boycott, Divestment and Sanctions (BDS) movement? I believe those campaigners want Israel declared an apartheid state so it becomes a pariah, open to the world's severest sanctions. Many want not just an end to the occupation but an end to Israel itself . . . .

How does that compare with the old South Africa? Under apartheid, every detail of life was subject to discrimination by law. Black South Africans did not have the vote. Skin color determined where you were born and lived, your job, your school, which bus, train, taxi, and ambulance you used, which park bench, lavatory, and beach, whom you could marry, and in which cemetery you were buried.

Israel is not remotely like that. Everything is open to change in a tangled society in which lots of people have grievances, including Mizrahi Jews (from the Middle East) or Jews of Ethiopian origin. So anyone who equates Israel and apartheid is not telling the truth.

So much for the argument that Israel proper, inside the Green Line determined by war (MAP 2), is an apartheid state. On the West Bank, the present story starts with the 1967 Six Day War . . . Israel is in military occupation of the West Bank. Day after day the actions needed to maintain it debase Palestinian victims as well as their Israeli occupiers. It means checkpoints, late-night raids and detentions, and killings, and administrative cruelties in regulating people's lives . . . It is wrong and must end. The point does not need to be embellished. Dragging in the emotive word "apartheid" is not only incorrect but creates confusion and distracts from the main issue.

EMILY BUDICK

Apartheid, as defined by BDS on its website, is "a social system that separates and discriminates against people based on race or ethnicity when that system is institutionalized by laws or decrees." It is, the statement continues, constituted by "acts committed in the context of an institutionalized regime of systematic oppression and domination by one racial group over any other racial group or groups and committed with the intention of maintaining that regime." However you want to characterize Israeli policy toward its citizens (and the Arabs are not the only minority in Israel), it is not apartheid and does not even meet the standards of BDS' own definition. The boycott against South Africa took a position in relation to a country that, similar to the slave-holding and then the segregated American South, deprived human beings of their citizenship, their basic human rights, equality under the law, and equal access to national resources. This is not the case in Israel, despite the BDS claim to the contrary. Indeed, the analogy to South Africa is not only a ploy for adducing sympathy for the boycott. More fundamentally, it is also another way of articulating the full right of return for Palestinian refugees. The analogy (which is a false one) is that just as South Africa was a country of an African majority that was oppressed and marginalized by a white minority, so, according to the BDS, is Israel a nation with a Palestinian majority (albeit many of them living outside of Palestine), which is being controlled by a Jewish minority. Yet, the State of Israel was established by international law as the homeland of the Jewish people in a place that already had, when the State was declared, a significant Jewish population, despite immigration restrictions imposed by the British, who were intent on preventing further Jewish immigration to British Mandated Palestine. The appeal to the example of the boycott of South Africa is nothing more than a rhetorical flourish, aimed at bringing the logic of one situation to come to bear on another very different situation, which requires a different set of terminologies and a different set of solutions.

Notably, the American Studies Association justified its 2013 boycott of Israeli academic institutions not on the basis of the occupation in the West Bank or the Israeli settlements but instead with a blanket condemnation of the substance of Israeli society as a whole: "As with South Africa, Israel's system of racial discrimination, at all institutional levels, constitutes apartheid." Support for the boycott depends on accepting the extremist credo that Israeli democracy is indistinguishable from South African apartheid, a myth that the ASA endorses, thereby undermining its credibility as a scholarly organization.

It is a fantasy that opportunistically trivializes the experience of apartheid in South Africa, while misrepresenting the reality of Israeli society. Support for the boycott requires the belief that the problem is not the unresolved Israeli occupation of parts of the West Bank but the existence of Israel altogether.

## ALAN JOHNSON

The idea that Israel is an "apartheid state" is the shaky intellectual foundation of the global movement to boycott, divest from, and sanction the Jewish homeland (BDS). In *The Apartheid Smear* (http://www.bicom.org.uk/analysis-article/18870/), I try to show that the comparison of Israel with racist apartheid-era South Africa is a malicious lie that does huge damage to the central goal of the peace process: the creation through negotiation of two states for two peoples, Israeli and Palestinian.

Readers can judge my argument by reading the pamphlet. In brief, I claim Israel within the Green Line is a multi-ethnic democracy in which every citizen is guaranteed equal rights under the law; save for those promoting a Greater Israel, beyond the Green Line, Israel's security policies are best understood as the tragic and continuing response to the failure of repeated peace negotiations and the terrible reality of terrorism, and not as an Israeli intent to rule over the Palestinians as superiors holding down inferior helots, apartheid style.

Here, I want to say something about the revealing historical background to the apartheid smear. There have been three key moments. Each—whatever the sincere hopes of many of its supporters—was a cynical attempt to demonize Israel as a pariah state in order to prepare the ground for its eventual destruction.

The smear originated in "anti-Zionist" campaigns that were waged without let up by the Communist states during the Cold War. Seeking Arab allies, these campaigns frequently descended into antisemitism, the word "Zionist" understood by all as a fig-leaf for "Jew." Many ideas that have since spread around the world, especially amongst "progressives," began here: Zionism equals racism, Zionism equals imperialism. Israel is the USA's "watchdog" in the Middle East, Zionism is complicit with, or even promotes, antisemitism, and, of course, Zionism equals South African apartheid.

It is hard to overstate how corrosive these ideas were to liberal intellectual culture in the West. For example, in 1975 an official publication of the communist Ukrainian Soviet Socialist Republic, *Zionism and Apartheid*, claimed that Israel shared with South Africa a "racial biological doctrine" based on the idea of a "chosen people" versus an inferior people. Fellow travelers of the communists produced a stream of books in this period that circulated widely in Western universities and often demonized Israel and Zionism. For example, *Zionism, Imperialism and Racism*, edited by AW Kayyali in 1979, included a chapter by Fayez Sayegh which claimed that "This century has witnessed three perfect racisms: Aryan or Nazi racism, Zionism racism and Apartheid Racism." (I cut my teeth in student politics in the 1980s resisting attempts by the Socialist Workers Party, and others, to ban campus Jewish societies. Yes, really.)

The smear got a huge boost in 1975 when a coalition between the Soviet Bloc, the authoritarian Arab states, and the so-called "Non-Aligned Movement" used its built-in majority at the UN General Assembly to pass Resolution 3379, which equated Zionism with racism. (The UN rescinded the resolution in 1991.)

The third key moment in the growth of the Apartheid Smear came in 2001 with the failure of the Camp David peace talks. This gave the smear an opening which was seized by a tightly-organized, politically motivated, and well-resourced group of NGOs and anti-Israel activists who hijacked the UN's World Conference against Racism, Racial Intolerance and Xenophobia in Durban, South Africa to launch a global campaign against Israel as a "racist, apartheid state" and Israel itself as a "crime against humanity."

South Africa's then Deputy Foreign Minister, Aziz Pahad, was appalled: "I wish to make it unequivocally clear that the SA government recognizes that … [the Durban Conference] was hijacked and used by some with an anti-Israel agenda to turn it into an antisemitic event."

The event was marked by hate speech. Pamphlets were circulated filled with grotesque caricatures of hook-nosed Jews depicted as Nazis, spearing Palestinian children, dripping blood from their fangs, with missiles bulging from their eyes or with pots of money nearby. In a Palestinian-led march with thousands of participants, a placard was held aloft that read "Hitler Should Have Finished the Job." Nearby, someone was selling the most notorious of anti-Jewish tracts, *The Protocols of the Elders of Zion*, a forgery which purports to be the minutes of a world Jewish Conspiracy, and which has been called a "warrant for genocide."

Mary Robinson, the former President of Ireland and the UN High Commissioner for Human Rights, has said "There was horrible antisemitism present—particularly in some of the NGO discussions. A number of people said they've never been so hurt or so harassed or been so blatantly faced with antisemitism."

Such is the history of the apartheid smear.

Politicians who stay silent when the smear is aired in parliament have a duty to find their voice and protest. Enough of letting it slide. The smear damages hopes for peace by encouraging extremists and demoralizing moderates. It fosters political polarization, eroding the chances of compromise, mutual recognition, and reconciliation. And it fosters a destructive "smear and boycott activism" here in the West, consuming energies that could be invested in something more constructive: a politics that is pro-Palestinian, pro-Israeli, pro-peace. Time to call time on the apartheid smear. ■

*Adapted from Benjamin Pogrund, "Israel has many injustices. But it is not an apartheid state," Emily Budick, "When a Boycott is Not Moral Action but Social Conformity and the 'Affectation of Love,'" and Alan Johnson, "The Ugly History of the Apartheid Smear."*

Also see ANTI-JEWISH BOYCOTTS IN HISTORY, ANTI-ZIONISM AS ANTI-SEMITISM, JEWISH ANTI-SEMITISM: THREE VIEWS, and BDS: A BRIEF HISTORY.

# BDS: A BRIEF HISTORY

## CARY NELSON

T he international Boycott, Divestment, and Sanctions (BDS) movement is the most influential current version of a long-term effort to delegitimize the State of Israel. A **boycott** can be defined as a way of withdrawing from commercial, professional, or social relations with a person, a people, a company, an institution (like a university), or a country. Both individuals and groups can advocate and initiate boycotts. **Divestment** refers to a process of selling an asset, as when an investor sells stocks or takes money out of a fund or an institution. It too can be carried out by both individuals and groups. **Sanctions**, on the other hand, are legal constructs, punishments or restraints typically initiated by legislative bodies. They carry the authority of state actions.

BDS supports all three strategies. In addition, it adopts specific principles and guidelines with far-reaching goals. The movement officially advocates an agenda that would bring Israel's Jewish identity to an end by allowing the Palestinians who were displaced by the new State of Israel in 1948 to return, along with their millions of descendants, thereby replacing the Jewish state with an Arab-dominated one. While BDS officially gives no detailed account of how a Palestinian "Right of Return" would play out, the fact that its website, its key advocates, along with all major Palestinian groups, insist on honoring the principle without qualification means that all who join the movement are effectively promoting the dissolution of the Jewish state, whether or not that is their intention.

BDS's most prominent advocates, including movement founder Omar Barghouti and American literary critic Judith Butler, explicitly call for the end of the Jewish state, but a deceptive version of "BDS lite" persists in some quarters. Columbia University Professor Bruce Robbins has worked to fudge the Right of Return principle by claiming that "BDS is not aimed at repairing the original injustice of the Nakba. It's much too late for that. Nor is it about achieving moral consistency. That it is always too late for." Robbins acts like it is a grand concession to admit we cannot bring justice to the dead; that would seem self-evident. But he insists "we inhabit the site of violent injustices committed long ago" and that the living "have been visibly shaped by those injustices." So we have a "debt to the living" that must be repaired. This is a distinction without a difference. Indeed the Palestinian narrative is centered on the foundational injustice of the Nakba, and the call for Israel to acknowledge its guilt. That we cannot achieve moral consistency is true, but BDS demands we address the inconsistency and repair it as substantially as possible, which centers both the present and the future on 1948.

The other versions of "BDS lite" include the occasional claim that BDS is not aimed at dismantling Israel but just with changing its policies. Although the endorsement of the Palestinian right of return contradicts that claim, it is equally notable that BDS has never organized around any set of specific policy changes. If you want policy changes, you advocate for them. You don't hope for indirect (and unspecified) policy change by boycotting Tel Aviv University or Ahava beauty products. Robbins mounts yet another disingenuous argument by asserting "the movement explicitly restricts the demand to lands colonized *since 1967*, in other words to the West Bank." But of course BDS demands the right of return to Israel within its pre-1967 borders. And BDS advocates also frequently claim that Arab citizens of Israel proper face apartheid-style abuses and thus insists they be lifted. BDS lite is essentially a bait and switch strategy. A comment Robbins made at the January 2016 meeting of the Modern Language Association was an effort to shape BDS's basic attitude toward such contradictions: he said it was important just to admit that BDS resolutions are not perfect. Then we could proceed to advocate for them without troubling ourselves with their flaws or their consequences. One such consequence was noted at the same meeting: a Palestinian doctoral student at a boycotted Israeli university might find it impossible to obtain an outside reader for her dissertation, a regrettable instance of collateral damage we would have to accept in the service of the greater cause. At a debate between BDS advocates and opponents on another day, one of the movement's critics accused it of anti-Semitism. The audience of 90, dominated by BDS, broke out in spontaneous laughter. Is anti-Semitism merely one further form of collateral damage the noble movement to boycott Israel generates, or is it fundamental to the movement's consequences and conditions of possibility?

The charge of anti-Semitism in fact is not the only challenge to the morality of BDS's tactics. For people in many countries—especially those with a history of violent territorial ambitions or colonialist, slave-holding, or genocidal legacies—there is the "glass house" phenomenon, the problem that critics of Israel do not speak from morally pure positions. Robbins echoes the unstated ethic of the anti-Israel movement by arguing that "the position you occupy ought to be irrelevant," that you can claim a position of absolute, unqualified, universal morality no matter how dirty your own and your country's hands are. That is certainly how many BDS activists behave, although most have perhaps not thought much about the matter. One consequence of promoting an unreflective morality, of leading the unexamined self-righteous life, is that you dismiss as irrelevant the only political actions likely to have any practical consequences, namely those directed toward your own country's policies and actions.

Robbins handles this objection to the BDS focus on delegitimizing the Jewish state by falsely arguing the only alternative would be to work to eliminate US military aid to Israel, a tactic Noam Chomsky has advocated. Robbins is correct in pointing out that isn't "a means to an end; it is the end. Pull that off, and it's game over." One might add that any effort to pressure the Israeli government to change its policies would discredit itself if it threatened a withdrawal of aid. It would also have exactly no chance of winning Congressional approval.

But if Americans want to promote the two-state solution they have many less apocalyptic options. They might publicize, criticize, and shame private individuals and foundations that fund West Bank settlement expansion. They might pressure Congress and the administration to make opposition to settlement expansion east of the security barrier a more central priority of US policy. They could support a UN Security Council resolution laying out a thoughtful set of principles behind a two-state solution, one without a deadline that accepted West Jerusalem as Israel's capital and East Jerusalem as the capital of a Palestinian state, one that provided for a Palestinian return to the West Bank but not Israel proper, one that insisted a Palestinian state be nonmilitarized, and one that incorporated the nearby settlement blocs into Israel by way of land swaps.

BDS's organizational incarnation and set of strategies originated in goals outlined in the summer of 2001 at the United Nation's World Conference Against Racism in Durban, South Africa. Instead of focusing on problems of racism throughout the world, however, the event developed largely into a focused attack on Israel and promoted the claim that Israel was an "apartheid state" exercising racist policies against the Palestinian people. Though that actual language was withdrawn from the text approved by the conference, a parallel meeting of NGOs, also in Durban in early September, adopted language equating Zionism with racism, language that had been withdrawn from the main meeting when the United States, Israel, and other nations objected. The UN General Assembly had endorsed the equation of Zionism with racism in 1975, but revoked it in 1991. Two days after the NGO meeting ended, more than 3,000 people died when the World Trade Center in New York City was destroyed, the Pentagon severely damaged, and an airliner brought down in Pennsylvania. Those events overshadowed the Durban meetings and limited the publicity they received. BDS has now revived the discredited slander that Zionism is fundamentally a form of racism.

BDS's academic boycott campaigns began in Britain and the US early in the new millennium. The first BDS campaign in the US was a February 2002 petition drive urging the University of California to sell (divest itself of) stock held in companies deemed as benefitting from their relationship with the Jewish state. That spring divestment drives followed at Harvard, MIT, and elsewhere. They all failed, but the publicity generated helped fuel BDS in the long term. Both then and since, these divestment drives proved highly divisive, generating mutual antagonism, accusations, and acrimonious debate on campus. BDS supporters target universities because faculty and students can become passionate about justice, sometimes without adequate knowledge about the facts and consequences. Like other targeted institutions in civil society, universities also offer the potential for small numbers of BDS activists to leverage institutional status and reputation for a more significant cultural and political impact. Campus divestment campaigns were launched again in 2009 and 2010, among them another Berkeley effort. They continued through 2016 and are likely to be ongoing.

Students for Justice in Palestine (SJP), a national group that claims about 100 campus chapters, was established at Berkeley in 2001 to support the BDS movement, frequently by urging student government bodies to adopt divestment resolutions. Some argue SJP's roots go back to anti-Israel organizing at San Francisco State University in the 1970s. SJP has an activist history that includes not only organizing anti-Israel rallies but also organizing occasional building occupations and demonstrations that interrupt pro-Israel campus lectures. In November 2015 both the University of Minnesota and the University of Texas at Austin saw pro-Israeli speakers interrupted by aggressive demonstrations aimed at preventing them from speaking or substantially delaying the event, actions that violate the basic standards for academic exchange. SJP has also been energetic in using social media to advance the BDS agenda. Their 2014 divestment campaigns included actions at the University of Michigan and the University of New Mexico. Northeastern University banned the group for a year in 2014 for actions that crossed the line between advocacy and intimidation. Divestment campaigns have also focused on companies doing business in Israel, along with pension funds and financial institutions investing in Israel, urging them to cease doing so, once again because a prominent company name can leverage a great amount of publicity.

In January 2016 an Israeli presentation at King's College, London, had to be cancelled when it was interrupted by a violent protest. Furniture was destroyed, windows broken, and fire alarms set off. A brief protest as a lecture is about to begin, perhaps a minute devoted to chanting slogans, is arguably an acceptable exercise of free speech in a university. But attempting in a sustained and relentless fashion to prevent an invited lecturer from speaking, as people in Minneapolis did, or actually blocking a speech, as the thugs at King's College did, violates the most basic principles of the university. We are witnessing a time when the opportunity to learn, to hear alternative views, is being overturned by mob action.

Meanwhile, the Palestinian Campaign for the Academic and Cultural Boycott of Israel (PACBI) was launched in Ramallah on the West Bank (MAP 3) in April 2004 and joined the BDS campaign the following year, with a website and incarnations worldwide, including the US Campaign for the Academic and Cultural Boycott of Israel (USACBI). In July 2004 the General Assembly of the Presbyterian Church in the US approved a pathway to divestment and a decade later sold shares in three companies targeted by the BDS movement. Attempting another version of BDS lite, the church stated it was not joining the BDS movement, but its Israel Palestine Mission Network, known for its anti-Zionist stances, formally embraced the BDS movement as did the United Church of Christ in 2015. In July 2005 an alliance of 171 Palestinian organizations called for BDS action against Israel, a date many BDS groups like to credit as their moment of origin, since it lets them claim they are answering a call from Palestinian civil society, even though the campaign was four years old at that point. The Palestinian BDS National Committee (BNC) was inaugurated in Ramallah in November 2007 to coordinate BDS activities with Palestinian NGOs and networks. Not all these efforts have causal relationships with one another, but they do influence each another, and the media often link them as evidence of an international movement.

The year 2005 also saw the emergence of "Israeli Apartheid Week," a mixture of rallies, lectures, exhibits, and film showings inaugurated in Toronto to support the BDS agenda and ideology. Now generally organized by campus groups and held in February or March, it may also include off-campus events as well. Locations in 2014 include over a hundred cities worldwide. MIT's Noam Chomsky has spoken at a number of Israeli Apartheid Week events, as has Israeli historian Ilan Pappé. Chomsky, though certainly hostile to Israel, is opposed to the BDS movement's current tactics, since he considers them politically counter-productive (Clark; Chomsky). Norman Finkelstein, implacably hostile to Israel, condemned BDS in 2012 because the movement lies about its aims, hiding a desire to eliminate Israel behind its three demands (Jordan Michael Smith). Although publicity for IAW events has often been limited to local coverage, the choice of the name was obviously designed to be provocative, disturbing, and a media draw.

The most difficult BDS goal to implement is the "S" in BDS, which refers to sanctions that nations or groups of nations might carry out against Israel. That requires considerable political clout, enough to leverage formal state action. Far easier to pursue and often enough successful are cultural boycotts of arts and humanities events, for which we provide a separate entry.

Another BDS strategy is the boycott of Israeli industries and products, which has a history long predating BDS itself, having been a concerted effort by Arab nations begun when Israel announced its statehood and continuing into the 1950s. The first Arab boycott of Jews in Palestine, though on a much smaller scale, dates from 1921. Jews throughout the world remember that the Nazis inaugurated their campaign against the Jews with boycotts of Jewish businesses. Most boycotts since have failed, but in recent years modest boycotts of West Bank products (or additional tariffs levied on them) have met with some success in the European Union and elsewhere. In 2015 the EU moved forward with a far less problematic plan simply to label products from the West Bank. At the same time, *Buycott* campaigns urging people to purchase products targeted for boycotts have worked well. The online *BDS Cookbook*, an anti-BDS guide (http://www.stopbds.com/?page_id=25), lists a number of the first Buycott projects, from the Canadian initiative (http://www.buycottisrael.com) that monitors campaigns to promote Israeli products targeted by BDS, to BuyIsraeliProducts.com, a website offering a range of products for sale.

Although nearly 450 college or university presidents issued statements opposing academic boycotts in 2007 and over 250 did so again in 2014—and although every major academic organization representing multiple academic disciplines (as opposed to those representing only one discipline) that has addressed the issue opposes them as well—faculty members in at least some disciplines continue to approve them as a political strategy. Proposals to boycott universities continue to receive faculty support and publicity in the press, and have a potential impact on public opinion and perhaps eventually even on national policy. The higher education associations rejecting boycotts include the American Association of University Professors, the American Council on Education, the Association of Public and Land-Grant Universities, and the Association of American Universities. The AAU, an association of 60 US and two Canadian public and private research universities, reaffirmed its opposition to boycotts of Israeli universities in January 2016.

One critical point to emphasize about faculty support for academic boycotts and the BDS movement overall is that it is concentrated in a group of humanities and social science disciplines. There is little or no support for BDS in the sciences, medicine, or in technical fields like engineering and computer science. A 2014 statistical analysis of "the institutional and primary departmental affiliations of 938 faculty members in 316 American colleges and universities, who have signed or endorsed one or more of 15 statements calling for an academic boycott of Israeli universities and scholars" shows that "the vast majority—89 (86%)—were in the Humanities (453 or 49%) or Social Sciences (336 or 37%). Only 61 (7%) of the boycotters were affiliated with departments in Engineering and Natural Science, and only 38 (4%) were affiliated with departments in the Arts division" (Rossman-Benjamin).

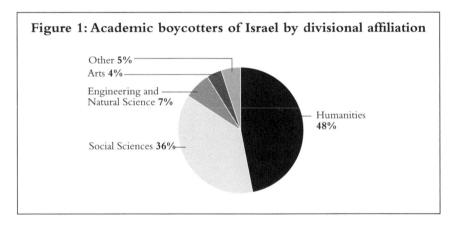

**Figure 1: Academic boycotters of Israel by divisional affiliation**

Other **5%**
Arts **4%**
Engineering and Natural Science **7%**
Social Sciences **36%**
Humanities **48%**

English and literary studies dominate the figures for faculty departmental affiliations, with 192 or 21%. That tells us both what academic discipline has contributed the most people to the BDS movement and suggests as well how much influence a given discipline has had on the movement, but does not make it possible to estimate what percentage of a discipline is committed to BDS, since the relative size of academic disciplines varies considerably. After English comes "ethnic studies (96 or 10%), history (68 or 7%), gender studies (65 or 7%), anthropology (53 or 6%), sociology (44 or 5%), linguistics or languages (43 or 5%), politics (39 or 4%), American studies (33 or 3%), Middle or Near East studies (32 or 3%) (Rossman-Benjamn). Support for BDS has no doubt grown in some fields since the data was gathered, but English has surely held its lead. It is a field where many faculty and students are notably moved by emotion and where facts have less influence.

# SUMMARY—THE TEN KEY PROBLEMS WITH BDS

1.  BDS demonizes, antagonizes, and delegitimizes one of the two parties who have to negotiate a solution to the conflict by working together, and BDS uncritically idealizes the other. That will inhibit negotiations, not promote them.
2.  BDS misrepresents its goal, which is not to change Israeli government policy but rather to eliminate the Jewish state.
3.  BDS offers no specific steps toward a resolution of the conflict and no detailed peace plan, merely a comprehensive condemnation of Israel.
4.  BDS misrepresents its conditions for a resolution of the conflict. BDS does not seek to negotiate a Palestinian right of return to the West Bank, but rather to impose a right for all Palestinians to return to Israel within its pre-1967 borders.
5.  BDS falsely claims to imagine a nonviolent route to ending the conflict. But there is no nonviolent way to achieve its goal of eliminating the Jewish state.
6.  BDS demands an end to all efforts to build mutual empathy and understanding between Israelis and Palestinians. This "anti-normalization" campaign rejects the communication, dialogue, negotiation, and unconditional interchange necessary to achieve a peaceful resolution of the conflict.
7.  BDS falsely claims to target institutions, not individuals. Its boycott guidelines prove otherwise, detailing numerous ways individuals will be targeted.
8.  BDS's academic boycott proposals would limit contacts with critics of Israeli policy, including Israeli Arabs teaching or studying at Israeli universities.
9.  BDS undermines academic freedom by limiting free expression and the exchange of ideas and undercutting faculty and student rights to collaborate with others as they choose and make their own decisions about what research and study opportunities to pursue.
10. BDS offers nothing to the Palestinian people it claims to champion. Perhaps the single most cruel and ironic feature of the BDS movement is that it actually offers nothing realistic and tangible to the Palestinian

people. The movement is really about capturing the hearts and minds of Americans and Europeans, not about helping the Palestinian people. Its message of hate is a route to war, not peace. ■

Also see ACADEMIC BOYCOTTS, ANTI-JEWISH BOYCOTTS IN HISTORY, BDS AND THE AMERICAN ANTHROPOLOGICAL ASSOCIATION, BDS AND THE AMERICAN STUDIES ASSOCIATION, BDS AND CHRISTIAN CHURCHES, CULTURAL BOYCOTTS, DIVESTMENT CAMPAIGNS, ECONOMIC BOYCOTTS, THE ONE-STATE SOLUTION, and PALESTINIAN THEOLOGY OF LIBERATION.

# BDS AND CHRISTIAN CHURCHES

CARY NELSON

## INTRODUCTION

One of the oldest traditions in both Judaism and Christianity, drawing on and amplifying exhortations by the Jewish Prophets and by Jesus in the Christian Gospels, focuses on the need to redress inequities, minister to the poor and the oppressed, and defend them against wealth and power. Once peoples are grouped as oppressors or oppressed, one group can be dehumanized and justice can easily become justice for the oppressed alone. In the last decade, for some Christian denominations that has meant championing the cause of the Palestinians and opposing the Israeli state, which is no longer perceived as vulnerable, given that it has a powerful army that oversees the administration of the West Bank. The conflict is consequently perceived as one between power and powerlessness, between the lion and the lamb. Those with power are expected to act benevolently, and those without power often have their aggressive or violent actions excused. While mainline Protestant activists may recognize suffering on both sides of the Israeli-Palestinian conflict, they are often convinced, with good reason, that the Palestinians presently suffer much more. For those who feel called to address that imbalance and who believe Israel must be held accountable for it, BDS is often the answer.

Some denominations also have longstanding relationships with Palestinian Christians, who understandably have a privileged voice when the Israeli–Palestinian conflict comes up for discussion and debate. The Sabeel Ecumenical Liberation Theology Center, a Jerusalem-based Palestinian organization founded in 1990, has been particularly influential. It supports a two-state solution, but sees it as a step toward a bi-national state. Sabeel's director, Rev. Naim Ateek, has also promoted much more aggressive rhetoric. His spring 2001 Easter message indicted Israel with echoes of an ancient prejudice: "It seems to many of us that Jesus is on the cross again with thousands of crucified Palestinians around him." Jerusalem's Bethlehem Bible College echoes that trope with its biennial "Christ at the Checkpoint" conferences. Sabeel's US-based affiliated group, Friends of Sabeel in North America (FOSNA), has promoted divestment resolutions both in mainline Protestant churches and on campus. In December 2009 a number of Palestinian Christians issued the Kairos Palestine Document urging Christians worldwide to join in fighting the Israeli occupation. The document's title echoes the 1985 Kairos Document, which focused on the Church's role in South Africa and urged strong action against the apartheid regime. BDS advocates in the Christian churches often call on Jewish Voice for Peace (JVP), a pro-BDS organization founded in 1996, to testify in favor of anti-Israel resolutions, thereby insulating the church from accusations of anti-Semitism by showing Jewish support for its agenda.

The pro-BDS sentiments in some Christian denominations often run counter to the widespread reevaluation of Christianity's relationship to Jews and Judaism that gained force after the Holocaust. Critical to that process has been the effort to repudiate supersessionist theological narratives in which Christians have supplanted Jews to become "the only legitimate heirs of God's covenant with Abraham." Unfortunately, old habits persist, and the long history of Christian anti-Jewish polemic lurks behind some anti-Zionist initiatives (Smith & Levine). Some 35 Christian religious institutions participated in the 2001 World Conference Against Racism in Durban, South Africa, that is credited with launching the BDS agenda. And BDS targets religious groups because of the moral authority they wield and the high publicity value of their pro-BDS votes.

The Christian group with the strongest anti-Zionist history is the once unequivocally pacifist American Friends Service Committee (AFSC), which actively supports BDS campaigns, trains students in BDS activism, and promotes anti-Israel rhetoric. AFSC pamphlets in the early 70s expressed sympathy for Palestinian violence. In 1973 the AFSC called for a US embargo on military aid to Israel. Now it works through the BDS movement to realize its goals. Dalit Baum is a prominent Israeli anti-Zionist activist who directs the AFSC's Middle East Program.

Some churches, especially in Europe, play a role in channeling government funds to BDS groups. The churches receive funds designed for humanitarian aid from government agencies but forward it to NGOs that sometimes have strong anti-Israel political agendas (http://www.ngo-monitor.org/data/images/File/BDS_Table.pdf).

# DIVESTMENT CAMPAIGNS IN MAINLINE PROTESTANT CHURCHES

For the most part, however, church groups in the US and Britain and international church groups with US affiliates have focused on divestment campaigns, in part because they have significant pension funds and stock holdings for which divestment from companies or international corporations doing business in the West Bank is a material action with practical consequences. In July 2004 the General Assembly of the Presbyterian Church (USA) approved a resolution setting a pathway to divestment from corporations operating in Israel. In 2005 the Central Committee of the World Council of Churches, meeting at its headquarters in Geneva, Switzerland, used similar language in encouraging its 342 member churches to adopt a "phased, selective divestment from multinational corporations involved . . . in the occupation." The WCC is the main global body uniting non-Catholic Christian churches.

The following year the Presbyterians' General Assembly rescinded its divestment language, but the denomination remained on the same pathway. Leading the effort has been the Israel Palestine Mission Network of the Presbyterian Church (USA), which published a fiercely anti-Zionist booklet and video, *Zionism Unsettled*, in 2014; *Zionism Unsettled* distorts and minimizes the ancient history of the Israelites based on the tendentious writings of a few fringe scholars. In June 2014, the General Assembly of the PCUSA passed a resolution by a vote of 310–303 to divest from Caterpillar, Motorola Solutions, and Hewlett-Packard, companies the PCUSA deemed complicit in and profiting from Israel's occupation of the West Bank and blockade of Gaza. They have now sold their shares in those companies. A number of outside groups and speakers had a major impact on the PCUSA process. Who Profits, cofounded by Dalit Baum, maintains a web site on "The Israeli Occupation Industry" (http://www.whoprofits.org) that helped the PCUSA to justify divestment. Jewish Voice for Peace (JVP) and Sabeel were active at the meeting. American psychologist Mark Braverman, a Jew who heads the pro-Palestinian Christian group Kairos USA, has been influential within the PCUSA for some years. He warns that "Christians . . . must not be intimidated by Jews who use [anti-Semitism] to muzzle legitimate protest against injustice" (339).

By that time the 200,000-member British Methodist Church, which had voted to endorse the boycott of settlement products in 2010, was in the process of considering more aggressive policies. In 2014 the United Methodist Church divested from G4S, a British-Danish firm providing security services to private prisons. It was misreported in *The New York Times* as a move related specifically to the company's contract work with Israeli prisons holding Palestinians. Although the UMC pension board issued a clarification, the damage from media misrepresentation was done. In June 2015 at its General Synod in Cleveland the 950,000-member United Church of Christ (UCC) passed a boycott, divestment, and sanctions resolution by a vote of 508-124. On the other hand, the same General Synod by a vote of 312 in favor to 295 against (and 31 abstentions) rejected a resolution branding Israel's West Bank practices acts of apartheid; the resolution failed to get the required two-thirds majority.

Even the votes in favor of divestment are not unanimous decisions. Presbyterians for Middle East Peace (PFMEP), a group of lay members and clergy in the PCUSA, remains critical of BDS initiatives, and early in 2016 they issued "Two States for Two Peoples," a substantial report and resource that should be useful both inside and outside the church. The battle waged in resolution votes is for the majority, since a majority vote often determines church policy. Moreover, even a close vote in favor of divestment that should not be considered a mandate is often treated as a major win by BDS advocates and the media alike. A number of Presbyterians have written letters protesting the 2014 vote, but that has little public impact. As one divestment opponent has written, "Jews have suffered at the hands of Christians for 2000 years" (Hallward 148). Another declared that "people that are promoting the BDS strategy have an incredibly grandiose vision of themselves and the power and the leverage that they might bring to bear on this thing" (Hallward 169). Others responded to the proposal to divest from Caterpillar by reminding the Church that many of its members work there. But some were troubled at the prospect that their own pension funds were implicated in social injustice.

More than 40 Commissioners to and Observers of the PCUSA's General Assembly signed *Reformed and Reforming: A Word of Hope* (http://www.reformingpcusa.org/AWordOfHope.pdf), a publicly available pamphlet decrying unfair and one-sided procedures at the meeting. It notes—among numerous other examples showing that "advocates for divestment have been given, in the past five General Assemblies, enormous advantages to make their case"—that during the debate in the Committee on Middle East Issues, pro-divestment speakers were allotted 18 hours of testimony, while opponents were granted less than 10 minutes (11). In the general meeting "peaceful local anti-divestment youth at the entrance to the assembly hall were harassed and asked to move while pro-divestment youth were given free access by GA staff" (14). The debate, they conclude, "in essence has become within the PC (USA) a Middle East war of proxy over the last decade" (6) in which "the denomination's historic commitment to fair and open debate of crucial issues" has been set aside (15). They plead for appropriate reform so discussion can be refocused on "spiritual discernment of what God is calling us to do and say as peacemakers" (4). One conclusion seems clear: like academic associations, religious organizations are ill-equipped to manage controversial political stands when their membership is deeply divided.

The General Assembly of the Church of Scotland accepted the controversial Church and Society Council report on Israel/Palestine titled "The Inheritance of Abraham? A Report on the 'Promised Land'" in May 2013. The report rejects Jewish scriptural and theological claims to the land, subjects Zionism to harsh criticism, and recommends church consideration of boycott and divestment resolutions. A revised version states that the report "should not be misunderstood as questioning the right of the State of Israel to exist." Meanwhile, the 1.8 million-member Episcopal Church's House of Bishops rejected three BDS resolutions at its 2015 General Convention, and the 97,000-member Mennonite Church voted 418-336 to postpone consideration of similar measures until 2017. In the summer of 2015, the Christian Empowerment Council, an Israeli Christian group, released *Test the Spirits: A Christian Guide to the Anti-Israel Boycott Movement* (http://eldarinn.com/CEC/images/BDS_PDF.JPG). Further consideration of boycott initiatives is likely in the United Methodist Church and Evangelical Lutheran Church in America.

The United Methodist Church took the first step in that direction in January 2016, when its pension board added five Israeli banks to a list of 39 companies from several countries it would not invest in for failing to meet its Human Rights Investment Policy guideline. The five Israeli banks are identified as being involved in settlement construction. Following a pattern similar to other Churches, Methodist advocacy has coalesced into competing groups. The United Methodist Kairos Response has submitted two resolutions for consideration at the General Conference in May 2016, one addressing companies supporting the occupation and another dealing with companies producing goods or services in Israeli settlements (MAP 4). On the other hand, a member of United Methodists for Constructive Peacemaking in Israel and

Palestine declared "we are not going to participate in the continuing demonization of one side over the other or the continuation of policies that bring about fear and isolation for one side over the other" (Richard Horowitz).

The practical Christian goal for those participating in the dialogue is to calibrate the relationship between the core of both Israeli and Palestinian narratives so as to address Palestinian suffering without becoming anti-Israel. That opens a conversation about whether the Jewish state has failed what many Christians see as its biblical imperative to act with justice. At this point the debate in mainline Protestant churches is confined to a conversation within the churches themselves—and often just to the activist core. Their long-term strategy seems clear, though: to call into question whether there should be a Jewish state, something that will be debated in a fashion at the PCUSA in 2016 as the denomination receives a report expected to call into question support for a two-state solution.

# ISRAEL AND THE EVANGELICAL MOVEMENT

There remains intense support of Israel and a complete rejection of the BDS movement among Christian Zionists in the large evangelical movement. Evangelical Protestant Christianity, which tends to take a more conservative view of biblical authority including the promise of the land to Abraham, Isaac, Jacob, and their descendants, encompasses some 286 million people worldwide, with roughly one quarter—or 61 million—residing in the US, where they are a potent political force (http://www.pewforum.org/2015/05/12/americas-changing-religious-landscape).

Many Evangelical Christian Zionists believe that the return of the Jews to the Holy Land, and often to all of Greater Israel, is a fulfillment of scriptural prophecy and thus that there is theological reason to support the existence of the Jewish state and to oppose a two-state solution. Some support Israel as a Jewish state in the hopes that Diaspora Jews will emigrate, with the return of Jews to Zion as a prerequisite for the return of Jesus to earth. Still others, who might be called "America Firsters," support Israel as a Jewish state because, on their reading Genesis 12.2-3 promises blessings to those who support Jews in Israel ("I will make of you a great nation, and I will bless you, and make your name great, so that you will be a blessing. I will bless those who bless you, and the one who curses you I will curse; and in you all the families of the earth shall be blessed"). Still others support Israel, and Jews, because they regard Jews as the "chosen people" and because it is from the Jews that Jesus was born. Finally, some Evangelical support for Israel is supported by a strong anti-Muslim view.

On the other hand, a number of prominent evangelical leaders have been allied with the political right, thus generating inevitable political tension with liberal Jews who share the evangelical's support for Israel. This tension is exacerbated by suspicions held by many Jews that evangelical support for Israel is grounded in prejudiced views of Arabs and Muslims, conviction that Palestinians have no rights to any of the land, conversionary imperatives, or eschatological beliefs, although the most common theological reason for evangelical support for Israel embodies a belief that the land is quite simply promised to the Jewish people. The Israeli government has found reason to make common cause with evangelicals in their shared belief that Israel should be supported. And any analysis of declining support for Israel among liberal Protestant denominations must keep in mind the sheer numerical and political force wielded by evangelicals. A substantial portion of the Americans who give Israel strong support are evangelicals. Those mainline Protestants who are active in the movement to question Israel's legitimacy often see themselves as a counterweight to the evangelicals. Indeed, some liberal Protestant anti-Israeli activity functions to define these Protestants over and against their Christian-Zionist counterparts. Thus in Christian contexts, the term "Zionism" needs to be precisely defined: Christian Zionism is primarily a religious view, namely, that God promised the land to the Jews. It is less often seen primarily in its historical view, namely, that Zionism is the Jewish quest for self-determination in their historical homeland. ■

Also see ACADEMIC BOYCOTTS, BDS: A BRIEF HISTORY, DIVESTMENT CAMPAIGNS, ECONOMIC BOYCOTTS, PALESTINIAN LIBERATION THEOLOGY, THE SOCIAL JUSTICE MANDATE IN HIGHEREDUCATION, ZIONISM AS PHILOSOPHY AND PRACTICE, and ZIONISM: ITS EARLY HISTORY.

# BDS AND ORGANIZED LABOR

CARY NELSON

I n November 1909 Clara Lemich, a 15-year-old Jewish worker from the Ukraine, rose to address a mass meeting of garment workers from numerous companies. Yiddish-speaking Jews from Eastern Europe who arrived from the 1880s on and settled in cities had gravitated to the garment industry. The industry was booming, with six hundred shops operating in New York City and sales of ready-made clothing, including "shirtwaists" (women's blouses) succeeding in mass markets, but wages were meager despite workweeks of 65–75 hours. As would become clear in the Triangle Shirtwaist Factory Fire of March 25, 1911, these factories were often death traps. Lemich had listened to several hours of speeches by men, although the workforce was over 70 percent female, about half Jewish and a third Italian. She took a pledge adapted from Psalm 137 ("If I turn traitor to the cause I now pledge, may my right hand wither from the arm I raise") and called in Yiddish for a general strike. Within two days, 20,000-30,000 workers went on strike. Lemich was arrested 17 times and had 6 ribs broken, but in February 2010 over 300 companies agreed to improved working conditions, wages, and hours. The National Women's Trade Union of America (NWTUL) and the decade-old International Ladies Garment Workers' Union (ILGWU) helped organize and publicize the effort. Five years of labor revolt followed that organized much of the industry. As a result, class consciousness was merged with feminism, and workers joined the suffragist cause.

Meanwhile there was already a Jewish labor movement in play and a significant Jewish role in the larger labor movement. Samuel Gompers (1850–1924), a Sephardic Jew who arrived from England in 1863, helped found the Cigar Makers Union in the 1870s and the American Federation of Labor in the following decade. He became the AFL's first president. The United Hebrew Trades was formed in 1888. In addition to the garment and cigar makers, Jews or Jewish unions would organize bakers, furriers, hat makers, painters, printers, and Yiddish actors. There was a strong socialist component in much of the Jewish labor movement, though Gompers was not sympathetic to it. Socialist leadership instead came, among others, from the Jewish labor leader Daniel DeLeon (1852-1914), who is credited with conceptualizing revolutionary industrial unionism. A rich union culture developed around these movements that linked union activism with a general commitment to education, cultural development, and social welfare. It was part of a generation that founded Yiddish schools and summer camps, reading circles, sports teams, old age homes, insurance plans, and orchestras through the Arbeiter Ring/Workmen's Circle. Earlier there had been significant Jewish participation in labor activism in the late 19th century. Hundreds of Jewish workers participated in the New York capmakers' general strike of 1874, the Cigar Makers' Strike of 1877–8, and the cloak makers' strike of 1890.

But it was partly the 1909–1910 "Uprising of the 20,000" among garment workers that decisively inspired a generation of Jewish labor activism, activism that had a transformative impact on the American labor movement. Although the labor movement suffered in the 1920s, it revived in the Great Depression under the New Deal. In 1937 eight American Federation of Labor unions split to form the Congress of Industrial Organizations (CIO); three of those were Jewish: the ILGWU, the Hat Makers and Milliners Union, and the Amalgamated Clothing Workers of America. The ACWA's president, Sidney Hillman (1887-1946) became FDR's main labor advisor and thus the best-known Jewish labor leader of the time. Jews were active in the mass strikes the CIO organized in the auto, steel, and textile industries during the Depression. The socialist-identified Jewish unions formed the Jewish Labor Committee in 1934. Under Baruch Charney Vladeck's leadership until his death in 1938, it warned about the rise of Nazism. It also lobbied on behalf of legislation admitting Jewish refugees to the US and later supported Jewish immigration from Europe to Israel. The Jewish labor unions also took the lead in pressing for equal status for African Americans in the workplace and in the union movement itself through the 1940s. American labor generally supported the founding of the Jewish state, indeed widely saw Israel as a labor endeavor and built working relationships with the *Histadrut*, the Israeli organization of trade unions founded in 1920:

The US trade union movement has a history of support for Israel going back three decades before Israel's independence, including statements in support of the Balfour Declaration. In fact, support for Israel's labor movement goes back to 1924 when the United Hebrew Trades in New York (UHT), now the New York Division of the JLC, started a fund-raising campaign among Jewish trade unionists to support the young *Histadrut*, now Israel's General Federation of Labor. Individual trade unions—from the needle trades to the Communications Workers of America—have established enduring relations both with their "sister unions" in Israel and directly with the *Histadrut*. Since the State of Israel was established in 1948, US trade unions have assisted in the construction of educational, health care-related, cultural and recreational facilities for workingmen and women in Israel, their families, and communities. These include the Max Pine Vocational School, the Glenn Watts Center, and the Morton Bahr education wing of the Yitzhak Rabin Center. Given the significant role played by the Israeli labor movement in the founding of the Jewish State and the creation of its infrastructure and institutions, it is not surprising that older US labor leaders view Israel as a nation-state created by organized labor. This is one of the reasons labor union pension funds, union banks and union insurance companies have invested heavily in State of Israel Bonds . . . . In recognition of the US labor movement's historical bedrock support for Israel, anti-Israel forces have in recent years made a concerted effort to break these ties.

—Jewish Labor Committee (17)

The 1950s saw the rise of McCarthyism; though Jews were on both sides of the conflict, many were among the Communists eliminated from the AFL and CIO. But Jews had also been moving into the professions. As public sector employees gained collective bargaining rights in the 1960s and 1970s, Jews took leadership roles in the American Federation of Teachers (AFT) and the American Federation of State, Country, and Municipal Employees (AFSCME) that represented them.

One cannot expect that union members throughout the United States today have this history in mind as they confront BDS efforts to organize labor movement opposition to the Jewish state. But the national union leadership often does, and it makes them sensitive to anti-Israel initiatives that cross the line into anti-Semitism. Overall, BDS inroads into British trade unions have been far more significant than their efforts in the United States. Though the US labor movement has resisted these efforts, a few US union votes have supported divestment as a result. In December 2014 the United Auto

Workers local 2865 representing 13,000 University of California teaching assistants and student workers officially declared itself a member of the BDS movement and voted to urge both UC and the UAW International to divest their investments and pension funds "from Israeli state institutions and international companies complicit in severe and ongoing human rights violations as part of the Israeli oppression of the Palestinian people." The resolution also called for an end to military aid to Israel and encouraged members to sign a personal pledge "refusing to take part in any research, conferences, events, exchange programs, or other activities that are sponsored by Israeli universities complicit in the occupation of Palestine and the settler-colonial policies of the state of Israel." Both the regional and the international UAW swiftly rejected their California local's position and remain opposed to divestment. The US Congress was of course no more likely than the UC Regents to answer this call, but the votes add some legitimacy to BDS among campus union members. Struggles over divestment resolutions culminated in pro-BDS votes in the UAW locals representing NYU and UMass Amherst graduate employees in April 2016. In November 2015 the Connecticut AFL-CIO adopted a resolution in support of BDS, but it was likewise overturned by the national AFL-CIO. In August 2015 the 30,000-member national United Electrical Workers Union became the first major national union to endorse the BDS agenda and urge an end to all military support for Israel.

The US campaigns follow upon and parallel a history of British and Canadian trade unionist opposition to Israel. In 2006, the Ontario local in the Canadian Union of Public Employees (CUPE), which represents 200,000 workers, voted to support a boycott of Israel. The British public sector trade union UNISON, with 1.4 million members, called for a comprehensive boycott of Israel in 2007. That year the British National Union of Journalists voted to boycott Israeli products but has not implemented the resolution. Nonetheless, these are the people who write the news, and the resolution may have helped strengthen anti-Israel reporting. In 2009 the CUPE Ontario University Workers Coordinating Committee proposed to ban Israeli faculty from speaking, teaching, or doing research at Ontario universities, but the CUPE national leadership forced the elimination of the blacklisting language. The Irish Congress of Trade Unions, IMPACT (the Irish public-sector union), the Northern Ireland Public Service Alliance, and Britain's Trade Union Congress issued boycott calls in 2009. UNISON renewed its call in 2010. That year the Scottish Trades Union Congress did much the same. In July 2014 Britain's largest trade union, Unite, committed itself to campaign for sanctions against Israel, accusing the country of being "guilty of the crime of apartheid." The following month the National Executive Committee of Britain's National Union of Students called for a boycott of "corporations complicit in financing and aiding Israel's military" and urged an arms embargo against Israel. In April 2015 a major Quebec labor federation, the *Confédération des syndicats nationaux* (CSN) announced that its central council had voted to join the BDS campaign. Its Montreal council had endorsed BDS in 2010. The CSN represents 325,000 workers in both the public and private sectors, in close to 2,000 unions throughout the province.

One arena in which BDS economic efforts have had noisy but only fleeting success is in organizing protests to block Israel-related shipping from being unloaded at west coast ports, actions that have concentrated on San Francisco, Seattle, and Vancouver. Despite a history of political solidarity, the International Longshoreman and Warehouse Union (ILWU) has not been willing to support BDS demands. A few current or retired ILWU members have joined picket lines, but the membership as a whole has remained ready to load and unload ships when demonstrators have not blocked their access to the docks. Here again there has been a difference between the US and Europe, as well as South Africa. In February 2009, dockworkers in South Africa refused to unload an Israeli ship. Port workers in Sweden and Norway refused to process Israeli ships for a period of a week in June 2010.

In August 2014, fueled by anger at Operation Protective Edge in Gaza, an umbrella group of about 70 BDS-allied Bay Area organizations coordinated demonstrations at the Port of Oakland under a "Block the Boat" banner. Their target was the *Piraeus*, a container ship operated by ZIM America Integrated Shipping Lines. The *Piraeus* isn't Israeli-owned or flagged, and its previous ports of call, including the duty-free zone at Colon, Panama, suggest it was not carrying Israeli goods. The ship's crew would typically be international, and there is no reason to expect it would include any Israelis. ZIM itself is a global company that provides services to contracting customers, but it is 32 percent Israeli owned and often provides services to Israeli firms. That was enough to make it a target of BDS activism.

The public is not allowed onto the docks themselves, but after weeks of preparation "Block the Boat" managed several days of demonstrations aimed at blocking the dock's parking lot entrances. These were not, however, actual labor picket lines, so support from area labor unions was not forthcoming. Oakland, moreover, only handles about nine percent of west coast shipping, so companies can easily shift to other ports, an effect that would hurt the Oakland economy and cut local dockworker wages, but have no appreciable economic impact on Israel. Demonstrations were highlighted with chants of "Netanyahu you can't hide. We Charge you with genocide," "1, 2, 3, 4, occupation no more," "5, 6, 7, 8, stop the oppressive Israeli State," and "Open the Siege, Close the Gate, Israel is a Terrorist State" that provided short-term emotional gratification. The effort delayed the ship from docking, but a similar effort failed in Long Beach because too few demonstrators showed up.

BDS groups had convinced a ZIM ship to turn away from the Oakland port in 2010, and they may succeed again in the Bay Area, but they have so far been unable to identify current efforts with the major actions taken against South African shipping in the 1980s. Bay Area ILWU Local 10 has an especially strong political history, but the ULWU as a whole became somewhat isolated from the broader labor movement after the AFL-CIO arranged a split in 2013 (Dyer).

At least in the US, we do not face a broad anti-Israel movement in organized labor. The union locals that have adopted BDS resolutions often represent anti-Israel constituencies that have evolved outside the union context. That is particularly true of graduate student locals. California has the only powerful state-wide campus opposition to Israel, so it is not surprising that the state UAW representing teaching assistants passed a BDS resolution. It is possible that other locals in hostile environments, like the UAW local at New York University, will pass such a symbolic resolution as well, even though the national UAW will nullify it. The labor movement as a whole has suffered in recent years, but collective bargaining remains the only proven organized way to improve wages and working conditions, secure fair grievance procedures, ensure worker safety, and give workers a voice in national affairs. ▪

---

Also see BDS: A BRIEF HISTORY, DIVESTMENT CAMPAIGNS, and ECONOMIC BOYCOTTS.

# BDS AND THE AMERICAN ANTHROPOLOGICAL ASSOCIATION

HARVEY GOLDBERG

The impetus to take steps against the state of Israel in the form of boy-cott may be seen in the context of long-term trends within anthropology, particularly American anthropology, and also in light of more proximate political developments.

## THE HISTORY OF THE DISCIPLINE

Anthropology took shape in the course of the 19th century, then underwent a major shift in orientation—both in England and in the United States—around the turn of the 20th century. In its formative period the field was based on accumulating data portraying customs, beliefs, and social patterns from societies around the world that had been unknown to European and European-grounded history in earlier centuries. The framework was unques-tionably Eurocentric, with cultural forms and social arrangements placed on developmental or evolutionary scales that took for granted the superiority of the ways of life that had emerged in Euro-America. Toward the end of the 19th century anthropologists who had conducted extensive research in small-scale societies remote from Western experience began to undermine the usefulness of grand evolutionary schemes. Franz Boas (1858–1942), working in North America, elaborated a concept of culture relevant to all human societies which—among other features—challenged schemes that assumed one set of societies was inherently more advanced than others. Bronislaw Malinowski (1884-1942), in the framework of British anthropology, insisted that long-term field work was necessary in order to penetrate particular cultural worlds and to bring forth the "native's point of view." Thus, foundations were laid for the discipline to question the "supremacy" of "the west."

The discipline remained small in terms of the number of practitioners, but the writings of some prominent anthropologists found resonance in wider American life. Cultural relativism was articulated boldly by Ruth Benedict (1887-1948), while Margaret Mead (1901–1978) utilized findings from New Guinea and elsewhere to direct the attention of Americans to their own culture as warranting reflection and rethinking. With some exceptions, most anthropological work continued to be conducted in societies considered "tribal" or outside the framework of large organized states, and most research among Native American groups emphasized "salvage" accounts of cultures before massive contact had affected them. This was to change significantly in the period after World War II.

The war itself helped re-imagine anthropology as relevant to large industrial societies. Some military recruits given intensive training in non-Western languages ended up in anthropological careers. The United States' need to comprehend societies formerly viewed as peripheral became apparent. Ruth Benedict's *The Chrysanthemum and the Sword* (1946) that sought to interpret Japanese culture is one example. After the war, a Harvard research center in which anthropologist Clyde Kluckhohn (1905–1960) was a leading figure focused on the Soviet Union. Another post-war scene that became central for anthropology was the emerging "third world."

As anthropologists became engaged in "third world" societies, where the United States and the Soviet Union competed for influence, new issues arose. The rural communities in which they worked were not "isolates." Villages were influenced by urban centers, the power of states, and international trade. Also, one could not understand "the culture" of such communities without viewing them as part of broad and ancient civilizations. "Peasant societies" was the concept used to analyze these situations as research expanded in Latin America, the Middle East, the Indian sub-continent, and elsewhere. In the 1950s the number of anthropological studies in the Middle East was still limited, with an emphasis on nomadic groups and village communities, but began to expand consistently. More generally, the number of professional anthropologists grew, as did membership in the American Anthropological Association.

Attention to broad economic and political factors was dramatically rein-forced by events in "the sixties" when questions of inequality arose in several realms: race, gender, and colonial rule, which entered American conscious-ness with the Vietnam War. Marxist perspectives, which had been marginal in the past, began to attract anthropologists. Political economy became a major analytic category and new formulations emerged such as post-colonialism. The study and "exposure" of power was a leading concern stimulated by writers like Michel Foucault (1926–1984) and Edward Said (1935–2003).

The discipline of anthropology itself came under attack. A common mantra was that it had been the handmaiden of colonialism. Historically the discipline developed during the era of imperialism and colonial rule, but connections between that background and the concrete work of anthropolo-gists were far more complex than, and at times directly at odds with, that formula. The general critique was reinforced by self-questioning like: "What gives me the right as a Western anthropologist to represent another culture?" Researchers felt the need to reflect upon the position from which they undertook fieldwork, which often reflected a power differential between where they stood and the life situations of those they studied. In the first half of the 20th century the implicit ethical imperative of anthropology had been to make sense of societies and cultures that were ignored or misunderstood, while in the second half a norm emerged that if an anthropologist is not critiquing or unmasking (Western) structures of power, he or she is complicit with them.

# THE AMERICAN ATHROPOLOGICAL ASSOCIATION (AAA)

By the turn of the 21st century, this hybrid moral-intellectual stance was poised to sympathize with various political positions and associate them with the AAA. Such a linkage was created with the BDS movement that criticized Israel while focusing on the 1967 occupation of lands in the West Bank of Jordan and the Gaza Strip whose Palestinian Arab populations were assert-ing demands for national recognition. By 2000 the occupation had been in place for 33 years, and attempts at resolving the conflict had failed. By then, and since, anthropological work took place in the West Bank, in refu-gee camps in other countries, and among Palestinians who were citizens of Israel. Some anthropologists who focused on the Palestinian situation began to demand AAA attention; some were activists within the wider BDS move-ment launched in 2004.

By 2010 BDS influence was felt at AAA annual meetings, with about 5,000 attendees. From that time on they included about 5 panels each year stressing a critique of Israel or advocating a boycott. This peaked in December 2014. In April of that year, the AAA executive announced a program highlighting the boycott issue in response to demands of the membership and with the goal of educating it. Executive committee backing was given to several panels. Five panels (featuring a few well-known BDS figures who were not anthropologists) advocated boycotting Israel, but only one session was organized in opposition (it did not include any anthropologists). A vote opposing academic boycotts was roundly defeated at the business meeting (by approximately 600 to 50). By this time, anthropologists in Israel had taken the first steps in organizing against an academic boycott and began coordinating themselves with American colleagues.

Conversely, anthropologists advocating boycotting Israel became active within the AAA's organizational structure, locating themselves within committees and formal deliberations regarding human rights and academic freedom. Arguments developed that drew on material selectively, and then were woven into academic presentations. Harmful or legally questionable aspects of the Israeli occupation were highlighted without mentioning human rights violations by Palestinians or acts of terror. Discourse developed based on a partial view of Israel. Salient was the labeling of Israel as a "colonial settler state," ignoring, for example, the centrality of refugees in Israel's makeup. The term "Palestinians" was used wholesale, often overlooking deep differences in the orientations of the Palestinian Authority and Hamas, or ignoring that there are Palestinians who are Israeli citizens. Overall, binary pictures dominated, dramatizing Israel's misuse of power and portraying boycotts as a non-violent strategy. The symbolic violence inherent in this description was masked, for it rarely drew a line between specific criticisms linked to the occupation and tropes that questioned the very legitimacy of the Israeli state.

On April 30, 2014, the AAA executive posted its plan "to open up these matters to association-wide conversation." About 25 members of the AAA were based in Israel, and the issue arose at the annual spring meeting of the Israel: Anthropological Association (IAA). Discussion continued during the summer and by email thereafter. Many IAA members were critical of the occupation, while there was a range of differences over how to express this, e.g.: as an association vs. individually, or alongside criticism of Palestine leadership or as a separate issue. There also were views sympathetic to boycotting and those opposing any criticism by the IAA.

At the end of August a letter from the IAA was sent to the AAA leadership stressing several points: academic boycotts are a breach of academic freedom; the AAA boycotting a country and its universities is unprecedented;

punishing scholars for the acts of their government is ineffectual and counterproductive; the claim to separate Israeli institutions from individual
anthropologists is—at the minimum—misleading; many Israeli anthropologists have been activists for the rights of Palestinians; a boycott would weaken
a source of liberal thought in Israel; why focus on Israel when there are many
places where people suffer because of conflict and unequal power?; and the
published program of the 2014 meeting does not match the promise to make
"a space for presentation of multiple perspectives." This letter was approved
by a large majority of voting IAA members.

In October, a group of anthropologists launched an on-line petition in
opposition to "ongoing Israeli violations of Palestinian rights." This was separate from a formal AAA initiative but obviously was coordinated to reinforce
pro-boycott sentiment within the association. By the end of 2014, about
one thousand people had signed the petition. Somewhat later, Israeli anthropologists along with others launched a petition: "anthropologists against the
boycott of Israeli academic institutions." By the end of the year there were
almost 400 signatories to that petition.

After the 2014 annual meeting, members of the AAA opposing a boycott
(including Americans and Israelis), formed a network: "Anthropologists for
Dialogue on Israel and Palestine" (ADIP, https://anthrodialogue.wordpress.
com/). It recognized the "ongoing Occupation of Palestinian lands and population by Israel in violation of the international consensus favoring a two-
state settlement." But rather than advocating a boycott, it sought to "encourage and support dialogue and engagement among Israelis, Palestinians, and
others concerned with the region…" Since then, it has backed nuanced positions that critique the continuing situation of the occupation while insisting
that academic boycott will not contribute to its amelioration. Encouraged
by a resolution of the IAA in June 2015, calling "upon the Israeli government to take key steps to bring about a just and viable future for Israelis and
Palestinians" and "upon anthropologists and others to recognize the important role that moderate segments in Israeli society—including academics—
have played in the difficult struggle for peace in the region," ADIP stepped up
efforts to bring attention to its views in advance of the AAA annual meeting
in November 2015.

## THE AAA LEADERSHIP RESPONDS

The AAA leadership responded to letters from the IAA with replies that only
partially made sense to the latter. It stated that the 2014 program reflected
"the submissions we received from our members," which left several points

unanswered. Why was the long statement justifying the Israel/Palestine emphasis published on April 30, after it was impossible to suggest further presentations? Also, it was the association, not the membership, that set the structure of the overall meeting in which most boycott-oriented panels took place in sequence over several days, in the same large hall, leading up to the annual business meeting. While working out this plan, why could the AAA not seek input from some of its Israel-based members? Further, did it not occur to anyone that the concern with issues like human rights might also be directed to the Palestinian side of the formula? Perhaps an answer is reflected in the first reply by the leadership to a letter from the IAA:"In recent months the Israel/Palestine situation has become a topic of increasing debate in the US media and, *thanks* to the Boycott, Divestment and Sanctions movement, in academic circles" (italics supplied).

At one point a shift in the program plan was initiated by the Executive. Initially, only one session, called the "members forum," was structured to encourage direct conversation among different views on boycotts. Speakers would be given two minutes at the microphone, and "names of members who wish to speak will be selected at random." In mid-autumn, the forum format was changed; it now consisted of a serious of roundtables spread around the hall, each led by a trained mediator. No explanation for the change was offered by the Executive; at the session itself there was no airing of views beyond what transpired at each table.

An innovative step taken by the AAA was to appoint a Task Force (TF) to study the Israel/Palestine issue and to submit a report in the fall of 2015. In the spring of 2015 it was decided that 3 members of the TF should visit the region. Various aspects of the TF project also raise questions. One is the attempt to achieve balance in the committee. Six active AAA members with specialties "almost all outside Israel/Palestine" and "with no public commitment to any given political stance on that conflict" were selected along with a Chair, Don Brenneis, a past president of the AAA. Choosing outside-the-region specialists who know neither Arabic nor Hebrew is surprising when Anthropological Linguistics constitutes a major sub-field within the association. This decision was taken after the April 30 announcement had stated that the Executive is "Considering organizing a task force. Our membership has considerable expertise on the Israel/Palestine issue, and on related questions." In response to a question from the IAA concerning the composition of the TF, the President of the AAA offered the following reply:"Above all, we have sought established scholars with a reputation for open-mindedness, rather than people who are known to represent entrenched constituencies on these issues." Did the executive conclude that there were no scholars with expertise who did not "represent entrenched constituencies?"

Another puzzling (even disturbing) episode in the process was when an email was sent by the AAA executive on April 28, 2015, stating that the Chair of the TF was stepping down for personal reasons. The same message announced the appointment of a replacement, Richard Bauman, emeritus at Indiana University. The ADIP quickly notified the executive that Bauman was a signatory to the pro-boycott petition circulated the past fall. Soon after that Bauman resigned from the position he had accepted. The incident disappeared from the AAA website and it was decided that the Executive Director would serve as the convener of the TF.

## The AAA TASK FORCE REPORT

The TF report itself, issued in October 2015, reveals clear imbalances. Here are four examples are. The first concerns background information. On pp. 72–74, the report presents "in chronological order, …a summary of the most relevant outcomes from scholarly societies to date." Missing from the list is a vote taken at the American Public Health Association in 2013. After two previous years of deliberations, the APHA rejected a pro-boycott resolution by a margin of 3 to 1 after opponents of the measure demonstrated the selectivity, errors of commission and omission, and lack of context in the materials that were brought before the association.

Another example, citation bias, was pointed out by David Rosen. The preponderance of anthropologists cited in the report are self-declared supporters of BDS (fourteen). Only six publically-declared boycott opponents are cited, while another four seem to have taken no public position on the issue. Selectivity also appears in the way specific topics are handled. In the subsection entitled "The 'Settler Colonialism' Frame" (p. 11), a problematic formulation as already indicated, some mention is made of Palestinians who are Israelis. We learn that within Israel itself, Palestinians "can also vote and have access to the Israeli court system if they want to try to assert their rights" (14). The phrasing suggests that Israeli Palestinians "assert[ing] their rights," occurs only now and then. Nowhere is the reader informed that there are Palestinian members of Parliament as well as lawyers and judges who are part of the Israeli court system (and many Palestinians study in Israeli law schools). Are typical AAA members, with no "deep histories of expertise in the region," expected to figure this out on their own?

Selectivity also appears in regard to tables and graphs. Figure 22 (Mortality rates for children under the age of 5 years in Palestine and Israel), is cited with two comments: that the "health environment for children appears to be dramatically better in Israel" and "between 1990 and 2013—mortality rates for children under age 5 years were four to five times higher than in Israel" (p. 38). The report does not mention that with the Oslo Accords (mid-1990s), the Ministry of Health of the Palestinian Authority became responsible for public health. In addition, an overall view of Figure 22 shows that child mortality among Palestinians declined consistently, at a rate faster than the decrease in Israel (Mel Konner). Readers examining tables or graphs in the report, or through links provided in it, will discover other findings going against the dominant grain of the text.

Along with these imbalances, the report is cautious about concrete boycott steps that might be taken. It points out that academic boycotts stand in sharp contrast to academic freedom, and how there already exist claims on both sides regarding intimidation for expressing one's views. It also underlines the difficulty that the AAA would face in determining when boycott demands are in fact met. In addition, the "Task Force repeatedly asked supporters of a boycott for specific examples of active anthropological complicity with the conflict / occupation. In the end, the Task Force could find almost no examples of such active collaboration…"(p. 66). This did not keep the pro-boycott resolution introduced in the 2015 business meeting from mentioning academic complicity several times.

## THE 2015 AAA BUSINESS MEETINGS

The 2015 AAA annual meeting took place in November, in Denver. The number of people who attended was about 1,800—more than double the 2014 number. Far beyond normal attendance, it represented mobilization for the boycott vote. Some younger people wore T-shirts supporting a boycott, posters were displayed, and cookies were handed out. Two paid advertisements were circulated to conference participants in advance, soliciting their vote: one was sponsored by Jewish Voice for Peace along with FOSNA (Friends of Sabeel, North America) and the second by ADIP. Two resolutions were on the agenda in advance: one proposed dialogue instead of a boycott and a second advocated a boycott. The first was defeated 1,173 (against) to 196 (for), and the second was approved by a 1,040 to 136 majority. Opponents to boycotting sought to introduce an amendment to the second resolution, but the question was called before any discussion of the amendment. In general, the pro-boycott majority used their overwhelming numbers to limit discussion (a procedure requiring a 2/3 vote), so the airing of views was limited. At several points, the chair requested participants to desist from cheering when decisions went their way.

In informal discussions many anthropologists opposed the boycott campaign for various reasons, but "voted with their feet" by not attending the business meeting. The boycott would not become AAA policy until after an electronic vote of the membership scheduled for April–May 2016. Depending on initiatives from members, other resolutions may appear on the spring ballot. In a comment to a blog soon after the vote, the Executive Director wrote: "The boycott's proponents suggested a blueprint for implementing such an institutional boycott. However, they do not speak for the Association, nor do they have the authority to dictate the terms of any such action, should the member-wide vote go in their favor." This is uncharted territory for all involved. ■

Also see ACADEMIC BOYCOTTS, BDS: A BRIEF HISTORY, BDS AND CHRISTIAN CHURCHES, BDS AND THE AMERICAN STUDIES ASSOCIATION, ORIENTALISM AND THE ATTACK ON ENLIGHTENMENT VALUES, and THE SOCIAL JUSTICE MANDATE IN HIGHER EDUCATION.

# BDS AND THE AMERICAN STUDIES ASSOCIATION

SHARON ANN MUSHER

## INTRODUCTION

On December 16, 2013, the 5,000-member American Studies Association (ASA), the "oldest and largest scholarly association devoted to the interdisciplinary study of US culture and history in a global context," was the first moderate-sized academic association to vote to boycott Israeli academic institutions (http://www.theasa.net/about/page/what_the_asa_does/). The action was widely condemned by university presidents, by academic associations representing more than one field, and by the press, since academic boycotts inhibit the free exchange of information and ideas, the core principle of higher education worldwide.

A small cadre of ideologically driven leaders within the association actively silenced opposition and railroaded the endorsement of a resolution that deviated from the association's declared goals: "The strengthening of relations among persons and institutions in this country and abroad . . . and the broadening of knowledge . . . about American culture in all its diversity and complexity." In doing so, they illustrated both the association's and the BDS movement's emphasis on activism over scholarship, dialogue, and complex moral thinking. They also helped to foster a boycott that, despite their claims, has led to the blacklisting of Israeli academics, promoted intolerance on some US college and university campuses, and divided academic colleagues.

87

# A FLAWED DECISION-MAKING PROCESS

Since the late 1960s, the ASA has exhibited a proclivity toward activism greater than that seen in many other professional associations. Today's scholars in the field, like those in Women, Gender and Sexuality Studies, Africana Studies, and Ethnic Studies, endeavor to link their academic and political commitments—assuming that intellectual work should also function civically. Thus, it is not surprising that a small cohort committed to the academic boycott of Israel began promoting their agenda within the association in 2006. After trying unsuccessfully to convince the Committee on American Studies Departments, Programs and Centers to put forward a boycott resolution, they turned to the Academic and Community Activism Caucus. In November 2012, at the annual meeting in San Juan, the Activism Caucus held a meeting attended by some eighty people to gather signatures for a boycott resolution. It then submitted the resolution to the National Council for adoption. More than half (ten out of eighteen) of the voting members of the Council, including the sitting and incoming presidents, Lisa Duggan and Curtis Marez, had already publically endorsed the US Campaign for the Academic and Cultural Boycott of Israel (USACBI). Three of them played leadership roles in the BDS movement, including Karen Leong, who had introduced a similar boycott resolution to the Asian American Studies Association, which, in April 2012, passed without objections or abstentions.

The Council made the boycott a central consideration in its planning for the 2013 annual conference, but it did not do so in an evenhanded manner. ASA leadership did little to advertise the resolution before the conference or to create space for alternative viewpoints either online or at the conference. Thus, most of the ASA's roughly 5,000 members were unaware that the association was considering a boycott prior to its enactment. At the annual conference, the Council organized a one-sided Town Hall during which there was very little discussion of specific Israeli policies or ways to end Israel's occupation of land beyond the Green Line in the aftermath of the Six Day War in 1967 (MAP 4). Instead the speakers uniformly articulated their opposition to the existence of the State of Israel, which they dubbed a settler-colonial entity and an Apartheid state engaged in ethnic cleansing. One of the Town Hall speakers, political activist and emeritus professor Angela Davis, received an award immediately after the Town Hall, followed by a presidential address by Marez, in which he advocated a boycott. The following afternoon, in an "Open Discussion" 45 people spoke in favor of the resolution and 7 opposed it. One ASA member who was present described the one-dimensional nature of the ASA's programming as "like being in North Korea."

In a false effort to appear democratic, the National Council returned the resolution to membership for a ten-day long voting period in December in the middle of exams and what many consider a holiday season. At no point did the ASA distribute arguments against the boycott to members, although substantial opposition developed both within and without the organization. A handful of ASA members who objected to the boycott organized an impromptu committee, ASA Members for Academic Freedom, which garnered signatures for letters that encouraged the association to engage in vigorous debate about the "Israeli-Palestinian conflict and how it should be resolved" while opposing an academic boycott. One hundred forty ASA members and non-member Americanists, including former presidents, prize winners, and lifetime members signed these letters. In addition, eight former ASA presidents wrote a letter to members encouraging them to vote against the boycott. The National Council refused to distribute either of these letters even as it continued to use its website to disseminate endorsements of the proposed resolution.

Furthermore, the National Council watered down the proposed boycott to ensure its passage. In explanatory materials posted on the ASA website, the National Council created a false dichotomy between boycotts of Israeli academics and academic institutions. Glossing over the dependence of individual scholars on the academic institutions that house them and financially support their scholarly work, including the sharing of it at academic conferences, the ASA suggested that members could boycott academic institutions—by, for example, refusing to attend a conference at Hebrew University, without blacklisting individual academics. They suggested that all academic institutions were complicit in maintaining the occupation, so regardless of the specific policies—including the programs specifically geared toward Palestinians at individual institutions—all academic institutions could be safely boycotted in an act of non-violent protest. The National Council further suggested that it was not calling for individual academics to engage in a boycott, but rather for the ASA to do so only when it acted institutionally "in its official capacities to enter into formal collaborations with Israeli academic institutions, or with scholars who are expressly serving as representatives or ambassadors of those institutions." Such collaborations had almost never occurred previously and, for obvious reasons, were highly unlikely to happen in the aftermath of the boycott. Furthermore, the Council attested that the boycott was not binding: ASA members were not obligated to follow it.

Despite these efforts at amelioration, support for the resolution within the ASA was tepid. Only a fraction of the organization's roughly 5,000 members approved it (820 voted for it; 420 voted against it or abstained). Within the association, eight colleges and universities dropped their institutional membership in the ASA (William A. Jacobson), and an additional twelve that were listed by the ASA as institutional members denied that status. Twelve recipients of the ASA's Turpie Award, the association's highest service award, wrote a letter to the ASA's Council expressing their dissent from the boycott. Furthermore, two regional associations of the ASA, in California and the Eastern American Studies Association, refused to comply with the boycott. Unsurprisingly, the ASA, which continued to post articles about the boycott on its website, only distributed the Turpie letter, ignoring articles documenting other dissent within the ASA.

But outside of the association, opposition to the boycott was growing. The American Association of University Professors urged the Council not to endorse the boycott, discouraged members from voting for it, and then expressed disappointment with the members' vote to endorse the boycott. Once enacted, the boycott was rejected by a number of professional higher education associations, including the American Council on Education, the Association of Public and Land-Grant Universities, and the Association of American Universities. Furthermore, the leadership of more than 250 US colleges and universities issued statements condemning the boycott.

In a move that only strengthened support for the boycott on the left, some universities and politicians attempted to boycott the boycotters, by refusing to pay institutional memberships, withdrawing support for conferences from organizations affiliated with the ASA, and seeking to pass legislation that would withhold tax dollars from institutions of higher learning that used state money to fund attendance at conferences sponsored by associations engaged in a boycott or that directly participated in such a boycott. Representing itself as a victim rather than a perpetrator of blacklists, political litmus tests, and legal bullying, the ASA initiated a $100,000 fundraising campaign under the logo "Stand with the ASA" (in contrast to "Stand with Us," a pro-Israel advocacy program) to defend the organization and pro-boycott individuals within it.

# THE CONSQUENCES
# OF THE ASA BOYCOTT

Commentators have disagreed about the consequences of the boycott. Supporters of the resolution viewed the conference as a watershed moment during which, to quote Edward Said, "America's last taboo"—understood as "any serious public discussion of . . . the systematic continuity of Israel's 52-year-old oppression and maltreatment of the Palestinians"—was shattered. They claim that the boycott "honor[ed] the call of Palestinian civil society to support the academic boycott of Israel" by embracing a symbolic boycott that sent a political message without stigmatizing individual academics (http://www.theasa.net/from_the_editors/item/asa_members_vote_to_endorse_academic_boycott/).

In contrast, opponents of the boycott have suggested that an institutional coup occurred in which a vocal minority largely followed the ASA's deliberative procedures to put into place a boycott that did not have widespread support. They dismiss the ASA as a relatively small and now quite fringe academic association and highlight the boycott's condemnation followed by the association's efforts to backpedal by disavowing some elements of the boycott or claiming others never existed. One-year after instituting its boycott, when the American Center for Law and Justice served notice to the Westin Bonaventure Hotel in Los Angeles for violating California's non-discrimination laws by housing the annual conference of an institution engaged in a boycott, the ASA's executive director John Stephens claimed that the resolution never intended to target individuals. Indeed, he insisted, even Israel's hawkish Benjamin Netanyahu could attend the ASA's annual conference as long as he did not do so as Israeli Prime Minister.

But despite the ASA's contention that the boycott is only institutional and symbolic, its consequences have been personal and real, especially for Israeli students and scholars. As Michael Zakim explained "The ASA boycott's first victim was a PhD student at Tel Aviv who recently completed his doctoral dissertation. His advisor was unable to recruit qualified outside readers to review the thesis due to its Israeli provenance. The fact that this same student is Palestinian (in this case, an Arab citizen of Israel) contributes an element of black comedy to an already unhappy situation" (Zakim and Mohamed).

The ASA's boycott has mobilized the BDS movement (Nelson, "The New Assault"). It inspired a handful of even smaller recently created professional associations, most of which had missions specifically geared toward minority groups or gender-based concerns, to initiate similar boycotts. Furthermore, groups within the MLA (Modern Language Association), AAA (American Anthropological Association), MESA (Middle East Studies Association), and AHA (American Historical Association) have pursued BDS-related resolutions at their annual meetings with growing intensity. Although couched in universalist terms, these resolutions make no effort to analyze dispassionately worldwide challenges to academic freedom. On the contrary, they should be recognized for what they are: the latest tactic in a political campaign focused exclusively on Israel.

Regardless of how the ASA ameliorated the tone of its boycott, by allying itself with the BDS movement it endorsed a set of boycott policies that have only grown more stringent. For example, in July 2014, the Palestine Academic and Cultural Boycott of Israel (PACBI) distributed a new set of guidelines that encourage the blacklisting of Israeli academics, staff, and students, and those who are funded by Israel and its "lobby groups." They furthermore call for withdrawal from collaborative events, projects, and publications that bring together Palestinians and Israelis. By lending support to an anti-normalization campaign against the State of Israel, the ASA—despite its attempts to differentiate its campaign from others—lent credence to the broader BDS movement, which has only become more severe in its efforts to isolate Israel, blacklist Israeli academics, marginalize American Jewish faculty and students, and discourage the types of interchange—including exchange programs—that are so vital for setting a framework for scholarship, negotiations, and the promotion of a two-state solution. ■

Also see ACADEMIC BOYCOTTS, ANTI-JEWISH BOYCOTTS IN HISTORY, ANTI-NORMALIZATION, BDS: A BRIEF HISTORY, BDS AND THE AMERICAN ANTHROPOLOGICAL ASSOCIATION, CULTURAL BOYCOTTS, ECONOMIC BOYCOTTS, ORIENTALISM AND THE ATTACK ON ENLIGHTENMENT VALUES, and THE SOCIAL JUSTICE MANDATE IN HIGHER EDUCATION.

# BDS RESOLUTIONS ON CAMPUS: THEIR LONG-TERM GOAL

"Those who will lead the US in 20 years are studying on campuses today at which there is anti-Israel propaganda."

—Amos Yadlin

Campus BDS campaigns are often waged over a particular divestment resolution scheduled for a vote by student government representatives. Yet such campaigns, notably, are often preceded by several years in which the campus climate and student attitudes are gradually turned against Israel by BDS sponsored speakers, public demonstrations, and anti-Israel advocacy and agitation by faculty members. BDS is clearly in this for the long haul, not just for a single student government vote.

—CN

SAMUEL M. EDELMAN AND
CAROL F. S. EDELMAN

Advocates of BDS understand that the movement's success on campus is not measured by the resolutions themselves. The resolutions are a means to a larger end. Thus supporters recognize that the movement has had an impact on how people think about and discuss the conflict. The resolutions create discussion, generate publicity, and attract attention. Publicity about Israeli West Bank human rights violations starts months and years before the vote on whether to adopt a resolution will take place. School newspapers, community newspapers, and social media spread the word. They engage students in an issue that most know very little about. They spearhead a public relations/propaganda campaign focused on the delegitimation and demonization of Israel.

A divestment campaign may be preceded by years of work in portraying Israel in a negative light with speakers, panels, and films. In the few months leading up to the vote, Students for Justice in Palestine will use Facebook and Twitter campaigns to drum up interest. They get editorials published in the student newspaper supporting divestment and demonizing Israel. Focusing only on the resolution and its possible implementation is too narrow. That ignores so much of what has always taken place on campus. Resolutions often fail, but what BDS does not fail at is weeks, months, and even years of constant attacks against Israel, portraying it as a pariah nation, an occupier, a human rights violator, a racist nation, and a denier of Palestinian rights.

Young college-aged men and women have thereby been exposed over time to repeated anti-Israel rhetoric. These include many young people who have little or no knowledge of the Middle East, really don't care that much about the issue, and have no affinity to one side or the other, who now have a kernel of doubt about Israel planted in their minds. Now Israel is connected with the important negative buzz words for this cohort—racism, apartheid, occupier, human rights violator. We can't predict what attitudes this "at risk" generation will have in the future but, as Nazi propagandist Julius Streicher (1885-1946) often said about his anti-Semitic messages, "something always sticks." While the BDS movement is losing most college campus resolution vote battles, their propaganda campaign may be successful in the long run.

We must never forget that each boycott, divestment, or sanction initiative contains within it long term seeds of doubt about Israel and Israelis; left to fester, those doubts may have long-term political consequences detrimental to all parties. The constant drip, drip, drip of accusation and the portrayal of Israel as evil will persuade some students that Israel should not exist. Those students graduate to become professionals, business leaders, and politicians. We can only hope that strong counter campaigns can provide students with a more full and realistic understanding of the complexity of both Israel and the Middle East as a whole. ■

*Adapted from Samuel M. Edelman and Carol F. S. Edelman, "When Failure Succeeds: Divestment as Delegitimization."*

Also see ACADEMIC BOYCOTTS, ANTI-JEWISH BOYCOTTS IN HISTORY, ANTI-NORMALIZATION, CULTURAL BOYCOTTS, DIVESTMENT CAMPAIGNS, and ECONOMIC BOYCOTTS.

# BI-NATIONALISM

Bi-nationalism refers to a concept whereby two recognizably different and coherent peoples would share one state, granting citizenship and equal rights to all. In the context of the Israeli-Palestinian conflict, that state could encompass Israel, Gaza, and the West Bank. Although everyone would vote for one parliament, Jews and Palestinians would likely retain some separate nation-like legal and political character. Whether this structure would provide a means to negotiate differences or a setting guaranteed to exacerbate them is open to dispute, but the odds are not good. As Alexander Yakobson and Amnon Rubinstein write,

> In order to believe that such a state would in fact be binational, a number of wildly implausible assumptions need to be made: that the Arab-Palestinian people would agree over the long term that its state—the only state it will have—would not have an Arab character and would not be regarded as part of the Arab world; that it would agree to be the only one among the Arab peoples whose state would not be officially Arab, would not be a member of the Arab League and would not share, by declaration, the aspirations for Arab unity; and that the Palestinian people would agree to make this concession—a declared relinquishing of Palestine's "Arabness," something which no Arab nation has agreed to do in its own state for the sake of the non-Arab native minorities—for the sake of the Jews, widely considered "foreign intruders" and "colonialist invaders" in Palestine, whose very claim to constitute a nation is no more than "Zionist propaganda" (10).

Bi-nationalism is one form of a one-state solution, but other versions of a one-state solution would retain no separate religious, ethnic, or national divisions. Those alternatives would likely produce either an Arab or a Jewish dominated nation. The continuing stalemate in efforts to reach a negotiated solution to the conflict has generated enough frustration to produce naïve calls for various one-state models. The likelihood that Jews and Palestinians would get along peacefully in such a bi-national state has no support either in history or in contemporary reality. Part of the tragedy of the present situation is that for many in Palestine and abroad bi-nationalism no longer seems more unrealistic than the two-state solution itself. Over time, separate Jewish and Palestinian states could build on areas of cooperation to create some form of federation, but that would rely on a much higher degree of separation than bi-nationalism offers.

—CN

## RACHEL FISH

The bi-national idea as a theoretical construct is appealing to some Jews and Arabs alike, as it attempts to recognize differences between peoples while in principle creating a united society, but in practice the establishment of a bi-nationalist state faces many challenges. Since no bi-national polity for the state of Israel has been created or defined, it has been possible for the term to be employed by those with a variety of perspectives and goals. From the 1920s through the present, Zionist theoreticians, Palestinian intellectuals, political activists, and academics—Israeli, Arab, Jewish, and non-Jewish—have used the term to advocate very different political goals and visions. Indeed the meanings associated with bi-nationalism have changed, from early Zionist proposals for a bi-national state to the way it is used in twenty-first-century non-Zionist and anti-Zionist calls for the dissolution of Zionist society and the Jewish state.

The 1967 war—when Israel gained control over areas of the West Bank, the Gaza Strip, East Jerusalem, the Golan Heights, and the Sinai Peninsula— is often considered a direct assault on the principles of bi-nationalism in that it exemplified and exacerbated accusations of colonialism. Non- and anti-Zionist supporters of bi-nationalism—as well as many Zionists—argued that controlling another people was unjust and would eventually erode and corrupt Israel's values. Recalibrating the perceived victims and the victim-izers—the David and the Goliath in this equation—resulted in a new para-digm. Unease over how Jews, particularly Israelis, held power and used power became an accepted trope in the debate over Israel's territorial conquests and ultimate relationship with the Palestinian Arab communities.

Bi-nationalist discourse had evolved from emphasizing coexistence and cooperation to focusing on deconstructing the Jewish character of the state as the way to ensure equality for all citizens irrespective of national identity, ethnicity, or religion. The Arab minority had always been part of the equa-tion, but the model of a homogenous ethnic nation-state was now deemed abhorrent and to be rejected in favor of a multi-national, multi-ethnic com-munity where each ethnic or national group would have its own political structure and framework. This was the new bi-nationalist position post-1967 that persists today.

If we skip ahead to twenty-first-century bi-nationalist discourse, we find but a skeleton of the original bi-national idea. Employing the language of democracy and multiculturalism, some Palestinian Arabs in Israel and elsewhere, particularly the elite and intelligentsia, condemn Israel for rep-resenting and thereby ultimately privileging one people's identity, religion, language, and culture over another. Claiming that the nation-state cannot allow a specific identity to be institutionalized by governmental authori-ties, some Palestinian Arabs of Israel advocate a bi-nationalism they refer to as the "One State" solution and demand the status of a recognized minority. Supported by a number of Israeli academicians, those Palestinian Arabs want to replace Israel with a bi-national state, a single state shared by Arab and Jewish citizens, and one that has no identifying Jewish characteristics mark-ing the public sphere. The current bi-nationalist vision prioritizes the desires of the Palestinian Arab community. It emphasizes and gives expression to Palestinian identity while de-emphasizing the role and concerns of the Israeli Jewish population.

The bi-nationalism of today focuses on the dismantling of the Zionist and Jewish nation-state as it exists and seeks to replace it with a bi-national arrangement (for which, it should be noted, there are no currently successful long term working models, and, arguably, some notable failures—Belgium, Cyprus, and Yugoslavia among them) that goes beyond the territory of Israel proper to incorporate the West Bank and Gaza Strip. While, within this imagined polity, Palestinian Arab public intellectuals imagine a frame-work of two national groups—Jews and Arabs—their bi-nationalist vision does not provide a solution to the fundamental challenges and needs of the

Jewish people that the Jewish state was intended to address (i.e. security and self-determination).

The idea of bi-nationalism has shifted its focus from coexistence and cooperation to asserting the claims of Israel's Arab citizens, a stand a number of international constituencies take. As a result, bi-nationalism has become a euphemism for a one-state solution or a "state of all its citizens" that effectively calls for the end of a state with any Jewish character or commitment to the development of Jewish culture. The contemporary discussion of bi-nationalism has thus devolved into a continuation by other means of the conflict between Arabs, Israeli Jews, Jews and non-Jews alike. The fantasy of a bi-nationalist framework is now the sanitized version of de-legitimating the state of Israel. ■

*Adapted from Rachel Fish, "The Bi-nationalist Fantasy within Academia."*

Also see ANTI-NORMALIZATION, COORDINATED UNILATERAL WITHDRAWAL, THE ISRAELI RIGHT AND RELIGIOUS SETTLER POLITICS, THE ISRAELI-PALESTINIAN PEACE PROCESS, THE ONE-STATE SOLUTION, and THE TWO-STATE SOLUTION.

# COORDINATED UNILATERAL WITHDRAWAL

CARY NELSON

oordinated unilateral withdrawal is a concept a number of Israelis have put forward as a means to begin resolving the future of the West Bank in the absence of a comprehensive peace agreement. Over time, a staged series of unilateral Israeli withdrawals from the West Bank would be coordinated with the Palestinian Authority and the international community and supported by significant economic investment and institution building. Careful attention would be given to guarantee Israel's security. This would be a very different process from that employed in Gaza. This is certainly not the only route to peace, but it is one worth discussing as we try to move beyond the arguments and accusations that now dominate debates on the Israeli–Palestinian conflict.

## POLITICAL CONTEXTS FOR COORDINATED UNILATERAL WITHDRAWAL

Confidence that Israelis and Palestinians can negotiate a final status agreement, settle the outstanding issues that have plagued them since 1948, and establish two secure states that enable their peoples to live in peace may well today be at its lowest point in decades. Due to the failure of previous negotiations and to the lack of faith in either party's willingness to continue, the international conversation about the Israeli–Palestinian conflict says more at the present time about anger and frustration than it does about how to move forward productively.

For many years, the international community has placed all of its hopes and its diplomatic efforts behind a model of negotiations between the two primary parties leading to a final resolution of all outstanding issues. While a comprehensive final agreement is obviously preferable—and Israelis and Palestinians will never settle all their disputes without one—the failure of this model suggests the need for alternative ways of conceptualizing what steps in the interim might advance a two-state solution. Many who support this strategy believe it is politically incumbent on Israel to take the first step because Israel is more powerful than the Palestinian Authority. The most consequential step would be to announce an end to all settlement expansion and new settlement development east of the security barrier (MAPS 3 & 4). That could be accompanied by steps to promote Palestinians' ability to export products for sale from both Gaza and the West Bank and to relax the blockade's limits on fishing in the Mediterranean. It is also in Israel's best interest to facilitate reconstruction in Gaza and to help improve living conditions both there and in East Jerusalem. The Palestinian Authority for its part must end all incitement to violence.

Yet neither side believes what the other side says any longer and neither the Israelis nor the Palestinians trust one another. There is as a result a considerable need for deeds, rather than words, to advance the peace process. Nonetheless, some words will have to accompany the deeds. Among the most fundamental commitments to be made are the key concessions each side must contemplate making.

# THE PRINCIPLES THAT COULD UNDERLIE AN AGREEMENT

Amos Yadlin (1951-)—former air force general, former head of the IDF Military Intelligence Directorate, and current director of Israel's Institute for National Security Studies (INSS)— has identified the concessions that should be part of a public commitment. Israel would (1) explicitly abandon all ambitions to establish a Greater Israel encompassing the West Bank; (2) commit itself to accepting a modified version of the pre-1967 borders; and (3) agree to the division of Jerusalem with East Jerusalem as the capital of a Palestinian state. The Palestinians would (1) specify that a final status agreement would settle all issues and end the conflict; (2) recognize Israel as a homeland for the Jewish people, as well as agree that the right of return for Palestinian refugees would be limited to returning to a Palestinian state (except for those who have family members who are Israeli citizens, who could return to Israel itself); and (3) accept a form of sovereignty for a Palestinian state that would include restrictions to guarantee Israel's security.

One might clarify the meaning of the Palestinian concessions by pointing out that acknowledgement of Israel as the Jewish homeland is not the same as declaring Israel to be a theocracy or possessing a state religion. It simply recognizes a historical fact. Combined with recognition of Israel's borders and the country's democratic status, it effectively concedes that the Jewish majority has the key role in shaping Israel's future. It is also important that Israel acknowledge the catastrophic character of the Nakba and Israel's role in it and support the principle of financial compensation for those who lost property. That would constitute acknowledgement of the core of the Palestinian narrative. Israel could also accept the return of a limited number of Palestinian refugees with a family member who actually resided there in 1948 and is now an Israeli citizen.

## A PLAN FOR COORDINATED
## UNILATERAL WITHDRAWAL

With these principles publicly established and internationally recognized, the belief is that it would be possible for Israel to consider a staged unilateral withdrawal from carefully calculated portions of the West Bank. This would serve to build trust, give Palestinians realistic hope for their own state, and provide opportunities for the kind of economic investment that must undergird a viable Palestinian state. Within the right constraints, the initial stages of withdrawal should not present Israel with any increased security risks.

One potential initial target area for withdrawal is in the north central area of the West Bank; it might be anchored in the north and the south respectively by the existing Palestinian cities of Jenin (population 300,000) and Nablus (population about 400,000) (MAPS 3 & 4). The eastern boundary in the north could extend as far as the Palestinian town of Bal'a. Much of it is classified as Area A or B under the Oslo Accords and is under at least Palestinian civil control, but Area B areas are crisscrossed by Israeli roads and thus do not constitute a fully contiguous Palestinian area. The region has a substantial population and business base on which to build, and there is also considerable area available for development.

A second phase withdrawal could extend from Nablus to Ramallah (MAPS 3 & 4). That would require evacuation of numerous Israeli settlements and outposts. Immediately south, between Nablus and Ramallah, a series of settlements cut through the center of existing Palestinian areas A and B. A realistic Palestinian state would require their elimination. Those settlements, with their 2014 populations, include Bracha (2,195), Yitzhar (1,279), Kfar Tapuah (900), Itamar (1,275), Eli (3,947), Ma'ale Levona (758), Shilo (3,113), Ofra (3,137), Bit El (5,700), and possibly others. There are also approximately 30 outposts in the area with a total estimated population of about 4,000 to be dealt with. Evacuating 26,000 or more people in both well established settlements and illegal outposts will be difficult. Thus the first phase of a unilateral withdrawal would likely have to have Nablus as its southern border. The Jenin to Nablus withdrawal could be carried out without evacuating any settlements, thereby leaving the government with a more limited political problem to confront. If that first withdrawal worked well and helped build trust, the more challenging withdrawal from the area between Nablus and Ramallah might follow. It might be possible to work further south in stages; general negotiations could be reopened at any point.

In the model very roughly sketched here, Israel would retain a buffer zone to the north and east as a security guarantee, but would cede control of the roads crossing the area to the PA, so as to create a substantial contiguous territory that could anchor a nascent Palestinian state. The fate of the few settlements in the area would partly determine the exact boundaries. In the meantime, Israel would not waive control of any West Bank air space, but a managed right of return would operate in the area identified as a prototype Palestinian state or an enhanced Area A. BDS would lose much of its appeal once such a process started.

Preparations could begin now for the potential second phase of withdrawal. The Israeli organization Blue White Future specifies that "Israel should prepare a national plan for the absorption of the settlers who would relocate to Israel proper, whether before or after an agreement is signed. Such a plan should have urban, vocational, social, psychological and other appropriate components." This "New Paradigm" thus recommends that the time to prepare psychologically, legally, and administratively for resettlement is now: "Israel should enact a law that allows for voluntary evacuation, compensation, and eventual absorption of settlers presently residing on the eastern side of the security barrier, to encourage settlers who wish to relocate within the Green Line or within settlement blocs, regardless of whether an agreement with the Palestinians is concluded" (MAPS 3 &4). It is not only that a clear plan would be reassuring; it would also help focus Israelis on practical steps and help make the option realistic, rather than hypothetical.

Unlike the purely unilateral withdrawals from Lebanon and Gaza, these withdrawals would be coordinated with the Palestinian Authority and with the international community. Yet they are still steps that Israel could take unilaterally. The likelihood that any given Israeli government would agree to do take such steps does not diminish the need to consider and promote such options. No government lasts forever, and it is a mistake to limit the analysis of options and possibilities and the character of political organizing to what a given government might approve. In any case, increasing international pressure and the unpredictable play of events may open possibilities that now seem out of reach. ■

Also see THE BI-NATIONALISM, THE ISRAELI RIGHT AND RELIGIOUS SETTLER POLITICS, THE OSLO ACCORDS, THE PALESTINIAN AUTHORITY, THE ISRAELI-PALESTINIAN PEACE PROCESS, THE SECURITY BARRIER, SETTLER COLONIALISM, THE TWO-STATE SOLUTION, and THE WEST BANK.

# CULTURAL BOYCOTTS

## CARY NELSON

The international BDS Movement devotes considerable energy to cultural boycotts of arts and humanities events, as the cancellation of concerts, performances, and exhibitions generates significant negative publicity for Israel. There have been some notable successes, but most individual artists resist the well-organized BDS movement pressure placed on them and appear in Israel as planned. Cancellation of cultural events, many of which by their nature tend not to be overtly political, eliminates opportunities for dialogue, mutual appreciation, and understanding.

Far easier to pursue than academic or economic boycotts—and more often successful—are cultural boycotts of arts and humanities events, which can be limited to pressuring one artist or speaker to cancel an Israeli tour, performance, or lecture. Once again, as with boycott agendas that impact students and faculty, this puts to rest the BDS claim that the movement acts against institutions, not individuals. The rhetoric devoted to one event can easily embody broad opposition to all exchanges with Israel. The PACBI/BDS campaign has been a dual one—devoted to both academic and cultural boycotts—since 2005, but the two campaigns have partly proceeded on separate tracks.

Cultural boycott campaigns are particularly brutal when they target a single person. The theoretical physicist Stephen Hawking canceled a 2013 visit to Israel following a public campaign to persuade him. Ironically, the computerized device he uses to enable him to function and communicate is a largely Israeli product. Yet the American Indian poet Joy Harjo gave a reading in Tel Aviv despite considerable criticism from the Native American community. Elvis Costello, Lauryn Hill, Thurston Moore, Sinead O'Connor, Tommy Sands, Carlos Santana, and Roger Waters cancelled Israeli concerts. Justin Bieber, Leonard Cohen, Bob Dylan, Lady Gaga, Elton John, Jon Bon Jovi, Alicia Keys, Cyndi Lauper, Madonna, Justin Timberlake, Kanye West, and the Rolling Stones refused to cancel and performed. The director Ken Loach pulled his film *Looking for Eric* from the Melbourne Film Festival in 2009 after discovering Israel was a cosponsor. Musician Brian Eno and filmmaker Jean-Luc Goddard also support the boycott, but Harry Potter novelist J. K. Rowling opposes it. In 2012 the American writer Alice Walker declined to authorize a Hebrew translation of her novel *The Color Purple*. The late Swedish novelist Henning Mankell (1948-2015) took the same stand. In 2014, however, the actress Scarlett Johansson refused despite intense public pressure to end her advertising relationship with the Israeli company SodaStream. In 2015, in response to pressure from a BDS local chapter, the organizers of a music festival in Spain dropped the American Jewish hip-hop artist Matisyahu from their lineup because he would not endorse a Palestinian state. Overwhelming Spanish and international condemnation, however, quickly led them to back down. Since Matisyahu is not an Israeli, there was no way the organizers could avoid recognition that they were targeting him because he is Jewish. Moreover, this was not a case of urging a performer to withdraw; it was an effort to get a venue to boycott an artist. In the end, he gave a triumphant performance of his signature song, "Jerusalem," with its chorus that adapts the 137th Psalm:

> Jerusalem, if I forget you,
> fire not gonna come from me tongue.
> Jerusalem, if I forget you,
> let my right hand forget what it's supposed to do.

Efforts to convince artists not to perform in Israel often include massive social media campaigns with their own hashtags and slogans promoted on Twitter. And they can take the form of harassment and intimidation. As was reported in *The Guardian*, Paul McCartney received death threats in connection with his 2008 concert in Israel (Michaels).

Other cultural boycott actions have been collective. A controversy erupted at the 2009 Toronto International Film Festival when a group of artists objected to a focus on Tel Aviv that highlighted the work of ten Israeli filmmakers. Their letter of protest was countered by a letter condemning the attempted boycott, and the boycott effort failed. In 2011 protestors disrupted a performance of the Israeli Philharmonic Orchestra at London's Albert Hall. In 2014, as part of their anti-normalization campaign, PACBI organized protests against the joint Israeli-Palestinian project Heartbeat, which has used music to bring both peoples together and build trust. PACBI considers Heartbeat an unacceptable effort to normalize relations between Israel and the Palestinians. BDS and PACBI reject any project that treats Israelis and Palestinians as equal parties to an event or program, including any tour that visits both Israel and the West Bank. In February 2015, a group of seven hundred artists said they would boycott Israel until its "colonial oppression of Palestinians" comes to an end. Such BDS efforts are guaranteed to continue.

Most of those promoting cultural boycotts see no need to reflect on what is lost in the process, given that cultural boycotts can affect broad public audiences. Since there aren't any symphonies and art museums doing military research, the marginal arguments used to justify boycotting universities as complicit in state power do not apply to arts institutions. BDS regards the humanistic outreach, vision, and aesthetic ambition central to the arts as simply expendable or as an affront when exhibited in Israel. Like universities, cultural events or institutions are basically targets of opportunity. A significant BDS victory took place in January 2014 when the opening of a UNESCO-sponsored exhibition on the 3,500-year history of Jews in Palestine was cancelled after Arab nations lodged a protest against it. Organized by the Simon Wiesenthal Center in conjunction with the Canadian government, the exhibit had been curated and was ready to open in Paris. Cancelling such events removes opportunities for dialogue, mutual appreciation, and understanding. And we never really know what we have lost, as efforts to establish relationships and seek solutions can grow out of specific cultural contexts. Meanwhile the campaigns to cancel arts and humanities events can turn them into polarized political arenas, which is precisely the BDS movement's intention.

If politics is defined broadly enough—as the meanings and values that structure our identities and our social interactions—then all culture either has political implications or can be assigned them by targeted interpretation. In line with the BDS conviction that the Israeli-Palestinian conflict is the defining issue of our time, the series of cultural boycotts aims to redefine the arts as necessarily implicated. Artists should not, from the BDS perspective, be able to think of their work or promote it as politically neutral.

The work that academics do is often relevant only to highly specialized audiences, whereas musicians, writers, and other artists can have devoted fans in the hundreds of thousands or more, often stretching across the world. The publicity value of a concert, performance, or exhibition cancellation is thus high, which is why BDS devotes a great deal of energy to the effort. When a popular artist cancels an Israeli performance it adds a political dimension to the work itself, implying that Israel is not a suitable venue for the values embodied in the music, poetry, or graphic works at stake. And that is why BDS celebrates artists who agree to cancel. If you like Elvis Costello's music, the implicit logic goes, how can you possibly like Israel if Costello refuses to perform there? Conversely, you can believe that love of Israel is consonant with your devotion to Bob Dylan.

Jewish artists and art projects, along with Israeli artists, curators, and academics—whether they live in Israel or elsewhere—face both group organized and individual boycotts. It is particularly stressful for an exhibition curator to face a series of withdrawals from an event already approved and scheduled.

A campaign to boycott universities is an attack on the fundamental principle of academic freedom. Some artists who reject boycott efforts comparably say boycotts are antithetical to the idea of art, but that principle is often overshadowed by the defense of an artist's right to perform anywhere he or she is invited. When an artist withdraws from an event, it amounts to a personal choice, so BDS does not risk the same degree of principled backlash by pursuing cultural boycotts. The focus of cultural boycotts is the hearts and minds of national and international audiences. They are urged to cast Israel out of the aura of universalism that attaches to artistic works of great emotional appeal. ▪

Also see ACADEMIC BOYCOTTS, ANTI-NORMALIZATION, ANTI-JEWISH BOYCOTTS IN HISTORY, BDS: A BRIEF HISTORY, DIVESTMENT CAMPAIGNS, and ECONOMIC BOYCOTTS.

# DIVESTMENT CAMPAIGNS

CARY NELSON

ivestment campaigns are organized efforts to get institutions to withdraw their investments in one or more companies based on political, rather than financial, considerations. The BDS movement has deployed this measure against both Israeli companies and US companies doing business in Israel across a variety of civil society arenas, including universities, labor unions, churches, and the socially responsible investing community. Most such efforts adopt a few basic principles (like the right of return) but avoid advocating for a detailed set of specific policy goals, let alone an agenda for achieving them. Without a plan for achieving change, they end up being aimed at delegitimizing Israel. Most have been unsuccessful, but even when they are successful the economic impact is negligible, although they generate considerable negative publicity for Israel. Most importantly, these campaigns do nothing to advance the goal of achieving peace between Israel and the Palestinians and in fact do the opposite. By demonizing Israel they make negotiated progress toward two states for two peoples more difficult. Those interested in more detail about divestment in specific arenas can consult the topics noted at the end of this entry.

# INTRODUCTION

The opposite of investment, divestment is an economic strategy or procedure focused on the purchase of bonds or shares of a company on the stock market. Divestment entails the sale of those stocks and a pledge never to invest in the company again unless it changes its employment practices, alters its product line, or stops marketing its products in a targeted country. Divestment campaigns are organized efforts to pressure an organization or institution to abandon its investments in an objectionable company or country. Such campaigns often act on moral, ethical, or political imperatives and amount to a form of economic warfare. The most widespread divestment campaign peaked in the 1970s and 1980s when campuses, countries, and cities divested from companies doing business in South Africa. In addition to the potential economic consequences divestment campaigns may produce, their impact comes from the publicity they generate, which can broadly shape public opinion—well beyond the members of the group that is being urged to divest. These campaigns are different from instances when companies divest themselves of some of their holdings or portions of their operations to obtain funds, better focus their business, or sever their relationship with a failing or underperforming enterprise.

Divestment campaigns often target a few companies in the hope that they will stop doing business in Israel and others companies will follow suit, especially those anticipating only modest income from their Israeli business. Some companies may quietly withdraw from Israel to avoid the controversy that a divestment campaign can generate. A focused campaign may cause a broader fear of controversy that affects companies not yet targeted. The ultimate goal, however, is all the same: to cripple the Israeli economy, but that is almost certainly unachievable. The immediate aim is to tar Israel as a racist state that has no right to exist.

BDS urges people to mount divestment campaigns against Israel in "churches, unions, universities, local authorities and pension funds" (http://www.bdsmovement.net/activecamps/divestment). The movement encourages people to realize that each divestment campaign "raises the profile of the BDS" movement and encourages support for the entire BDS agenda, including approval of a right for millions of Palestinians to return to Israel proper and overwhelm the Jewish majority. BDS leaders like Ali Abunimah, Omar Barghouti, and Judith Butler make it clear they believe Israel has no legitimacy as a country and no right to exist. They dismiss the historical record in which Jews bought land from its legal owners before Israel was created as a country, and they dismiss the UN vote that gave Israel international recognition.

Like economic boycotts, divestment campaigns alone tend to have minimal actual economic impact. As Siew Hong Teoh, Ivo Welch, and C. Paul Wazzan wrote in a 1999 study of the South African case, "Despite the prominence and publicity of the boycott and the multitude of divesting companies, the financial markets' valuations of targeted companies or even the South African financial markets themselves were not visibly affected. The sanctions may have been effective in raising the public moral standards or public awareness of South African repression, but it appears that financial markets managed to avoid the brunt of the sanctions." Put simply, when a given investor sells stock, someone else tends to buy it.

# COMMUNITY IMPACT

These different divestment campaigns have one notable characteristic in common: they produce passionate advocacy and intense debates, but they tend not to polarize communities and generate widespread acrimony. In other words, except perhaps in the early stages of advocacy, they do not typically threaten the social fabric of the communities in which they are waged. But one group of contemporary divestment campaigns do exactly that, especially in campus communities. These highly divisive campaigns are devoted to divesting from companies that do business on the West Bank or in Israel itself.

Many Jewish students, faculty, and community members have deep emotional, cultural, religious, and political commitments to the homeland of the Jewish people. They recall the Holocaust, revelations about which helped lead some United Nations member countries to vote to found the Jewish state in 1947. Other nations regarded a Jewish state as the best way to deal with all the displaced Jews they preferred not to invite into their own counties, but that too was a World War II legacy. Jews in other countries may have relatives in Israel. And they watch the disturbing and frequently fanatical rise of anti-Semitism in Europe and the Middle East. They may disagree strongly with present Israeli government policy, but they are uncomfortable or even threatened by an activist campaign focused on dismantling Israel itself. Instead, many look for positive ways to encourage movement toward two states for two peoples, Israelis and Palestinians. BDS-promoted divestment campaigns are not focused on policy changes or the two-state solution. They are aimed at delegitimizing and demonizing Israel and eliminating it as a Jewish country.

At that point the "anti-Zionism is not anti-Semitism" mantra becomes more than a little disingenuous. Of course a minority of leftist Jews are anti-Zionist, but support for Israel's continued existence remains an over-whelming majority consensus among the world's Jews. To ignore or dismiss this, as BDS often does by publicizing the views of Jewish Voice for Peace, is to say that what the Jewish people wants—alone among all historically marginalized peoples—simply does not matter.

# SOCIALLY RESPONSIBLE INVESTING (SRI)

There is a long history of divestment from tobacco companies, which mar-ket a carcinogenic product that has no public benefits, and divestment from arms manufacturers, though weapons have the benefit of defensive uses. More recently, college campuses have witnessed campaigns to divest from fossil fuel-producing companies. The online "Divest Coal" campaign focuses on the fossil fuel that does the most environmental damage. The economic impact of divestment on a company or a campus is usually negligible; instead the campaigns aim to educate both the campus and the general public about the dangers of global warming and the need for alternative energy sources. Campaigns increasingly combine divestment from fossil fuel company stocks with divestment from companies doing business in Israel so as to give the appearance of positioning divestment from Israel within a progressive socially responsible investing agenda. This is a manipulative strategy designed to give the impression that divestment from Israel is a public good. There are likely to be more SRI-oriented divestment and investment campaigns both on campus and in corporations in the near future.

Until recently, BDS has largely ignored the investment side of the divest-ment paradigm. But it was always implicitly there. If one sells one's stock in a particular company, one may well invest the funds in another. BDS has now committed itself aggressively to investment options organized under the Socially Responsible Investment (SRI) strategy. SRI is an investment disci-pline that, in addition to its economic agenda, looks closely at the social con-sequences of investment in companies and mutual funds. Unlike the divest-ment campaigns that target companies that do business in Israel, anti-Israel SRI campaigns package together noncontroversial progressive industries that do not do business in Israel. The resultant funds can be promoted without mentioning Israel at all. In November 2015 the US Department of Labor issued new guidelines for pension fund investment covered by the Employee Retirement Income Security Act (ERISA). Those guidelines give approval to economically targeted investments (ETI) that observe environmental, social, or governmental (ESG) standards. This may prove a major opportunity for

SRI investing in the massive world of government pensions and thus an important opportunity for BDS.

# DIVESTMENT ON CAMPUS

Divestment campaigns against Israel on US campuses had their most notable origin in the 2002 campaigns at Harvard and the Massachusetts Institute of Technology (MIT). These campaigns then multiplied in 2005 after a group of 170 West Bank Palestinian organizations endorsed divestment and called for further action. Since then, universities in California have witnessed numerous student government–initiated divestment campaigns. They include University of California campuses at Berkeley, Davis, Irvine, Los Angeles, Riverside, and San Diego. The campaigns have produced resolutions calling on the UC Regents to divest from companies doing business in Israel, "profiting from the occupation" of the West Bank, or complicit in the "violation of Palestinian rights." UC Santa Barbara's student government bucked the trend by narrowly defeating a divestment resolution in 2015, the third year in a row. BDS is expanding its California initiative to include the California State University system. Meanwhile, DePaul, Evergreen, Loyola (Chicago), Northwestern, Oberlin, Stanford, Toledo, and Wesleyan have seen resolutions succeed.

Few people expect that any boards of regents or trustees will change their investment policies because of student votes. Thus the resolutions in that sense are ineffective, but BDS leaders acknowledge that winning the votes is not important. They aim instead to win hearts and minds, to turn students who will become business leaders, professionals, and politicians against Israel, and to create a campus climate where hostility toward the Jewish state prevails. Already these campaigns have radicalized and embedded opposition to Israel in many graduate students in the humanities and social sciences who will be the next generation of college teachers. Despite the intensity of time-bound campaigns, BDS is in this struggle for the long haul.

# DIVESTMENT IN LABOR UNIONS

See BDS AND ORGANIZED LABOR.

# DIVESTMENT IN CHURCHES— TARGETING COMPANIES

The most successful US divestment campaigns have taken place in some Protestant church denominations. Those campaigns are addressed in a separate entry. The church groups share with others overlapping lists of companies targeted for divestment. High on the list are Hewlett-Packard, Motorola, and Caterpillar because their products are actually used by Israeli authorities on the West Bank. BDS promotes a distinctly unsubtle condemnation of the three companies and fails to promote any detailed knowledge of how their products are used.

Hewlett-Packard sells Israel software and produces biometric I.D. cards for both Israelis and Palestinians. The I.D. cards are designed to facilitate and speed the flow of Palestinians through West Bank checkpoints; one benefit is that they eliminate more intrusive physical contact between Palestinians and the soldiers monitoring the checkpoints. The smart card system was developed with support from the US and the European Union and was reflected in an agreement between Israel and the Palestinian Authority. Given that the checkpoints are not going to disappear so long as Israel continues to have security concerns, HP's product is actually devoted to making Palestinian lives easier. Is the company's willingness to do business with Israeli military authorities sufficient grounds for moral outrage even if it enhances daily life for Palestinians?

Caterpillar is a different case. Its heavy-duty bulldozers are used in West Bank house demolitions, an IDF strategy that many consider ill-advised, counter-productive, and inhumane. But they have also been used during war in the Sinai and elsewhere, where they are tasked with towing mobile bridges, clearing land mines, and building defensive barriers. Palestinians also use Caterpillar products, and there is a West Bank Palestinian Caterpillar dealership, which complicates any general divestment or boycott initiative. Israel produces an add-on armor kit that shields the bulldozers against land mines and protects the occupants with bullet-proof glass. In any case, Caterpillar does not sell these tractors directly to Israel. The bulldozers are obtained through the US Foreign Military Sales Program, a government-to-government program for selling US-made equipment that is financed by the US Defense Department. Thus the supply chain for the bulldozers is distinct from that of other American products that arrive in Israel. It is unrealistic to expect Caterpillar to refuse to sell its products to a US government program. As many have suggested, Caterpillar itself is not an appropriate target for a protest against the defense department's programs and policies.

BDS's tactics raise a series of questions. Does a company have the ethical responsibility to track and investigate how a buyer uses its products? Is this a realistic expectation? Is this a valid model for commercial activity? Should a company initiate sales bans in response to selective political pressure absent comprehensive knowledge of how its products are used elsewhere in the world? Should companies try to ban product sales on their own initiative, absent legal national or international prohibitions? It is easy to arouse people to oppose companies whose products are used as part of a military occupation, but accurate information can make such political agendas more complex than BDS advocates wish to admit.

Some divestment advocates on campus or in religious groups believe they can promote such campaigns without being identified with BDS or its fundamentally anti-Israel agenda. But BDS predictably embraces such "independent" divestment campaigns, applauds and publicizes their efforts, and welcomes the campaign to its cause. Should that campaign succeed, both BDS itself and the press will count it a win for the BDS movement. And indeed it is. It is in fact naïve to suppose one can distinguish oneself from a well-publicized political agenda when one adopts its tactics. The difference one establishes in one's own mind does not necessarily carry weight in the public sphere. ▪

Also see ACADEMIC BOYCOTTS, ANTI-JEWISH BOYCOTTS IN HISTORY, ANTI-NORMALIZATION, BDS: A BRIEF HISTORY, BDS AND CHRISTIAN CHURCHES, BDS RESOLUTIONS ON CAMPUS: THEIR LONG-TERM GOAL, CULTURAL BOYCOTTS, ECONOMIC BOYCOTTS, and SOCIALLY RESPONSIBLE INVESTING.

# ECONOMIC BOYCOTTS

## CARY NELSON

## INTRODUCTION

The history of efforts to boycott Jewish businesses in many countries is long and sordid. They have generally been a part of broader campaigns to exclude Jews from the social, economic, and political life of their nations or of the international community. Explicitly anti-Semitic economic boycotts were common in 19th century Europe, often as a reaction to liberal efforts granting Jews equal citizenship rights. They reached their zenith in Nazi Germany, where they were implemented soon after Adolf Hitler came to power. At the same time, Arabs organized boycotts of Jewish businesses in the years of Mandate Palestine, before Israel was founded as a country. Starting in 1945 and continuing throughout most of the life of the state of Israel, Arab nations, under the auspices of the Arab League, have promoted an economic boycott of Israel. Egypt, Jordan, and the Palestinian Authority terminated their boycotts after signing peace treaties with Israel, or, in the case of the PA, interim agreements, and in the wake of the Oslo Peace Accords of 1993, other Arab nations relaxed or declined to enforce their boycotts. Nonetheless, considerable Arab aversion to economic cooperation or commerce with Israel has remained.

The focus here is not on that long history but rather on the recent boycott agendas promoted by the Boycott, Divestment, and Sanctions (BDS) movement and its allies. Divestment campaigns are also addressed in a separate entry. This entry will address economic boycotts and their potential impact on Israel itself, the broader cultural and political aim to delegitimize the Jewish state, and the effects on local communities where many boycott campaigns have been carried out over the last decade.

BDS language is explicit in supporting the right of Palestinians worldwide to return to Israel and the need to demolish Israel's security barrier, but the international movement has been less clear in distinguishing among the alternative models for economic boycotts. Indeed in practice boycott advocates often do not know precisely what they aim to accomplish, other than to demonize and isolate Israel. In August 2015, after Iceland's Reykjavik City Council passed a resolution advocating the boycott of all Israeli products, Knesset member Yair Lapid published a series of questions in *Fréttabladid*, Iceland's largest circulation newspaper: (http://mideasttruth.com/forum/viewtopic.php?t=11934):

- Does the boycott include products made by Israel's Arab minority which is 20 percent of the population?
- Does the boycott include the 14 Arab Israeli parliamentarians who sit beside me in Israel's parliament?
- Does the boycott include Israeli factories which employ tens of thousands of Palestinians for whom this is the only opportunity to provide for their children?
- Does the boycott include Israeli hospitals at which tens of thousands of Palestinians are treated every year?
- Does the boycott include produce made by the 71 percent of Israelis who, according to the latest survey, support a two-state solution and the creation of a Palestinian state alongside Israel?
- Among the products being boycotted is Copaxone, for MS sufferers, included?
- Does the boycott include "Tulip" wine, which is made by people with special needs and those who suffer from autism?
- And what about the books of Israeli Nobel Prize Laureate in literature, Shai Agnon?
- Does the boycott include Microsoft Office, cellphone cameras, Google—all of which contain elements invented or produced in Israel?

Lapid's list of questions effectively made the point that any boycott, whether of Israel as a whole or of the West Bank, was bound to be in some respects inconsistent, incoherent, and unenforceable. Israel is well integrated into the global economy, and although the boycott movement could ultimately have harmful effects should it gain enough adherents, resolutions such as the Reykjavik City Council's serve more as political gestures rather than as considered actions designed to achieve results. Indeed, almost immediately after the city announced the resolution, the Icelandic national government disavowed it and Reykjavik's City Council backpedaled, revising it to limit the scope to products produced on the West Bank. In any case, the resolution was purely symbolic, there being no national policy or mechanism in Iceland to enforce either a limited or a comprehensive boycott. In fact there are few Israeli products sold in Iceland at all, which reduces the resolution to a form of virtuous posturing. And yet, because Reykjavik is Iceland's capital, the symbolism had publicity value and potential cultural weight. It could contribute, for example, to the political movement to delegitimize Israel entirely.

## THE EUROPEAN UNION'S LABELING AGENDA

Clearly the current round of calls for economic boycotts of Israel take a variety of forms. The European Union in 2015 moved forward not with a boycott but with a plan to require that products produced in the West Bank and the Golan Heights be so labeled. Although such a labeling plan has some resemblances to a boycott, and can be fairly questioned for singling out the West Bank among occupied or unfree territories worldwide where goods are produced, there are also significant differences. Moreover, such a plan will have to address the complex question of what constitutes a West Bank product. Is a product made in Israel proper with West Bank raw materials a West Bank product? What percentage of West Bank material turns a product manufactured elsewhere into a West Bank product? Is 10 percent sourced from the West Bank enough to make something a West Bank product?

The EU's plan is is not a boycott per se. It does not prohibit the import of West Bank products. It is a labeling regimen that gives both businesses and individuals a choice about whether to purchase West Bank products. It also enables people to identify Israeli products that are not manufactured in the West Bank and buy them. People who want to buy West Bank products can do so—indeed they can make a point of doing so if they wish—whereas those who oppose the expansion of West Bank settlements can make a personal ethical and political statement through their choices as consumers. But they can also take advantage of the quality guarantees built into the vast majority of Israeli products without worry that they may have been manufactured on the West Bank. People might well prefer to buy medicines made in Israel than in countries with less reliable manufacturing safeguards. With some countries, "Made in" can serve as warning not to buy a product manufactured without clear safety and efficacy standards. It is information that consumers should have for all products.

Gerald M. Steinberg has argued the opposing case, echoing the stand taken by both the Netanyahu government and the opposition: "The next step would be to ban these products, and then to single out all Israeli items . . . . Product labeling is the embodiment of a strategy to delegitimize Israel and the right of the Jewish people to sovereign equality. It is central to the political war embodied in BDS—boycott, divestment and sanctions—whose stated objective is not peace, but rather 'the complete international isolation of Israel' . . . Although those promoting this agenda use different methods than the terrorists stabbing Israelis in Jerusalem, Petah Tikvah and Tel Aviv, they have the same goals." Although a selective ban on Israeli products has a progressive logic that leads toward a comprehensive economic boycott, product labeling does not. Moreover, many of those who support—or at least tolerate—product labeling would not sign on to any actual Israeli boycott. To claim that those promoting the EU strategy share links with anti-Semitism, as Steinberg goes on to say, appears to be unwarranted.

The EU's labeling agenda is also a challenge to those BDS advocates who contradictorily support boycotting all Israeli products, no matter on which side of the Green Line (MAP 4) they are manufactured or produced, while claiming they are not hostile to the existence of the Jewish state. For the labeling protocol enables people to engage in a more politically focused form of symbolic politics. And it thereby clarifies which people are fundamentally opposed to Israel. Of course, in addition to those who oppose singling out Israel for criticism, those who embrace the concept of a Greater Israel may not be happy with a labeling regime that distinguishes between Israel proper and the West Bank; that distinction is the only genuine slippery slope in play. In any case, it may be a better political strategy to discount the significance of product labeling, rather than escalate the war against it and increase its symbolic and political power.

## PRODUCTS TARGETED FOR BOYCOTT

The irrationality of product boycotts is on display in the website of the Sacramento, California, BDS chapter. It offers a long list of Israeli companies and products to be boycotted, along with the reasons for doing so. Their examples (with their analysis quoted) include

**Sabra hummus**: Sabra hummus, baba ghanoush and other foods is co-owned by Israel's second-largest food company The Strauss Group and PepsiCo. On the "Corporate Responsibility" section of its website, The Strauss Group boasts of its relationship to the Israeli Army, offering food products and political support.

**Intel**: This technology company that manufactures computer processors and other hardware components employs thousands of Israelis and has exports from Israel totaling over $1 billion per year. They are one of Israel's oldest foreign supporters, having established their first development center outside of the US in 1974 in Haifa. Al-Awda (the Palestinian Right to Return Coalition, www.al-awda.org) has urged action against Intel for building a facility on the land of former village Iraq Al Manshiya, which was cleansed in 1949.

**TEVA**: An Israeli company that is one of the largest generic drug manufacturers in the world. Ask your pharmacist and doctor to find another brand.

**Estee Lauder**: This company's chairman Ronald Lauder is also the chairman of the Jewish National Fund, a quasi-governmental organization that was established in 1901 to acquire Palestinian land and is connected to the continued building of illegal settlements.

**Ben & Jerry's Ice Cream**, sold in illegal Jewish-only settlements in Palestine's West Bank in violation of international law.

**Naot shoes**. Naot maintains a factory outlet in one of Israel's illegal settlements inside Palestine's West Bank.

These are neither West Bank companies nor West Bank products. Naot shoes and Ben & Jerry's ice cream are targeted merely because they are sold on the West Bank, along with stores throughout the US and other countries. Products from Arab countries are also sold on the West Bank. TEVA is selected because it is an Israeli company. Estee Lauder is denounced because BDS doesn't like the politics of the company chairman, Intel because it has a factory on land vacated more than half a century ago. Intel's factory is located on farmland outside a former Arab village, not on the site of the village itself. On that basis there could be hundreds of boycotts targeting businesses and institutions in Israel. For several years, BDS called for a boycott of SodaStream because it maintained a plant on the West Bank, but when SodaStream moved its factory from the West Bank to the Negev in 2015, BDS insisted its boycott campaign against SodaStream should be maintained—now based on the BDS claim that the new factory, which is near the Bedouin city of Rahat, is built on land "stolen" from the Bedouins. But SodaStream in fact has a constructive ongoing relationship with the Bedouin community: 30 percent of SodaStream's employees come from Rahat. In September 2015, SodaStream's CEO Daniel Birnbaum and Talal Al-Krenawi, the mayor of Rahat, indicated their willingness to take in Syrian refugees and give them employment. BDS is unwilling to credit such practices, to recognize that the Bedouins near the factory have no interest in boycotting it, or to make a functional distinction between Israel and the West Bank. Echoing the radical Arab nationalist claim that no land in Israel proper belongs to the Jews, BDS's continued SodaStream boycott campaign aims not to change Israeli policies but rather to launch a comprehensive economic and cultural boycott that leads to the elimination of the Jewish state.

That BDS goal is highlighted by the demand on the same website to boycott "Wine from Occupied Golan Heights," hardly a response to the call from "Palestinian civil society" that BDS routinely cites as a reason for acting. Indeed, in the current political configuration to whom would Israel return the Golan Heights? ISIS? Hezbollah? Does Syria still exist? It would be hard to imagine a less rational action than for Israel to cede the Golan Heights now to anyone, though when Ehud Barak was Prime Minister it still seemed to many Israeli leaders a plausible issue for negotiation. In any event, Israel extended civil law to the Golan in 1981, which makes it quite unlike the West Bank, though relations with the Druze population there remain tense and complicated. The EU is equally misguided in requiring Golan Heights product labeling.

Should actual organized boycotts, as opposed to labeling, of West Bank products take hold, their economic impact on Israel would still be modest: West Bank products make up a small percentage of Israeli exports overall and less than one percent of exports to the European Union. The scholarly literature, moreover, demonstrates that limited economic boycotts like this have only minimal impact. Despite the excitement BDS advocates display when a boycott campaign or its attendant publicity seem to affect company practices, such campaigns typically leave official state policy untouched. Politically speaking, limited economic boycotts are not game changers. They give advocates momentary psychological satisfaction—and they may draw people to the BDS cause—but they are largely impotent as direct political weapons.

One continuing BDS strategy is to target an individual company doing business in Israel or the West Bank and urge it to cease doing so, as they did with SodaStream. BDS launched such a campaign against the giant French construction company Veolia in November 2008. The company was involved in a West Bank landfill and various water and transportation projects; it also had a five percent share in Jerusalem Light Rail, which connected settlement communities with Israel proper and could thus be accused of trying to "normalize" the status of the settlements. After several years of controversy, Veolia decided to cut its losses, selling its share in bus lines in 2013, jettisoning most of its other business operations there in April 2015, and liquidating its 5 percent share in JLR in August. Veolia insisted its decision was purely economic, but it is more likely to have been economics influenced by politics. Given that the West Bank projects represented only a tiny fraction of Veolia's international business, the time and cost involved in defending itself did not make economic sense. It has been suggested that BDS targeted Veolia for exactly that reason, because Veolia was such a minor player in the Israeli economy and Israel was a small portion of Veolia's portfolio (Scheindlin). Needless to say, none of this dissuaded BDS from trumpeting Veolia's decisions as a triumph of the largest order.

## COMMUNITY AND CAMPUS BOYCOTT CAMPAIGNS

Despite their limited economic impact, local boycott campaigns can have psychological and cultural power. In 2012 members of the Park Slope Food Co-op in Brooklyn voted 1,005 to 653 against boycotting Israeli products. The battle gained national attention. People did not want their daily life branded with antagonism to the Jewish homeland; many could no longer shop at the co-op if it became an outpost of the BDS movement. Typically, the store carried few Israeli products in the first place, but among them, ironically, was a line of tapenades and pestos produced by PeaceWorks Foods with olives from Palestinian villages. PeaceWorks is a US specialty food company that supports both Israeli and Palestinian businesses in an effort to promote coexistence. BDS followers tried to press for a boycott on Brooklyn again in 2015. Like several similar drives in California and Washington state, such battles are fought over what kind of community people understand themselves to be living in and whether they can perceive it as their home.

Among the more narrowly focused campaigns against Israeli products was the 2009 effort by the Code Pink group to boycott the Israeli cosmetic company Ahava's beauty products made partly from mineral-rich Dead Sea mud. Billed as the "Stolen Beauty" campaign, it featured Code Pink demonstrators dressed in bikinis and smeared with mud demonstrating in front of cosmetics stores demanding that Ahava "come clean" about the fact that West Bank mud should belong to Palestinians. The Ahava store in London's Covent Garden did finally decide to close in 2011 after years of disruptive protests that included demonstrators chaining themselves to concrete blocks inside the store.

Campaigns at Harvard, UC Riverside, Wesleyan, Vassar, and elsewhere have focused on whether the university cafeteria should stop selling Sabra hummus as a protest against Israeli policy. But Sabra Dipping Company is actually a US based company, which is co-owned by Strauss and Pepsico. The claim is that it donates money to a charity that benefits Israeli soldiers. At all four of these schools, administrators stepped in and directed that both disputed and non-disputed brands of hummus should be available so students could choose. At DePaul students held a referendum to decide whether to remove the hummus; it failed. At Princeton, students voted not to sell alternative brands.

As much as anything else, these campus campaigns seek not only to recruit people to a broad anti-Israel agenda but also to turn the campus into an environment hostile to pro-Israel students. While a pitched battle over serving a brand of hummus in the cafeteria might seem more appropriately considered theatre of the absurd rather than politics, hummus is obviously chosen because the cafeteria is a common space that students frequent where public demonstrations can be staged. Refusing a food product is also hardly a major sacrifice. If students' chests swell with a sense of righteous triumph when they pick another brand, they might be challenged to abandon that laptop with an Intel processor. Or they might be asked whether their prescription glasses have Shamir lenses. Widely considered the best such lenses in the world, they are manufactured on an Israeli kibbutz.

Universities themselves, in any case, are not appropriate vehicles for institutional political opinion; students and faculty instead are free to develop and express both individual and group views, but the institution needs to remain neutral. Indeed, a college's nonprofit tax status mandates that it not engage in political activity.

Sometimes local protests cross the line into anti-Semitism. When a Sainsbury store in central London stripped all kosher food, including British company kosher products, from its shelves in 2014, it turned an anti-Israel BDS protest into an attack on Jewish culture as a whole. The corporate headquarters pledged never to let it happen again. No such reversal of fortunes accompanied the 2011-2014 anti-Israel demonstrations against the Max Brenner chocolate shops throughout Australia. Headquartered in New York, the restaurant/chocolate bar establishments are a subsidiary of an Israeli food and beverage company, the Strauss Group, which donates care packages to the

Israeli army. That was enough to lead Australian protestors to block entry to Max Brenner shops, a franchise owned by Australian Jews, and chant "there is blood in your chocolate." Signs read "You Can't Sweeten Israeli Apartheid!" When a student group in Cape Town, South Africa, placed pigs' heads in the kosher sections of local supermarkets in 2014, they also crossed a line.

## COMPARISONS WITH SOUTH AFRICA

Finally, although economic boycott campaigns targeting Israel are sometimes justified by contentious comparisons with apartheid South Africa, there is little interest among the major national governments in mounting a comprehensive South Africa-style economic boycott of Israel. The United States, of course, would not support it. Nor would Canada, Germany, or numerous other countries. There is nothing even marginally comparable to apartheid to the west of the Green Line in Israel. Within its pre-1967 borders (MAP 2), Israel is a democracy, although one with an ongoing problem of discrimination against its Arab citizens. ■

Also see ACADEMIC BOYCOTTS, ANTI-JEWISH BOYCOTTS IN HISTORY, ANTI-NORMALIZATION, APARTHEID, CULTURAL BOYCOTTS, DIVESTMENT CAMPAIGNS, and SOCIALLY RESPONSIBLE INVESTING.

# FATAH

CARY NELSON

Now the chief political party represented in the Palestinian Authority, Fatah, originally the Palestinian National Liberation Movement, was founded in 1959 as a terrorist organization dedicated to overthrowing the Jewish State. The organization's flag includes crossed swords superimposed over a map of Israel, with a hand grenade below. The name Fatah is a reverse acronym based on an Arabic phrase that translates as "opening," "conquering," or "victory." It was founded by a group including Yasser Arafat (1929-2004), Khalil El-Wazir (1935-1988), Salah Khalaf (1933-1991), Khalid al-Hasan (1928-1994), and Faruk Qaddumi (1931-), all Palestinians working in the Gulf states. Fatah had no single leader at first, but Arafat eventually took charge and Fatah was strongly identified with him until he died. Fatah's first attacks against Israel occurred in the winter of 1964-65. Fatah became the most influential group in Palestinian politics after 1967's Six Day War. Khalid al-Hasan died of natural causes, but El-Wazir and Khalaf were both assassinated, the former by Israel and the later likely by a rival terrorist group.

In 1968, when Fatah headquarters were located in the Jordanian village of Karameh, Israel Defense Forces launched a major assault against the group. After the Jordanian Army committed itself to aid Fatah fighters in the village, the IDF withdrew to avoid a major escalation of the conflict. Building on the Israeli withdrawal, Fatah began jockeying for greater power in Jordan. In 1970, simmering tensions between Fatah and Jordan's ruling monarchy erupted into armed conflict. Several thousands of Fatah militants and Palestinian civilians died in the fighting, and Fatah fled to Syria before crossing into Lebanon and establishing its headquarters there.

In the 1970s Fatah attacked Israeli targets both in the Middle East and in Western Europe. In March 1978, for example, Fatah hijacked a bus on the coastal road between Haifa and Tel Aviv, killing 37 people. Meanwhile Fatah benefitted from weapons and training provided by the Soviet Union. The most famous terrorist attack of the period was the murder of eleven Israeli athletes and a German police officer at the 1972 Olympics in Munich. The massacre was carried out by Black September, which was billed as a Fatah splinter group, but in fact was established by Fatah and likely relied on Fatah's intelligence and security resources. Black September's other efforts included the 1972 hijacking in Vienna of a Belgian aircraft headed to the Israeli city of Lod and the hijacking of a Lufthansa plane in Rome the following year. In the Lufthansa case the hijackers demanded the release of the three surviving terrorists of the Munich massacre, and the Germans complied. In September 1972 the group sent dozens of letter bombs from Amsterdam to Israeli diplomats, successfully killing one in Britain. The destinations and the number of letter bombs intercepted are as follows: Austria (5), Australia (5), Buenos Aires (5), Cambodia (1), Jerusalem (11), London (17), Montreal (1), New York (3), Ottawa (6), Paris (2), Tel Aviv (1). An undisclosed number arrived at the Israeli embassy at Zaire. Letter bombs to the same location often arrived on different days. In October the efforts switched to Malaysia, with letter bombs sent to Hadassah executives in New York and a series of Jewish families in Rhodesia. Then several letter bombs addressed to American officials were found in Israel, possibly mailed by an infiltrator from Lebanon. In November police intercepted twenty letter bombs addressed to Jewish targets in Britain, fifty-two addressed to Jewish firms in Europe, and five targeted to Geneva. Some of these exploded and caused injuries. Several attempted or successful assassinations took place in 1972 and 1973.

Fatah and the PLO (Palestine Liberation Organization) became involved in the Lebanese Civil War in 1975. More than one group committed atrocities and war crimes. After Christian militias killed over 1,000 civilians in the Palestinian refugee camp Karantina, the PLO killed 684 civilians in the town of Damour in retaliation. When Israel invaded Lebanon in 1982, Fatah was compelled to move its headquarters to Tunisia, though some Fatah military leaders and fighters remained behind to continue in the Civil War.

Fatah was able to return from exile after the Oslo Accords in 1993. At that point Israel and the PLO recognized one another, and organized mass violence came largely to an end. Absent progress on the peace front, more localized but lethal violence, often organized by Hamas cells, has continued.

Fatah lost the legislative elections in Gaza to Hamas in 2006, and Fatah and Hamas engaged in a civil war. Fatah was cast out of Gaza as a result, leaving it with the Palestinian Authority (PA) in the West Bank as its power base. Despite their vexed and violent history, Israel and Fatah/PA have no other partners with whom to pursue a negotiated peace. ▪

Also see GAZA, HAMAS, THE LEBANON WARS, THE OSLO ACCORDS, THE PALESTINE LIBERATION ORGANIZATION, THE PALESTINIAN AUTHORITY, and THE WEST BANK.

# FROM FERGUSON
# TO PALESTINE

CARY NELSON

T he anti-Israel BDS movement has sought to link its cause with that of the Black Lives Matter movement, and by doing so gain enhanced legitimacy among progressives. But this analogy is fundamentally flawed. African-American citizens seeking civil rights and equal treatment under law within the United States cannot be compared to the Palestinian quest for self-determination and sovereignty—historically often using violent means rather than negotiation—in a separate state of their own.

## BACKGROUND

In 2015 many Americans had to acknowledge that white policemen in the US can kill unarmed Blacks, particularly Black men, with near impunity. This fact overlays the longest running social wound in the United States: the history that begins with slavery, continues through the American Civil War and Reconstruction to Jim Crow, and encompasses decades of lynching, violence, and discrimination. Even in the post Civil Rights era, the mass incarceration of Black men in the US, often punishing nonviolent drug offenses with disproportionately long prison terms, distinguishes and shames the United States among all nations. The fact that public schools in poor neighborhoods, including those dominated by African Americans, are financed with local property taxes has helped ensure that the schools remain separate and unequal. Black voting rights won at great sacrifice in the 1960s are once again under assault throughout the South. While there have been significant gains in opportunity for African Americans since the Civil Rights era, including the rise of a Black middle class, inequality and poverty remain widespread and systemic. But there is little comparable to the progress in US race relations among Jews and Palestinians on the West Bank.

## JEWS AND BLACKS

The inequality and discrimination highlighted above deeply trouble many Jews, both because of the fundamental injustice they embody and because Jews have themselves been victims of both discrimination and murderous violence for centuries. Their economic success and success at assimilation in the United States does not for many erase the longer historical memory that speaks to a different reality. Their long commitment to social justice has also led Jews to commit themselves to the civil rights movement in the US. That does not mean that Jewish communities have been free of prejudice or that Jews have had no complicity in American injustices, but it does mean that an effort to erase or discount Jewish civil rights advocacy or the deep social justice traditions in Judaism itself is singularly painful. Since their arrival in the United States, Jews have overwhelmingly tended to support movements for racial equality and they still vote in patterns closely resembling their Black compatriots. Many Jews recall Martin Luther King's opposition to anti-Semitism in the Black community and his support for Israel and a Zionist narrative. They take pride in the presence of prominent rabbis as speakers in the 1963 March on Washington, the disproportionate numbers of Jews who participated in the 1964 Mississippi Freedom Summer, and in the strong Jewish participation in many legal challenges to racial discrimination over the years.

Many Zionists too see their movement as a freedom struggle, and legitimately so. The historic resonances between the Jewish and Black narratives ("Let My People Go"), the characterization by southern Blacks of the north as "the promised land" during the Great Migration, are not coincidental. The installation of an anti-Zionist narrative within African American struggles erases both the essence of Zionism and its deep kinship to American Blacks' quest for freedom.

There have also been political differences, of course, between the two communities, which have erupted from time to time since the 1960s, such as over the Ocean Hill-Brownsville teachers' strike of 1968 or Jesse Jackson's presidential campaigns in 1984 and 1988 or over the wisdom of certain public policies like affirmative action. But the recent spread of slogans such as "From Ferguson to Palestine" and "Palestine2Ferguson" is a source of particular pain to many American Jews, who tend to support the aspirations of today's Black activists but recoil at the analysis of Middle East politics that some in the movement are now championing.

# FROM FERGUSON TO PALESTINE

"From Ferguson to Palestine," "Palestine2Ferguson," "Justice from Ferguson to Palestine," "Resistance is Justified from Gaza to Ferguson," and "From Ferguson to Palestine, occupation is a crime" are slogans that spread across the US in 2014 and 2015 in an effort by the Boycott, Divestment, and Sanctions (BDS) movement and by some Black activists to link the struggle for justice and Black rights in the US with the struggle for Palestinian rights in the Israeli–Palestinian conflict. The connection they make is drawn in part from the fact that a number of US police departments have sent officials to Israel to receive anti-terrorist training. But the slogans reflect a larger effort to demonstrate how African American and Palestinian narratives intersect. These slogans also serve as a platform through which BDS organizes multi-ethnic campus resistance to Israel and multi-ethnic support for the movement. BDS did not create the Black Lives Matter campaign, but it did rapidly link itself to the movement when the campaign gained momentum in 2014, in part by building influential relationships between BDS and African American leaders.

The Black Lives Matter campaign began in 2013 as a protest against the failure to bring justice to 17-year-old Trayvon Martin's killer George Zimmerman in Florida. It gained national prominence with its protest against and conceptual framing of the August 2014 police shooting of Michael Brown, an unarmed 18-year-old African American in Ferguson, Missouri. The protest placed Brown's killing in a long line of other recent police shootings of Black men and sought to highlight the failure in most cases to punish police officers who used force, especially lethal force, against African Americans without sufficient justification. Over time, the movement took on broader goals and critiques, including of Israel. In August 2015 more than 1,000 activists (http://www.blackforpalestine.com/view-the-signatories.htm) signed the Black Solidarity Statement with Palestine (http://www.

blackforpalestine.com/read-the-statement.html) occurring "on the anniversary of last summer's Gaza massacre." It declared, in part: "We remain sickened by Israel's targeting of homes, schools, UN shelters, mosques, ambulances, and hospitals. We remain heartbroken and repulsed by the number of children Israel killed in an operation it called 'defensive.' We reject Israel's framing of itself as a victim . . . We offer this statement first and foremost to Palestinians, whose suffering does not go unnoticed and whose resistance and resilience under racism and colonialism inspires us." The statement went on to endorse the right of all Palestinians to return to Israel and to urge the end of all US economic and military aid to Israel.

As Black journalist Mark Lamont Hill declared in a January 2015 demonstration in the Israeli Arab city of Nazareth organized by Black Lives Matter co-founder and BDS advocate Patrisse Cullors, referencing Israeli "greed" and the slaughter of innocents in a way that resonates uncomfortably with historic anti-Semitic tropes, "We come to a land that has been stolen by greed and destroyed by hate. We come here and we learn laws that have been cosigned in ink but written in the blood of the innocent" (https://electronicintifada.net/blogs/rania-khalek/watch-ferguson-activists-bring-message-love-and-struggle-palestine). Fueled by demonstrations that put posters with slogans on the national news, the campaign made its initial impact through social media, with Facebook posts and Twitter feeds. Aggressive social media campaigns are notable for their effectiveness in promoting both solidarity and political conformity and indeed for blurring the difference between the two. At its most hostile, the media campaign spreads the claim that Zionism equals white racism.

The justification for the relevance of the Palestinian cause to the Black Lives Matter movement, and for the wholesale adoption of a particular, militant Palestinian narrative, is a presumed resemblance of the plight of African Americans and of Palestinians in the occupied territories. As Bassem Masri, a Palestinian and Black Lives Matter activist who was involved in the Ferguson demonstrations puts it, "the people of Palestine and Ferguson are reaching out to each other because they are fighting a common system of injustice, control and racism . . . In both Saint Louis and Jerusalem, segregation is alive and well. Both areas are zones of occupation overseen by violent police departments enforcing regimes of racism." Once the analogy is established, the next step is the articulation of a common cause: as Masri writes, the link between the movements shows "that oppressed people could make alliances across oceans and heavily fortified borders in a joint struggle to achieve justice." Similarly, two anti-Zionist activists, Sandra Tamari and Tara Thompson, wrote: "When Palestinians are called violent for their freedom demonstrations against the Israeli military we are reminded of our liberation protests on the streets of Ferguson where we were treated as state enemies." Some, such as BDS activist and self-described independent journalist Rania Khalek, go so far as to claim, as she did in 2015, that Zionism points to the ideology underlying state violence throughout the world: "From the killing fields of Gaza to the teargassed streets of Ferguson and beyond, Zionism is an engine for cutting edge in the development of the technology of repression that sustains racism and inequality across the globe." In its most ambitious version, the Ferguson-to-Palestine movement seeks to bind the situations and destinies of Palestinians and Black Americans. When *Electronic Intifada* co-founder Ali Abunimah spoke at the University of Illinois during the Israeli Apartheid Week of 2015, he argued that Black Americans would never be free until Palestinians were free as well.

Although not everyone wants to acknowledge it, the parallel between African Americans and Palestinians is based partly on the conviction that Israelis are white and Palestinians are people of color. It certainly helps the left's settler-colonialist mantra if one opportunistically racializes the Israeli-Palestinian conflict, but the conflict itself historically has not been about race, but rather about how nationalism, religion, ethnicity, and history create peoplehood. If Palestinians are people of color, then surely Egyptian, Ethiopian, Iraqi, Moroccan, and Yemini Jews, among others, are as well. Less than half of Israelis are of European origin, but ignorance and opportunism permits people to think otherwise. In the US, of course, Arabs long identified themselves as white, and some still do. If skin color, a minor genetic feature, is to be the guide, then many Palestinians and Israelis appear equivalently white or brown. In fact many Jews and Palestinians share considerable genetic material. Using race to essentialize the parties to the conflict is an invidious political decision. Racializing the conflict makes it more difficult both to understand its complexity and to devise solutions to solve it, but it does facilitate BDS's depiction of it as a Manichean struggle between good and evil, between justice and injustice.

The academic justification for linking African American and Palestinian struggles often relies on the developing theory of "intersectionality," which proposes that injustices and systems of discrimination, oppression, and domination "intersect" within a society. That has been helpful in understanding the relationship between race, class, and gender, among other social categories, and it is a useful way to compare how those forms of social differentiation and discrimination compare and contrast in different societies. The Ferguson-to-Palestine logic rests on a far more speculative claim—that injustices intersect even if they occur in different parts of the world in different contexts under different political systems. Then the "intersection" often occurs only in the mind of the beholder in or a political manifesto, and it begins to function like a conspiracy theory. It is the rationalizing glue that holds together a series of historically and culturally unrelated political causes and builds alliances based on them. As David Bernstein writes, "Much more than a theoretical framework, intersectionality is a comprehensive community relations strategy."

That is because intersectionality has been transformed from a theory into a political slogan, into a rallying call, in Angela Davis' words, for "an internationalism that always urged us to make connections among freedom struggles" (53), thereby honoring "the intersectionality of movements" (21). In his Foreword to Davis' 2016 *Freedom is a Constant Struggle*, Cornel West defines intersectionality as "a structural intellectual and political response to the dynamics of violence, white supremacy, patriarchy, state power, capitalist markets, and imperial politics" (viii).

Unfortunately, as a slogan, intersectionality aims to resist the possibility that the structural relations between the forms of power and discrimination in different times and places might not be the same. As a slogan used to mobilize solidarity, it sweeps such differences aside, even denies they exist. Intersectionality did not in itself constitute a theory of how race, class, and gender intersect, but it named one and gave encouragement to develop such a theory. Simply invoking the word now constitutes proof of a connection, as if the term itself had evidentiary status. The slogan thus eviscerates the analytic usefulness of the theory. When the slogan in turn is then used as an analytic tool it acquires the status of a totalizing account of both politics itself and the politics of social life. It has the totalizing power of Marxism but without the rich theoretical content Marxism acquired over more than a century. Despite the empty symbolic character of the term, Angela Davis may, in light of her Marxist history, be drawn to its totalizing power. It is an instance of theory returning as farce. In a telling moment, Davis regrets that "too often people feel that they are not sufficiently informed to consider themselves an advocate of justice in Palestine" (21). These are, she reminds us, issues of justice, as indeed they are. But political solidarity should be a consequence of understanding, not its alternative. Even if fans of intersectionality actually tracked injustices worldwide, rather than limiting examples to Israel and the US, it is not clear the effort would help us do the political work necessary in combatting racism.

## CONCLUSIONS

To say that no people on earth will be free until all peoples are free has the same idealist appeal that folk music did in the 1960s. But the Ferguson to Palestine slogan does not link all liberation struggles. Instead it singles out the denial of Palestinian rights as the singular and preeminent injustice in the entire world and thus an international cause Americans need urgently to embrace. It does so based on a false analogy—that the plight of Black citizens in the American state where all citizens are promised equality before the law is the same as or is linked with the plight of Palestinians in a conflict between two peoples seeking self-determination who do not share a common state.

There remains a split in the Black Lives Matter movement about whether to make a fundamental bond with the Palestinian struggle. Some Black Americans properly believe they would be better advised to prioritize the political defense of their voting rights, where so much is directly at stake, for neither their political power in the US nor their capacity to win changes in local police practices are dependent on Palestinians winning their rights on the West Bank. Neither is the Tibetan freedom movement or any other. The world is not yet that globalized, and there is little reason to suppose it will be any time soon. To the degree that the BDS movement succeeds in actually coopting the US struggle for racial justice, it presents at best a distraction and at worst a potentially serious setback for Black Americans. That is despite signatures by Angela Davis and Cornell West to the Black Solidarity Statement with Palestine.

But Abunimah's interpretation of the "Ferguson to Palestine" slogan has additional purposes as well. It is designed to delegitimize progressive American solidarity with the Black Lives Matter campaign unless and until progressive opinion demonizes Israel. It is thus a divide-and-conquer strategy that is largely directed at both civil rights activists and the American left. Like efforts to compare Israel's security barrier (MAP 3) with the fence on the US border with Mexico, it is also aimed at building a broad anti-Israel alliance among peoples of color. In this framing, the only true progressives are those who denounce Zionism as a form of racism and who promote the dissolution of the Jewish state. People who have fought racism in their professions and in their communities for years are suddenly disqualified from continuing to do so. As a result, long-standing inter-racial relationships on campus and elsewhere have been broken. The anti-racist community is thus divided and turned into a battlefield. Susan Talve of St. Louis was one of thirty Rabbis who participated in civil disobedience demonstrations in Ferguson. That kind of solidarity and commitment should be welcomed, not challenged.

Talve has also been outspoken in support of Israel and a two-state solution; she reiterated her support for Israel during 2014's Operation Protective Edge. In the wake of the Ferguson demonstrations, a photo of Talve circulated on the internet with a caption accusing her of being a "supporter of genocide and international apartheid," along with the hashtag #realterrorist.

A week before Talve officiated at a 2015 White House Chanukah celebration, the St. Louis chapter of Jewish Voice for Peace (JVP) sponsored an open letter challenging Talve and those who found her a sympathetic figure: "To whitewash the lived alliances between Ferguson and Palestine is to silence the very voices we seek to hear" (Guttman & Lokting).

Progressive Jews and others who find themselves deeply moved by the wakeup call the Black Lives Matter campaign has issued—but who do not share a demonic view of Israel— should resist allowing this wedge to be driven between them and their Black comrades. But that will not be an easy battle to win. "From Ferguson to Palestine" is the most disturbing slogan and the most divisive strategy BDS has formulated in some time.

Superficially a means for African Americans and Palestinians to find common cause in combatting their oppression, at its core the BDS campaign to identify Palestine with Ferguson is an effort to reduce the Israeli-Palestinian conflict to a struggle over race, whereas it is actually a story about two peoples with separate national aspirations for self-determination and sovereignty. Unlike the struggle for equality in the US, the Israeli–Palestinian conflict is fundamentally not about people seeking shared and equal citizenship but rather about two groups seeking their separate cultural and political destinies. In addition to distracting Americans from their own struggles for justice and alienating Black Americans who identify with Israel's story, the BDS campaign promotes a fundamental misrepresentation of the cultural, historical, and political realities of the Middle East. As Black activist Chloe Valdary observes in a piece by Shiryn Ghermezian, "it is a shame that the BDS movement has hijacked the historical Black struggle in an attempt to build solidarity with a blatantly antisemitic campaign that seeks to strip Jews of their rights to their homeland." It denies and erases the history of Jews who found haven and promise in Israel, and it misrepresents the dynamic of Palestinian aspirations for national and religious sovereignty.

"Black Lives Matter" is an important slogan that produces a timely shock of recognition—in part because it introduces a concept that should not have to exist. All lives matter; that should be self-evident. And yet, to America's shame, after centuries of racial trauma, apparently it is not. America's shame deserves its singularity. It should not be diluted by or confused with fictitious intersections with other peoples' histories. If American courts, legislatures, and the Congress are to be turned away from their current course, it will not be by linking the necessary cultural, educational, and political work with the fate of Palestine. The Black Lives Matter slogan symbolizes a diverse and decentralized movement with some segments focused on mass protest, others organizing to challenge candidates for political office and use the traditional political process to effect change. There is still time and opportunity to orient most segments toward eliminating inequality and injustice in the US. The struggle to right the wrongs American racism continues to generate deserves the dedicated focus of all who seek justice. ■

Also see ANTI-ZIONISM AS ANTI-SEMITISM, APARTHEID, BDS: A BRIEF HISTORY, BDS AND CHRISTIAN CHURCHES, THE IDIGENOUS PALESTINIAN, THE "JEWISH CONSPIRACY," SETTLER COLONIALISM, and THE SOCIAL JUSTICE MANDATE IN HIGHER EDUCATION.

# GAZA

## CARY NELSON

aza, or the Gaza Strip, is a narrow, 25-mile long land area on the east coast of the Mediterranean Sea with a 6.8-mile border with Egypt on its south and a 32-mile border with Israel on its west and north. Gaza had a population of 1.8 million as of 2014. Long part of the Ottoman Empire, the area came under British control in 1918 after World War I and remained so until the 1948 war, after which, except for a few months of Israeli control following the Sinai War in 1956, it was occupied by Egypt for 19 years. About 200,000 refugees entered Gaza during that war with the new state of Israel. An Egyptian military authority governed the strip thereafter and severely restricted movement into and out of it. Israel conquered the area in the Six Day War in 1967 and established 21 settlements in Gaza, using about 20 percent of the land area. In accordance with the 1993 Oslo Accords, the Palestinian Authority gained administrative authority over Gaza's population centers in phases, while Israel continued to control the air space and territorial waters. Egypt continued to control the main point of exit and entry, the Rafah crossing in the south. The border with Egypt is a recognized international border, established in 1906.

In 2005, under Ariel Sharon (1928-2014), Israel took a further step and decided unilaterally to abandon its settlements in Gaza and leave the area. By then, many Israelis had concluded Gaza was a liability. Unilaterally leaving Gaza also tended to freeze international efforts toward a jointly negotiated peace and thus helped sustain the West Bank status quo. Conversely, the move delegitimized the goal of a Greater Israel that could include Gaza, Israel proper, and the West Bank.

Hamas won the legislative election the following year, engaged in a bloody civil war with its rival party Fatah in 2007, and took full control. Some 600 Palestinians died during the fighting between Hamas and Fatah. Having routed Fatah militarily and assumed political power in Gaza, Hamas thus divided the Palestinian community into separate ideological as well as geographic entities. Considerable hostility has continued to undermine the PLO/PA relationship with Hamas and its leadership, despite occasional flirtations with "unity." For Hamas, the secular nature of the PA and the extensive financial and political corruption that characterized Arafat's nation-building years have cast doubt on the PA's capacity to govern and reinforced the view that the PA betrayed the Palestinians by agreeing to a peace process. For the PA and Fatah, the largest party within the confederated multi-party PLO, Hamas' political and religious extremism, its refusal to recognize Israel and renounce terrorism, and its isolation by the international community have so far made Hamas a political liability for Palestinians in their attempts to create an independent state. It has also meant that Israel has been willing to take steps to prevent Gaza under Hamas from becoming a fully functional state. Some argue that Hamas and the Israeli far right both contribute to the cycle of violence and to the resistance to diplomatic progress.

In hindsight, Israel's decision to leave Gaza precipitously was ill-considered. The Palestinian Authority needed more time to strengthen its security forces and the international community needed to make and honor more binding commitments to economic aid and sound economic options for Gaza's people. Social services needed to be gradually strengthened with reliable infrastructure. In other words, Israel should have found opportunities to help Gaza transition to a place that offered employment opportunities and hope to its people. And Israel should have provided more appealing resettlement opportunities to the 9,000 Jews who were forced to leave their homes. Yet relatively few Israelis even now, after the 2014 war, would be eager to reoccupy Gaza permanently.

In the months between its June 2007 victory and early 2008 Hamas fired hundreds of rockets into Israel. Over 3,000 rockets were fired into Israel in 2008. In response, Israel launched Operation Cast Lead, which lasted from December 27, 2008, to January 18, 2009. This return to Gaza in a military operation was intended to stop the rocket and mortar launches from Gaza to Israel (over 1500 were fired at the Israeli city Sderot in an eight month period from mid-2007 to February 2008, for example) and end weapons smuggling into Gaza. Aerial bombardment of weapons caches, police stations, and political and administrative buildings took place in Gaza, Khan Yunis, and

Rafah, all densely populated cities, followed by a ground campaign. Having accomplished its mission, Israel declared a unilateral ceasefire and withdrew its forces. Because over 1,000 Palestinians died, the international Boycott, Sanctions, and Divestment movement embraced and promoted hyperbolic characterizations of Operation Cast Lead as genocidal, a concept, one might note, whose meaning and utility is being nullified by such irresponsible use. Others condemned the war in less hyperbolic terms. Yet the rocket attacks had turned Israeli towns within range into environments of unremitting stress and considerable danger. Every public setting, even bus stops, were hardened against rockets, and air raid shelters were added to every apartment and schoolyard, a necessity given that some border communities had only seconds' warning of an attack. Those measures cut down civilian deaths in Israel, but not the grave psychological trauma of living under bombardment, a price particularly unsettling to see children pay. Nonetheless, when Israel entered Gaza, BDS could play up the disparity between Israeli and Palestinian military power and death rates to garner international support, though the group has not attempted to estimate what the comparative death rate should be. Israel's military actions in Gaza thus succeeded tactically by limiting the rocket attacks but failed strategically by increasing support for the BDS movement and decreasing worldwide support for Israel itself.

Faced with the certain prospect of serious offensive weapons arriving in Gaza by sea, Israel maintained a naval blockade. The UN's 2011 "Report of the Secretary-General's Panel of Inquiry on the 31 May 2010 Flotilla Incident," also known as the Palmer Report after its chair Sir Geoffrey Palmer, acknowledged "the enormity of the psychological toll on the affected population" (40) of rocket attacks from Gaza and concluded that "a blockade in those circumstances is a legitimate exercise of the right of self-defence" (41). That does not, however, mean that elements of the blockade should not be modified. Israel also restricted Palestinian fishing rights to three miles, rather than the twenty miles specified in the Oslo Accords. That cut into Palestinian income as well as an important food source and helped justify continued hostility.

With Hamas continuing to fire rockets into Southern Israel, the IDF launched Operation Pillar of Defense (November 2012) with the killing of Ahmed Jabari (1960-2012), chief of the Gaza military wing of Hamas. Just days before, 100 rockets had been launched into Israel. During the operation, nearly 1,500 more rockets landed in Israel, but 142 misfired and fell back into Gaza. Israel's Iron Dome system successfully intercepted a number of rockets. Of the 174 Palestinians who were killed during the eight days of the operation, some died from Hamas' own failed rockets. Eight Palestinians accused of collaborating with Israel were executed by the Izz ad-Din al-Qassam

Brigades, Hamas' military wing. Exactly what constitutes "collaboration" in Hamas' view remains unclear, though the summary executions were war crimes in any case. Egypt mediated a ceasefire, announced a week after the operation began. Afterwards, Human Rights Watch accused both sides of violating the rules of war, though the record of any war being conducted without war crimes is not inspiring. In December, maintaining his bravura in the face of IDF attacks, Hamas leader Khaled Mashal (1956–) called for Israel's elimination.

The relative calm did not last long. On June 12, 2014, three West Bank Israeli teenagers were kidnapped; for days the government withheld information about their fate. Then on June 30th their bodies were found, and it was revealed that three Hamas members had abducted and murdered them, though not on order of the Hamas leadership, although Israel arrested most of the Hamas leadership on the West Bank. In retaliation, Israeli thugs captured a 16-year-old Palestinian boy on July 2nd and murdered him, apparently burning him alive. The murders helped trigger a new round of violence in the Israeli-Palestinian conflict.

On July 8 the IDF initiated Operation Protective Edge with air strikes against military targets in Gaza. The primary aim was to restore security to Israeli civilians. The preceding three weeks had seen 250 rockets fired into Israel. With rocket fire continuing, the IDF launched a ground campaign on July 18. Ground operations revealed a more extensive network of concrete-reinforced underground assault tunnels branching into Israel than the IDF had been aware of. The destruction of those tunnels—some 32 were located and destroyed, of which 14 crossed into Israel—became a higher priority as the campaign evolved. Some 4,500 rockets and mortars were fired at Israel between July 8 and the end of the operation. Iron Dome intercepted 86 percent of those judged to be headed toward Israeli cities. The campaign lasted fifty days and was especially costly to the Palestinians, with, according to some reports, over 2,100 losing their lives and thousands more wounded. The percentage of Hamas fighter versus civilian casualties remains in dispute, but it is likely final figures will demonstrate it is roughly half of each. Some 10,000 homes were destroyed and many more severely damaged. Hamas' tactic of launching rockets from civilian areas and using schools, mosques, and hospitals as weapons depots and firing sites made them targets for IDF strikes and increased the damage to civilian infrastructure. After several cease fire agreements failed, eventually one held, and Operation Protective Edge came to an end.

Hamas intensified its rocket barrage once Israel began its air campaign in an effort to draw Israel into a ground campaign that would increase civilian casualties. As "An Assessment of the 2014 Gaza Conflict," an October 2015 report issued by an international group of military officers details, Hamas had turned "civilian neighborhoods into pre-prepared battlegrounds, with elaborate networks of tunnels and firing positions." These pre-prepared strongholds included those at Shejaiya and Rafah; they used civilian buildings to mask an extensive military infrastructure. Civilian settings thus became 360 degree battlefields, with both great risks to Israeli soldiers and vastly increased probabilities of noncombatant casualties. Yet the IDF had to enter these strongholds, which hid extensive tunnel networks, if it was to destroy the infiltration tunnels and degrade Hamas' military infrastructure. These 360 degree battlefields meant that the IDF was not merely vulnerable to being outflanked. It was surrounded by potential fire and indeed by the rearming of positions previously destroyed. As the report observes, "the urban environment rebalances asymmetric conflict to a considerable extent, depriving the technologically and numerically superior combatant of advantage."

Hamas' use of these urban settings for military purposes constitutes a serious violation of the laws of armed conflict. As the report cited above details in section 107,

> Violations included, but were not limited to, flagrant breaches of Article 51.7 of the Additional Protocol to the Geneva Conventions prohibiting the embedding of its military apparatus in civilian structures, as well as Article 58 requiring the evacuation of civilians from the vicinity of military objectives. Further, Hamas clearly violated Articles 18-19 of the 4th Geneva Convention and Articles 12-13 of the 1st Additional Protocol, prohibiting the use of medical facilities for military purposes, and Article 37 prohibiting the feigning of civilian, non-combatant status in order to harm an adversary.

The practices at stake in these violations were many, among them, for example, the use of civilians as wartime Hamas messengers and the use of ambulances to transport Hamas fighters. Hamas turned the al-Wafa hospital in Shejaiya into a military site with weapons storage, firing positions, surveillance stations, and tunnel infrastructure; abandoned sections of the still medically functioning al-Shifa hospital in Gaza City were used as interrogation and torture centers (Amnesty International). Meanwhile, Israel took on considerable risk to its soldiers to protect civilians, notable among them the practice of notifying Gazans in advance of planned military actions so civilians could evacuate, despite the fact that that enabled Hamas to position its fighters in advance for ambushes. Israel also established multi-level review and approval procedures for air strikes planned in advance. And in 2014 Israel largely limited artillery strikes to open areas with no civilian presence, though civilians did die in air strikes. That is not to say that Israel made no mistakes during the war, as local commanders no doubt made some errors in judgment and not all individual soldiers will have behaved without malice. No military logic, moreover, can free us of being haunted by images of dead children.

One 2014 military action that has been frequently faulted in BDS resolutions in academic associations is the August 2, 2014, strike against the Islamic University in Gaza City. Israel has said that the campus was "being used by Hamas for the building, testing, and at times, even launching of rockets from certain locations within the University grounds," a condition that made it a valid target under the laws of war. Given Hamas' wide use of schools and mosques, this use of the campus for military purposes is not surprising, but it is also important to recognize the special character of the campus. As Thanassis Cambanis pointed out years earlier, this is "a different place from the Western universities it resembles." Founded by members of the Muslim Brotherhood in 1978, it has established itself as "the brain trust and engine room of Hamas . . . the overlap of the party and the school is nearly seamless . . . . Many faculty members share Hamas' most hard-line beliefs . . . . The scholarship and instruction at the Islamic University offer a map of the world Hamas's leaders would build if they had no constraints."

Part of the political and economic pressure Hamas faced in the lead up to the 2014 war was the loss of its ties with the short-lived Muslim Brotherhood government in Egypt. Indeed Egypt became even more hostile to Hamas in the aftermath of the war. Egypt has since faced growing assaults from the ISIS-affiliated group in the Sinai, Ansar Beit al-Maqdis, a group that is alleged to have an ongoing relationship with Hamas. Beginning in late 2014 and extending into spring 2015 Egypt destroyed over 2,000 Palestinian homes in the Gaza Strip along the southern border to create a buffer zone near the Rafah crossing. That followed a smaller scale Egyptian house demolition operation in 2013. Although Amnesty International protested the 2015 action, there was no international protest at the level that would have resulted had Israel done the same thing. Meanwhile, at least as of 2015, the jihadist insurgency in Sinai led Egypt to keep the Rafah crossing—Palestinians' main access to the outside world—closed but for a few days. By the time this book appears in print, that crossing may have been reopened. Closure of the crossing has made it difficult or impossible for Palestinians, including those needing advanced medical attention, to get travel permits. But the relevant state power is Egypt, a fact that once again does not interest the international community. In the fall of 2015 Egypt began pumping sea water into the Rafah area in order to flood and destroy the smuggling tunnels under the border, tunnels Egypt saw as vehicles for transporting jihadists into North Sinai. In what has become a pattern, much of the international aid promised to make reconstruction possible in Gaza has either not arrived or not made its way to those who need it. According to the World Bank, international donors had pledged five billion dollars for rebuilding. Six months after the 2014 war had ended, the US had delivered 84 percent of its promised aid, whereas Qatar and Saudi Arabia had delivered but ten percent of theirs. Kuwait, Turkey, and the United Arab Emirates had delivered none. Overall, about 35 percent of promised aid had been delivered by August 2015. Meanwhile reports continue that Hamas is directing incoming supplies toward reconstruction of its assault tunnel network. The nearly 10,000 homes destroyed in Operation Protective Edge remain in rubble as of 2016.

Israel inspects the supply trucks going through its Kerem Shalom crossing carrying construction materials, food, electronic equipment, and medical supplies to Gaza carefully. It is a slow process and a necessary one, as Israel does discover efforts to disguise military supplies as a result, but it is also too frequently an inconsistent process, with shipments inexplicably blocked; even so, hundreds of trucks carrying thousands of tons of material nonetheless regularly pass through daily. Israel supplies Gaza with 125 MW of electricity and with fuel daily; it continued to supply both during Operation Protective Edge, despite the obvious fact that electricity and fuel have military uses. This humanitarian commitment is highly unusual for a country at war, though it reflects the status of Gaza under International Law, which still sees Israel as having responsibilities for the survival of those in Gaza. Israel also supplies Gaza with 10 million cubic meters of water daily.

Unfortunately, the movement of goods into Gaza is only half the story, and the other half is not good. The Gaza economy is nearly obliterated. Unemployment as of 2015 was at 60 percent; 80 percent of Gaza's residents live below the poverty line. Palestinians need at the very least to be able to sell agricultural products, light manufacturing goods, and crafts to Israel, the West Bank, and other countries, which will require vastly improved abilities to export goods from Gaza into and through Israel. Economic conditions in Gaza make an excellent basis for breeding hatred and recruiting fighters and terrorists, conditions Hamas is happy to exploit, thus winning public support for its rocket attacks, its construction of cross-border attack tunnels, and its promotion of lethal West Bank violence. It is in Israel's strategic interest to help improve the Gaza economy—and to do so as both a humanitarian and a strategic response, not one conditional upon a truce negotiated with Hamas.

One humanitarian consequence of area politics is the difficulty Gaza students have in traveling to study abroad. For decades, students heading for study abroad have left Gaza through the Rafah crossing and flown to their destination from Cairo. But the current Egyptian government is hostile to

Hamas and has kept the Rafah crossing mostly closed. The Islamist insurgency in Sinai has made matters worse. In response, Israel has relaxed its prohibition against undergraduates exiting Gaza through the Erez crossing at Gaza's north end. From there they travel across Israel and the West Bank into Jordan to fly abroad from Amman. That route, however, raises its own political problems. Jordan requires them to have travel visas, visas that are issued based on lists provided by the Palestinian Authority. But the PA's relationship with Hamas is also hostile, so the PA is wary about taking responsibility for students who may also be committed to political agitation. The PA as a consequence is very slow to produce the required lists. Jordan used to issue the visas in ten days. Now, uneasy about Gaza students as well, Jordan takes several months to issue visas, when it issues them at all. The result of these combined delays means that fellowship offers expire and school terms begin and end. In an exceptionally ill-informed gesture, some BDS resolutions in academic associations blame all this on Israel and count it a reason to boycott Israeli universities.

Meanwhile there is a new danger abroad in Gaza—the potential for ISIS recruiting among Gaza's disaffected youth, its generation without hope. In October 2014 an ISIS-inspired explosion started a fire at the French cultural center in Gaza city. The center was attacked again that December. The following June, ISIS in Syria posted a video denouncing Hamas for collaborating with "secularist entities." Hamas in response ramped up its attacks on ISIS supporters in Gaza, provoking a series of car bombs. Whether Hamas can succeed in suppressing its still more violent new rival is unclear, but "the nightmare of being locked inside Gaza with the ISIS monster is worse than all other nightmares the Gazans have faced" (Helm 20). It would also be a nightmare for Israel. ■

Also see HAMAS, THE PALESTINE LIBERATION ORGANIZATION, PROPORTIONALITY IN ASYMMETRIC WAR, and IRON DOME.

# HAMAS

CARY NELSON

F ounded in 1988 as an offshoot of the Muslim Brotherhood Movement (a transnational Islamist organization founded in Egypt in 1928), Hamas is a Palestinian Islamic organization that operates with political, social welfare, and military wings. Canada, Egypt, Israel, Japan, the United States, and the European Union have designated Hamas a terrorist organization. Australia and the United Kingdom reserve that designation for Hamas' military wing, the Izz ad-Din al-Qassam Brigades, though the distinction between the political and military wings is partly a strategic fiction designed to help liberal Western constituencies invest hope in the former and to speculate about tensions between the two, though Hamas does have political offices in two locations—Gaza and Qatar. A Turkey office has directed Hamas' West Bank activities but is promised to be closed. Hamas is banned in Jordan. Brazil, China, Iran, Norway, Qatar, Russia, Switzerland, and Turkey do not classify Hamas as a terrorist organization.

Although Hamas boycotted the 2005 Palestinian presidential election, it participated in the 2006 legislative election in Gaza, winning 132 seats to its rival Fatah's 43 and triggering violent confrontations between the two groups. The following year the PLO's Fatah and Hamas took up armed conflict; 600 Palestinians died, and Hamas seized full control of the Gaza Strip. Hamas has not held elections since its 2006 victory, though neither has the Palestinian Authority. Hamas severely limits freedom of speech in Gaza; some criticism can place your life in danger.

The group's founding covenant, a 9,000-word charter, was adopted on August 18, 1988. Its Introduction announces that "Israel will exist and will continue to exist until Islam will obliterate it, just as it obliterated others before it." An early section, Article 6, embraces the Islamic Resistance Movement and declares "it strives to raise the banner of Allah over every inch of Palestine." As Article 11 elaborates, "The land of Palestine is an Islamic Waqf [holy possession] consecrated for future generations until Judgment Day. No one can renounce it or any part, or abandon it or any part of it." Thus, as Article 32 states, "Hamas regards itself the spearhead and the vanguard of the struggle against World Zionism," for "Zionist scheming has no end, and after Palestine, they will covet expansion from the Nile to the Euphrates River . . . Their scheme has been laid out in *The Protocols of the Elders of Zion*." The Protocols, of course, is a notorious anti-Semitic fabricated text first published in Russia in 1903 that purports to be a report of plans for world domination written by Jewish leaders. Hitler was a fan, and German schools taught it as authentic after he came to power.

In a passage from Article 7 that some Palestinians quote approvingly to the present day, the Hamas charter adopts traditional tropes in its homicidal stance toward Jews: "The Day of Judgment will not come until Muslims fight Jews and kill them. Then the Jews will hide behind rocks and trees, and the rocks and trees will cry out: 'O Muslim, there is a Jew hiding behind me, come and kill him.'" Article 22, The Powers Which Support the Enemy, mounts an anti-Semitic rant against a worldwide Jewish conspiracy, echoing Nazi propaganda at several points:

> The enemies have been scheming for a long time, and they have consolidated their schemes, in order to achieve what they have achieved. They took advantage of key elements in unfolding events, and accumulated a huge and influential material wealth which they put to the service of implementing their dream. This wealth [permitted them to] take over control of the world media such as news agencies, the press, publication houses, broadcasting and the like. [They also used this] wealth to stir revolutions in various parts of the globe in order to fulfill their interests and pick the fruits. They stood behind the French and the Communist Revolutions and behind most of the revolutions we hear about here and there. They also used the money to establish clandestine organizations which are spreading around the world, in order to destroy societies and carry out Zionist interests. Such organizations are: the Freemasons, Rotary Clubs, Lions Clubs, B'nai B'rith and the like. All of them are destructive spying organizations. They also used the money to take over control of the Imperialist states and made them colonize many countries

in order to exploit the wealth of those countries and spread their corruption therein. As regards local and world wars, it has come to pass and no one objects, that they stood behind World War I, so as to wipe out the Islamic Caliphate. They collected material gains and took control of many sources of wealth. They obtained the Balfour Declaration and established the League of Nations in order to rule the world by means of that organization. They also stood behind World War II, where they collected immense benefits from trading with war materials and prepared for the establishment of their state. They inspired the establishment of the United Nations and the Security Council to replace the League of Nations, in order to rule the world by their intermediary. There was no war that broke out anywhere without their fingerprints on it.

Although the charter remains both aspirational and inspirational for Hamas members, its official status has deliberately been made ambiguous. Some argue that Hamas' participation in the political process in the 2006 parliamentary elections in Gaza shows that the group has moved on from the historical ferocity of the charter. But the rockets since showered on Israel and the extensive network of cross-border assault tunnels exposed during the July 2014 war in Gaza make it clear that war and terrorism remain Hamas priorities.

Hamas for a decade has suggested intermittently that it could endorse a multi-year truce (*hudna*) with Israel, especially if a West Bank Palestinian state were to be recognized, but nothing indicates Hamas would cease strengthening its military and terrorist options or its long-term commitment to eliminating the Jewish state even if a such a truce were to be successfully negotiated. It has continued to rearm itself and rebuild infiltration tunnels since the conclusion of Operation Protective Edge. Whether any of those tunnels cross into Israel is unclear. A technology to detect tunnels under construction is more likely than one to detect tunnels already completed. Some argue that Hamas' social service activities suggest it could evolve into a political partner, and certainly there are Hamas members for whom that is true, but it is equally apparent there are many others for whom Israel will remain the unacceptable "Zionist entity," not a country but an "entity." Indeed that phrase, the Arab media's standard way of referring to Israel without speaking its name has now come back into fashion for Iran, Hezbollah, Syria, Hamas, and others. Hamas continues to embrace its conviction that permanently ceding any territory to a Jewish state would amount to a violation of religious principle. It has also engaged in Holocaust denial throughout its history, though it is important to remember that "in the West, radical Holocaust denial is relatively marginal, while in the Muslim world it is relatively mainstream" (Patterson 333). More serious still are the many instances when Hamas and its allies have urged not only the annihilation of Israel but the extermination of all Jews. Consider "Hamas spokesman Osama Hamdan's public claim in August 2014 that Jews use Christian blood to make matzos; in May 2014, a Hamas television show for children calling for the killing of Jews; a Hamas cleric's vow in July 2014 on Al-aqsa TV to exterminate all Jews 'until the last one'; and the dissemination of a music video in November 2012 by Hamas's Al-Qassam Brigades in which killing Jews is presented as a form of worship" (Jikeli 66).

Officially founded in 1992, Hamas' military wing has steadily increased its offensive capacity and varied its primary strategies, graduating from suicide bombings to rocket attacks and increasing the range of its rocket stockpile. Its Al-Qassam Brigades carried out both suicide bombings and paramilitary attacks against Israeli civilian and military targets from 2000 to 2005 during the Second Intifada. During the July 2014 war in Gaza Hamas used mosques, hospitals, and schools as weapons depots and launched rockets from these and other civilian areas, thereby guaranteeing there would be civilian casualties when Israel struck the launch sites. As the High Level Military Group's 2015 "Assessment of the 2014 Gaza Conflict" reports (sections 71, 103), Hamas' main operational headquarters during the 2014 conflict was in the al-Shifa hospital, Gaza's chief medical facility. The *Washington Post* describes it as "a de facto headquarters for Hamas leaders, who can be seen in the hallways and offices" (Booth). Civilian casualties serve as Hamas' greatest weapon in the war for international political opinion and in its effort to delegitimize the Jewish state. It must be recognized that Hamas seeks military confrontations with Israel that will produce civilian casualties, the more the better. Hamas of course has not announced such a motivation, but its actions confirm that tactic. This inhumane and cynical tactic violates the international Law of Armed Conflict (LOAC) developed over decades, but it is highly effective.

Over the course of three conflicts with Israel in Gaza, Hamas has developed a set of linked military and propaganda strategies that have served its ends well. As "An Assessment of the 2014 Gaza Conflict," an October 2015 report issued by an international group of military officers details, Hamas combines traditional military operations with terrorist actions in a hybrid model that not only ignores international norms for conflict but also takes advantage of Israel's commitment to observe them. Reflecting on the last twenty years in Gaza, Israelis often observe they traded land for terror.

As of 2016 Hamas and the Palestinian Authority remain at odds. When Hamas incites or organizes West Bank violence—either through the internet, sermons at the mosques it controls, or agitation from its West Bank members and allies—it not seeks not only to terrorize Jewish settlers but also to destabilize the Palestinian Authority. Hamas' hostility meanwhile reinforces those in Israel who argue that no accommodation with Palestinians is possible and only a Greater Israel can guarantee Israel's security. In 2015 debates erupted about Hamas' relationship with ISIS. ■

Also see FATAH, GAZA, HEZBOLLAH, THE PALESTINE LIBERATION ORGANIZATION, THE PALESTINIAN AUTHORITY, and THE WEST BANK. THE WEST BANK.

# HEZBOLLAH

CARY NELSON

Hezbollah (Arabic for "Party of Allah" or "Party of God") is a Lebanon-based Islamist paramilitary group and political organization that is financed and supported by Iran. Its original leaders were followers of Iran's Ayatollah Khomeini (1902–1989). Hezbollah's (also transliterated as Hizbollah or Hizbullah) formation was announced in 1985, though elements of the group were in operation as early as 1982-83. The group coalesced in the wake of the 1982 Israeli invasion of Lebanon. Many consider Hezbollah responsible for the October 1983 bombing of American and French military barracks in Beirut which killed 299 servicemen. Australia, Canada, France, the Gulf Cooperation Council, Israel, the Netherlands, and the United States categorize Hezbollah as a terrorist organization, whereas Britain and the European Union single out its military wing only. Canada, Israel, and the United States view the "Islamic Jihad Organization" as synonymous with Hezbollah.

Hezbollah's initial priority from 1982-2000 was to oppose the Israeli occupation of South Lebanon. It conducted what was at the time a non-conventional war whose tactics included murder, hijacking, and suicide bombings, along with the more conventional strategy of rocket attacks against northern Israel.

Hezbollah's power and influence have grown considerably since 2000. Its paramilitary forces are more effective than the Lebanese army and extend beyond the Lebanese border. Iran has continued to provide funds, training, and weapons. Hezbollah and its allies now control a substantial number of positions in Lebanon's cabinet. Since 2012, Hezbollah has fought in Syria on behalf of the Assad government, describing the opposition as a "Zionist plot." Hezbollah's support for the repressive Syrian government has largely cost it any lingering status as an authentic revolutionary group within the Arab world. In Lebanon, Hezbollah has been described as "a state within a state." In addition to wielding military and political power, it supervises hospitals and educational activities.

Hezbollah's hostility toward the state of Israel is fueled by anti-Semitism: As historian Robert S. Wistrich has written in *A Lethal Obsession*,

> The anti-Semitism of Hezbollah leaders and spokespersons combines the image of seemingly invincible Jewish power . . . and cunning with the contempt normally reserved for weak and cowardly enemies. Like the Hamas propaganda for holy war, that of Hezbollah has relied on the endless vilification of Jews as 'enemies of mankind,' 'conspiratorial, obstinate, and conceited' adversaries full of 'satanic plans' to enslave the Arabs. It fuses traditional Islamic anti-Judaism with Western conspiracy myths, Third World anti-Zionism, and Iranian Shiite contempt for Jews as 'ritually impure' and corrupt infidels. Sheikh Fadlallah typically insists . . . that Jews wish to undermine or obliterate Islam and Arab cultural identity in order to advance their economic and political domination (766-767).

In 1992 a Hezbollah statement proclaimed, "It is an open war until the elimination of Israel and until the death of the last Jew on earth." Ten years later Hezbollah's leader, Sheikh Hassan Nasrallah (1960-), encouraged Jews to move to Israel. "If they all gather in Israel," he said, "it will save us the trouble of going after them worldwide."

Hezbollah's ideological and religious-based goal of obliterating Israel is supported by a formidable military arsenal, one now highlighted by perhaps as many as 100,000 missiles and rockets. During the 2006 Lebanon War, after Israel invaded southern Lebanon in response to a cross-border raid in which Hezbollah kidnapped and killed several Israeli soldiers, Hezbollah waged a guerilla war against the Israeli Defense Forces. Hezbollah also launched thousands of rockets against northern Israeli towns and cities in an indiscriminate assault on civilian targets. Already in 2006 its rockets successfully reached Haifa. Now its long-range rockets may well be capable of reaching all major Israeli cities. A war between Israel and Hezbollah would now present far greater risk to the Jewish state than any confrontation with Hamas. Protecting Israeli citizens would require massive military action by the IDF.

For the present, however, Hezbollah's 2015–2016 losses while fighting in Syria may constrain its anti–Israel ambitions. ▮

---

Also see FATAH, HAMAS, THE LEBANON WARS, and THE PALESTINE LIBERATION ORGANIZATION.

# HOLOCAUST INVERSION

Unlike Holocaust deniers, practitioners of Holocaust inversion do not claim that the Holocaust did not exist. Instead, they try to turn the images, meaning, and legacy of the Holocaust against Zionism and the Jewish state. Instead of becoming perhaps the signal tragedy of modernity, the Holocaust becomes a weapon to be used in delegitimizing Israel. But Holocaust references and comparisons with Nazism employed to defend Israel also dishonor the unique character of modernity's greatest moral tragedy.

—CN

## ROBERT WISTRICH

A particularly obnoxious "anti-Zionist" form of Holocaust inversion—suggesting that the Israelis are "Nazis" and the Palestinians are "Jews" . . . is increasingly common not only in Germany but also in Poland, Hungary (where far-right antisemitism is on the rise) and many other EU nations. By pretending that the Jewish State is pursuing a "genocidal" policy today, the need to face the scale of European guilt and complicity in the mass murder of Jews during the Holocaust can be more easily deflected.

## LESLEY KLAFF

What has been called "Holocaust Inversion" involves an inversion of reality (the Israelis are cast as the "new" Nazis and the Palestinians as the 'new' Jews), and an inversion of morality (the Holocaust is presented as a moral lesson for, or even a moral indictment of 'the Jews'). More: those who object to these inversions are often told . . . that they are acting in bad faith and merely concerned to deflect criticism of Israel. In short, the Holocaust, an event accurately described by Dan Diner as a "rupture in civilization" and by Alon Confino as a foundational historical event—an event organized by a regime that, as the political philosopher Leo Strauss observed, "had no other clear principle except murderous hatred of the Jews"—is now being used, instrumentally, as a means to express animosity towards the homeland of the Jews. "The victims have become perpetrators" is being heard more and more. That is Holocaust Inversion . . . Anthony Julius, author of a landmark study of British antisemitism, notes that Holocaust Inversion is becoming part of the iconography of a new antisemitism. Headlines such as "The Final Solution to the Palestine Question," references to the "Holocaust in Gaza," images of IDF soldiers morphing into jackbooted storm troopers, Israeli politicians morphing into Hitler, and the Star of David morphing into the Swastika, are all increasingly common.

The 2009 Report of the European Institute for the Study of Contemporary Antisemitism, *Understanding the 'Nazi' Card: Intervening against Anti-Semitic Discourse*, reported that equating Israel with the Nazis is an important component of incitement and racial aggravation against Jews in the UK today . . . By inverting reality and morality, and by recklessly spreading accusations of bad faith, Holocaust Inversion prevents us identifying the changing nature of contemporary antisemitism and is an obstacle to marshaling active resistance to it.

## HOWARD JACOBSON

Berating Jews with their own history, disinheriting them of pity, as though pity is negotiable or has a sell-by date, is the latest species of Holocaust denial . . . Instead of saying the Holocaust didn't happen, the modern sophisticated denier accepts the event in all its terrible enormity, only to accuse the Jews of trying to profit from it, either in the form of moral blackmail or downright territorial theft. According to this thinking, the Jews have betrayed the Holocaust and become unworthy of it, the true heirs to their suffering being the Palestinians . . . One particularly popular version, pseudo-scientific in tone, understands Zionism as a political form given to a psychological condition—Jews visiting upon others the traumas suffered by themselves, with Israel figuring as the torture room in which they do it.

## ALAN JOHNSON

"Among all the harms produced by Hitler's politics and the Holocaust," suggests the Heideggerian-Communist Italian philosopher Gianni Vattimo, "one can also list the creation of Israel as a Jewish state in 1948" (15). Once it was the "devilish Jew," notes David Hirsh; but now, for anti-Zionists, it is Israel doing what the devilish Jew used to do: "standing in the way of world peace . . . being responsible for stirring up wars . . . being uniquely racist or apartheid or dangerous in some other way." Jewish nationalism, he points out, is now viewed as "essentially different from all other nationalisms . . . nothing at all but a mode of exclusion . . . more like a totalizing and timeless essence of evil than a historical set of changing and variegated beliefs and practices" (Anti-Zionism, 20, 27).

For example, Israeli journalist Yitzhak Laor claims that Israel Defense Force "death squads" are guilty of "indiscriminately killing," and of acts of "sadism," including "mass starvation" (130-31). Omar Barghouti claims Israel has an "insatiable appetite" for "genocide and the intensification of ethnic cleansing" ("A Secular"). (One is reminded here of those inter-war cartoons of gigantic Jews looming over and eating up the world.) According to Israeli sociologist Yehuda Shenhav's *Beyond the Two-State Solution*, Israel is "built on the ruins of the indigenous people of Palestine, whose livelihood, houses, culture, and land had been systematically destroyed"; the country is "an aggressive war machine," pregnant with genocide; Israel's "violence-generating mechanisms" drive it into "killing Arabs regularly," the 1956 Kafr Qasim massacre, for example, being not an exceptional event but "the political model of Jewish sovereignty." Israel, seen through the lens of anti-Zionist ideology, is on course to achieve "the annihilation of the Palestinian people" (21, 181n.51, 191n.76, 48, 84, 3).

The unhinged portrayal of Israel as a genocidal state often takes the form of what has been called "Holocaust Inversion." Four forms can be identified. First, the depiction of Israelis as the new Nazis and the Palestinians as the new Jews; an inversion of reality. As British legal scholar Lesley Klaff notes above, "We see headlines like 'The Final Solution to the Palestine Question,' references to the 'Holocaust in Gaza,' images of Israeli IDF soldiers morphing into jackbooted storm troopers, or of Israeli politicians morphing into Hitler, or of the Star of David morphing into the Swastika" ("Political and Legal Judgment"). Noam Chomsky described the IDF as "those who wear the jackboots" (8), while Jacqueline Rose falsely claimed that the IDF "provided a guard of honor" at the tomb of Baruch Goldstein, the Jew who massacred 29 Arabs in Hebron in 1994 (131). Shenhav quotes approvingly from the testimony of a person who "describes the wrongs forced upon the Palestinians in the territories as 'Sabra and Shatilla times a million'" (99).

Second, Zionism is made to appear as *akin to Nazism*, or is considered alongside of, or in comparison to, or even collaborating with Nazism. For example, writer-activist Tikva Honig-Parnass finds in the socialism of the early Zionists "a local version of National-Socialism that retained the main tenets of organic nationalism" (9). A theme in historian Shlomo Sand's work is "[t]he relative inaction and indifference of Zionist leaders towards the annihilation of European Judaism" (167), while other anti-Zionists such as American writer Lenni Brenner radicalize the notion of "indifference" and claim there was active "collaboration" between Zionists and Nazis during the Holocaust.

Third, the Holocaust is turned into a "moral lesson" for, or a "moral indictment" of the Jews—an inversion of morality. Rose argues that after "escaping the horrors of Europe, the Jews are in danger of transporting their own legacy of displacement, directly and perilously, onto the soil of Palestine ... the displacement of one history of suffering directly onto another" (47). The anti-Zionist writers Hazem Saghiyah and Saleh Bashir are perhaps the most candid in treating the Holocaust as laying a special moral burden on the Jews. They write: "The dissociation between the acknowledgment of the Holocaust and what Israel is doing should be the starting point for the development of a discourse which says that the Holocaust does not free the Jewish state or the Jews of accountability. On the contrary, *the Nazi crime compounds their moral responsibility and exposes them to greater answerability.*"

Fourth, *Holocaust memory* appears within anti-Zionism *only* as a politicized and manipulated thing, a club wielded instrumentally, with malice aforethought, by Jewish bullies, for Jewish ends. Ilan Pappé devotes a chapter of *The Idea of Israel* to lambasting the "official and collective manipulation" of Holocaust memory by the Israeli state, praising the work of Idith Zertal because there "one encounters Israel as a necrophilic nation ... [o]bsessed and possessed by death . . . yet quite able to use and abuse [Holocaust] memory for the sake of its political aims" (177, 166). Gianni Vattimo goes further. The Shoah is not just used as "an all-encompassing justification for all the actions of Israel." Israel is guilty of "much more than a simple and cynical political expediency." And what is this "more"? It is a "radical and vindictive executionism" (21). With Vattimo, it is clear, anti-Zionist ideology is brought (hardly kicking and screaming, it has to be said) to the very threshold of antisemitism.

# KENNETH L. MARCUS

Holocaust inversion is analogous to other forms of what might be called "human rights inversion": the practice of accusing victims of the very wrong that they have suffered . . . Among its myriad variants, Holocaust inversion includes portraying Jews (especially Israeli Jews) as Nazis, crypto-Nazis, Nazi sympathizers, Holocaust perpetrators, or Holocaust copycats.

Holocaust inversion, like other human rights inversions, has several functions: to shock, silence, threaten, insulate, and legitimize. First and most unmistakably, human rights inversion is *shocking*, even when it is repeated frequently, which is why it is repeated frequently. No one tells Holocaust survivors—or a nation of Holocaust survivors and their children—that they are Nazis without expecting to shock.

Human rights inversion is shocking in a particular manner, a manner that tends to *silence*. Given the sensitivity of many Jews to issues concerning the *Shoah*, Holocaust inversions have the power not only to shock but also to silence expression of Jewish viewpoints, including speech sympathetic to the state of Israel. Moreover, the stereotype of Jewish conspiratorial power, combined with the use of Nazi motifs, has a particular chilling effect. Beyond silencing, human rights inversion is *threatening* because the ascription of guilt carries with it the threat of punishment. This is after all the point of the allegation . . . Finally it is legitimating . . . The Israelis-as-Nazis analogy serves to justify not only anti-Israeli but also anti-Jewish activity that otherwise is socially or legally repelled. Bernard-Henri Levy has explained that Holocaust inversion erodes social conventions that have developed as a safeguard against recurrence of genocidal murder, enabling "people to feel once again the desire and, above all, the right to burn all the synagogues they want, to attack boys wearing yarmulkes, to harass large numbers of rabbis . . . in order for anti-Semitism to be reborn on a large scale (63-64).

## KENNETH S. STERN

The use of the Nazi label to tar Jews in general and Israelis in particular is itself a form of Holocaust denial, because, while such comparisons unfairly defame Jews, they also belittle the crimes of the Nazis. The watering down of what "Nazi" meant made it easier for others to use that eviscerated and misunderstood adjective to target Jews and the Jewish state. The linkage is carefully calculated (especially in Europe) and has two purposes: to grant moral license to forget how Jews were victimized in the mid-twentieth century, and to produce in the speaker a feeling of moral smugness in targeting Israel.

If Holocaust denial was not complicated enough, it is given a boost by Holocaust relativism. This term refers not to denial of the Holocaust outright, but to its minimizing by unfair, and usually ignorant, comparisons.

(Many antisemitic myths, by the way, have a "lite" version. The claim that neocons—read Jews—exercised inordinate influence over

President George W. Bush leading up to the war in Iraq is a "lite" version of the claim that Jews are secretly in control of the U.S. government, for example.) Sure, Hitler was a mass murderer . . . but so was Stalin. Sure, the Nazis put Jews, Gypsies, Jehovah's Witnesses, and others in camps . . . but America put Japanese-Americans in camps too. Sure the Nazis targeted innocent civilians . . . but the Allies bombed Dresden. Sure the Nazis passed the Nuremberg laws . . . but America had Jim Crow. Like Holocaust denial, these immoral equivalencies rest on distortions. As horrid as the internment of Japanese-Americans was, they were not worked to death, systematically shot, selected, or sent to gas chambers or crematoria. Whether or not it made sense for the Allies to bomb Dresden (some say it was justified by legitimate military goals, while others are not convinced), civilians had nothing to fear once the Allies gained territory; civilians had everything to fear once the Nazis gained territory. And so on.

Some years ago I attended a conference of the Northwest Coalition against Malicious Harassment. Two plenary speakers brought up the Holocaust in the most gratuitous and disturbing ways. A Native American woman, speaking eloquently about the discrimination her people face daily, said in passing that the genocide of American Indians was "worse than" the Holocaust and that Hitler could not get his hand on any Indians, so he went after Jews. Forgetting the absurdity of the notion that Hitler at the time wanted to go after American Indians, the idea that the genocide of American Indians was "worse than" the Holocaust is bizarre. On what scale can one measure genocide? How can you rank these tragedies? It makes no sense to say that the Holocaust was "worse than" slavery, for example. How do you factor in the number killed, the percentage of the population destroyed, the time it took to commit the murder? Each genocide is unique. (What is unique about the Holocaust to me was the priority that killing Jews took over winning the war effort.) Each is another example of people's capacity to classify an "other," to dehumanize that "other," and when dehumanization becomes either central to one's ideology or commonplace and unremarkable, to kill that "other," including babies. The attempt to enlist the Holocaust in a contest of victimization is counterproductive, and this American Indian speaker, who should have known better, unfortunately did not.

Then came a Hispanic poet who spoke passionately about the problems of getting quality public education for Hispanic children. He said that many teachers just assumed that a Hispanic child would not amount to much, so these children were neglected and not challenged to succeed. "This is a crime worse than Hitler," he said. "While Hitler attacked the body, these teachers attack the mind." Later he talked about the deportation of farm workers across the border back to Mexico in the first half of the twentieth century and said, "This was the same as the Holocaust." Even allowing for poetic license, this was too much. As racist as those deportations were, farm workers were not lined up on the border and summarily shot nor taken to gas chambers, killed, had their gold fillings removed, and their bodies burned.

The people at this conference had worked in the trenches in the Northwest, combating groups such as the Aryan Nation and the racist militias. They should have been the last people who felt a need to minimize and distort the Holocaust to make the case that other racism should be taken seriously. They were speaking to a self-selected audience of sympathetic people. How much of this was latent antisemitism, and how much of it was ignorance of the Holocaust? It is difficult to know, just as it is not easy to gauge how much was a tactic designed to win over an audience, and the related question of what that says about contemporary culture (91–3).

## PASCAL BRUCKNER

[A new kind of anti-Semitism has appeared] in the post–World War II era: the envy of the Jew as a victim, the paragon of misfortune. In this way, the Jew becomes the model and the obstacle; he usurps a position that should, by all rights, redound to the Blacks, the Palestinians, the Muslims, the Russians, the Poles, and so on. The suffering of the Jews has become the universal measure of suffering, its characteristic features—pogroms, diaspora, genocide—are claimed by everyone, and the Shoah has become the founding event that provides access to the understanding of mass crimes . . . it fascinates people not as an abomination but as a treasury from which they think they can draw advantages . . . being able to say that you are the object of a new Holocaust means shining the brightest floodlights on your own case; it also means purloining the maximum misfortune and declaring oneself its only legitimate owner ("Antisemitism" 15).

## BERNARD HARRISON

[T]o treat the Holocaust as a crime against humanity rather than against a specific people, the Jews, is not merely to render its nature and origins impossible to understand, except in terms of some vague and explanatorily vacuous notion of evil or the darkness of the human heart. It is to erase Jews and Jewishness from the historical record . . . ("Uniqueness" 294). ■

*Adapted from Robert Wistrich, "Anti-Zionism and Anti-Semitism in the 21st Century," Lesley Klaff, "Holocaust Inversion and contemporary anti-Semitism," Howard Jacobson, "Let's see the criticism of Israel for what it really is," Alan Johnson, "Intellectual Incitement: The Anti-Zionist Ideology and the Anti-Zionist Subject," Kenneth L. Marcus,* Jewish Identity and Civil Rights in America, *Kenneth S. Stern,* Antisemitism Today, *Pascal Bruckner, "Antisemitism and Islamophobia," and Bernard Harrison, "The Uniqueness Debate Revisited."*

Also see ANTI-ZIONISM AS ANTI-SEMITISM, HAMAS, HEZBOLLAH, JEWISH ANTI-ZIONISM: THREE VIEWS, and THE "JEWISH CONSPIRACY."

# THE INDIGENOUS
# PALESTINIAN

The BDS movement and its advocates for at least a decade have promoted the claim that Palestinians or their Arab predecessors are the only people native (indigenous) to the area from the Mediterranean to the Jordan River. BDS did not invent the claim; it appears, for example, in the notorious 1974 Weather Underground pamphlet *Prairie Fire*, but it has gained more currency recently. Some go so far as to assert that neither the Hebrew tribes nor ancient Israel ever existed. Others simply dismiss all the archeological and historical evidence of the Jewish presence in Palestine, including the testimony in non-Jewish texts. In truth Jews have had a continuous presence in the Holy Land for thousands of years. They have a history in Jaffa and Hebron. They sustained a center of learning in Tiberias from the 3rd century, despite the city being sacked in the 7th and 13th centuries and being devastated by an earthquake in 1837. In 1845 the population of Jerusalem was 16,410, including 7,120 Jews, 5,000 Muslims, and 3,390 Christians; in 1912 it was 70,000, with 45,000 Jews, 12,000 Muslims, and 13,000 Christians (Gilbert). Israel represents the evolution of the existing Jewish community that preceded it. In addition to denying or discounting the Jewish history in Palestine, those opposed to the Jewish state argue that its citizens are settler-colonialists. While Jews may have the more ancient claim to the land, there has been continuous Muslim governance of the region, except during the Crusades, for thirteen centuries, along with a large Arab population. Both Jews and Arabs are at once indigenous and immigrant populations. Many Arabs settled in Palestine in the 7th century, along with the expansion of Islam. As the *Yishuv* developed further in the early 20th century, improving area health, more Arabs were drawn to Palestine as well. A rich Arab community evolved in Haifa in the 1930s. Although the dismissive and false historiography denying Jewish history must be contested, the most rational option is to set aside both Jewish and Palestinian claims to "original" indigenous status and agree that neither people's connection to the land trumps the other's. The plan to divide the land between Jews and Arabs itself has nearly a century of history behind it, and that is the dispositive perspective.

—CN

## ILAN TROEN

The concept of indigenousness is a frequent weapon in the arsenal of attempts to de-Judaize Israel/Palestine. The insistence that only Arabs are the indigenes, the native residents of Palestine, is ubiquitous in the discourse of academic boycotts. It is one of the concepts that Palestinian academics inside Israel use in arguing for transforming Israel from a Jewish state into a "state of all its citizens." Consider the opening statement of the *Future Vision of the Palestinian Arabs in Israel* (2007): "We are the Palestinian Arabs in Israel, the indigenous peoples, the residents of the State of Israel, and an integral part of the Palestinian People and the Arab and Muslim and Human Nation." This assertion underlies the claim that Jewish settlement is illegitimate. It supports the right and indeed the imperative to oppose a Jewish state in the 1948 war, even if defeat resulted in a *nakba* (catastrophe). It upholds demands for far-reaching autonomy in a Jewish state and the right of Palestinians to return to anywhere in the State of Israel even as the legitimacy of Jewish settlement everywhere is questioned.

This morphing of "native" into "indigenous" is not accidental. Since the 1960s the idea of indigenous rights has become increasingly part of an international legal system. First initiated by the International Labor Organization to protect Indian tribes in Central and South America, it quickly came to embrace Australian aborigines and Canadian First Peoples as well as American Indians in the Southwest. In the original and pristine meaning, indigenous referred to peoples like the Aborigines whose claim of continued presence for 35,000 to 40,000 years in Australia is unchallenged.

That standard is too stringent for less isolated areas of the world where there are all manner of records for the last 3,000 or 4,000 years. It was for more ancient and unprotected populations that in 2007 the UN issued a Declaration on the Rights of Indigenous Peoples. The US and Canada ultimately signed this convention but only with the expressed reservation that indigenous rights do not trump those of the modern, sovereign state. It had become apparent that assigning newly constructed rights to rectify ancient injustices can cause contemporary mischief. This potential was exploited by Palestinian activists who in the 1990s adopted it as a new tactic in the campaign against Israel (Yahel; Frantzman).

The first practical challenge to the authority of the State of Israel was made by the Bedouins in a case brought before Israeli concerning ownership of lands in the Negev. Their case failed due to lack of evidence: they provided no valid documents verifying ownership at any time since the Ottoman period nor proof of residence in the area prior to the 19$^{th}$ century. The latter assertion to ancient presence was an attempt to claim rights of the indigenous. Indeed, how does a Christian Arab prove that he is a "living stone" (1 Peter 2:5) and descended from forbearers who were present at the time of Jesus? How, too, does a Muslim Arab substantiate descent from Jebusites, other Canaanites, or any pre-Israelite peoples or, for that matter, anyone from but a few centuries previous?

The historic reality is that Palestine had no more than 250,000 inhabitants from the Jordan to the Mediterranean in 1800. It was an under-populated area that had had many times that population in the ancient world but had since been depopulated. During the 20$^{th}$ century, the region became a magnet for both Jewish and non-Jewish immigration. Indeed, the Albanian, Mehmet Ali (1769-1849), moved to Egypt to become its leader in the second quarter of the 19th century and sought to extend Egyptian control into the area; thus Egyptians settlers entered the area in significant numbers. Circassians arrived in Palestine from the Caucasus in the 1870s. From the Turkish coast to Beirut and on to Jaffa and Alexandria the entire eastern Mediterranean littoral of the Ottoman Empire attracted migrants to a region poised for development as it began to be incorporated into the periphery of the European economic system. This migration included Jews from former Ottoman territory and from Europe who then constituted the country's majority with more than 6,000,000 inhabitants. It is not obvious why all others could become or be known as natives except Jews.

The claim of "indigenousness" is a political issue everywhere. Few peoples have such status in Africa and Europe. In the Middle East and Northern Africa, for example, only the Marsh Arabs south of Basra in Iraq and the Berbers of North Africa are generally considered authentically indigenous peoples in UN registries. Nevertheless, the push to include Negev Bedouins and Palestinians in general in this category is an integral part of the campaign to discredit Jews as foreigners and colonial settlers. ▪

*Adapted from Ilan Troen, "The Campaign to Boycott Israeli Universities: Historical and Ideological Sources."*

---

Also see ANTI-ZIONISM AS ANTI-SEMITISM, BDS: A BRIEF HISTORY, JEWISH HISTORY BEFORE ZIONISM, THE NAKBA, and SETTLER COLONIALISM.

# THE INTIFADAS

CARY NELSON, RACHEL S. HARRIS,
AND KENNETH W. STEIN

## THE FIRST INTIFADA

In December 1987, a grassroots Arab uprising in Gaza and the West Bank that began with a campaign of civil resistance, including strikes and commercial shutdowns, grew into stone throwing, hurling Molotov cocktails, and assaults with knives—the weapons of an unarmed popular insurrection. Known as the Intifada (literally "shaking off" in Arabic) this insurgency began as a reaction to Israeli control of Gaza and the West Bank, the persistent and ongoing state of economic deprivation for Palestinians in refugee camps, and the widespread use of Israeli checkpoints at roads and bridges, limiting access to Israel for Palestinians from the occupied territories. While the PLO had done much to raise the public profile of Palestinians, the organization operated outside the law before Oslo and could do little in a practical sense to improve the lives of Palestinians within the West Bank and Gaza. With these impoverished communities alienated from the PLO, the organization would have little impact on the opening months of the Intifada.

Yet the explosion of anger also turned inward, and many of the Palestinian deaths during the Intifada were caused by intra-ethnic violence, as widespread executions of suspected Israeli collaborators and informers took place. Israel had established a network of informers, but the extra-legal execution of those alleged to be among them violated fundamental norms of justice and human rights. By the end of 1992, approximately 1,800 Palestinians had died, about

800 of them at the hands of other Palestinians. The Israeli army responded to the uprising with a large show of military strength, but the images of young stone throwers operating against tanks severely damaged Israel's public image and did little to quell the uprising. Nor did it mitigate the economic damage caused by the strikes called by Palestinian organizations. The Intifada forced the IDF into a policing role for which it was not trained. And the IDF's tactical decisions were sometimes counter-productive. Thus the decision to close down West Bank and Gaza schools and universities during the 1987-1988 school year simply sent unsupervised students into the streets.

Along with increasing public media support and rising international attention to the Palestinian cause, the Intifada enhanced Palestinian self-esteem and demonstrated their agency: no longer relying on other Arab countries, they would negotiate for their own survival and political future. As the PLO—with its leaders in Tunisia—worked to regain a role in directing events, its status as the Palestinians' political representative increased. Yet the single most significant result of the Intifada was no doubt King Hussein's July 31, 1988, announcement that Jordan was relinquishing all claims to the West Bank and would instead honor a Palestinian state. That legitimated a Palestinian place at the table in the peace negotiations of the 1990s. The Intifada lasted at least until 1991, though some historians date its end to 1993 and the signing of the Oslo Peace Accords. It also had serious repercussions for Israel, including the blow to its public image internationally and the intensification of powerful internal criticism. The loss of public support for past expansionist policies pushed the country toward revising its legal position on administering the territories and made some of its leaders for a time more willing to trade land for peace.

# THE SECOND INTIFADA

Despite the shift in Israeli attitudes and Israeli offers to return as much as 95 percent of the West Bank to a Palestinian state, the Israelis and Palestinians could not resolve all their differences and were unable to settle the conflict. Nearly a decade after the first Intifada, with ordinary Palestinians frustrated and no nearer independence, the Second Intifada erupted in 2000 after the failure of the negotiations at Camp David outside Washington, DC. The Second Intifada was named for the Al-Aqsa mosque where the first violent uprising broke out in response to an ill-conceived, incendiary September 2000 visit by Ariel Sharon (1928-2014). The mosque is located on Temple Mount (or al-Haram al-Sharif, "Noble Sanctuary," in Arabic) in the Old City of Jerusalem. It is a holy site for both Muslims and Jews, but had long been under Muslim supervision. Considered the site of the Second Temple, many Jews honored the tradition of not visiting it for fear of violating the unknown spot where the Holy of Holies was located. Sharon's visit provoked fears that Israel would take control of the site and symbolized the conviction some Jews hold that a Third Temple should be constructed there. The Temple Mount is a site where religious and nationalist passions converge to the present day.

Unlike the First Intifada, which was largely directed at the Israeli military, this Second Intifada targeted Israeli civilians within Israel. Restaurants, markets, shops, and buses were targeted in Jerusalem and Tel Aviv. Israel faced an onslaught of suicide bombers; Jews, Arabs, Christians, and tourists alike were caught up in the violence. On May 25, 2001, two Palestinians drove a car full of dynamite into a bus in the coastal town of Hadera, killing four plus themselves and wounding 63. On June 1, a suicide bomber detonated his bomb at the Dolphinarium, a popular seaside Tel Aviv discotheque, killing 21 and wounding more than 80, most of them teenagers. That August, targeting the summer vacation crowds, a Palestinian teenager blew himself up in a Jerusalem pizzeria, killing six children and thirteen adults and injuring 90 others. Three days later a Haifa café was the target, this time with 20 casualties. On the November 29 anniversary of the UN Partition Resolution, a Palestinian detonated his suicide vest on a bus traveling from Netanya to Tel Aviv, killing four and injuring nine. That attack turned out to be a combined Fatah/Islamic Jihad operation. On December 1, powerful bombs in Jerusalem's main pedestrian mall killed 11 and wounded 180. Twelve hours afterwards, a suicide bombing on a Haifa bus took 16 lives and injured 45 more. The following March, 25-year-old Muhammad Abd al-Basset Oudeh, a Hamas recruit, videotaped his plan, donned a wig and dressed as a woman, then walked into a Passover seder being held in the dining room of the Park Hotel in the seaside town of Netanya. The explosion he triggered killed 29 and wounded 150. A June 18 Jerusalem bus bombing, one of 47 bombings that year, killed 19. On July 31, a Hamas-organized blast in the Hebrew University of Jerusalem cafeteria killed nine, four American students among them, and injured approximately 100. Between September 29, 2000, and June 4, 2003, 820 Israelis were killed and nearly 5,000 wounded. Two thirds of the dead were civilians. Although the many suicide attacks in Israel proper are the hallmark of the Second Intifada, a large number of other attacks, including shootings into Jewish crowds, took place in the occupied territories.

In a harbinger of future strife, Palestinian Israeli citizens staged demonstrations throughout northern Israel from October 1 to 9, 2000, in solidarity with the occupied West Bank. The demonstrations moved to civil disobedience, then turned violent. Hundreds of Jews rioted in response. The Israeli police trying to quell the escalating riots faced gunfire and Molotov cocktails. In the course of the week, the police shot and killed twelve Israeli Arabs. As Chaim Herzog writes, "Although the struggle was broadly directed by Palestinian Authority Yasser Arafat and his associates, the actual operations were carried out by members of the Palestinian security forces and of the many other organizations that had formed in the territories. Attacks were planned and prepared without co-ordination or centralized control, and the relation of individual terrorists to their nominal groups was often vague to the point of being arbitrary" (428). Though Israel was hesitant to carry out military operations in the areas for which the PA was responsible, and in which many of the terrorists and agitators were sheltering, the international political climate changed after the 9/11 attacks on the United States, and Israel mounted retaliatory attacks.

In April 2002, a sustained battle took place in the Jenin refugee camp in the West Bank. The town was estimated to be the source of at least 28 suicide attacks, so neutralizing the threat from the area became a military priority for the IDF. Since Jenin was heavily fortified with booby-traps and snipers were positioned throughout, the Israeli army was reluctant to enter the area and was forced to reject air bombardment for fear of causing civilian casualties. So the IDF entered on foot, conducting dangerous house-to-house searches through the narrow alleys. When thirteen Israeli reservists were trapped in an ambush and killed, the army was forced to change its tactics and began bull-dozing houses to flatten access routes and clear the way. In total, 23 Israelis and 52 Palestinians died in Jenin, but news reports accompanied by photo-graphed bodies made much of the event, accusing the Israelis of conducting a massacre. As Ahron Bregman writes, "These scenes of death and destruction had a strong effect on Palestinians, galvanizing many of the younger genera-tion to join the ranks of the militants ready to fight the Israelis" (242).

Though President George W. Bush called for the establishment of a Palestinian state, reinforcing Bill Clinton's commitment, it was unclear how such an endeavor could proceed. The following year UN Resolution 1397 was the first Security Council Resolution calling for a two-state solution to the Palestinian-Israeli conflict, and in 2003 the Quartet (the US, European Union, UN, and Russia) proposed a performance-based, goal-driven road-map for a negotiated Palestinian-Israeli agreement.

But as the violence continued, persistently terrorizing the whole Israeli population, Israel began building a security fence or wall to reduce the infil-tration into Israel of Palestinians and suicide bombers from the West Bank and Gaza. In July and August of 2003, the first continuous segment of Israel's security fence was constructed. Most of the fence consists of multi-layered wire, but about ten percent is constructed as a concrete wall (in areas where civilians might be vulnerable, for instance, to gunfire). Although it is not an official border fence, it can be compared with many border fences in the world—among them fences in Cyprus, Egypt, Ireland, Korea, Kuwait, Malaysia, Saudi Arabia, and the United States—some constructed for security reasons as well, but this one is politically implicated in the Israeli-Palestinian conflict and proves endlessly controversial. It has helped reduce suicide bombings by 80 to 90 percent, but its administration causes hardships to Palestinians who must regularly negotiate the checkpoints controlling passage through the wall. Moreover, the location of parts of the fence has provoked accusations that Israel is annexing Palestinian land and has cut villages in two or separated farmers from the land they work. The hostility and conflict of the mid-2000s suggested that all hope for peace had disappeared. Yasser Arafat was besieged from all sides: He was pursued by Israel for orchestrating the violent attacks on Israelis, meanwhile losing popularity with his own citizens for the increased corruption of the economy and failed national politics. In 2004, Arafat died, and the Intifada began to lose some of its energy; though it had at least one decisive long-term effect on Israel—the substantial weakening of the Israeli left.

In the fall of 2015 a new and distinctive round of violence erupted and continued into 2016, with Palestinian teenagers and young adults taking it on themselves to attack Israelis with knives, while others drove cars into crowds with sometimes fatal results. Although promoted on social media, encouraged by Hamas, and proliferating in copycat fashion, the actions otherwise seem to be unorganized individual efforts. The intimate character of the attacks and the young age of many of those committing them are as unsettling as the deaths on both sides. Whether this constitutes a third, "slow-burning" or "silent" Intifada is widely disputed, but it is surely compelling testimony to Palestinian frustration and hopelessness. A full-scale third Intifada would destroy the Palestinian economy and likely lead the Palestinian Authority to disintegrate, presenting Israel with the responsibility for maintaining social services and taking over policing for Palestinian cities. There would then indeed be no partner in peace negotiations. ■

*Adapted from Cary Nelson, Rachel S. Harris, and Kenneth W. Stein, "The History of Israel."*

Also see FATAH, THE OSLO ACCORDS, THE PALESTINE LIBERATION ORGANIZATION, THE ISRAELI-PALESTINIAN PEACE PROCESS, TEMPLE MOUNT / HARAM AL-SHARIF, THE SECURITY BARRIER, and THE WEST BANK.

# IRON DOME

## CARY NELSON

S ince Iron Dome is an exclusively defensive system, it may seem surprising that it has attracted a degree of controversy. BDS advocates sometimes imply that the system's success means that rocket attacks are unimportant and that Israel should simply tolerate them, indeed that the presence of Iron Dome renders a military response to Hamas immoral. Some treat the system as a hated symbol of the power differential between Israel and the Palestinians. Some in the peace movement worry that because Iron Dome curtails Israeli casualties it reduces Israel's need to reach an accommodation with the Palestinians. Given all this, it seems useful to establish some facts about the technology, its uses, and their political consequences.

Iron Dome is an Israeli-developed mobile air defense system designed to intercept and destroy rockets and artillery shells fired toward population centers. It works on rockets fired from distances of at least 2.5 miles and as much as 43 miles. Iron Dome is not effective against mortars, which can be fired from still shorter distances and thus detonate in less time. Iron Dome was developed by Rafael Advanced Defense Systems and Israel Aircraft Industries in collaboration with the Israeli Defense Force (IDF) and is designed to operate under all weather conditions. Additional funds for development and deployment came from the United States. Future plans include increasing its operational range and integrating it with a multi-level system that could deal with rockets from still greater distances and rocket barrages fired in greater numbers over short time periods. The technical demands on the system effectively require that a defensive rocket intercept and destroy an offensive one. Until the concept for Iron Dome began to take hold in 2004, it was widely believed this goal was unachievable.

Israel's motivation for developing a short-range rocket defense system was never in doubt. Hezbollah had fired rockets toward northern Israeli towns as early as the 1990s, though the consensus then was that no anti-rocket or anti-missile defense system would work. During the Second Lebanon War in 2006 Hezbollah fired perhaps 4,000 rockets into Israel. Some struck Haifa, Israel's third largest city. A quarter of a million Israelis evacuated, while perhaps a million sought cover in bomb shelters. Forty-four civilians were killed. Meanwhile, between 2000 and 2008 Hamas fired another 4,000 rockets and an equal number of mortars from Gaza into Israel's south, putting another million Israelis at risk. People living in Israel's border towns have as few as 15 seconds to get to a shelter after a warning siren sounds. In Sderot near the border with Gaza every apartment has a bomb shelter, and they are placed at every bus stop and on every school playground. Children subjected to incessant rocket attacks often suffer from post-traumatic stress syndrome (PTSD). The rate of pre-teen PTSD has increased over the years that rocket attacks have continued, with rates now calculated at 50-90 percent (Bedein; Israel Today Staff).

In 2007 the Israeli Ministry of Defense approved plans to develop the system. It was engineered and tested between 2008 and 2010, becoming operational in March 2011. Iron Dome intercepted its first offensive target, a rocket fired from Gaza, in April 2011. One of the system's key capacities is its ability to calculate an incoming rocket's trajectory and the place it will strike, thereby making it unnecessary to intercept rockets destined to land in unpopulated areas. That helps moderate demands on Iron Dome's capacity and reduce the overall cost of interceptions.

The system first proved its success at dealing with a substantial number of rocket attacks in March and November of 2012, when it intercepted 52 and 420 rockets respectively. During Operation Protective Edge in July 2014, by which time 70 percent of Israel's population was within reach of Hamas rockets, Iron Dome intercepted 735 projectiles headed toward civilian population centers or structures, a success rate of 90 percent. In reducing Israeli civilian casualties and preventing rockets from landing on Ben Gurion airport, Iron Dome enabled Israel to moderate its military response. Had the thousands of Hamas rockets landed in the population areas to which they were directed, Israel's actions in Gaza would have to have been more severe and more rapid. As it was, Iron Dome made it possible for Israel to maintain diplomatic efforts to reach a ceasefire. But most 2014 Gaza casualties could have been avoided had Hamas simply agreed to the ceasefire terms it eventually accepted on

August 26 when they were offered on July 15. As the High Level Military Group's "An Assessment of the 2014 Gaza Conflict" reports (section 138), it is possible that Qatar encouraged Hamas to believe (falsely) it could extract further concessions by continuing the conflict. Earlier news reports raised that possibility as well (Schreck). Qatar has been home to Hamas political leader Khaled Mashal (1956–) since 2012 and has become a key funder for Hamas. One might also note that Hamas could have protected civilians by using concrete to build bomb shelters rather than assault tunnels. ■

Also see GAZA, HAMAS, and PROPORTIONALITY IN ASYMMETRIC WAR.

# ISRAEL: DEMOCRATIC AND JEWISH

## CARY NELSON

O ver the last decade, there has been an ongoing debate about whether Israel's dual identity as both a democracy and the homeland of the Jewish people represents an insurmountable contradiction. Both the BDS movement and other critics of Israel highlight the tensions within Israel's dual identity to argue it creates structural inequities and injustices that cannot be overcome and that suggest Israel has no moral and ethical right to exist as a Jewish country. The list of countries that identify with or grant special status to one religion is a long one, but one may cite a few examples. Christianity has a privileged status in Argentina, Bulgaria, Denmark, Greece, Norway, and the United Kingdom, while being a dominant cultural force in many others. Buddhism has special status in Bhutan, Catholicism in Costa Rica, Islam not only in the Middle East, but also in Bangladesh, Malaysia, and Pakistan. It dominates all other faiths in Indonesia.

The argument that Israel cannot be both Jewish and Democratic ignores the fact that Israel's 1948 proclamation of independence guarantees complete equal rights to all its citizens—Jewish and Arab—without regard to religion, race, ethnicity, national origin, or sex. Israel is a democracy in which all citizens have the right to vote. Israel is a Jewish state, but it is not a theocratic monarchy like Saudi Arabia or a theocracy like Iran. The Christian community in Israel, numbering 161,000, continues to grow. Moreover, the long and productive history of debate over what it means to be a Jew continues both within Israel and throughout the world. It is unlikely it will ever be settled.

Yet Israel is also the homeland of the Jewish people. One cannot understand what that means without first reflecting on what it means to be a Jew. Jews do not only share a religion. Indeed many Jews in Israel and elsewhere are nonobservant. And one can become a Jew by converting to Judaism. Yet, as Gil Troy and Martin Raffel write, "being Jewish is not merely a religious category like Christianity or Islam; it also means belonging to a people with a culture, language, shared history, and national identity." Jewish identity has a three-thousand-year history that continues to link Jews worldwide, however assimilated, to a community with a sense of shared destiny. Part of that destiny has been the long dream of reestablishing a Jewish homeland in Israel. Jews are a people with national aspirations, a status the United Nations has recognized.

The argument that a nation that links its identity to a particular cultural group cannot be democratic needs to be tested against all the countries besides Israel that do so. As Alexander Yakobson and Amnon Rubinstein point out, Article 116 of the German constitution grants automatic citizenship to refugees and displaced persons of German ethnic origin (127); the Greek Law of Citizenship confers automatic citizenship on ethnic overseas Greeks who volunteer for Greek military service. Since the fall of the Soviet Union, some 200,000 ethnic Greeks have emigrated and been granted automatic citizenship as well; Greece defines them as returning to the homeland (129). Israel of course has handled Russian immigrants in the same way. Finland "regards itself as responsible for the fate of ethnic Finns who live in Russia and Estonia" and also defines their immigration as a return to the homeland (130). Poland grants citizenship to Russian Poles "on condition that they have preserved their Polish cultural identity" (130). Irish policy has been to confer immediate citizenship to any applicants of Irish descent. The Irish Nationality and Citizenship Act gives the Justice Ministry the power to waive naturalization requirements "where the applicant is of Irish descent or Irish associations" (130). The Armenian Republic awards citizenship to any person of Armenian descent who requests it (131). Turkey grants sanctuary to refugees of Turkish origin and facilitates their obtaining citizenship (132).

As Yakobson and Rubenstein also point out, "national or ethnic minorities exist in many democratic nation-states. In every such case, the country's public character is determined primarily by the majority and influenced mainly by its culture and identity, with consideration given to the rights of the minority" (3). Some claim that national symbols in such cases must be neutral, "but the sign of the cross, which appears on the national flags of the United Kingdom, Australia, New Zealand, Switzerland, Greece, Hungary, and Scandinavia's exemplary democracies . . . is not a 'neutral' symbol, and not all the citizens of these countries can identify with it" (3). Minorities in all these countries, including Israel, experience a degree of alienation as a consequence. Many Israeli Arabs live in segregated communities. It is the duty of all to make certain that the benefits of citizenship far outweigh the sense of alienation. Israel has a way to go in securing those benefits for all, but it is making progress despite the persistent racism in some quarters. A full sense of equality is not likely, however, until Arab political parties can be brought into Israel's governing coalition.

What militates against that progress is the conviction that Israel is not just a Jewish state but rather a state wedded to and defined by internal ethnic conflict. There is no inherent contradiction in a democratic state that honors its Jewish identity. But a state that internalizes its external conflicts with Arab states or its undemocratic relations with West Bank Palestinians does indeed put its democratic character in danger. It has been said repeatedly that Israel can be a Jewish state, a democratic state, or an occupying state, but not all three at once. It must choose two of these identities.

## EMILY BUDICK AND SHIRA WOLOSKY

The call for Israel to become a democratic state for all its citizens is tautological. Israel is today a democratic state for all its citizens. This is not to claim complete social justice across all sectors, or to disclaim the urgent need for greater opportunity, access, and investment across all sectors.

In terms of education, Arabic is an official language of Israel; Arabs run their own educational system, teaching their own cultures in their own language. This system does not receive equal investment. Nor is the access of Arab students to higher education equal. Yet a fifth of Israel's medical students are Arab, as are a third of the students at the University of Haifa and about 17 percent of those at Technion University. Israeli Universities have been committed for several years to increasing Arab participation in higher education. As Israel's Central Bureau of Statistics reports, in 1999/2000 only 9.8 percent of bachelor's degree students were Arabs. By 2015 the figure had risen to 14.4 percent. More dramatically the percentage of Israeli Arab masters degree students rose from 3.6 percent in 1999/2000 to 10.5 percent in 2015, and the percentage of Israeli Arab doctoral students went from 1.8 percent to 5.9 percent in the same period. In Tel Aviv, 30 percent of Israeli universities' medical school students are Arab.

Thus considerable progress is being made. That has required additional recruitment efforts and scholarships, remedial courses for Arab students not ready for college classes, and enhanced mentoring and advising programs to increase retention and assure that those students can complete their degrees. It should be self-evident that universities that are working hard to solve a problem and having quite substantial success in doing so do not deserve to be boycotted for doing so. In the West Bank as well, there are a respectable number of institutions of higher education: the Arab American University, Al-Quds Open University, Al-Quds University, An-Najah National University, Bethlehem Bible College, Bethlehem University, Birzeit University, Edward Said National Conservatory of Music, Hebron University, Ibrahimieh College, Khodori Institute, Tulkarm, Palestine Polytechnic University, Al Ahlia University of Palestine.

There is no need to compel Israel into "recognizing the fundamental rights of the Arab-Palestinian citizens of Israel to full equality." Such "full equality" by law, for all of it citizens, is already a part of Israeli law. Israeli Arabs (whether or not they identify themselves as Palestinians or Bedouin or Druze, Moslem or Christian or secular Israelis) do by law enjoy full civil rights: they are represented in the parliament, in municipal governments, in professions like medicine, law, and teaching; and at universities throughout Israel and so on and so forth. They own property. They run businesses. Any visit to an Israeli hospital or college campus dispels any notion of what BDS identifies on its home page as "Israeli Apartheid."

Is there unequal distribution of wealth in Israel? Absolutely, and the Arab sectors of Israel are victims of this, disproportionately, in ways that are not to be tolerated by any of us. Discrimination, lack of equal opportunity, and lack of equal investment should and must be addressed within Israeli democratic society. Nonetheless, Israeli democracy is legally committed to minority rights, in ways that are outstanding in the Middle East, even if some on Israel's political right do not share those values. This is one context in which the extraordinary self-subversion of the academic boycott of Israel is apparent. Besides the self-contradictory and self-defeating nature of any academic boycott—how can a boycott for freedom of speech itself boycott freedom of speech?—one directed against Israel attacks the very place where freedom of speech is most intense. Academic boycotts institute the very transgression they are protesting—restriction of freedom and rights of expression.

To be a state with a cultural identity is not anti-democratic —Norway and Denmark, The Netherlands and France, Germany and Britain all are democracies with specific cultural identities. As Michael Walzer has repeatedly argued, one project of Norway is to promote Norwegians and Norwegian culture: its language, its way of life.

Many Arab countries and most Palestinians themselves are committed to the continuity and heritage of Islam, as of Arab social forms and language. They militantly claim this right to be who they are in a variety of forums, including political ones. What then makes them deny this right to Israel? The claim to accept Israel as one state so as to create a true democracy is basely prevaricating. Aside from the fact that today there are no examples of multicultural Arab democracies that grant equal rights to minorities (Turkey struggles with its Kurds, has a violent history with its Armenians, and is now in a state of internal struggle over its democratic norms; Lebanon, which long was offered as the model for peaceful and respectful co-existence, experienced a fifteen year civil war and today sees its Shia and Sunni populations on the edge of violence; Iraq and Syria are riven places; throughout the Middle East minorities are under threat, including whatever Jews remain after their expulsion). Most importantly, democracy does not necessarily prevent the suppression or denial of cultural identities. Even the United States as a "nation of immigrants" undefined by exclusionary ethnicity, has a decided cultural identity of shared history, values, political forms, and norms. The denial to Israel of its right to self-determination while claiming such a right for the Palestinians gravely contributes to the conflict between them rather than towards its solution. A narrative that denies the legitimacy of Jews to self-determination is one that cannot be reconciled to a two-state solution or to the mutual respect for difference which alone can be the basis and foundation of peaceful co-existence and hopefully positive recognition.

That Israel is a Jewish state (even if that were the equivalent of another state being Christian or Moslem rather than Arab or American, which it is not) does not have to mean that it is not a democratic state, for all its citizens. It can mean no more than that there is a majority population or culture within that nation, as is the case in almost every nation on earth. Democracy does not depend on whether the majority in a particular nation is Catholic or Jewish or Muslim. It does not depend on whether the nation is called the United States of America or Palestine. Democracy depends on a nation's genuine attempt to insure equality for all its citizens. Most nations, including most of the nations in the Middle East, have failed in this endeavor, at least to some degree. Some nations, like Israel, continue to try to implement the fundamental principles of democratic government and society. The fact that Israel is a "Jewish" state rather than a Muslim or French state, is irrelevant. ■

*Adapted from Emily Budick, "When a Boycott is Not Moral Action but Social Conformity and the 'Affectation of Love'" and Shira Wolosky, "Teaching in Transnational Israel: An Ethics of Difference," with introductory material.*

Also see ISRAELI-PALESTINIAN UNIVERSITY COOPERATION, THE ISRAELI RIGHT AND RELIGIOUS SETTLER POLITICS, and ZIONISM AS PHILOSOPHY AND PRACTICE.

# THE ISRAELI-PALESTINIAN PEACE PROCESS: A BRIEF HISTORY

CARY NELSON, RACHEL S. HARRIS, AND KENNETH W. STEIN

Though Yasser Arafat (1929-2004) ambitiously declared Palestinian independence and a virtual Palestinian state as early as 1988, his refusal to renounce terrorism against Israel abruptly ended US efforts to open a dialogue with the Palestine Liberation Organization (PLO) leadership. Moreover, the first Intifada had opened the way for other political groups including Hamas, the Palestinian wing of the militant Muslim Brotherhood that dominated Gaza. Notoriously anti-Semitic, Hamas proclaimed its plans for an Islamic State free of both Jews and Christians, vilifying Jews in its charter which cited the infamous anti-Semitic forgery *The Protocols of the Elders of Zion* as evidence of a Zionist plot of world domination. Advocating Jihad against Zionism and refusing any negotiation or recognition of Israel, Hamas took a position more extreme than that of the PLO, which by the 1990s had come to see political maneuvering as a more effective strategy for nation building than terrorism.

But the Palestinian cause was sidelined in the winter of 1990-1991 when Saddam Hussein (1937-2006) invaded and annexed Kuwait, and allied forces responded with Operation Desert Storm, which resulted in the first Gulf War.

Asked by the US to stand down, Israel waited while Tel Aviv and northern Israel were shelled by Iraqi Scud missiles. International sympathy returned for the besieged Jewish state. Meanwhile, the Palestinians unwisely threw their support behind the show of Iraqi Arab militarism and lost some of the ground they had worked so hard to gain. The regional conflict soon silenced quieter struggles at home. Meanwhile, at the 1991 Madrid Peace Conference, Israel for the first time engaged in direct, face-to-face negotiations with all of its immediate neighbors and their political rulers, also launching a multilateral process that brought Israeli diplomats into contact with representatives of Arab states from North Africa and the Persian Gulf. Though these interactions would lead nowhere, the increasingly stable relationship between Israel and Jordan would be formally recognized through the signing of a peace treaty in 1994. Israel had signed a peace treaty with Egypt in 1979 and normalized relations the following year. Though debates about the relationship between and interdependence of the Israeli-Palestinian and Arab-Israeli conflicts and peace processes have waxed and waned, in fact the changed relationships with Jordan and Egypt, along with the more recent disintegration of Syria and Iraq, have altered the chemistry of the process and the character of the political pressures Israel has faced.

The growth of the peace movement in Israel and the changing political temperature heralded promise for an era of reconciliation and security. In recognition, the Knesset in 1993 repealed a 1986 law banning Israeli-PLO contacts, thereby enabling potential agreements between Israelis and Palestinians to be signed. On September 9, the PLO and Israel mutually recognized each other, and on September 13, the Oslo Peace Accords were signed in Washington by Prime Minister Yitzhak Rabin (1922-1995) and Arafat, with American president Bill Clinton as witness. The Oslo Accords, or the Declaration of Principles on Interim Self-Government Arrangements (DOP), provided for Palestinian self-rule. Following months of negotiations, initially between nongovernmental parties, an agreement was signed that gave Palestinians control over most of Gaza and of the West Bank city of Jericho, and set a timetable for negotiations to enable further transfer of authority.

Though both the Israeli and Palestinian public broadly supported these efforts, both also possessed a strong rejectionist minority. On Israel's right, resistance to the peace process would become increasingly vocal and, with the subsequent stalemate of the Oslo process, dominate Israel's political landscape in the twenty-first century. In the early 1990s, the Palestinians who rejected the accords noted that East Jerusalem remained under Israeli control, that the settlements remained in place, and that Palestinians had gained authority over only a tiny portion of the West Bank. These Palestinians also rejected the PLO's secular apparatus. Hamas and Islamic Jihad opted to undermine the process with terrorist attacks. At first, Israel maintained its determination to continue with the process, and the IDF withdrew from Jericho and most of Gaza in 1994. By mid-May, Arafat had arrived in Gaza and declared Gaza City the capital of the Palestinian Authority (PA), the political body that served as an embryonic government for a future independent Palestine.

In response, on October 19, 1994, a Hamas suicide bomber killed 21 and wounded 23 on a bus in Tel Aviv. This would be part of a wave of suicide bombings—including a Palestinian Islamic Jihad attack by two suicide bombers on January 22, 1995, that killed 21 soldiers at a crossroads bus stop in central Israel—that would terrorize Israel over the coming decade and erode public support for the peace process among the Israeli public. Nevertheless, in an attempt to resist the pressures of a minority, in 1995, the two sides signed the "Israeli-Palestinian Interim Agreement on the West Bank and Gaza Strip," which provided for the election of an 82-person Palestinian Council and a head (Ra'is) of an Executive Committee. The West Bank was divided into three categories of territory. Area A, which includes West Bank cities, was evacuated by the Israelis, with the Palestinian Authority responsible for security and policing. Area B, including most Arab towns and villages, would be controlled by the PA, which would be responsible for civil authority and normal policing, while Israel would retain ultimate responsibility for security. Area C, encompassing unpopulated territory and Israeli military outposts as well as Jewish settlements, would be shared, with the PA overseeing health, education, and other public services for Arabs and Israel doing the same for Jews. Israel would also control security and public order. Later that year, the IDF withdrew from Bethlehem, Jenin, Nablus, Qalqila, Ramallah, and Tulkarm (MAP 4).

Hopeful for the positive outcomes that the new autonomy would provide, Palestinians were eager about the future, but Arafat, a successful wartime leader, lacked the skills needed to be an effective nation builder. The anticipated economic benefits that self-determination was supposed to provide never materialized, as the Palestinian Authority was compromised by bribes and political corruption. The Legislative Council and presidential elections in the West Bank and Gaza, as prescribed in the Oslo Accords, proved hollow, as Arafat, once elected president, ignored the will of the Legislative Council and operated by fiat and tribal allegiances. The assassination of Yitzhak Rabin alone was a tremendous blow to hopes for peace. The democracy that Israelis enjoyed failed to become a reality for Palestinians, while the Palestinian economic situation deteriorated as travel between the different zones and cities, with their delays and Israeli checkpoints, proved burdensome, time consuming, and humiliating. Moreover, the Intifada eliminated work in Israel for many of the Palestinians in the West Bank; they were replaced by a foreign labor force, further limiting their economic opportunities.

Despite the terrorist bombs during the 1990s, in 2000 Prime Minister Ehud Barak (1942-) moved forward with final stage negotiations. Arafat, Clinton, and US Secretary of State Madeleine Albright (1937-) met with Barak at Camp David to pursue a definitive peace treaty. Barak offered to divide Jerusalem, giving the PA sovereignty over the outer East Jerusalem neighborhoods, and to cede 84-90 percent of the West Bank overall. With Barak having taken office after defeating the incumbent Benjamin Netanyahu (1949-) in 1999 on a peace platform, the potential for success seemed high, though Barak was politically weakened by the time of Camp David. But Arafat initially held firm to a demand for PA control of all of the Old City, though he moderated that position as the talks proceeded. He also insisted on Palestinian control of the entire raised portion of the Temple Mount, though he was willing to cede sovereignty of the Western Wall. He continued to insist on a Palestinian Right of Return, which would offer all Palestinians who left, and all of their descendants, the right to live in Israel. For Israel, acceding to such a request would be a demographic, political, cultural, religious, and financial disaster, not only burdening Israel with the potential immigration of millions of new citizens, but also transforming the makeup of the country, already with a population of one million Arabs, into an Arab country with a Jewish minority. With such a move, Israel would become an Arab country, and the only country where Jews have a sovereign right of national self-expression would disappear overnight. In a symbolic gesture Barak offered to accept several thousand Palestinian refugees, but this was rejected by Arafat as well. In a final attempt to resolve the disputes, Barak offered Arafat roughly 90 percent of the West Bank, but neither was willing to compromise over the issue of sovereignty over the Temple Mount. In the end it was the status of East Jerusalem and most of all the Temple Mount that produced a stalemate. In the West Bank the Arab press claimed that it was only Barak who refused to compromise.

In truth all parties contributed to the failure. The Israelis thought of the West Bank as theirs to cede or control, whereas the Palestinians felt they had already ceded 78 percent of historic Palestine and saw little reason to give up still more territory. Neither party, moreover, felt they could sell its respective public an agreement ceding sovereignty over the Temple Mount.

Yet Arafat thus tragically rejected not only the best overall territorial offer Israel had ever made, but also quite possibly the best offer the Palestinians will ever receive. As Anita Shapira writes, "Some argue that his years at the Palestinian Authority demonstrated to Arafat that what awaited him at the end of the road was a relatively small, poor state burdened with economic and social problems, and that he preferred the romanticism of the struggle rather than the dejecting routine of being president of the Palestinian state. So long as there was no peace, he was a national hero, a media figure at whose door the world's luminaries came calling." It is also likely that Arafat was fearful. All area leaders remember what happened to Sadat. Many observers consider the Second Intifada the substantive Palestinian response. It may reflect a conclusion, based on Hezbollah's success in Lebanon, that a dispersed low-tech policy of violence can defeat a sophisticated modern army.

Meanwhile, the failure of the peace negotiations in 2000 and the outbreak of the Second Intifada, with its constant suicide bombs, also persuaded many Israelis that the peace camp had decisively failed. That led to Israelis in 2001 choosing a right-wing government that they thought would be better able to suppress the constant daily violence. Four years later, in 2005, several factors seemed to bring significant change to the political landscape. With Arafat's death, the election of Mahmoud Abbas as chairman of the PLO in 2005, and the sudden stroke that left Sharon in a coma until he died nine years later, the traditional positions on the conflict could be rethought. In one of his final acts in office, Sharon had ordered a unilateral withdrawal from the Gaza Strip and the evacuation and removal of its 21 civilian settlements. A movement in support of the settlements sprang up through the country, but despite the government's worst fears of a Jewish civil war, the disengagement was ultimately peaceful and conducted ahead of schedule. Israel's withdrawal from Gaza was intended to facilitate the PA's sovereignty as part of the Oslo Accords, but almost immediately, in what amounted to a bloody revolt, Hamas overthrew the PA in Gaza and divided the Palestinian community into separate ideological as well as geographic entities. Great animosity permeates the PLO/PA relationship with Hamas and its leadership. For Hamas, the secular nature of the PA and the extensive financial and political corruption that characterized Arafat's nation-building years have cast doubt on the PA's capacity to govern and promoted the assumption that they betrayed the Palestinians by agreeing to a peace process. For the PA and Fatah, the largest party within the confederated multi-party PLO, Hamas' political and religious extremism, their refusal to recognize Israel and renounce terrorism, and their isolation by the international community have made them a political liability for Palestinians in their attempts to create an independent state. A collaboration Hamas and the PLO announced in 2014 soon collapsed.

In 2009, on a visit to Egypt, the recently elected President Barack Obama affirmed the strong bonds of the US-Israeli relationship but criticized Israel for continuing to build settlements that served as an impediment to peace. In June the same year, Israeli Prime Minister Benjamin Netanyahu gave what appeared to be a historic speech where he offered a five-point plan for a negotiated agreement with the Palestinians that included the establishment of a demilitarized Palestinian state on condition that Israel would be recognized as a "Jewish state." The Palestinian leadership rejected his terms. With no changes in the status quo, and Hamas continuing to fire rockets into Southern Israel, the IDF launched Operation Pillar of Defense in November 2012. Egypt mediated a ceasefire, announced a week after the operation began. Netanyahu's more recent comments and actions raise doubts about whether he was ever actually willing to see a Palestinian state be realized.

Despite intensive efforts during 2013 and 2014 by Secretary of State John Kerry and the US government to lead Israelis and Palestinians into an agreement, little progress has been made between the PA and Israel. Moreover, Hamas was left out of these negotiations, as were the other Arab countries like Lebanon that continue to maintain populations of Palestinian refugees, often with few rights and opportunities. Ultimately, any real solution will need to reflect a regional consensus that recognizes Israel's legitimate security concerns and accommodates the Palestinian drive for self-determination, but limits it to the West Bank and Gaza.

Looking back over all of Israel's history from the current vantage point, the series of short wars and discrete military actions amount, in effect, to one long war that has sometimes paused but never really stopped. The number of belligerent states, combined with paramilitary or terrorist organizations, means that no one nation seems able to prevent the region from repeatedly slipping into war. For Israel itself, with the most powerful military and non-oil dependent economy in the Middle East, the risks of terrorism and of Iran's obtaining nuclear weapons loom large. Hamas and Hezbollah are insurgent groups who openly seek Israel's destruction. Israeli governments to date have not been willing to risk temporary or permanent withdrawal from the West Bank over concern for security, commitment to the settlement movement, and the possibility that a West Bank Palestinian state would be similar to the Hamas-dominated Gaza Strip that makes a true peace process impossible. For now, Israelis seem more willing to accept responsibility and criticism for retaining control over the West Bank than to confront a potentially radical new Palestinian state. Indeed the expansion of settlements deep inside the West Bank steadily decreases the odds of a just peace. The demographic challenge posed by large numbers of Palestinians under Israeli control is equally real. And the restrictions on Palestinians in the West Bank are incompatible with Israeli democracy. As it has since the end of the June 1967 war, the overarching premise of Arab-Israeli negotiations remains: under what conditions and over what period of time will Israel relinquish territories won in the 1967 war and what will Israel receive in terms of a treaty or promise of non-war in return for territorial concessions? For those goals to be realized, Israel's justified security concerns regarding the West Bank will have to be dealt with. ■

*Adapted from Cary Nelson, Rachel S. Harris, and Kenneth W. Stein, "The History of Israel."*

Also see COORDINATED UNILATERAL WITHDRAWAL, THE OSLO ACCORDS, THE PALESTINIAN AUTHORITY, THE TEMPLE MOUNT / HARAM AL-SHARIF, and THE TWO-STATE SOLUTION.

# ISRAELI-PALESTINIAN UNIVERSITY COOPERATION

A dvocates of academic boycotts of Israeli universities often have little knowledge of what those universities are actually like. Absent knowledge of the institutions themselves, it is easy to imagine they serve Israeli Jews only, easier still to assume Jews and Palestinians and universities in Israel and the West Bank exist in entirely separate worlds, with no meaningful interaction and no collaboration either in research projects or in providing services. Although the BDS movement objects to the kinds of projects described below as examples of "normalization" and urges that they be eliminated, they bring many benefits to Palestinians. The cause of peace would be better advanced by increasing, not decreasing, their number.

—CN

# ILAN TROEN

There is incontrovertible evidence of active cooperation between Israeli educational institutions and those in the Palestinian Authority. During the British Mandate and under Jordanian rule, foreign Christian groups typically supported small Palestinian educational institutions. It was not until after 1967 under the Israeli administration and with its encouragement that these were transformed into public universities.

Enrollment and graduation rates have grown exponentially with more than 200,000 students in the PA's 49 recognized higher education institutions, 34 of which are in the West Bank. Higher education in the PA is growing at such a rate that it intends to capitalize on this success and convert this sector into a "Palestinian Export," bringing in students from all over the region (European Commission).

The Coordinator of Government Activities in the Territories (COGAT) is a division of the Israeli Ministry of Defense that coordinates civilian issues between the government, the Israel Defense Forces, international organizations, diplomats, and the Palestinian Authority. It has offices in Palestinian cities and separate branches to facilitate activities like infrastructure, foreign relations, and economics and business.

Jewish outreach to Palestine's Arabs began well before Israel's establishment, when individual Jewish physicians set up clinics to treat diseases like trachoma. Perhaps the best-known example of Israeli inaugurated medical cooperation is the Hebrew University's affiliated Hadassah Medical Center in Jerusalem that serves the city's Jewish and Arab populations, and well beyond. It is an integrated institution with Arab and Jewish medical staff, patients, and support workers.

There are other examples. Specialized trilateral programs bring together Israeli, Palestinian and Jordanian health professionals to target cerebral palsy victims. This largely forgotten population would not likely receive care were it not for the involvement of Israeli researchers. Emergency Medicine is another area of cooperation. Israel has among the most skilled personnel anywhere, due in large measure to the need to respond to terrorist attacks. These painfully acquired skills are shared with Jordanians and Palestinians, with expenses often entirely underwritten by Israeli institutions.

From cerebral palsy and cancer to public health and drug-abuse, Israeli academics engage with Palestinian counterparts to address problems across the Green Line. Professor Khulood Dajani, an Al Quds University Vice-President and Founding Dean of its Public Health faculty, holds a doctorate in this area from Ben-Gurion University. Her observation, made during the last Intifada bears quoting here: "The Israeli–Palestinian experience in collaborative projects in public health has demonstrated that despite tragic hostile events and marked fluctuations in the political atmosphere cooperation could be carried on. Thousands of people of both sides were involved and vital health services were provided to populations in need."

Palestinians who work with colleagues at the Technion, the Weizmann Institute, Ben-Gurion, and Hebrew Universities have expressed similar appreciation for what has been achieved through joint projects. A succinct summary of the ongoing significance of cooperation between Palestinians and Israelis was brought before the American Public Health Association meetings in Boston in November 2013 where a precursor to subsequent BDS resolutions was presented. The APHA rejected the divestment resolution by a 3-1 margin when confronted with these substantial facts, an impressive selection of which bear quoting. They included referencing the "long history of formal and informal collaboration between many Israeli and Palestinian public health and medical communities in service, training and research"; "substantial Israeli-Palestinian collaborations and Israeli contributions to progress in public health, preventive medicine, water and sanitation, nutrition, agricultural irrigation, immunization —notably polio, detection and prevention of lead poisoning, and medical care and education and training"; "the data on the huge numbers of Palestinians receiving medical care in Israeli hospitals and other care facilities over the years—over 200,000 in 2012 alone, an 11 percent increase from the previous year"; "the implications of time trends in improvement in public health indicators, notably for children between 1967 and 1995. Since Palestinian administration began, these indicators have remained stable. The lack of major continued improvement since 1995 (when the PLO took control) appears to be attributable to waste, misuse of funds, and mismanagement" ("Victory for Israel at APHA").

In addition to medicine, there are at least two other essential and active areas of cross-border collaboration. The first is the struggle with desertification. The inhabitants of Palestine/Israel/Jordan and Egypt share a similar arid or semi-arid climate. The most significant place for combatting desertification—outside the American Southwest—is in the research spearheaded at Israeli universities. Zionism has made the desert bloom. Collaborators from China (the Gobi is larger than the Negev), across Africa and elsewhere come to Israel. This includes Palestinians and Arabs from neighboring countries. Jewish and Arab scientists and students work together in research and the transfer of technologies. A sampling of the collaborative research projects between Arabs and Israelis—beyond public health—clearly illustrates the fact that problems of natural disaster, water supply, and pollution do not recognize geo-political borders and therefore neither do the scientists who contend with them to make a better world. A sampling of such projects includes:

- Collaboration with the PA on Water Research with a grant from MERC (Middle East Regional Cooperation, a US funded agency) to increase the clean water supply around Israel and the Middle East. This study brings together Israelis and Palestinians to address clean water issues in the West Bank area of Nablus over a five-year period. Additionally, a group of Israeli and Palestinian environmental researchers are working together to test the area's water supply for potentially health-altering endocrine-disrupting chemicals. Unequal distribution of water supplies for Israelis and Palestinians does, however, remain a problem. A new water line announced in 2015 should help.
- A Bi-Annual Conference on Drylands, Deserts and Desertification sponsored by Ben Gurion University's Blaustein Institute to deal with desertification. More than 500 people from 50 countries—including presenters from American universities and US government agencies—attend, as do Palestinian and Jordanian delegates. The conference is held in cooperation with the United Nations Educational, Scientific and Cultural Organization (UNESCO).
- Desalination; solar energy; desert architecture; arid zone agriculture; animal husbandry; ensuring the viability of the Dead Sea (a body of water that Jordan, Palestine, and Israel share)—are but a few among many others.

These life-sustaining projects are supported not only by the participating institutions but also by the international community, especially Europe, the United States, and Arab countries such as Oman, which is particularly interested in desalination. These collaborations not only result in new technologies to afford a better life for millions who live under harsh climate conditions, but serve to promote mutual respect, shared understanding, and peaceful coexistence.

The second area is the construction of narratives. For approximately 20 years, scholars at Israeli and Palestinian universities have attempted to contribute to mutual understanding by sharing our national narratives. We initially imagined we might construct one inclusive narrative out of the conflicting claims and interpretations of the Arab/Israeli conflict and then integrate it into Palestinian and Israeli education. That strategy proved misguided, as Sami Adwan of Bethlehem University and the late Dan Bar-On of Ben-Gurion University explained. Instead of a unitary homogenized narrative, they suggested, there are parallel ones. In human discourse, as in nature, these parallel lines do not meet. Nevertheless, Adwan and Bar-On deemed the exercise essential, for it has the potential of engendering empathy—a quality that can diminish, even if it cannot eliminate, conflict.

In 2013, *Israel Studies*, an Israeli-based journal co-edited for Indiana University Press, published a special issue on "Shared Narratives" that brought together the work of scholars from Israel and Palestine. This project will now be republished by a Palestinian research center for even wider distribution in the Arab world. Such shared enterprises mitigate the prolonged conflict that has so diminished our lives. Significantly, similar projects are taking place in many Palestinian and Israeli universities and colleges.

The dissemination of knowledge should have no boundaries. Israeli and Palestinian scholars and students, who are so vocal in so many areas, are not clamoring before any academic association for support of an academic boycott of Israel. On the contrary, Israeli and Palestinian Jews and Arabs want and need more, not less, of Israeli science and higher education. Both within and across the border, cooperation between Israeli and Palestinian institutions and academics is ongoing and fruitful. It should not be diminished but encouraged for the benefit of all. ■

*Adapted from Ilan Troen, "The Israeli-Palestinian Relationship in Higher Education: Evidence from the Field."*

Also see ANTI-NORMALIZATION, ISRAEL: DEMOCRATIC AND JEWISH, and TEACHING ARABS AND JEWS IN ISRAEL.

# THE ISRAELI RIGHT AND RELIGIOUS SETTLER POLITICS

CARY NELSON, RACHEL S. HARRIS,
AND KENNETH W. STEIN

W hen the first religiously driven Jewish settlers established themselves in Hebron after the 1967 war, it was with a deep sense of homecoming. They were reestablishing an indigenous Jewish community whose members were massacred in 1929. They also believed they were reversing a broader Diaspora that had exiled them from where they belonged. Possessing a messianic sense of destiny, as Michael Feige describes it, "they return to Hebron like Abraham, reside in Tekoah like the prophet Amos, and live in Beit Horon where the Maccabees have fought" (49) "The Bible is omnipresent in the settlers' world; many of their villages have biblical names, as do their children" (48). They were fulfilling a divine promise. "In other words," Feige continues, "the connection between the people and the land is metahistorical; it precedes history and constitutes it" (43). Accordingly, they felt any compromise with the Palestinians or withdrawal from the occupied territories constituted a severe religious transgression. Even today, many settlers view their actions as realizing the true meaning of the State of Israel, a view quite different from what one might call the "survival Zionism" that supported the existence of a Jewish state before 1967. On the other hand, the religiously motivated settlers can be distinguished from the large number who moved to the West Bank because it offered much cheaper housing and better access to social services.

When the settlers noticed Palestinians at all, they thought of them fundamentally as Arabs, not as Palestinians, and thus as part of that larger people, not a group meriting their own independent homeland. Feige again: "Like the pioneers, the settlers went to live on a dangerous frontier to fulfill their ideas of a better society. Both groups of settlers regarded themselves as avantgarde, hoping that others would follow once they 'saw the light' or realized the success of the colonization project" (54). Like some early Zionists they also embodied the Orientalist assumption that the local Arabs would benefit economically and culturally from their arrival and thus should welcome it. The more religiously driven settlers tend to view Israelis in the coastal plain who criticize them as weak and fearful of non-Jewish opinion, a view that extends to Diaspora Jews as well.

The ideologically oriented settlements tend to be physically isolated, located farthest from the Green Line and surrounded by Palestinians. The settlers living close to the 1967 borders (MAP 4) are more likely to have come for good jobs, better and more affordable housing, and other economic benefits, rather than out of religious conviction. They are also therefore likely to be living on the Israeli side of the security barrier (MAPS 3 & 4). The religious settlers are very much aware that this physical barrier puts them on the wrong side of what seems to be a de facto national border, despite official Israeli denial that it is a border. The majority of Israelis, moreover, do not identify with the religious settlers' sense of mission. Palestinians and their allies criticize the wall unsparingly, but it actually offers the potential for a unilateral Israeli withdrawal from 90 percent or more of the West Bank, effectively establishing a Palestinian state.

The fate the isolated religious settlers face, therefore, may be decisive. Most problematically of all, the Palestinians see themselves as inheriting hundreds of years of history in the land. Yet "the area ceded to the Palestinian Authority was chopped up into a bizarre archipelago to accommodate the needs of the settlers" (Feige 35). Though some Palestinians have gained economic opportunities through the occupation, others find their lives disrupted intolerably. Paradoxically, however, the Palestinian project of disrupting the settlers' daily lives had the effect of hardening their hearts, rather than persuading them to leave. "As the ability to go shopping or take a bus became a declared act of bravery and a national achievement, the banality of normal life became consecrated" (Feige 259). Meanwhile, the extremist elements among the settlers have their own history of violence. Members of a "Jewish

Underground" attempted to assassinate several mayors of Arab towns and were planning to bomb the Dome of the Rock until the plot was uncovered and they were arrested in 1984.

On February 25, 1994, Baruch Goldstein (1956-1994), a Jewish doctor from the neighboring settlement community of Kiryat Arba, donned his reserve officer's IDF uniform, entered nearby Hebron's holy place called the Tomb of the Patriarchs by Jews and the Ibrahimya Mosque by Muslims during morning prayers and massacred 29 Muslim worshippers and wounded 150 others. The survivors proceeded to beat him to death. In the riots that followed, the IDF killed about 30 Arabs and injured hundreds. Goldstein was born in New York and immigrated to Israel in 1983. He was a member of the racist and extremist Jewish Defense League and was acting out of his personal rage and his opposition to the peace process. "Beforehand, Goldstein told friends he had a plan for ending the Oslo process" (Gorenberg *The Unmaking* 107). Simply categorizing him as insane thus hides the incendiary political and cultural movement that focuses and encourages radical violence. Indeed there is a monument to Goldstein in Meir Kahane park in Kiryat Arba.

In 1995, fringe groups on the Israeli far right ramped up zealous, extremist agitation in response to Prime Minister Yitzhak Rabin's (1922-1995) peace initiative, describing him as a traitor and calling for his death. Although the Oslo Accords did not commit to creating a Palestinian state, they pointed in that direction. Extremist elements of the religious right regarded any effort to divide the sacred land of Israel as sacrilege. The incitement to violence produced results. On November 4, Rabin was assassinated by Yigal Amir, a 27-year-old law student at Israel's religious university, Bar-Ilan. The assassination took place at a peace rally designed to show support for Rabin. Amir was a graduate of Orthodox and ultra-Orthodox schools and yeshivas. After his arrest, he declared that he aimed to derail the peace process. For many right-wing supporters who had opposed the peace movement, seeing it as a betrayal of Zionist values, these actions had gone too far, and many worked to distance themselves from this extremism, including rabbis who saw that their comments against the government had spilled over from political protest to violence and even treason.

But the failure of the peace negotiations in 2000 and the outbreak of the Second Intifada, with its constant suicide bombings, also persuaded many Israelis that the peace camp had decisively failed. That led to Israelis choosing more conservative governments that they thought would be better able to suppress the constant daily violence. In 2001, Ariel Sharon (1928-2014) was elected Prime Minister; by then he had arguably moved toward a center-right stance, but he remained the premier symbol of the political right and a leader inclined to address problems with the use of force. Having first served as Prime Minister from 1996–1999, Benjamin Netanyahu formed a decidedly right-wing coalition in 2009 and was reelected repeatedly, beginning his fourth term in 2015.

## CARY NELSON

Underwriting the ideology of the religious right and the religious settler movement are the teachings of Avraham Yitzhak Hacohen Kook (1865–1935), chief rabbi during the British Mandate. He fused European nationalism with Jewish mystical doctrine to proclaim that the return to Israel was part of a divine plan to redeem the world. After the Jewish state was created and Israel later gained control over the West Bank, those who believed peace could only follow the arrival of the Messiah found reason to place no faith in a negotiated peace. As this stand evolved and was elaborated by others, "it taught that the world's spiritual condition was measured by Jewish military power and territorial expansion. Religion swallowed whole the hard-line ultra-nationalism of soil, power, and ethnic superiority, and took on its shape. Settling in 'redeemed' territory [in the West Bank] was a way of consciously advancing God's plan" (Gorenberg *The Unmaking* 92). Charles S. Liebman identified three components of Israeli ultra-nationalism: territorial maximalism, exclusionary ethno-nationalism, and cultural hegemony.

This ideology made it psychologically and politically acceptable to dehumanize Palestinians, steal their land, and carry out harassing forms of violence on a regular basis. The annual West Bank olive harvest is one recurring opportunity, with extremist settlers regularly stealing Palestinians' olive harvest and uprooting or setting fire to the groves. Jews who participate in the Palestinian harvest in solidarity are subject to opportunistic violence from thugs in the settler community.

Religious Jews who set up small illegal West Bank outposts—about a hundred of them were established in the decade leading up to 2005—found themselves in a curiously contradictory position. On the one hand, they showed disrespect for the rule of law by establishing these encampments outside the planning process that makes settlements legal in Israeli terms. Yet they also relied on government ministries to purchase the mobile homes that were quietly redirected for outpost use. A pattern was established: a theologically driven mission to take over land so as to diminish the size of a potential

Palestinian state or block it entirely regarded the state and its peace negotiations as fundamentally illegitimate, while relying on the state both for material support and military protection. *Haredi* (strictly Orthodox) men who believe God gave the Jews Judea and Samaria, but do not work and rely on the government for financial support while devoting themselves to lifetime study complicate the paradox still further. As a generation that has never lived west of the Green Line matures (MAP 4), this contradiction becomes more intractable. Meanwhile government agencies hid outlays for outpost support in budgets that failed to honor the financial transparency principle critical to the democratic process. In that way West Bank practices tend to undermine the principles intended to govern Israel itself.

Ever since the Israeli government removed its settlements from Gaza in 2005, hostility in some quarters of the settler movement has focused not only on the Palestinians but also on the government itself. A "price tag" movement evolved to exact a cost from both as a reaction to policies, actions, or events to which the participants object. The movement's tactics most commonly involve acts of vandalism directed against Palestinians, Arab-Israelis, the Israeli left, the police, and the Israeli Defense Forces. The movement's members are most often young, often in their teens and 20s, with the number of active participants decreasing as the level of violence increases. Damaging property, uprooting olive trees, stone throwing, and defacing homes are the most common forms of aggression and retaliation. There may be anywhere from several hundred to several thousand Israelis involved in various activities. A few rabbis have encouraged the movement. Although the price tag activists are a minority, they often feel they have the tacit support of the mainstream settler leadership, even if the leadership simply remains silent in the face of their actions because they find it difficult to condemn their own people. Over the last decade the government has mostly declined to pursue, identify, and prosecute perpetrators. That has, in effect, encouraged them to continue their efforts. It also corrodes Israeli society as a whole by encouraging general disrespect for the law and discounting the violence done to Palestinians and undermining commitment to their human rights.

About fifteen percent of all settlers are American born, a percentage that likely applies to the price tag movement as well. Some feel the liberal values they learned in the US just cannot function in the very different West Bank environment. Others are "all for Palestinians having jobs and being able to have access to some civil institutions and other forms of social care, but where they draw the line is that they're not interested in Palestinian sovereignty" (Hirschorn). Some give decisive priority to Jewish rights and benefits. And some are drawn to the most extreme forms of violence.

More serious violence is generally carried out by small, closely-knit groups. Estimates of their total number top out at no more than a few dozen people. They often live in isolation on hilltops or in caves, cut off from larger communities, and have been dubbed the "hilltop youth" (Caspit; Gershuni). They typically reject the traditional forms of Zionism and seek to replace the existing form of government with a revived ancient Kingdom of Judea. The October 1, 2015, firebombing murder of the Dawabsha family in the West Bank Palestinian village of Douma is one graphic example of such violence at its most horrific. It helped incite the Palestinian knife and auto attacks that followed through the rest of 2015 and into 2016. Though the hilltop youth represent a fringe movement among the settlers, the political impact of their extreme violence can be substantial. ■

*Adapted from Cary Nelson, Rachel S. Harris, and Kenneth W. Stein, "The History of Israel," with concluding material added.*

---

Also see THE OSLO ACCORDS, THE ISRAELI-PALESTINIAN PEACE PROCESS, SETTLER COLONIALISM, THE WEST BANK, and ZIONISM AS PHILOSOPHY AND PRACTICE.

# JEWISH ANTI-ZIONISTS: THREE VIEWS

The Zionist commitment to the Jewish right to a homeland remains a strong component of Jewish culture worldwide. Early Zionist history includes Jewish opposition to the creation of a Jewish state, but support for that position declined decisively once the reality of the Holocaust was revealed and Israel was founded as a country. Objection to a hypothetical Jewish state is altogether different from opposition to a country with a population of eight million people. Jews in Israel and elsewhere are often relentlessly critical of Israeli government policy—criticism that comes both from the right and the left—but most draw a line between criticism of government policy and a conviction that Israel should be eliminated entirely or cease to be a Jewish state. Despite efforts to muddy the issue by asserting the reverse, criticism of Israeli government policy does not amount to anti-Semitism. The experience of intense Jewish anti-Zionism, however, is particularly painful for Jews who support Israel's existence, whether or not they are advocates of current government policy. At the same time, Jews who break with Israel sometimes compensate for the inner conflict that creates by adopting an anguished hostility that generates a serious rift within the Jewish community.

—*CN*

## KENNETH L. MARCUS

Many who dispute the connection between anti-Semitism and anti-Zionism observe that many of Israel's sharpest critics are Jewish. The presence of these Jewish anti-Zionists has been used to rebut accusations of anti-Semitism on the purported ground that a Jew cannot be an anti-Semite (Ottolenghi, 425). This argument has been described as "Jew Washing," referring to the enlistment of Jews to provide cover for activities that would otherwise be seen as anti-Semitic (Santis and Steinberg). In fact, the presence of Jewish participants within the BDS movement does not disprove its anti-Semitic character.

Their presence can be partly explained on the ground that some Jews absorb anti-Israel and even anti-Jewish attitudes tacitly as a function of their choice of ideologies. Like anyone else, Jews often adopt broad ideologies that resonate with them across a range of issues and then maintain views and behavior that follow from these over-arching ideologies (Hillman 62). If they choose to embrace certain progressive ideologies, they may adopt the positions on Israel that come with the package, even if these positions are based on anti-Jewish stereotypes. Moreover, insofar as anti-Israel attitudes have become part of this "package deal," they have become a cultural code marking their adherents as belonging to a particular subcultural milieu (Volkov). Sina Arnold has argued that this "collective identity" approach best explains anti-Zionist attitudes among progressive Jews, thus eliminating the need for psychological and speculative concepts such as "Jewish self-hatred."

A full treatment of this issue, however, cannot ignore the reality that Jews, like members of other persecuted groups, sometimes embrace the perceptions of their group that circulate within the larger society. Just as there are Jewish anti-Semites, there are many Jewish critics of Israel, including some whose criticisms are devoid of anti-Semitism and others whose criticisms are not. The concept of Jewish self-hatred is now considered impolitic in some circles, just as there are other circles in which its existence is beyond question. Sander Gilman has persuasively argued that "self-hatred" is a valid term for a form of self-abnegation that has existed among Jews since ancient times. The power of common prejudices, the "persuasive wisdom of what 'everyone knows'" can cause members of any minority group, to believe even the worst that others say about them (Julius 67). Gordon Allport explained self-hatred as a "subtle mechanism" through which a victim comes to agree with his persecutors and to see his group through their eyes. He observed, for example, that a Jew "may hate his historic religion . . . or he may blame some one class of Jews . . . or he may hate the Yiddish language. Since he cannot escape his own group, he does in a real sense hate himself—or at least the part of himself that is Jewish" (147). Indeed, members of persecuted groups have powerful incentives to reject the markers of their otherness. In anti-Semitic environments, this has generated efforts to deny or escape from Jewish origins in environments that attach stigma or inferiority to Jewishness. In such cases, Jewish self-hatred reflects a persecuted group's identification with its aggressor.

In many cases, Jewish dissidents have stressed their Jewish origins in order to support projects hostile to the Jewish people. In this way, they have responded to an assimilationist fantasy, whether in medieval Spain or on contemporary California university campuses: "Become like us—abandon your difference—and you may be one with us" (Gilman 2). Thus, for example, Jews were among the first medieval polemicists to write against Judaism, and they stressed their Jewish origins in doing so (Julius 34). Indeed, many of the Jewish people's greatest persecutors throughout history have been rumored to be converted Jews, although historians have cast doubt on some of these rumors (Poliakov 52). Over the centuries, anti-Jewish polemicists within the Jewish community have used the authority of their Jewish background to legitimize virtually every anti-Jewish canard, from blood libel to international Jewish conspiracies. (Julius 34-37).

At the end of his classic treatise on *Jewish Self-Hatred*, Sander Gilman writes that "one of the most recent forms of Jewish self-hatred is the virulent opposition to the existence of the State of Israel" (391). Jewish progressive and intellectuals are often responsible for some of the most virulent criticism of Israel. Noam Chomsky, Norman Finkelstein, Ilan Pappé, and Jacqueline Rose, for example, have been among Israel's most unrelenting critics. It should not be surprising that some leading supporters of the BDS movement, including Judith Butler, are Jewish as well.

## CARY NELSON

Some Jews, including some who testify in the Bruce Robbins film *Some of My Best Friends Are Zionists*, experience an overwhelming need to expel Israel from themselves, to convince both themselves and everyone else that they do not harbor it—to use a Derridean metaphor—encrypted within. That helps explain the intensity with which some Jews reject the very existence of an

Israeli state. And yet for Jews Israel always seems to be encapsulated, warded off within, so their passion for expelling it escalates. It is a dynamic and progressive process. The well-known accusation of Jewish self-hatred is thus a simplification and a slander. They hate and fear but part of themselves. Asked why they are determined to condemn Israel for practices comparable to those many other nations engage in, some Jews claim their right to do so as a birthright. At public events, most recently at MLA in 2014, Bruce Robbins, a Columbia University English professor and long-time BDS advocate, always responds to the "Why Israel" question by answering "because I am a Jew, and I object to what Israel is doing in my name." He delivers the statement with enough anguish and vehemence so as to forestall further discussion. As I suggest in *No University is an Island: Saving Academic Freedom* (2010), I have heard some opponents of Israel, both Jewish and non-Jewish, speak with such uncontrolled venom that I am convinced that they are anti-Semitic whether they know it or not. Hostility toward Israeli government policy does not in and of itself constitute hostility toward Jews, but when it escalates to opposition to the very existence of the Jewish state, it crosses a line into anti-Semitism. It is much easier to cross the line now than it was even as little as a generation ago, because there is now an organized, often hyperbolic, movement to eliminate the Jewish state that did not exist before. It sets a standard of passion for anti-Zionist Jews to meet and provides collective rein-forcement for them when they do so. The philosophical anti-Zionism that flourished in the late nineteenth century has been replaced by something far more visceral and emotional.

## RICHARD LANDES

Anti-Zionism among Jews is one of the greatest contributors to the ability of the Jihadis to enlist the progressive left in their ranks, one that permits the false consciousness of good intentions—this is for peace!—to operate far longer than it should among people who unintentionally but consistently contribute to war. In leadership positions both within the BDS movement and supporting it from without, there are a host of Jewish progressives who want to show their commitment to world redemption by accepting the lethal narratives about Israel, and thus *prove* their bona fides. Scholars have extensively chronicled this old and disturbing phenomenon that goes back at least a millennium (Gilman; Rubin; Wistrich).

A new contingent of such Jews has cropped up with particular vigor in France, people who had made careers as successful, if invisible Jews, all of a sudden feeling they must, "as a Jew…" denounce the crimes of the Israelis. These "alter-juifs," as their critics call them, dominated public discussion in the aughts (Trigano, Steinberg and Santis). In Anthony Julius' apt phrase, they're "proud to be ashamed to be Jew." Anyone who had the slightest whiff of *communautarisme* (partisanship) got sidelined. Among such Jews, we find Judith Butler, who applies her most stringent standards of pacifism to Judaism (thou shalt not exercise sovereignty) even as she accepts Hamas and Hezbollah into the "anti-imperialist" global progressive left. Indeed, one might even identify an actual *religious* movement among such Jews, a *tikkun olam* (repairing the world) that believes that in sacrificing Israel, Jews will contribute to global peace (Landes, "Does Burston").

This is a messianic syndrome, a kind of masochistic omnipotence fantasy, in which everything is *our* (we Jews') fault. If only *we* could change, we could fix everything. It invokes the prophetic tradition to insist on moral perfectionism, although the prophets did not write their scathing (and rhetorically inflated) criticism for a non-Jewish audience. It's not enough for these Jewish critics that Israel matches or surpasses every marker of the most "advanced" armies in respect for enemy civilian lives, for the civic and human rights of populations in wartime, for tolerance of criticism. No. Israel must live up to its own exalted standards. And anything short of that standard deserves public denunciation in the most uncompromising rhetoric.

We end up with a post-modern moral inversion. If the tribal attitude is "my side right or wrong," and the civil attitude is "whoever's right, my side or not," then one current position has become, "their side right or wrong." Some Jews have become leaders in the poisonous marriage of pre-modern sadism—"you, the imperialist, racist whites are evil and we must kill you"—and post-modern masochism—"you, the subaltern indigenes, are right; we deserve it." Hence, Jews, even Israelis, who compare their own people to Nazis.

Of all the Western answers to the Jihadi prayer for allies, none has proven so valuable: they gave legitimacy to his lethal narratives even as they attack as "Israel-firsters" those who resist. Of all the people duped by Jihadis, one might argue, these are the most lamentable. Those Jewish academics and public intellectuals who have consistently denounced Israel, who are suddenly alarmed at the hostility on campus not just to Zionism but to Jews, need to ask themselves how much they, in ignoring the forces at work, in dismissing their critics as "right-wing fanatics" and in obsessing publicly on Israel's crimes, actually fueled that hostility.

But leave the Jews aside. Why on earth would sound non-Jewish minds want to take such troubled advocates as guides either to morality or to empirical reality? On the contrary, I'd argue that the only way for the democratic, multi-cultural, tolerant, self-critical, progressive West to survive the Jihadi attack is to resist those juicy morsels of moral *Schadenfreude* about Jews behaving badly and the unconscious racism of moral expectations involved, even (especially) when offered up by Jews. All the more reason to resist the temptation when the lethal narratives are not only inaccurate, but wrapped up as descriptions of an apocalyptic evil.

Ironically, to save itself, the West must *genuinely* renounce its long romance with Judeophobia which, right now, constitutes is single greatest vulnerability. ▪

*Adapted from Kenneth L. Marcus, "Is BDS Anti-Semitic," Cary Nelson, "The Problem with Judith Butler," and Richard Landes, "Fatal Attraction: The Shared Antichrist of the Global Progressive Left and Jihad."*

Also see ANTI-ZIONISM AS ANTI-SEMITISM and HOLOCAUST INVERSION.

# THE "JEWISH CONSPIRACY"

CARY NELSON

Anti-Semitism since the Middle Ages has often taken the form of conspiracy theories about the Jews. Among other things, it was fantasized and believed that Jews poisoned wells to spread disease, killed Jesus, and used Christian blood in their rituals. The blood libel that Jews kill non-Jewish babies to obtain their blood for use in making Passover matzos dates from that period, though other elements have precursors in antiquity. Some Muslim religious figures repeat the blood libel slander to the present day. Such conspiracy theories led to the mass murder of Jews, or pogroms, and to policies that Jews must live only in prescribed areas. The Nazis promoted several Jewish conspiracy theories, among them that Jewish bankers control international capitalist finances and that Jews seek world dominance through Communism. Anti-Zionism now often embodies the myth that Zionists seek complete control of the Middle East, along with continuing fantasies about outsized Jewish power and influence in the US and elsewhere. BDS not infrequently draws on these sentiments to promote its agenda.

On the lunatic fringes of the BDS movement conspiracy theories about Israel don't require so much as a grain of truth. All they require is a single credible referent to Jewish culture or Israeli history. The pattern is much the same as the blood libel fantasies about the use of Christian blood in baking matzos; after all, there is no question the matzos themselves exist, so any hallucinatory embellishments to the baking of them one wants to make are welcome. In Rutgers University faculty member Jasbir Puar's paper "Inhumanist Biopolitics: How Palestine Matters," presented at Vassar College in February 2016, she expands on the fact that some Palestinians are wounded and maimed in confrontations with Israeli forces to lay out a whole argument that Israelis have a formal policy of maiming and stunting as many Palestinians as possible, preferable even to killing them. She offers no proof beyond her own conviction. Whether Puar herself is anti-Semitic I cannot say, but her conspiracy theory surely is. The fact that it attacks Israel does not in itself make it anti-Semitic, but its content does. While Vassar faculty had every right to invite her, anyone has the right to criticize the wisdom of doing so and to fault its content for its anti-Semitism. Academic critique is not a form of silencing.

## DEREK J. PENSLAR

Classic, nineteenth-century anti-Semitism identified the Jew with modern capitalism and the rapid transformation of society and culture that came in its wake. Ancient and medieval tropes of Jewish avarice, murderous hatred of Gentiles, and black-magical practices mutated into the modern stereotype of an international Jewish conspiracy . . . In the nineteenth century, notions of a Jewish international political and financial conspiracy were exported to the Middle East, largely via French and Francophone Christian clerics . . . [The 1030s and 1940s saw] the adoption of common European views of the Jew as universal solvent, the destroyer of social order and bringer of chaos . . . Nonetheless, up to 1948, Arab anti-Semitism did not routinely function, as it did in Europe, as a totally unbounded discourse, attributing every ill of modern humanity to Jewish influence . . . As opposed to traditional Muslim Judeophobia, post-1948 Arab anti-Semitism featured a transition from a view of the Jew as weak and degraded to a belief in Jewish global power . . . Israel's military victories in 1948, 1956, and 1967 generated a tidal wave of anger and compelled a search for explanations for the Arabs' ignominious defeat in the arcane realms of anti-Semitic fantasy . . . There are strains of post-1948 Arab anti-Semitism that absorbed the Manichean qualities of Nazism, elevating the Jew into a global, even cosmic, evil, which must be annihilated, not only within Palestine but wherever he may be found.

Such viewpoints are espoused vigorously by Muslim fundamentalists in many lands ("Anti-Semites" 15, 25, 26, 27, 14, 28).

# PAUL BERMAN

The argument in favor of boycotting Israel and the Zionists has gone through, by my calculation, three main phases or waves, with a fourth phase presently floating in our direction. The earliest of these phases, back in the 1920s and '30s, was simple, practical, and Palestinian—an Arab boycott of the Jews, intended to put up a fight against the tide of Jewish refugees that was beginning to rival and outrival the Palestinian Arabs for control of the land. This was a boycott that, if anyone had been in a mood to work out a compromise between the two populations, might have conferred a much-needed negotiators' advantage on the Palestinian leaders. The spirit of the age did not smile on people who attempted negotiations, however, and the argument for a boycott entered its phase more or less simultaneously with the first.

The second phase was more than regional. It was international, and it rested on supernaturalist doctrines about the Jews and their cosmic menace to the world. The 1920s and '30s were an era of anti-Jewish boycotts in several parts of the world, sometimes secular, sometimes Catholic, and in all of those places the analytic tendency underlying the boycotts ascribed to the Jews a sinister and not-quite human plan to dominate the world, as described in *The Protocols of the Elders of Zion* or sundry other documents with similar themes, on to *The International Jew: The World's Foremost Problem*, which was Henry Ford's American contribution to the literature. And the same supernaturalist interpretation of Jewish power and evil, except with an Islamic twist, took root among the Palestinian leaders, or at least the most influential of them, which proved to be a hugely unfortunate development for Jews and Palestinians alike. The anti-Jewish boycott in the Middle East, when it spread outward from Palestine to the wider Arab world—Cairo, 1936, the Muslim Brotherhood in command, riots in the streets—rested all too firmly on the supernaturalist argument, with its peculiar and fateful fusion of European conspiracy theory and Islamic tradition.

In the years after the Second World War, an anti-imperialist aspect within the boycott's justification began to loom a little more prominently. In this next phase of the argument, the old Nazi idea, which regarded Zionism as a plot against the Europeans, was turned upside down, and Zionism was accused, instead, of being a European plot, directed against everyone else for the purpose of maintaining the system of European imperialism. Third World solidarity, together with the need to protect Islam from the diabolical Jewish conspiracy, became the boycott's fundamental appeal, now under the administration of the Arab League. The anti-imperialist side of the new argument proved to be fairly convincing, too, here and there around the world, perhaps with a little help from the oil exporters. Only, in sketching these phases of the argument, I do not mean to ascribe too much simplicity or logic to the arguments or to the progress that led from one phase to the next. Certain of the supernaturalist arguments against Zionism and the Jews collapsed when the Nazis collapsed. Post-war Vatican reforms put an end to certain others. Some of the force in the anti-imperialist argument against Israel drained away when the Soviet Union drained away. The boycott itself, in its commercial aspects, went into decline.

And yet, as if to demonstrate that not every new step in the world of ideas is a forward step, the supernaturalist argument for a boycott of Israel underwent a revival, late-twentieth century. The Islamist revolution in Iran brought this about, and the revival grew stronger yet with the success of the Muslim Brotherhood, under the name of Hamas, among a portion of the Palestinians. It is daunting to consider that a document as barbarous as the Hamas charter, from 1988, could figure significantly in the political and cultural developments of our own moment—the Hamas charter, with its intermingled citations to *The Protocols of the Elders of Zion* and Islamic scripture and its call to murder the Jews. And yet, Hamas and its ideas do play a role in world affairs, and they play a role even in the politics of European book fairs and book prizes, and maybe they play more of a role in our own high-minded American debates than we like to imagine.

And just now has come the newest or fourth phase of the pro-boycott argument, which, if you are a professor, has been filling your own mail slot at the office for the past few seasons. This is the argument that begins by likening Zionism to the old Afrikaner ultra-right in apartheid South Africa, and goes on to appeal to the liberal principles of human rights and the legacy of the anti-apartheid boycott of thirty or forty years ago.

# ALAN JOHNSON

Anti-Zionist ideology also drinks deep at the well of conspiracism, including wildly inflated estimates of the power of the "Jewish lobby." John Mearsheimer's and Stephen Walt's 2007 book *The Israel Lobby* gave a stamp of academic legitimacy to conspiracism, by claiming to prove that only the power of the Israel lobby to shape US foreign policy could explain the US decision to invade Iraq, although the Bush administration's internal illusions were clearly the primary factors (229-262). A shiny new Ivy League stamp of approval was given to the smelly old idea that hidden Jewish power pushes states into wars and revolutions to serve Jewish interests. In this vein, Ilan Pappé claims that in 1947 "the Truman administration was probably the first ever to succumb to the power of the Jewish lobby" and today's US policy in the region is "confined to the narrow route effectively delineated . . . by AIPAC" (118), a claim now pretty thoroughly undone by AIPAC's (American Israel Public Affairs Committee) failure to defeat the 2015 Iran nuclear deal. More: "In the United States today," Pappé writes, "one cannot ignore the level of integration of Jews into the heights of American financial, cultural and academic power" nor "the exploitation of the fruits of successful integration into American society for the benefit of a foreign country" (Chomsky and Pappé 35). He doesn't quite call American Jews a fifth column, but he is getting there.

The *Haaretz* commentator Carlo Strenger has expressed his frustration at Judith Butler's conspiracist view of Zionism, but he might have had the entire anti-Zionist ideology in his sights. "Judging from [Butler's book] *Parting Ways*," he wrote, "you might think that Zionism was a unitary ideology run by some politburo. At no point would you recognize how complex the history of Zionism is, and how different its various shades can be. You would not guess that there are committed liberal Zionists who argue for a secular constitution for Israel that would give full equality to Arabs and lead to a complete separation of religion and state." He went on: "Quite remarkably, Butler, whose life's work is about nuances, unquestioningly accepts simplistic premises about Zionism."

# RUSSELL BERMAN

Fantasies about an all-powerful Jewish lobby are one of the most common examples of contemporary conspiracy theories about Jews. Following the low road through online comment sections or in social media, one finds boycott promoters quick to label their opponents as part of the "Zionist lobby." To dismiss a critic as part of a lobby means to deny him or her the right to independent thinking; defamation replaces argument. To treat lobbies as inherently corrupt betrays a simplistic view of modern liberal democracy, where lobbies, foundations and other organizations fill the political landscape. (The boycott movement itself depends on extensive foundation support even as it pretends to represent Palestinian "civil society.") ▪

*Adapted from Paul Berman, "Preface," Alan Johnson, "Intellectual Incitement: The Anti-Zionist Ideology and the Anti-Zionist Subject," and Russell Berman, "Scholars Against Scholarship: The Boycott as an Infringement of Academic Culture."*

Also see ANTI-ZIONISM AS ANTI-SEMITISM, JEWISH HISTORY BEFORE ZIONISM, and JIHAD.

# JEWISH HISTORY
# BEFORE ZIONISM

The area that today is the State of Israel was dominated by Jewish life and periods of sovereignty for about one thousand years before most Jews were expelled by the Romans in 135 CE (CE refers to the "Common Era," an alternative designation for "AD" embodying the same numbering system). The Jewish people maintained a physical presence in the land from that time forward as well as a deep spiritual connection among Diaspora communities. Jewish history through the last two millennia is replete with anti-Semitism and persecution, which provided impetus for the emergence of a Jewish national movement called Zionism in the 19th Century. Over the last decade or so, the status of Jews in the ancient period in particular has become a subject of considerable acrimony as some BDS advocates have claimed that Jewish or Hebrew tribes and kingdoms never existed and thus that there has been no long-term Jewish presence in Palestine. At the same time, contemporary echoes of Medieval blood libel accusations have been put into circulation again, while the character of Jewish culture during and after the Enlightenment has faced dispute. All these historical areas have been politicized and those political positions feed into efforts to delegitimize the Jewish state.

*—CN*

CARY NELSON, RACHEL S. HARRIS,
AND KENNETH W. STEIN

As early as the tenth century BCE (before the Common Era), Israelite kings ruled in the Land of Israel, a territory that stretched from the Mediterranean Sea to beyond the western banks of the Jordan River. Archeological evidence confirms biblical accounts of a Temple in Jerusalem, constructed about 960 BCE during King Solomon's reign. After its destruction in 586 BCE, many (though not all) Jews were exiled to Babylon but returned and rebuilt a second temple in 515 BCE that stood until the Romans razed Jerusalem in 70 CE. But rabbinic Judaism developed in Jamnia, then Usha, then Caesarea. Jews continued in the land from antiquity to today. It is this religious and political legacy that forms Jewish historical claims to a region with which the world has associated the Jewish people since ancient times, and with which they have maintained a spiritual and physical connection, despite centuries of exile, persecution, and domination by foreign powers within the area, and within the countries to which they have been dispersed.

As a minority that kept its own customs and traditions, Jews lived at the favor of local religious and political leaders. At times they would flourish under benevolent rulers, but in a moment they might find themselves subject to cruel tyranny and excessive taxation, often becoming victims of violence and murder. Casualties of world history, Jews were left with little political agency and few methods of defense when Christian and Muslim societies turned against them. The inventory that follows is but a partial account.

For the Christians of Medieval Europe, Jews were the killers of Christ; virulent myths about child kidnapping and blood libel were propagated, triggering violent anti-Jewish riots that led to massacres and expulsion from communities that Jews had for a time been able to consider home. By the end of the Middle Ages, Jews had lived in and been expelled from England, France, Spain, Germany, Bavaria, Italy, Belgium, Hungary, Slovakia, Austria, the Netherlands, Warsaw, Portugal, Prussia, Lithuania, Bohemia, and Prague, sometimes on multiple occasions, and later from Ukraine, Poland, and Russia. Between the 11th and 19th centuries, Jews were repeatedly massacred; they were expelled more than 30 times from major European cities and states. They lost their property, they were murdered, they were accused of blood libels (kidnapping and murdering Christian children in order to obtain blood for use in preparing Passover matzoh), they experienced forced conversions often at the point of a sword, they were accused of spreading the plague and poisoning wells, and during the crusades they were repeatedly attacked by

Christian armies on their way to fight Muslims in the Holy Land. In 1096 more than 5,000 Jews were murdered in Germany. In 1290, King Edward I issued an edict expelling all Jews from England, following 200 years of persecution, including the massacring of 100 Jews in York (1190), when they were burned to death after taking shelter in a tower. Five thousand Jews were killed in France in 1321 after they were accused of prompting lepers to poison wells. Thousands were killed in riots in Germany in 1389. Over 10,000 Jews were massacred in Spain in 1391. Following the wishes of Father Tomas de Torquemada, head of the Spanish Inquisition, 200,000 Jews were expelled from Spain on July 30, 1492, under an edict issued by King Ferdinand and Queen Isabella, and tens of thousands died in the effort to reach safety after being expelled. While Jews were tolerated to a greater extent under Muslim rule—as people who shared a holy book and as "dhimmis" ("protected" infidels) were not persecuted for their religious beliefs—they still experienced discrimination, taxation, and at times faced violent prejudice that again led to massacre and expulsion.

The beginning of the Modern period, the end of feudal Europe, and the rise of the nation state opened new opportunities for Jews. While many continued to live an almost medieval existence in parts of Eastern Europe, by the 19th century those in the West could take advantage of booming industrialization and the rapid development of major European cities. Two clear paths presented themselves for those who sought new opportunities for economic and intellectual growth: emancipation ended or reduced civil, economic, and political restrictions for some; others could attempt the cultural choice to assimilate. For those who chose assimilation, conversion to Christianity and marriage to a Christian were the most radical choices, but others chose the route of acculturation, modernizing their dress, habits, and religious practices to be more like the Christians among whom they lived. As Jews began to move out of the ghettoes in the eighteenth century, they were forced to confront their own traditionalism. For many a dichotomy existed between simple assimilation versus innovation in Jewish practice, which led to reframing of Jewish praxis particularly in central Europe. Yet this descent into modernity also inspired a backlash by those who preferred embracing the primitive nature of religion and foregrounding spirituality as evident in Hassidic movements. This too resulted in concerns over the dilution of religious observance, and the nineteenth and twentieth centuries produced anxieties over Judaism that led to divisive religious factionalism. Moreover, the destruction of historical centers of Jewish life, many of which had existed for millennia, brought together Jews with all manner of customs and traditions leading to a muddling of distinctions and creating new forms of hybridity.

The Jewish Enlightenment (the Haskalah), which developed during the 18th and 19th centuries in keeping with European Enlightenment ideals, frightened the traditional orthodox groups by calling for greater integration into modern secular society. As the map of Europe was rapidly transforming, Jews who had embraced Enlightenment ideals saw an alternative to conversion and the abandonment of Jewish faith; instead they identified a place for Jews within the broader brotherhood of man. This belief in the possibility of Jewish emancipation led to political efforts throughout the 19th century to have Jews included as equal citizens within continental European countries, and particularly in the newly created states emerging from the former Ottoman Empire. In Eastern Europe, these same ideals translated into political activism, and Jews believed that in a new Russian democracy they would be free from the violent prejudices of the past. But for many, the dream that Jews would finally be treated as equals in a new modern Russian republic was shattered with the anti-Semitic violence that erupted in the wake of the failed Russian revolution of 1905.

The combination of Haskalah ideals, the relentless violence against Jews in late nineteenth-century Russia through a series of pogroms, and the increasing manifestations of anti-Semitism in the press of apparently enlightened Western European societies, provided strong impetus for a Jewish national movement—one that believed the only truly safe haven for Jews would come through Jewish self-determination. Thus arose the political movement to establish Jewish sovereignty in the ancestral homeland, a movement we know today as Zionism. ■

*Adapted from Cary Nelson, Rachel S. Harris, and Kenneth W. Stein, "The History of Israel."*

Also see THE "JEWISH CONSPIRACY," ZIONISM: ITS EARLY HISTORY, and ZIONISM AS PHILOSOPHY AND PRACTICE.

# JIHAD

*ihad* is an Arabic word whose meanings are contested. A neutral translation might be "struggle," but that does not capture the many uses of the term over the centuries. The concept of Jihad points to the duty Muslims have to sustain their religion and strive to honor God's purposes on earth. It thus can refer both to internal efforts to be a good Muslim and to external efforts to defend the faith and resist its enemies real and imagined. As an obligation imposed on believers, it has often had a military component. Jihad has often been translated as "Holy War," and it is that meaning that has helped inform terrorism and religious war in our own day. Although a substantial number of Muslims embrace fundamentalist Islam, only a small percentage embrace Jihadist violence, but that percentage nonetheless represents a significant threat. Islamist terrorists like those organized in Palestinian Islamic Jihad, founded in 1981, or ISIS, the Islamic State of Iraq and Syria that declared a worldwide caliphate in 2014, draw selectively on primary Islamic sources to justify acts of extraordinary barbarism and see themselves as engaged in a clash of civilizations with the West. Some on the international left are unwilling to criticize such movements or accept the movements' self-definition for fear that such criticism amounts to Islamophobia. But beheading captured troops and civilians, throwing homosexuals off rooftops, and institutionalizing female slavery cannot count as culturally relative practices beyond criticism. As Salman Rushdie has put it about Islamophobia most bluntly, "A new word had been created to help the / blind remain blind." As Pascal Bruckner challenges us, "In a democracy, one has a right to reject all religious denominations, to regard them as fallacious, backward, or stultifying . . . Why does one and only one religion escape the climate of raillery and irony that is normal for the others" (10-

11)? It is a question still more powerfully relevant after the *Charlie Hebdo* and Hypercacher kosher supermarket massacres in Paris on January 7 and 9, 2015.

—CN

## RICHARD LANDES

The "global, progressive, left" has gradually adopted a secular version of the Jihadi apocalyptic scapegoating narrative in which Israel and the US are the "great and little Satan" (or vice-versa). This overlap between two ostensibly completely different value systems has served as the basis for mobilizing a common struggle against the US and Israel over the last decade or so. In so doing, the left has ironically welcomed, within its "anti-imperialist" mobilization, one of the most ferociously imperialist movements in the long and dark history of mankind, a trend that has culminated in ISIS and its Caliphate. The Jihadist movement opposes not merely Israeli and American "imperialism," but also targets the very culture of progressive values—human rights, peace, tolerance for diversity, human freedom. BDS is a symptom of the self-destructive disorientation wherein progressives who sympathize with, join forces with, or refuse to criticize Jihadis have effectively embraced their own worst enemies.

This apocalyptic narrative is a cosmic/global story, or scenario, about how, at some point in the future, the forces of good and evil will enter into a final stage of conflict and the good will emerge on the other side to live and share in a just, abundant, peaceful society, while the bad are cast out. The most destructive form of apocalyptic narrative sees a massive battle between the forces of good (us) and evil (them). In the Book of Revelation, for example, the battlefield is littered with the corpses of the slain, upon which the birds of carrion feast– from kings to slaves. In passive apocalyptic scenarios (e.g. Revelation) divine forces carry out the destruction, not humans; in active scenarios, the believers themselves become the divinely appointed agents of that cataclysmic violence. In these latter "active" scenarios, the "them"– the apocalyptic enemy—embody evil; and their elimination brings redemption. Historically, when movements with such violent apocalyptic scenarios gain power, they have proven capable of wholesale massacre and genocide. In the worst cases (five in the last two centuries), this has produced mega-death in the tens of millions of human lives. My analysis of the apocalyptic dimension of Islam draws on books by Timothy Furnish, Laurent Murawiec, David Cook, and Jean Pierre Filiu, as well as my own *Heaven on Earth*.

Despite the spectacular attacks on the West, most Westerners have little familiarity with the *Jihadi* narrative that animates the movement across a broad range of groups, a narrative that made its first "real-world" appearance in Khomeini's Iran. It varies significantly in some ways from traditional Muslim apocalyptic thought, which focused on a Last Judgment at the *end* of the world. Instead, this apocalyptic scenario focuses on a *this*-worldly *millennium* (messianic era) envisioned as the global victory of Islam. Those who join this movement fight in an apocalyptic battle in which the Jews will be slaughtered and other non-Muslims would be subjected, either by conversion or by accepting the *dhimmi* (*"protected infidel"*) contract of submission: a "Second Global Islamic Kingdom," to cite the words of Bassem Jarrar, a Palestinian apocalyptic writer immensely popular with Hamas. Globally, in the battle, no mercy should be shown to those who resist Islam's dominion. Everything to kill and die for: suicide martyrs go straight to heaven; their victims, straight to hell.

Muslim apocalyptic believers hold that virtually all traditional great and small "signs of the end" have been fulfilled in our day with the advent of modernity. The power of the godless West has grown so great that it threatens Islam with annihilation. With its progressive values of tolerance and equality for all, including women, the West incarnates the rebellion against Allah's will, the triumph of diabolic forces, including women misbehaving. And is not that one of the most fatally poisoned "gifts" of a gender-transgressing modernity?

But behind the scenes of this global battle with a modernity that aggressively presses for a civil, tolerant, global community of universal "human rights" lies a second more important battle. The US and the rest of Crusader Christianity (i.e. the European West) are mere pawns in a cosmic drama where the Jews have duped and manipulated them. They now serve the Jewish conspiracy to degrade and enslave all of humankind. First the Jews got the Christians to take the tendered bait (democracy), and now they bow to every Jewish whim. And now these Jews, with their duped Crusader Christians, want similarly to degrade Islam: "the Zionist world government, which governs the entire world . . . the Zionist American government . . . the United Nations and the Security Council . . . the Zionist world government, which are managed from behind the curtain by the Antichrist and Satan, just as the book of Revelation points out" (H. Abd al-Hamid, 1996; Cook 199-200), a narrative constructed despite the fact that the Book of Revelation never mentions the "Antichrist."

While this "apocalyptic enemy" working to destroy Islam takes many forms, from military invaders to the NGOs spreading the gospel of "human rights" and "women's equality," none of the enemies loom so central to contemporary Muslim apocalyptic imagination as the Jews. Israel constitutes the most unbearable of the mortal insults to Islam of the modern world. It is an unbearable blasphemy—an independent *dhimmi* state in *Dar al Islam* (the land/realm of submission to Allah, where Muslims rule), a beachhead of Western decadence (including women's liberation), an infuriatingly small group of (historically cowardly; i.e., unarmed) Jews who hold their own in wildly asymmetrical fight with Arab might and honor, the headquarters of the conspiracy to exterminate Islam. But Israel itself is only the visible tip of a vast Jewish conspiracy to enslave mankind, which has already subjected and degraded the Christian World:

> Thus the Jewish slap on the faces of the Christians continues, who apparently enjoy and allow this sort of humiliation and attack, and give them their other cheek so that the Jew can continue to slap the Christians— just as we see—ruling them in Europe through the Masons who dig the grave of Western civilization through corruption and promiscuity. The Crusader West continues like a whore who is screwed sadistically, and does not derive any pleasure from the act until after she is struck and humiliated, even by her pimps—the Jews in Christian Europe. Soon they will be under the rubble as a result of the Jewish conspiracy. (Muhammad Izat Arif, Nihayat al-Yahud, cited in Cook 220)

Having accomplished that, the Jewish conspiracy now manipulates Christians into inflicting the same subjection on the Muslim world. Israel is the "Little Satan."

Traditional Muslim apocalyptic writing has few references to the Jews since, for most of Islam's fourteen-century-long existence, the Christians represented the military foe. With the advent of Israel, however, everything changed: for Muslims the world over, and especially for Arab Muslims neighboring her, Israel posed the most terrifying threat. The embodiment of a modernity that has repeatedly eluded the other countries in the Middle East, tiny Israel has managed to win war after war with a vastly more powerful enemy. The humiliation, on a global scale, embodies the catastrophe (*Nakba*) of history gone wrong.

Muslim apocalyptic literature responded with a previously rarely invoked hadith that declared that the Day of Judgment (i.e. the Day of Vindication for the true followers of Muhammad and Allah) will not come until Muslims kill every last Jew: "The day will not come until the Muslims fight the Jews, and the Jews will hide behind rocks and trees, and the trees and the rocks will say, "*O Muslim, O servant of Allah, there is a Jew behind me, come and kill him.*"

Hadith are the collections of sayings attributed to Muhammad; they are the major source of Islamic guidance apart from the Koran itself. Hamas cites this hadith as a call to action in its charter (¶7); and its theologians developed the justification for "Shahid operations," or martyrdom, even though Sharia forbids suicide, as a sacred duty in the apocalyptic battle (Oliver and Steinberg). Recently a Hamas official expressed his dual preference for the fate of the Jews: dead in Palestine, dhimmi elsewhere:

> We must massacre [the Jews]... to prevent them from sowing corruption in the world . . . We must restore them to the state of humiliation imposed upon them . . They must pay the jizya security tax while they live in our midst . . . However, in Palestine, where they are occupiers and invaders, they cannot have the status of dhimmis. (Hamas MP Sheik Yunis Al-Astal, March 6, 2014, on the Hamas-owned Al-Aqsa TV, broadcasting from Gaza, MEMRI translation; http://www.memri.org/clip_transcript/en/4202.htm.)

In short, Jihad views its path to global domination via genocide against the Jews in Israel.

Nor will Allah abandon his faithful in this time of need. He only asks that those faithful take up Jihad and strive with every fiber of their being for the promised victory: the global Caliphate. Now is the time when one must fight back. Now is the time to destroy the conspiracy. Now is the time to restore Islam to its rightful place, dominating the world. Indeed, the very process of modern globalization that has so terribly humiliated Islam will become the vehicle for Islam's global domination. Not all Muslims believe this, and still fewer believe that dominion should come about through violent imposition, but it is unquestionably a belief within Islam, and lies at the heart of the current Muslim millennial dream: global Sharia. Western global hegemony is the *Praeparatio Califatae*. The day will come when Muslims will have uprooted Israel, when the green flag of Islam will fly from the White House, when the Queen of England will wear a burkah.

The current generation of apocalyptic Jihadis, a small but dangerous percentage of Muslims worldwide, agree that virtually all preliminary signs of the Last Days have been fulfilled in our day (Cook 49-58). They live in apocalyptic time; and they have identified the apocalyptic enemy against whom they fight in this final war of extermination. The overwhelming choice in the literature—to the point of monotony—is some combination of the U.S. and Israel: "the Great and Little Satan" (Cook, chaps 2, 7, & 9). And it is the sacred task of the Jihadis to destroy that enemy in order to redeem the world by the global imposition of Sharia. ▪

*Adapted from Richard Landes, "Fatal Attraction: The Shared Antichrist of the Global Progressive Left and Jihad."*

Also see HAMAS and ORIENTALISM AND THE ATTACK ON ENLIGHTENMENT VALUES.

# THE LEBANON WARS
## (1978, 1982, 2006)

Three times in recent years Israel has taken military action in Lebanon. When the Palestine Liberation Organization (PLO) was expelled from Jordan in 1970 it retreated to Southern Lebanon, established a quasi-state there, and initiated a series of cross-border attacks on Israel. Israel invaded Lebanon in response in 1978 and pushed the PLO north, but the attacks continued. As a result, Israel returned to Lebanon in 1982 and expelled the PLO. Israel then kept control of a 12-mile buffer zone, but intermittent conflict continued with a new terrorist group, Hezbollah. Israel withdrew from Lebanon in 2000, but occasional cross-border attacks once again continued. After Hezbollah captured two Israeli soldiers, Israel entered Lebanon again in 2006.

—CN

## CARY NELSON, RACHEL S. HARRIS, AND KENNETH W. STEIN

In 1978, in response to terrorist attacks, Israel first crossed the border into Southern Lebanon to drive out the Palestinians firing at Northern Israel. In March 1978, a Fatah raiding party crossed into Israel from Lebanon, killed an American tourist on the beach, and hijacked an Israeli bus on the coastal road near Haifa. Thirty-five Israelis were killed, and Israel launched a 7-day offensive in response. Though the Israelis pushed the Palestinians back from the border, Israel invaded again in 1982, after responding to requests for aid and military training from the Lebanese Christian (Catholic) Maronite Phalange Party headed by Bashir Gemayel (1947-1982). The Maronites are a Christian Catholic religious group concentrated in Lebanon and the Lebanese diaspora. Prime Minister Menachem Begin (1913-1992) was moved by the Maronite appeal, for in his mind the Lebanese civil war was a battle between Muslims and Christians. As the Israeli historian Benny Morris writes, "For millennia the Christian world had oppressed and killed the Jews. Now a Christian community was appealing to the Jews for succor— after Europe, particularly France, had turned its back. Begin was not one to resist the opportunity of showing the world how his people, in their magnanimity and humanity, would help and protect the Christians of Lebanon from Muslim 'genocide' as Europe and the United States had failed to do for the Jews" (404-5).

As Muslim Syrian forces advanced into Lebanon, Gemayel responded by sending his own fighters into Syrian dominated territory in 1981, but his militia was overextended and the Syrians launched an artillery barrage that killed hundreds of Christian civilians. In a curious alliance, the IDF had become partners with the Maronite Lebanese, if only to protect Israel's northern borders from Palestinian violence. Their air attacks on Palestinian-controlled Lebanese towns reached as far as Beirut, where they destroyed PLO buildings and killed several hundred people. Israel believed that by eliminating the PLO and restoring Christian dominance to Lebanon, they would be able to negotiate a peace treaty with the new government. Their aims tallied with Gemayel's own desires for Christian political rule, though he was not as comfortable admitting his association with Israel publicly as he had been in receiving aid. Despite a slowdown in Palestinian provocations by the end of 1981 and into the spring of 1982, Minister of Defense Ariel Sharon (1928-2014), who would serve as Prime Minister from 2001 to 2006, pressed for the 1982 invasion of Lebanon. When the Israeli ambassador to London Shlomo Argov (1929-2003) was shot in the head and badly wounded (in an attack carried out by a Palestinian splinter group and ordered by the Iraqi intelligence service), Sharon had the provocation he needed, and despite PLO condemnation of the assassination attempt (and their denials of involvement in its orchestration), Israel bombed several PLO targets in retaliation, and the Israeli cabinet agreed to a limited invasion of Lebanon. Sharon, with more expansive ideas for the campaign, manipulated and misled the cabinet to give piecemeal approval for further steps; they finally agreed to put the IDF into armed conflict with the Syrian forces in Lebanon. After a two-month siege of the city, the IDF entered West Beirut.

Ongoing skirmishes between the PLO and the IDF on the ground and the brutality of urban guerilla warfare left innocent victims in the line of fire. The local PLO militias dug in to fight, using the refugee camps as shelter. Hundreds of Palestinians were killed, and though the IDF sought not to fire on civilians, only a heavy bombing campaign forced the PLO to evacuate. Though the Lebanese Army refused to empty the refugee camps, the Phalangists agreed to take on the job. What happened next continues to be a subject of intense debate, with some scholars and writers quite convinced that Israeli forces were more fully aware than others believe. On the evening of September 16, 1982, Phalangist men moved into the Sabra and Shatilla refugee camps without Israeli intervening to stop them. Two days earlier, Gemayel, already elected president, had been assassinated; those responsible remain unknown. Eager for revenge, the Phalangists moved from house to house, killing whole families. The Phalangists were out of sight of the Israelis, who were stationed beyond the walls of the camp, and the Israelis thus did not know what was happening or intervene, ultimately failing in their responsibility to care for the residents' safety.

Yet the Israeli military leadership, under Sharon's authority, certainly had ample reason to be wary of the Phalangists' intentions. Whatever else, it was a deadly case of gross negligence on Israel's part. After the brutality of the bombings, as Israeli historian Anita Shapira writes, the massacres "sparked a conflagration among the Israeli public. The possibility that the IDF was even indirectly responsible because it stood aside and did not intervene . . . subverted the army's image as moral in the eyes of civilians and soldiers alike . . . Intellectuals, media figures, and writers felt that 'their' country was disappearing and being replaced by a country that was not theirs" (384). Israel had gone beyond gestures of self-defense to invade another country; accordingly, the government lost public support for the war. Officers signed a letter of protest that became a powerful symbol for Israel's early peace movement, and hundreds of thousands of civilians demonstrated in Tel Aviv against the Sabra and Shatilla refugee camp atrocities, demanding an Israeli commission of inquiry be formed. Begin resisted at first but was compelled to concede and finally resigned in 1983, a victim at once of public pressure and his own growing sense of personal depression. Sharon remained in the Cabinet but lost his portfolio and was effectively ousted from political life for almost two decades. For many, Lebanon was the moral nadir of Israel's wars.

Having forcibly expelled the PLO, whose leaders now fled to Tunis, Israel withdrew to a slim borderland buffer zone policed by the Southern Lebanon Army (SLA) where Israel also maintained a military presence of its own. Meanwhile, however, the PLO had been replaced by Hezbollah, an Iranian-backed Palestinian terror group that would use the next twenty years to wage guerilla warfare against the SLA and IDF. In 1996, after constant low-level conflict, Israel and Hezbollah signed a ceasefire treaty agreeing to forgo attacks on civilians. But Israeli soldiers continued to remain targets and Hezbollah adopted a policy of killing or kidnapping them and releasing them in exchange for Palestinian political prisoners held in Israel. Israel continued to fund the SLA, but in 2000 the Southern Lebanon Army collapsed under an onslaught from Hezbollah and from concern the Israelis might abandon the SLA as part of a peace agreement with Syria.

After becoming Prime Minister in 1999, Ehud Barak sought to fulfill a campaign promise to withdraw all troops in Lebanon, but a hope that this might be part of an agreement with Syria faded. Then, in elections, the political wing of Hezbollah won all the parliamentary seats allotted for Southern Lebanon. An Israeli withdrawal might have eliminated Hezbollah's legitimacy as a force opposing an occupying power, but it could also have destroyed the SLA. In 2004, the UN called for a dismantling of militia groups and a withdrawal from Lebanon by foreign powers. Syria withdrew in 2005, but Hezbollah refused to lay down its weapons and continued attacking Israeli targets. Tensions in the area led to constant accusations of terror actions by both Hezbollah and Israel, and though Israel had expressed a desire to sign peace accords with Lebanon, the possibility now seemed unlikely. When word of Barak's plans to withdraw leaked, SLA forces began to desert, leaving Israeli troops dangerously exposed in many places. On May 24, 2006, the IDF completed a withdrawal and Israel ended an eighteen-year presence in Lebanon.

Assisted by Iranian and North Korean instructors, Hezbollah thereafter began building an elaborate system of concealed bunkers connected by tunnels throughout what had been the security zone. The bunker system, which still exists today, is stocked with sufficient supplies and weapons to survive a siege. Rocket launchers were established underground and mounted on lifts that could raise them into firing position. In July 2006, Hezbollah attacked a patrol on Israel's side of the border, kidnapping and killing Israeli soldiers. Israel responded with air strikes. Hezbollah then began an aggressive campaign of rocket launches into Israel. An extensive air campaign proved effective in eliminating Hezbollah's medium- and long-range rockets, but had little effect on its 10,000 to 16,000 short-range rockets with a range of 18 to 28 km that could be fired from mobile launchers. From July 12 until August 14, when a ceasefire went into effect, over 4,000 rockets struck Israel, killing and wounding ordinary citizens and substantially disrupting daily life. Just before the UN-brokered ceasefire went into effect, Israel sent in ground troops, but the bunker system, like that used by the North Vietnamese, proved resilient. As Ahron Bregman writes, "Hezbollah had embraced a new doctrine, transforming itself from a predominantly guerilla force into a formidable quasi-conventional army . . . A semi-military organization of a few thousand people, carrying relatively primitive weapons, was able to survive against what was regarded as the strongest army in the Middle East" (292). This, the second Lebanon War, displaced a million people in Lebanon and half a million in Northern Israel. Thousands of Lebanese sought refuge in Syria. Israeli retreated south in their own country. The UN finally brokered a ceasefire and since then there have been only limited outbreaks of violence. But Hezbollah has continued its substantial buildup of offensive resources, both for use in Syria and in anticipation of another war with Israel. ■

*Adapted from Cary Nelson, Rachel S. Harris, and Kenneth W. Stein, "The History of Israel."*

---

Also see HEZBOLLAH and THE PALESTINE LIBERATION ORGANIZATION.

# THE NAKBA

## CARY NELSON

The Nakba (in Arabic "al-Nakbah," literally "disaster," "catastrophe," or "cataclysm") names the exodus of more than 700,000 Palestinians from their homes during the 1948-1949 Arab-Israeli War, much of it taking place in the spring of 1948. Initially the Palestinian elite left the new state of Israel in a considered decision to escape the conflict. That left the bulk of the local Arab population without many of its leaders. Some fled in fear; others were forced out. Neighboring Arab states encouraged men to stay and fight, but many inevitably accompanied their families as they escaped to Lebanon (104,000), Syria (82,000), the West Bank (360,000), Transjordan (100,000), and Gaza (200,000). For many Palestinians the Nakba refers not only to a specific event in time but also to a continuing process and legacy of exile:

> If I was not a Palestinian when I left Haifa as a child, I am one now. Living in Beirut as a stateless person for most of my growing up years, many of them in a refugee camp, I did not feel I was living among my "Arab brothers." I did not feel I was an Arab, a Lebanese, or as some wretchedly pious writer claimed, a "Southern Syrian." I was a Palestinian. And that meant I was an outsider, an alien, a refugee, a burden. To be that, for us, for my generation, meant to look inward, to draw closer, to be part of a minority that had its own way of doing and seeing and feeling and reacting.
>
> —Fawaz Turki (8)

The bulk of the 1948 Palestinians fled their homes, villages, and land primarily because of mortal fear created by systematic terror campaigns conducted by the Israeli state forces. Even as they took flight, however, there was never a question of return: It was always a matter of when and how, not whether they would return. As time went on and the tragedies accumulated, the mystique of "the return" became even stronger. In many a Palestinian home in the diaspora, families display olive wood carvings or framed needlework pictures with the words "*Innana raji'oun*" or "*Innana 'ai'doun*" (We shall return).

—Samih K. Farsoun (127)

It was the revisionist Israeli historian Benny Morris who first did the important archival research to show that some Arab residents of Israeli towns and cities were forced out and others fled in fear, not simply in a voluntary exodus. Morris argues that there was no centralized, coordinated plan to achieve that end; the actions that spread fear were opportunistic products of war. One such pivotal event that triggered Palestinian flight, especially from villages near Jerusalem, was the April 9, 1948, massacre at Deir Yassin, a Jerusalem area Arab village. Fighters from the paramilitary Irgun (a militant underground Zionist group founded in 1931) and the Stern Gang (a paramilitary Jewish group founded in 1940 with the aim of evicting the British) entered the village to clear it—with Haganah approval—ostensibly as part of an effort to secure the Western approaches to Jerusalem. When they encountered unexpected armed resistance, they reacted brutally, killing an estimated 107 men, women, and children, partly by blowing up their houses. Several captured men were then executed. All parties to the conflict then overstated the number of deaths—the Irgun to sow fear and demonstrate their prowess, the Arabs to rally support for the invasion. Arab propagandists fabricated and broadcast stories of widespread rape at Deir Yassin in the aftermath of the massacre. While the stories did build support for the invasion of Israel by Arab countries, the stories also drove thousands of Palestinians to flee. The furor led to an Arab massacre carried out at least in part for revenge. On April 13, 1948, hundreds of Arab militiamen attacked a largely unarmed convoy that was taking students, faculty, doctors, and nurses to the Hadassah Hospital at the Hebrew University campus. After the few defenders ran out of ammunition, the Arabs moved carefully to the line of buses, wet them with gasoline, and set them alight. All told, 78 Jews died, many burnt alive, most of them students and medical personnel. The Deir Yassin and Hadassah convoy massacres were neither the first nor the only opportunistic acts of violence against civilians carried out by either side. When Gush Etzion fell to Arab forces on

May 13, 1948, two days before Israel was declared a state, 127 Jewish soldiers and civilians who had surrendered were massacred.

More influential for the general reading public has been the Lydda chapter in Ari Shavit's 2013 *My Promised Land*. Shavit was not the first to discuss the Israeli massacre and expulsion of Lydda's Arab population, but his widely read and reviewed journalistic account reached people who had not yet confronted the fact that the 1948 war included inhumane violence by Jews as well as Arabs. In an ideal world, some Arab villages would have been recreated on the West Bank nonviolently. That would have enabled population transfers of the sort envisaged in the July 1937 Peel Commission Report, which judged that two states for two peoples was the only way to secure peace in the area, but that was not to happen in the midst of the 1948 war.

The 700,000 people who fled or were forced out had their lives completely disrupted; they lost their homes and their communities. The family, rather than the village, for a time became the only functional social unit. But they were not yet a clearly defined and politically unified Palestinian people. They were residents of a geographical area called Palestine that named the boundaries of the British Mandate. But there was no country called Palestine. The retroactive use of the term "Palestinian" modifying refugees tends to promote anachronistic confusion. In the aftermath of the war, Israel decided as policy to bulldoze and eliminate abandoned Arab villages, thereby making their reestablishment less likely.

The refugees divided into two groups. Middle-class and upper-class Arab refugees settled when possible in cities, especially Amman (Jordan), Beirut (Lebanon), Cairo (Egypt), and Damascus (Syria). Some eventually took up residence in Saudi Arabia and other oil-producing countries and became wealthy. Others left for Europe and the Americas. About a million Palestinians now live in the Western hemisphere. The mass of poor, destitute, illiterate, and thoroughly desperate refugees, many essentially peasants, ended up in refugee camps in Gaza, Lebanon, Syria, Transjordan, and the West Bank. Half a century later there were nineteen camps in the West Bank, twelve in Syria, ten in Jordan, and eight in Gaza. They began as tent cities without proper sanitation. After more than a year the United Nations Relief and Works Agency (UNRWA) stepped in to help provide food and health care. Gradually a shantytown mix of wood, tin, and corrugated iron structures replaced tents. By 1970 cinder block and concrete construction began to replace corrugated iron as the refugees acquired construction skills. The camps were evolving into congested miniature cities with their own shops and social institutions.

Had the Arab states sought to assimilate the refugees, a shared Palestinian identity might never have fully developed. But they did not. They preferred to sustain a refugee crisis so as to block normalized relations with Israel. But most Arab countries also felt politically and economically threatened by this "other" in their midst. Lebanon and Syria had complex national and religious divisions that might have been unbalanced by fully absorbing the refugees in 1948, though that concern lost validity over time and does not justify maintaining the camps for decades. Jordan alone offered citizenship but not universal voting rights. Still, Jordan felt increasingly threatened by growing Palestinian opposition and explicit challenges to the Hashemite monarchy, enough so to launch full-scale military assaults and slaughter thousands of Palestinian refugees in 1970 and 1971. "The Jordanian authorities saw virtually any independent Palestinian organization as subversive and as a threat to the unity of the kingdom, and ruthlessly combatted political activity of most kinds" (Khalidi 136). Although Fatah and the PLO had been willing to coexist with Jordan, the more radical splinter groups called for the regime's overthrow, initiated plane hijackings to Jordan, seized a Jordanian oil refinery, and mounted several unsuccessful attempts to assassinate King Hussein. They drew the PLO into their orbit and made Yasser Arafat (1929-2004) the head of a unified military command (Tessler 456-464). Jordan then moved to eliminate the Palestinian threat once and for all.

The other Arab states imposed segregation and various forms of repression on the refugees. As their identity cards confirmed, most refugees in the camps thus remained refugees; they were essentially stateless exiles. But their educational levels increased, especially in the West Bank after the 1993 Oslo Accords. The refugees were thus ripe for a political awakening. The Nakba had created "a sort of tabula rasa" (Khalidi 135) on which a Palestinian identity could be inscribed. Social segregation and second-class status, distrust of the countries in which they were living, personal aspirations that were politically linked by the rise of the PLO, all these contributed to the formation of a Palestinian national identity and a conviction that only Palestinian statehood could answer their needs. They became what Benedict Anderson calls an "imagined community" with a shared ideology and historical narrative like any other nation. And the only place that nation could be realized was historic Palestine, namely Gaza, Israel, or the West Bank.

Some supporters of Israel tend to dismiss Palestinian peoplehood because it developed two thousand years after Jewish peoplehood did, but that has only limited bearing on today's political realities. It does bear on efforts to deny the Jewish people the right to political self-determination in their ancient homeland, but it does not override the sense of specifically Palestinian identity that has been strengthened over time. As a result, the Nakba now has two linked meanings for Palestinians: it is not only the catastrophe of the exodus from Israel; it is also what many Palestinians consider to be the catastrophe of the formation of the Jewish state. Marked by speeches and rallies, and sometimes by clashes with Israeli soldiers, Nakba Day is commemorated annually on May 15, the day after the Gregorian calendar date for Israel's Independence. Some supporters of Israel dismiss Palestinians as an "invented" people, but in fact every people was invented at some point in time.

The Nakba is at the core of the Palestinian historical and political narrative. Recognition of its centrality to Palestinian identity is a prerequisite for the sense of mutual empathy that must undergird the peace process. While there are many exaggerated or unfounded claims put forward by both Israelis and Palestinians, there is a compelling element of truth in each people's historical narrative. Those core truths must be mutually accepted if peace is to be realized. People are notably not inclined to evaluate their historical tragedies comparatively. Individuals as well tend to understand their own suffering within its own terms. Thus efforts to rank tragedies in order of importance are not likely to promote understanding. Objective measures—the number of people involved, the nature of the planning and execution of a tragedy, the length of time it took to unfold, the character of the harm done—all this may suggest that the collective traumas at the core of different peoples' national narratives are not comparable, but that has little bearing on their psychological and political impact. ■

Also see FATAH, THE LEBANON WARS, THE 1948 WAR OF INDEPENDENCE, and THE PALESTINE LIBERATION ORGANIZATION.

# THE 1948 WAR OF INDEPENDENCE

The 1948 War, which immediately followed Israel's establishment and actually lasted from November 1947 to July 1949, was Israel's war of independence. Fighting against resident Palestinians and five Arab armies, Israel proved to the international community that it could defend itself and prevail. The armistice lines set at the end of the war substantially expanded Israel's boundaries beyond what were the fundamentally indefensible borders allocated to it by the United Nations in 1947 (MAPS 1 & 2).

—CN

CARY NELSON, RACHEL S. HARRIS,
AND KENNETH W. STEIN

Even before the British withdrew from Palestine on May 14, 1948, Jewish and Arab forces were at war, with the local Palestinian Arab militia supported to a degree by a military coalition of neighboring Arab states. It began with actions like Arab attacks on Jewish convoys, sometimes followed by reprisals, and gradually escalated into a five-month civil war. The main Jewish force was the Haganah, with about 45,000 men and women once large numbers of civilians were mobilized. There were also two dissident paramilitary groups, the Irgun and the Lehi, or Stern gang, totaling about 3,000 fighters, who often coordinated with the Haganah. In addition to responding to resident Arabs who took up arms and preparing for the expected invasion by Arab countries, the Israelis had to secure supply routes to thirty-three Jewish settlements the UN partition plan had left in what was to be the Arab state. There were also numerous Arab villages in what was to be Israel, but the majority of their residents fled or were forced out. Initially the Arabs appeared to be winning. The Haganah lost most of its armored vehicles and hundreds of its best-trained troops in March, but in the spring of 1948 the tide turned. With a series of disasters having taken place on the roads, the Haganah had to switch strategies to attacking Arab villages.

As war loomed in 1948, there was little confidence in the world that Israel could prevail. In February, the US State Department sought to have the US government rescind its support for partitioning Palestine into Arab and Jewish states (MAP 1). Policy Planning Staff member George Kennan (1904-2005) told Secretary of State George Marshall (1880-1959) that a Jewish state would offend Arab interests and hurt US-Arab relations. He feared that the Zionists would be overwhelmed in a war with the Arabs, forcing the Americans to send troops to defend the Jews, in turn causing the Soviets to dispatch troops to the Middle East, which would put Washington and Moscow in armed confrontation. The US tried but failed to have UN trusteeship established for Palestine's future in hopes of preventing the Jewish state from emerging. Among the groups rallying to Israel's support that year was the National Lawyers Guild, reflecting American progressive support for partition. A Guild resolution called for the US State Department to "permit American volunteers to go to the aid of those who are defending and complying with the dictates of the UN in the enforcement of the Partition Plan," and called upon the UN Security Council to "equip the Haganah," "defend the Jewish State," and "prevent Arab infiltration of men and arms into Palestine for the purpose of creating strife and the defeat of the Partition Plan."

In April 1948 the Palestine Zionist Executive, designated as the Jewish agency called for in the Palestine Mandate and which was renamed The Jewish Agency, established a People's Council to serve as an embryonic parliament and a People's Administration to function as an embryonic government, and on Friday, May 14, David Ben Gurion (1886-1973), soon to be Israel's first Prime Minister, gathered the People's Council in Tel Aviv and read the Declaration of Independence, establishing the State of Israel. The US recognized the new state that evening. One of the first acts of the new Israeli government was to revoke the immigration and land purchase restrictions imposed by the May 1939 British White Paper, which sought to limit Jewish immigration to a total of 75,000 over five years and to prohibit further Jewish land purchase.

At that point in 1948, the first phase of the war, the internal civil war between the Yishuv (the Jewish community in Palestine prior to the creation of the Jewish state) and the Palestinian Arab community, essentially ended. Israel now faced a conventional war with the surrounding Arab nations and Palestinian irregulars. While the Arab countries, with exception of Jordan, were united in their determination to push the Jews out of Palestine, they largely distrusted one another and failed to coordinate their operations fully. The one Arab nation with a clear goal was Jordan; it aimed to annex the West Bank, which was part of the British Mandate for Palestine from 1920-1948. Jordan occupied it from 1948-1967 but only Britain and Pakistan recognized the annexation. In retrospect, because the Arab states only mobilized but a portion of their immense collective resources, Israel was likely to win, but Israelis had no way to be confident of that at the time. While the Israelis were exhausted from the civil war, they were also defending their homes. Virtually the entire country was on the front lines; Tel Aviv was bombed fifteen times with several hundred casualties. The Israelis feared annihilation.

Arab armies invaded across every land border. There would follow three periods of combat, interrupted by two periods of UN-brokered truce. The Arab Legion moved from Transjordan through the West Bank into East Jerusalem, but held back from trying to push further. Its intense battles with Israel were limited to Jerusalem itself. Two columns of Egyptian troops entered the Sinai from the south. The Syrian army to the north crossed into land the UN partition plan had allotted to Israel. Iraq contributed 18,000 troops to the war, with the aim of crossing Israel's narrow waist and taking Haifa, but its forces were repulsed. The Lebanese and the Israelis clashed several times over the northern Palestinian village of al-Malkiyya, but the Lebanese army never crossed into Israel itself. Israel was most in danger during the first few weeks when it was at a disadvantage in available weapons. It had virtually no artillery or tanks, no combat aircraft, and limited ammunition. On June 11, a UN-brokered truce went into effect for a month, the same time a siege of Jerusalem was lifted; the road to the city was blocked, but it was bypassed after a dirt track through abandoned villages was discovered and proved passable at night without lights. After fighting resumed, the Israeli Defense Forces were better organized and arms from Czechoslovakia had begun to arrive. Syrian forces in the north disintegrated under fire, and the Israelis destroyed the southern arm of the Egyptian army.

Between 583,000-609,000 Palestinians left their homes (Karsh 264-267). This migration is known to Palestinians as the Nakba ("catastrophe") and forms the central narrative in the creation of Palestinian national identity.

Exactly why so many Palestinians or were forced out remains a subject of continuing debate in the scholarly literature, partly because there are competing preferences for uniform, simplified narratives both within and outside the scholarly community. In truth there seem to be multiple causes. The urban Arab elite left early on; the departure of upper-class Arabs, along with professionals and the intelligentsia, delivered an unspoken message that others should leave as well. Some villages were forced out by the Israelis, though the reasons were often but by no means always strategic. Other villages fled in fear, responding to stories of real, exaggerated, or fabricated violence. In some cases, such as in the Arab village of Deir Yassin, Israeli paramilitaries killed large numbers of civilians. In the case of Deir Yassin that occurred on April 9, several weeks before the war officially began. An Arab strategy of encouraging Palestinian women and children to leave Israel so men would be free to fight—reported by some Arab and Jewish writers but contested by others—backfired when men left with their families. In the cities, "conflicting economic interests, political differences, and social and interdenominational schisms diminished the appetite for fighting, generated successive waves of evacuees, and prevented national cooperation. There was no sense of an overarching mutual interest or shared destiny" (Karsh 240). None of this, including the refusal of the Arabs to accept the UN's partition plan (MAP 1), eliminates Israel's role in the Nakba, but it does justify arguing that the responsibility for solving the problem now is shared.

When floods of Arab refugees arrived in the Arab countries, only Jordan would offer the Palestinians citizenship, while in Gaza (held by Egypt) and Greater Syria (including modern day Lebanon) they were held in refugee camps and granted neither civil rights nor nationality. Palestinian refugees were trapped in a cycle of poverty and suffering, with little reason to imagine a viable future for themselves. Although World War II in Europe produced population transfers numbering in the millions, the Arab states uniquely refused to absorb the Palestinian refugees. Instead, a myth was promoted by the Arab governments that all the displaced and exiled Palestinians would return home once Israel was destroyed, thereby perpetuating the refugee problem and making permanent peace with Israel politically impossible. "Throughout history, problems created by similar population movements had been solved not by repatriation and the creation of large hostile and disruptive national minorities, but by resettlement in the countries chosen by the refugees in the hour of decision" (Sela 78). (About 1.5 million permanently fled the 1917 Russian Revolution or the civil war that followed it. The 1923 forcible population exchange between Greece and Turkey involved about two million people. The largest single such population movement in history was the 13.5 to 16.5 million Germans expelled or who fled from Eastern or Central Europe after World War II.)

Given that a roughly equivalent number of Jews fled or were forced out of Arab countries in 1948 and following years, gave up all their property, and came to Israel, the Israeli government argued that a population transfer had taken place. The US had recognized Israel on May 14, and by the summer of 1948, a sometimes reluctant US State Department had come to accept Israel as a reality. Yet the celebration in Israel was short lived as riots broke out in many Arab capitals against Jewish citizens who had lived there for centuries. Between 1948 and 1951, Israel accepted 700,000 new immigrants, doubling the Jewish population. The Jewish exodus from Arab countries varied from country to country and in its timing. Some 90% of the Jews left Libya, Yemen, and Iraq, though Iraq initially forbade emigration realizing it would increase Israel's Jewish population. That was despite 1941 anti-Semitic Baghdad riots that left 180 Jews dead. Prior to the UN vote establishing the Jewish state, both Iraq's prime minister and its foreign minister warned of violent consequences for Jews in Arab countries. When Iraq briefly lifted the travel ban in March 1950, some 120,000 Jews left within months. The Exodus from Egypt did not peak until the 1956 Suez crisis. After a series of pogroms in Libya, 30,000 Jews left beginning in 1948. About 5,000 Jews left Syria for Israel in 1949; thereafter restrictions on emigration meant others had to be smuggled out.

Two thousand Israeli Arabs and 3,700 foreign Arab troops died in battle; perhaps twice that many Arab civilians died or went missing, though exact numbers are uncertain. The war cost 6,000 Jewish lives, 1 percent of the Jewish population in Palestine, and many more were injured. But Jews had held onto enough land to establish a state, viewing this War of Independence as a battle for survival. Under the partition plan, the Jews were to receive 14,900 square kilometers, the Arabs 11,700 (MAP 1). As a result of the war, Israel's territory grew by 37 percent, to 20,770 square kilometers (MAP 2). Egypt and Jordan occupied Gaza and the West Bank respectively, a total of 5,500 sq. km., until the 1967 war. The war also heightened inter-Arab divisions and produced internal upheavals in Arab countries. The comprehensive failure of the Arab armies, in company with earlier predictions of victory, triggered ultra-nationalist sentiment in several Arab states.

The character of postwar settlements suggests that the Arab countries overall viewed Palestine either as a possible extension of a pan-Arab nation that included Syria and Jordan, or as an opportunity to add to their own sovereign territory. Nothing suggests they aimed to create an independent Arab nation for Palestinians. In time, however, the Arab states would adopt the Palestinian cause because they realized it would help them to secure both domestic and regional legitimacy. In the final resolution to the war, Israel set up an independent state, while Egypt, Jordan, and Syria annexed different portions of Palestine. The Arab armies had acted separately, and in 1949 the UN armistice agreements were negotiated separately as well, primarily by the US-provided mediator, Ralph Bunche (1903-1971). Egypt signed first, followed by Jordan. The agreements created new boundaries that came several decades later to be known as the Green Line, but they amounted to armistice lines (MAP 2), rather than recognized borders. The state of war between the Arab states and Israel continued, with Arab attacks on Jewish citizens persisting after the war was over.

After the war, the Israeli government slowly expropriated much of the land in Israel previously owned by Arabs who had fled or been expelled, often to help settle new immigrants. To decrease the feasibility of a large-scale Palestinian return, they also bulldozed abandoned villages and gave Jewish immigrants access to abandoned Arab homes in city neighborhoods. Those Arabs who remained within the newly formed state of Israel were held under martial law, and were often viewed as a fifth column by successive Israeli governments, but in 1966 they were granted full citizenship, receiving equal treatment under the law. Many have acquired college degrees and become accomplished professionals.

Overall, "the experience of the war stamped a sense of unity and common destiny on the psychic fibre of the Israelis, who had emerged from it with a new national consciousness, a unity of purpose overriding party conflict and internal feuds" (Bregman 37). But the war also left Israel and the rest of the area with the new, unresolved burden of Palestinian refugees that continues to haunt us today. ▪

*Adapted from Cary Nelson, Rachel S. Harris, and Kenneth W. Stein, "The History of Israel," with new material added.*

Also see JEWISH HISTORY BEFORE ZIONISM, THE NAKBA, WORLD WAR II AND THE FOUNDING OF ISRAEL, and ZIONISM: ITS EARLY HISTORY.

# THE ONE-STATE SOLUTION

CARY NELSON

What Muslim Arab society in the modern age has treated Christians, Jews, pagans, Buddhists, and Hindus with tolerance and as equals? Why should anyone believe that Palestinian Muslim Arabs would behave any differently . . . ?

—Morris, *One State, Two States* 168-69

So if it is so difficult to arrive at a solution of end of conflict, why not have one state? Because the one-state cure is the proverbial cure that kills the patient. I cannot think of any place on earth where two nations locked in conflict for over 100 years are offered a solution to be thrust together in a boiling pot of coexistence that would end no doubt in mutual destruction . . . . Mostly I would say the reason why this is a bad idea is because most Jews in Israel and most Palestinians in the West Bank and Gaza don't want it. There are people in the Diaspora who may wish for such a solution, but they won't face the music and probably couldn't care less about it . . . . We, the Israelis, have to come to terms with the fact that we may have to withdraw for less than peace, that land for peace may be desirable, but not necessarily fully attainable. Why should we withdraw in the absence of full peace? If we don't, we are allowing those who resist the idea of peace with Israel, like Hamas and company, to dictate to Israel what kind of country we will live in in 10, 20, or 30 years' time.

—Susser, "The Two-State Solution"

There are several constituencies behind advocacy for a one-state "solution." BDS's most prominent spokespersons consider Israel to be an illegitimate country that should be dissolved, a position that some Palestinians both allied and not allied with BDS endorse. It would be replaced by a Palestinian majority nation stretching from the Jordan River to the Mediterranean Sea. That majority would be assured by inviting the five million or more descendants of the 700,000 Arabs who fled or were forced out of the new state of Israel in 1948 to return. Some believe Jews would largely leave Israel as a consequence. Others insist Jews could then live peacefully in a Palestinian state, a state that would either be a Muslim theocracy or at least a state with a Muslim majority. Little in history suggests that is a result in which most Israelis should or would place much confidence. Indeed the troubling results of the Arab Spring confirm Benny Morris' tough judgment that "the Palestinian Arabs, like the world's other Muslim Arab communities, are deeply religious and have no ... tradition of democratic governance" (170). That doesn't mean Arab countries cannot develop democratic institutions over time, but it does mean that a minority Israeli population will have reason to fear that neither their rights nor their physical security would be guaranteed in the critical first years of a Palestinian majority state's existence.

But perhaps civil war or pogroms would not unfold immediately. Perhaps two roughly equal populations of Jewish and Palestinian populations could try to coexist. But could their long-standing desire for ethnically based national sovereignty be set aside? Could their religious differences be minimized or adjudicated? Would Temple Mount hysteria and hostility suddenly disappear? As Gershom Gorenberg has written,

> two nationalities who have desperately sought a political frame for cultural and social independence would wrestle over control of language, art, street names, and schools. Psychologically, it would be a country with two resentful minorities and no majority. Even in the best case, the outcome would be the continued existence of separate Jewish and Political parties ... Israel would become a second Belgium, perpetually incapable of forming a stable government. In the more likely case, the political tensions would ignite as violence ... The transition to a single state would mark a new stage in the conflict ... A single state would not be a solution—or even a workable arrangement, which is what politics ordinarily offers in place of solutions. It would be a nightmare (*The Unmaking* 225).

Which leads us to the question of motivation. Some on both sides of the conflict are convinced the expansion of West Bank settlements and the increase in the Jewish settler population mean either that Israel is drifting inexorably toward a one-state solution or that the window of opportunity in which to create two separate states has closed. Oddly enough, both the far right in Israel and rejectionist Palestinians think that this trend will hand them victory. The Israeli far right apparently deludes itself into thinking the status quo can be sustained, with West Bank Palestinians tolerating second-class status indefinitely. Some Palestinians who reject a negotiated two-state solution suppose international pressure and West Bank protest will eventually give them most of what they want. Both in the US and Israel the stalemate has produced yet another one-state constituency, one based on political and cultural naiveté. Its underlying ethos is a version of liberal humanism: surely Israelis and Palestinians can just get along. Others believe a divorce is the only route to realistic coexistence. Others still endorse a one-state solution out of frustration with the failure of negotiations. But there are also darker motivations behind some one-state advocacy. Alan Johnson finds them in what he calls "The Vindictive One-State Movement."

## ALAN JOHNSON

The vindictive version of the one-state movement is primarily interested in ending Israel, rather than creating a Palestinian state. It effectively denies the right to national self-determination to **both** fiercely nationalist peoples.

Vindictive one-statism seeks to end Israel by rewinding the film of history and undoing 1948. "Nationhood is not a right ... self-determination is a myth" says Jacqueline Rose (44). Omar Barghouti, a founder of the BDS movement, rejects *any* expression of Jewish self-determination because "by definition it infringes the inalienable rights of the indigenous Palestinian to part of their homeland" ("A Secular" 198). The leading one-stater, Ali Abunimah of *Electronic Intifada*, writes that "self-determination ... cannot apply to Israelis as a separate group due to the settler colonial nature of Zionism." Gabriel Piterburg, notes Zeev Sternhell, "holds that Israel can only obliterate the original sin of its birth by disappearing" ("In Defense"). More: the idea of conquest lies just beneath the surface of vindictive one-statism. Coercion is necessary, implies Yehudah Shenhav, because Israel is an example of what Herbert Marcuse called a one-dimensional society, that is, a "pseudo-democracy" in which all critical thought has been "paralyzed" (Shenhav 9). Saree Makdisi, an English professor at UCLA, is blunter still. "No privileged group in the history of the world has ever voluntarily announced its privileges," he says, so "the Israelis will never relinquish their privileges until they are *compelled* preferably by non-violent means . . . to accept the parameters of a single democratic state" (96–97).

The program of vindictive one-statism also pushes the anti-Zionists into trying to play the role of the conscience of the Palestinian national movement, policing it from the left, attacking Mahmoud Abbas (1935–) as a "sell-out" and prettifying Hamas as "the resistance." It all makes for a ludicrous spectacle. Judith Butler, an apologist for Hamas and Hezbollah as "part of the global left," wags her tenured Berkeley finger at the Palestinian president Mahmoud Abbas, rallies opposition to the two-state solution he seeks to negotiate, and charges him with "abandon[ing] the right of return for diasporic Palestinians" ("The End of Oslo"). The *London Review of Books* routinely denounced the two-stater Salam Fayyad, when he was prime minister of the Palestinian Authority, as a collaborator. "Fayyad's critics," wrote Adam Shatz, "call him a 'good manager of the occupation,' a 'builder of apartheid roads,' 'the sugar daddy who got us hooked on aid,' and it's all true." Ilan Pappé simply defines the entire Palestinian Authority as a bunch of hopeless "collaborators." The US-born Palestinian academic Saree Makdisi expressed his disdain for "those Palestinians who cling to what is manifestly an outmoded form of political thought . . . centered on the nation-state" (90). Tikvah Honig-Parnass spits at the "collaborative" PA as a "police force to keep Palestinians under control" (211, 77). Noam Chomsky spits at the PA as "nothing but a quisling regime" (9). Makdisi spits at the PA because "its main function is to facilitate the ongoing occupation and colonization of the West Bank" (93). Pappé spits at the Oslo traitors . . . *of Fatah*, because they have embraced "a concept of peace that altogether buried 1948 and its victims" (Chomsky and Pappé 72). Shenhav is just glad Israel does *not* have a partner for peace, because the two state solution is "immoral" (34, 38). And so on.

The anti-Zionist one-state movement, in short, encourages Palestinian rejectionism and maximalism, echoes the obstructionism of Hamas, stokes the fantasy of a full untrammelled right of return for every last Palestinian refugee, and can find no place in its heart for the right of the Jewish people to national self-determination. ▪

*Adapted from Alan Johnson, "Intellectual Incitement: The Anti-Zionist Ideology and the Anti-Zionist Subject," with introductory material added.*

Also see HAMAS, THE TWO-STATE SOLUTION, THE ISRAELI RIGHT AND RELIGIOUS SETTLER POLITICS, TEMPLE MOUNT / HARAM AL-SHARIF, and THE WEST BANK.

# ORIENTALISM &
# THE ATTACK ON
# ENLIGHTENMENT VALUES

CARY NELSON

The most neutral definition of orientalism is as a field of study and subject of artistic representation focused on the countries, cultures, and history of Asia and the Middle East. For some, though not all, that field has always had an exoticist component, in which the Orient became the West's "other." It served to mark a fundamental and collective difference with the West, a complex of traditions and values that symbolized not only itself but also what was different and special about the West. It was Edward Said (1935-2003), a Palestinian born in Egypt who became a major literary theorist and public intellectual in the US, more than anyone else who emphasized the misrepresentation and self-aggrandizement in Orientalism, elevating this self-defining perspective to the status of a colonialist and deeply racist cultural bias and, indeed, arguing that the Orient as a whole in the West is a fictional social construct. As Said's followers would argue, the Orient became not only exotic, but also too often inferior, uncivilized, and dangerous. As an "other" constructed by Western fantasy, they argued, the Orient was inaccessible to Western understanding. In the end, Said's valid insight became a form of political correctness, as even serious Western scholars were deemed incapable of saying anything true or accurate about the Orient's history or its widely varied cultures. In the contemporary world this sometimes means we are told we must treat all national practices within the Orient as relative, resisting making any moral or political judgments about them. The most pathological example is the reluctance among some to judge Islamic Jihad or ISIS by Western standards and condemn them:

> In accounting for the prominence of the left (liberals and radicals alike) in the articulation of the new anti-Semitism, there are additional causes at work. First, in the last half-century, the left has regularly championed the cause of Third World, non-Western peoples. It has viewed them as victims of Western oppression (imperialism, colonialism, capitalism, globalization, racism, orientalism, etc.) and their use of violence as morally justified. At the same time, it has turned a blind eye to the tyranny, corruption, and mass murder that have flourished in so many postcolonial Third World states. The left enthusiastically mobilizes to denounce Israel, but not the gangster-like rule of Robert Mugabe in Zimbabwe, or the slave trade carried on by Muslims in the Sudan. Most importantly, the left has romanticized postcolonial peoples and their struggles, making them the bearers of progressive values and representatives of moral authority, regardless of whether there is any factual basis for this . . . It is a species of orientalism—that is, of the Western world's discursive use of non-Western peoples for its own ends . . . the Palestinians play the same role in the imagination of the European left that other progressive, freedom-loving peoples, including the Cubans, the Vietnamese, the Nicaraguans, and the Chinese, played earlier.

> —Todd M. Endelman (75-76)

Of course the progressive values the Enlightenment promoted were accompanied in the 18th century by genocidal wars against native peoples in the Americas and the enslavement of millions of Africans. European colonialism flourished in the 19th century and beyond, underwritten by a conviction that non-Europeans would benefit from their subjection. Then with the Holocaust a supposedly enlightened Europe descended into collective madness and barbarism. Though the effort to promote the best enlightenment ideals needs to confront the West's willingness to betray them, there is little hope for us if we abandon advocacy of our better impulses and traditions as a result.

## SABAH A. SALIH

Western culture has frequently been in the healthy habit of looking at itself. One could argue that the whole Modernism project was just that: a prolonged and rigorous effort to subject the culture's values and practices to debate. Indeed, the best criticism of Western culture is made, not by its detractors, most notably Islamism, but by Western culture itself. Yet the achievements of the Enlightenment are now routinely the subject of ridicule and attack in academic and journalistic circles. Even the claim that "science and reason are somehow superior to magic and witchcraft," writes education historian Diane Ravitch, is now considered by many to be simply "the product of Euro American ethnocentrism," whose aim has always been "to establish the dominance of European forms of knowledge" over non-Europeans. This revolutionary project that liberated humanity from the monarch and the feudal lord, from the tyranny of unverifiable claims, from fear of the unknown, and gave ordinary people a sense of dignity and revitalized society with such things as representative government, sexual freedom, gender equality, and the spread of scientific knowledge: this project is now generally derided in Christopher Hitchens' memorable words as "white" and "oppressive." Some would now go further, arguing that the Enlightenment was a curse; rather than setting us free, it enslaved us.

Reason and its accomplishments were now the problem. Where once culture was understood as an affirmation of universal values, and in Steven Pinker's apt phrase "a tool for living," it has now become an affirmation of tribal loyalties, more grandly called identity politics. Historian Niall Ferguson has shown that the reason why the Western way of life has become "a kind of template for the way the rest of the world . . . [aspires] to organize itself" is because for the last 500 years or so most major developments in science, politics, architecture, social life, and economy have come from the West, and that this domination has been accomplished "more by the word than by the sword." But the view some progressive faculty and university departments promote these days is very different. Ignoring the fact that cultures when in contact shamelessly borrow from one another and that some cultures in Pinker's words "can accomplish things that all people want (like health and comfort) better than others," our academic fundamentalists never seem to get tired of bashing Western culture. It is this dim-witted way of thinking that has been a major factor in helping BDS flourish in the West.

Probably no book has probably been more instrumental in popularizing this form of fundamentalism than Edward Said's 1978 book *Orientalism*. In class discussions and conference papers Said's book had the final say; its style of thinking was not to be questioned. Everyone seemed to proceed according the book's blueprint: it was nearly mandatory for certain things to be said; it was also nearly mandatory for certain other things not to be said. The book had arrived at the right time . . . in 1978 American intellectual life had all but lost faith in America . . . knowledge was to be suspected, since its arrangements and accumulations were supposed to be mostly the result of Western exploitation and domination. It wasn't just America that was the problem; it was the whole Western experiment in civilization. Because of its cultural and strategic ties to the West, Israel too came in for the same criticism.

Said described orientalism as "a Western style for dominating, restructuring, and having authority over the Orient." The book's purpose was "to show that European culture gained in strength and identity by setting itself off against the Orient as a sort of surrogate and even underground self." Arab states could now describe all criticism of their actions as a new form of colonial intervention.

Said's Orientalism and Western culture's war against itself shielded Arab tyrannies from criticism, but the book and the war also paved the way for something else: the intellectual colonization of the West by anti-Enlightenment values. That in turn boosted the fortunes of BDS. Terrible things would be said about Israel, but Islamism, much to its delight and disbelief, would be immune from scrutiny. It would be welcomed and championed as the voice of the oppressed and those opposing it—including non-Islamist Muslims—would be attacked as supporters of imperialism and racism. That Islamism did not believe in thinking for oneself, that Islamism was sexist through and through, that its agenda was totalitarian, that it was the sworn enemy of the life of the mind—none of that mattered. ■

*Adapted from Sabah A. Salih, "Islamism, BDS, and the West"*

Also see BDS AND THE AMERICAN ANTHROPOLOGICAL ASSOCIATION, BDS AND THE AMERICAN STUDIES ASSOCIATION, JIHAD, and THE SOCIAL JUSTICE MANDATE IN HIGHER EDUCATION.

# THE OSLO ACCORDS

CARY NELSON

The Oslo Accords refer to a series of agreements jointly signed by the Israeli government and the Palestine Liberation Organization (PLO). The first formal document, the Oslo I Accord—or more properly the Declaration of Principles on Interim Self-Government—was signed in Washington, DC, on September 13,1993. The Oslo II Accord, or the Interim Agreement on the West Bank and the Gaza Strip, was first signed in Taba, a town on Egypt's border with Israel, on September 24, 1995, and then formally adopted at a White House ceremony four days later.

The negotiations leading to Oslo I were conducted in secret in Oslo, Norway, with the document itself signed at a public ceremony in Washington. The agreement created the Palestinian National Authority (PA) and gave it responsibility for governing areas now under its control. The West Bank and Gaza were treated as one territorial unit. The signing was made possible by Letters of Mutual Recognition agreed to in Oslo. In those letters the PLO acknowledged Israel's existence and agreed to reject violence. Israel in turn recognized the PLO as the Palestinian peoples' representative and Israel's formal negotiating partner. This was the first formal mutual recognition between Israel and the PLO.

A number of factors made this breakthrough possible. The Intifada that began in 1987 highlighted the intolerable living conditions Palestinians faced under the military occupation. That put the PLO under pressure to find a way to break the political impasse that sustained the occupation and in turn brought to an end a nearly fifteen-year struggle within the PLO over what its goals and strategies should be. "The PLO was in need of a breakthrough in order to rebut the charge that its political strategy was bankrupt and that advocates of armed struggle thus had a better chance of securing Palestinian rights" (Tessler 759). The result was the November 1988 decision to accept UN General Assembly Resolution 181 that called for a two-state solution (Golan 118). The PLO had also lost much of its Arab financial backing when it supported Saddam Hussein (1937-2006) in the 1990 war over Iraq's invasion of Kuwait. Meanwhile the PLO's 1988 decision strengthened the peace movement in Israel and encouraged some Labor party constituencies to accept negotiations with the organization. Labor came to power with Yitzhak Rabin (1922-1995) as prime minister in 1992. But overall the experience of the Intifada motivated the Israeli public to consider negotiations worth the risk. It was clear the status quo could not be sustained; the Palestinians would simply no longer accept it. A successful result of negotiations could strengthen Yasser Arafat's hand in dealing with Hamas, which was founded in 1988.

Oslo I included plans for Israel to withdraw from portions of Gaza and the West Bank, including the city of Jericho (located near the Jordan River), actions that were initiated after the Gaza–Jericho Agreement or Cairo Agreement, was signed on May 4, 1994. The Palestinians would establish a police force to handle internal security, while the Israelis would be responsible to provide for external security, though the question of what constituted external security would become a source of considerable tension. The Palestinians would also be responsible for education and culture, health, social welfare, direct taxation, and tourism, responsibilities that, along with the police force, would enable them to begin building the institutions necessary for self-governance.

Oslo II took the process further by creating Areas A, B, and C on the West Bank, and providing for Israeli withdrawal from the rest of the West Bank Palestinian cities. The PA was to have complete authority only over Area A, while Israel and the PA would share responsibility for Area B, and Israel would retain full control over Area C. Areas A and B combined represented but 27 percent of the West Bank and were divided into over 200 noncontiguous zones, some as small as a few square kilometers. Area C would end up encompassing the expanded system of Israeli settlements, a development the international community did not foresee.

While settlement expansion did not technically violate the Accords, Palestinians reasonably saw it as undermining the likelihood of their ever having a state of their own. Clearly the effort to encircle Jerusalem with Jewish housing was designed to make division of the city difficult at best. Neither of the Accords made a commitment to establishing a full-fledged Palestinian state, but they envisioned a 5-year negotiation process that would settle all outstanding issues, including the status of Jerusalem. For the Palestinians, that meant a state. Rabin, however, perhaps seeking to assuage Israeli fears, insisted the goal was "an entity which is not a state," which would nonetheless provide for Palestinian self-rule. A different way of approaching the issue is to define the limitations a Palestinian state might have in the context, such as the absence of offensive military weapons (see the entry on Coordinated Unilateral Withdrawal). Seeking a more affirmative term for that limitation in 2001, President Clinton described it as a "non-militarized," rather than a demilitarized state, suggesting a capacity that would not be implemented, rather than one stripped away.

The five-year process never fully materialized; the 1999 deadline for reaching a final status agreement came and went and those issues remain unresolved today. Given that, the Oslo process is widely regarded as a failure, but it did give Palestinians a measure of control over daily life in their cities. It also triggered the institution building that would almost certainly have to precede any workable form of sovereignty. Yet the multiple and separated segments of Area A made for a fragmented patchwork of communities with the spaces between bisected by Israeli roads and by an increasing number of Israeli settlements and illegal Israeli outposts. A system of Israeli-controlled roadblocks and checkpoints evolved that made travel between Palestinian areas still more difficult—frustrating, time-consuming, and sometimes humiliating. Some checkpoints are mostly unmanned, except in periods of crisis. While there are obvious security benefits from being able to monitor movement, as a long-term arrangement the internal West Bank checkpoints have proven to be oppressive.

All this helped trigger the Second Intifada in 2000, but in fact the Second Intifada had been preceded by numerous terrorist attacks inside Israel that followed the signing of the Declaration of Principles. The parties did a reasonably good job of honoring their commitments for over two years, but after that the process deteriorated. Actions by spoilers among both Palestinians and Israelis—including, most dramatically, the November 1995 murder of Yitzhak Rabin by an Israeli— helped undermine Oslo, but Hamas and Islamic Jihad terrorism had the stronger impact. More Israelis died in 1994, 1995, and 1996 than had been killed before the Accords were negotiated. Following the established pattern, Israel's responses to terrorism produced yet further resistance. Benjamin Netanyahu's government, meanwhile, which came into power with the 1996 elections, was explicit in opposition to Oslo. The new government demanded "reciprocity" in carrying out the Oslo obligations, and the Palestinian Authority did not begin to fulfill its obligation to suppress terrorism soon enough. "By demanding reciprocity and then claiming that Palestinians had not fulfilled their obligations, the new prime minister had a ready justification for Israel's own failure or unwillingness to implement the agreed-upon timetable" (Tessler 786).

The post-Oslo expectation of building mutual trust was thus undermined. As Galia Golan has suggested, "deeply engrained psychological factors, the sense of victimhood, and fear were still present even as support for the process was apparent" (132). Hope does not simply replace fear; trust does not extinguish skepticism. These emotions remain in contention, available to be manipulated by events. It is not easy "to overcome years of hatred and dehumanization of the enemy" (136).

In late 2002, the Road Map for Peace was promoted by the US, with a final text issued in April 2003. It envisioned creation of a Palestinian state after further negotiations. But all effort at negotiation failed. Despite repeated efforts to restart it, the Oslo process has remained fundamentally in stalemate. Had it produced further tangible results, had continued practical steps established the mutual confidence-building the Accords were designed to promote, had settlement expansion deep into the West Bank not taken place, had the Second Intifada's violence not erupted, had more widespread economic development among Palestinians occurred, had Yasser Arafat (1929-2004) not maintained monopolistic control over the economy, had Benjamin Netanyahu supported the process after he became prime minister, we might not call Oslo a failure.

Immediately upon the signing of the Accords, the Palestinian scholar Edward Said (1935-2003) published an exceptionally vitriolic piece, "The Morning After," in the *London Review of Books*. He decried "the fashion-show vulgarities of the White House ceremony," found that the agreement made too "many unilateral concessions to Israel," and deplored the fact that "the PLO has ended the intifada, which embodied not terrorism or violence but the Palestinian right to resist." The rejectionist narrative has not changed since. University of London lecturer Adam Hanieh argued twenty years later that Oslo made goals like a right of Palestinian return

> seem fanciful and unrealistic, normalizing a delusive pragmatism rather than tackling the foundational roots of Palestinian exile. Outside of Palestine, Oslo fatally undermined the widespread solidarity and sympathy with the Palestinian struggle built during the years of the first Intifada, replacing an orientation toward grassroots collective support with a faith in negotiations steered by Western governments . . . As it weakened the Palestinian movement, Oslo helped to strengthen Israel's regional position. The illusory perception that Oslo would lead

toward peace permitted Arab governments, led by Jordan and Egypt, to embrace economic and political ties with Israel under American and European auspices.

As a consequence, he argues for a one-state solution, a solution that would either eliminate the Jewish state or decisively undermine its democratic character. Although the more dystopian elements of Said's essay—"one can already see in Palestine's potential statehood the lineaments of a marriage between the chaos of Lebanon and the tyranny of Iraq"—are overwrought and his intense hostility toward Arafat and the Palestinian Authority were counter-productive, he was nonetheless on target in predicting that Oslo would not soon lead to justice on the West Bank. Oslo nonetheless provides a model for moving forward in stages, absent a final agreement along the way. ■

Also see COORDINATED UNILATERAL WITHDRAWAL, THE INTIFADAS, THE PALESTINE LIBERATION ORGANIZATION, and THE ISRAELI-PALESTINIAN PEACE PROCESS.

# THE PALESTINE LIBERATION ORGANIZATION (PLO)

CARY NELSON

T he Palestine Liberation Organization was founded at an Arab League summit meeting in Cairo in 1964 with the aim of liberating Palestine and eliminating Zionism in the Middle East through armed struggle. Although Yasser Arafat (1929-2004) did not become the organization's chairman until 1969, he shaped much of the organization's history and identity. The PLO was considered a terrorist organization by both Israel and the United States until the Madrid Conference in 1991. The Madrid Conference was an international effort to revive the Israeli–Palestinian peace process. The PLO was designed to be both a kind of government in exile and a secret military organization, functions that were inherently in conflict. Some of its terrorist activities mandated a top-down structure, while its governmental face needed at least the appearance of representative democracy. Terrorism and hierarchy won out until the organization decided to place more emphasis on a political agenda, though the representative character of its governing parliament, the 740-member Palestinian National Council, has been undermined by the failure to hold elections for a decade. The PLO also has an eighteen-member Executive Committee, a group that has also not been tested or renewed by elections, and many of its seats are unoccupied. It includes no members from Hamas. In 1993 the PLO renounced violence and terrorism, accepted Israel's right to live in peace, endorsed key UN resolutions, and gained Israel's acknowledgement as the representative of the Palestinian people. The PLO achieved observer status at the UN in 1974 and the right to non-voting participation in General Assembly debates in 1998. In 2012 it gained non-member observer state status, enabling it to join specialized UN agencies.

The PLO's 1964 Palestinian National Covenant, later more commonly called a "Charter," was unreservedly hostile to the Jewish state, describing Palestine as "an indivisible territorial unit," characterizing Israel as an "entirely illegal" entity, and demanding the ethnic cleansing of Jews from Palestine. Notably, this predated the 1967 war and the occupation of the West Bank and Gaza; the PLO objection was to Israel proper. Although Arafat periodically qualified the Charter's hostility in oral remarks and written communications, the document stood. As part of the Oslo Accords, Israel's Prime Minister Yitzhak Rabin made revising the Charter a requirement. Although the Palestinian National Council voted in 1996 to drop the offending clauses of the Charter and posted the text of the consequent amendments, a promised full revision of the Charter has never taken place. Some Palestinians have suggested the actual revision awaits the test of Israel's conduct. As recently as 2009, Fatah claimed the Charter would be unchanged. These ambiguities leave the PLO's philosophy and intentions inherently open to interpretation and dispute. Some observers vehemently claim one meaning or another, but many are left with the sense that the PLO is simply speaking contradictorily to different constituencies or that the organization can say one thing and mean another.

Within a few years of its founding the PLO focused its mission on destroying the Jewish state, using its bases in Lebanon, Syria, Gaza, and the West Bank to launch terrorist attacks. It also evolved to become partly an umbrella organization encompassing multiple factions with their own leaders and agendas. When the PLO decided to work through political pressure rather than organized violence, two of its factions—the Popular Front for the Liberation of Palestine (PFLP) and the Democratic Front for the Liberation of Palestine-Hawatmeh (DFLP-H), both with Marxist ideological loyalties—withdrew to continue their terrorist activities. Others of the PLO's followers over the years have left to join Hezbollah or Hamas to embrace continued violence.

Some of the terrorist acts committed by PLO member organizations include the 1970 Avivim school bus massacre carried out by the DFLP; the attackers killed nine children and three adults and crippled nineteen others. In 1972 Black September massacred eleven Israeli Olympic athletes and officials at Munich. In 1974 the DFLP captured a Ma'alot school bus in Israel and killed 26 students and adults and wounded over 70. In 1975 Yasser

Arafat's Fatah killed eight hostages and three soldiers at the Savoy Hotel in Tel Aviv, and in 1978 Fatah carried out the Coastal Road massacre, killing 37 and wounding 76 who were traveling on a bus Fatah hijacked.

From 1970-71 the PLO fought a civil war with Jordan. At issue was whether the PLO or Jordan's Hashemite monarchy would rule the country. Thousands of Palestinians died at the hands of the Jordanian Armed Forces, and Jordan expelled the PLO leadership, which retreated to Lebanon. Lebanon thus became the PLO's main base of operations until the Israeli invasion of 1982, when the PLO leadership was forced to flee to Tunis, Tunisia, where it remained until 1991. That put the leadership at a distance from its main constituency and at an organizing disadvantage.

The PLO has not always helped itself by its decisions. On October 7, 1985, four members of the PLO organization Palestine Liberation Front (PLF) hijacked the Italian ocean liner *Achille Lauro* when it was on its way from Egypt to Israel. They proceeded to murder Leon Klinghoffer, a 69-year old Jewish American man confined to a wheelchair and force crew members to throw him overboard. PLO Foreign Secretary Farouq Kaddumi (1931–) later crudely claimed Klinghhoffer's wife had murdered him for the insurance money, but the PLF finally admitted guilt in 1996, and the PLO reached a settlement with the family. Such actions undermined the claim that terrorists were actually "freedom fighters." In 1990, after Saddam Hussein (1937-2006) invaded, the UN's Security Council ruled Iraq's annexation of Kuwait and its oil fields "null and void" and authorized the use of force to eject the Iraqis. Although the Arab League condemned the invasion of Kuwait and approved the UN stand, the PLO supported Saddam Hussein. Kuwait castigated Arafat as a traitor and, when the war was over, expelled the remaining 200,000 Palestinians who had been living there, 200,000 having left earlier. Most held Jordanian passports and thus returned there. The Palestinian community in Kuwait had been a relatively affluent one, "a crucial pillar of the PLO's prosperity and independence" (Khalidi 147).

The first chairman of the PLO's Executive Committee, occupying the position from 1964 to 1967, was Ahmad Shukeiri (1908-1980). He was followed by Arafat, who was chair until his death in 2004. Arafat for many years played the various Arab states off against one another in an effort to undercut their competing efforts to shape the Palestinian future. In the process he managed to win international acceptance of the PLO as the sole representative of the Palestinian people, but he also centralized power in himself in a way that curtailed efforts to create the independent institutions a Palestinian state would need. "Most of the leaders of the PLO, from Arafat on down, had spent their entire careers in the atmosphere of a clandestine, underground liberation movement, and proved to be poorly suited for the task of state building, for transparent governance, or for a stable structure of governance based on law" (Khalidi 159). But the PLO under Arafat did develop state-like departments that acted like "ministries carrying out a variety of financial, educational, medical, and social tasks" (Khalidi 175). Arafat also created numerous competing security services, first in the PLO and then in the PA, a tactic that helped prevent the emergence of a coherent alternative source of power that might challenge his own authority, but the result was a liability in state-building, one his successor would work to eliminate by unifying the security force. Mahmoud Abbas (1935–), who also uses the name Abu Mazen, assumed the position in 2005. Both Arafat and Abbas served simultaneously as chairman of the PLO and president of the Palestinian Authority governing the Palestinian-controlled areas of the West Bank. Inevitably the PLO's influence began to decline once the Palestinian National Authority came into existence, though that trend has been partly minimized by Arafat and Abbas occupying both positions. ■

Also see FATAH, GAZA, HAMAS, THE NAKBA, THE PALESTINIAN AUTHORITY, THE ISRAELI-PALESTINIAN PEACE PROCESS, and THE WEST BANK.

# THE PALESTINIAN
# AUTHORITY

CARY NELSON

The Palestinian National Authority (PNA or, more commonly, simply PA) was constituted in 1994 in the wake of the 1993 Oslo Accords and tasked with governing both areas A and B of the West Bank and most of the Gaza Strip. The Accords led to a Declaration of Principles jointly agreed to by Israel and the Palestine Liberation Organization (PLO). The Accords defined Area A as a series of noncontiguous segments that include the major Palestinian West Bank urban centers. Those are classified as being under full Palestinian authority. Area B, composed of additional noncontiguous segments amounting to about 27 percent of the West Bank, includes substantial rural territory where the PA handles civil matters and Israel oversees security. Area C, which includes the Israeli settlements, is contiguous and is under full Israeli control. By the end of 1995, Israel had withdrawn from five West Bank Palestinian urban centers as agreed. The sixth was to be Hebron, but the agreement was renegotiated so the plan was not carried out as originally planned. Before long, the PA became the major employer in the territory under its authority. Aid from other countries was also transferred through the PA, which helped cement its influence. And the PA established radio, television, and newspaper outlets.

When Israel withdrew from Gaza in 2005, the whole strip came under the PA's governing authority, but after Hamas won legislative elections in

Gaza the following year, followed by a civil war in 2007, Hamas expelled the PA from Gaza and its authority was limited to the West Bank. A unity government was jointly formed by Hamas and the PA in 2014, but it disintegrated soon thereafter, and as of this writing hostility between the two groups remains intense.

The first elections to the PA presidency and the Palestine Legislative Council took place on January 20, 1996. Eighty percent of eligible Palestinian voters in Gaza and seventy percent of those on the West Bank participated. Hamas officially boycotted the proceedings but encouraged its allies to vote for independent candidates. Yasser Arafat's Fatah party candidates won more than half of the contests and independent Fatah candidates won enough of the others to give the combined forces 75 percent control. Yasser Arafat (1929-2004), the Chairman of the PLO, won the presidency of the PA and occupied the office until his death in November 2004. Mahmoud Abbas (1935-) was elected to succeed him in January, with a term expected to end in 2009, but as of spring 2016 the anticipated next elections have not been held. The supposed right of Palestinians to vote in their own elections is thus no longer credible.

The PA as a legal entity was intended to represent Palestinians living on the West Bank and Gaza, but not those living in the Palestinian diaspora. The PLO remains the internationally recognized representative of the Palestinian people worldwide. It represents them in the UN as "Palestine." As mentioned above, both Yasser Arafat and Mahmoud Abbas headed both the PA and the PLO.

Tasked with overseeing security of the major population centers under its control, the PA established the Preventive Security Force in 1994; its size grew rapidly, with duties that include counter-terrorism. Its success at handling that role did not inspire confidence. As the *Jewish Virtual Library* describes it,

> The PA's performance came under growing Israeli public criticism as a result of continued terrorist attacks on Israelis both in the occupied territories and within the Green Line [Israel's pre-1967 border—MAP 2], carried out mainly by Hamas and the Islamic Jihad. The debate in Israel about Arafat's policies turned increasingly toward the view that he had been avoiding decisive measures of repression against Islamist terrorism and its sponsors because he was not interested in putting an end to violence and in fact perceived it as a legitimate means of struggle even in the course of the Oslo process. Arafat was forced to take decisive measures against Hamas and the Islamic Jihad following the suicide bombings of February–March 1996 in Jerusalem, Tel Aviv, and Ashkelon. However, the scope of his measures then was never repeated. In fact, Arafat used

the Islamic opposition as an instrument in the face of Israeli delays and procrastination in the peace process, using rapprochement and antagonism vis-à-vis his own opposition in accordance with his needs vis-à-vis Israel. In December 1995, prior to the elections to the PLC slated for January, Arafat's delegates tacitly gave the green light to Hamas' leadership in Cairo to continue its attacks against Israel as long as it did not "embarrass" the PA, namely, did not leave signs that the action had been initiated from PA-controlled areas. Arafat's policy in this respect became a major obstacle in the peace process and a primary arguing point for all the opponents of the Oslo process in Israel . . . By 1997 internal criticism of the PA grew vehement, revolving around Arafat's authoritarian rule, the PA's centralized decision-making process, mismanagement of financial allocations, and growing manifestations of corruption, abuse of power, and human rights violations by the security agencies and senior officials of the PA. ("The Palestinian Authority")

Meanwhile the economic viability of the West Bank was damaged by the terrorist actions of radical groups opposing the PA and by the actions Israel took to manage the security situation, from curfews to checkpoints to blockades. That culminated in 2002 when Israeli forces entered Area A centers and confined Arafat to his offices in Ramallah (MAP 3). Arafat's death in 2004 and Mahmoud Abbas' new role as president made it possible to begin reconstituting the PA's security forces whose authority had been undermined in 2002. In the years since the Second Intifada, Palestinian security forces in the West Bank have cooperated with Israel to contain large-scale violence to a significant degree and track militant West Bank groups. Yet the PA has been willing to encourage protests that include potential violence, such as the protests over Israeli access to the Temple Mount in the Old City of Jerusalem. Nonetheless, Israel and the PA are now dependent on one another to maintain a fragile status quo. ■

Also see COORDINATED UNILATERAL WITHDRAWAL, GAZA, HAMAS, THE ISRAELI RIGHT AND RELIGIOUS SETTLER POLITICS, THE OSLO ACCORDS, THE PALESTIN LIBERATION ORGANIZATION, THE ISRAELI-PALESTINIAN PEACE PROCESS, THE SECURITY BARRIER, SETTLER COLONIALISM, TEMPLE MOUNT / HARAM AL-SHARIF / THE TWO-STATE SOLUTION, and THE WEST BANK.

# THE PALESTINIAN RIGHT OF RETURN

The Palestinian right of return refers to a political position that asserts that both surviving Palestinian refugees who fled or were forced out of Israel in 1948 (now fewer than 50,000 of the 700,000), along with their descendants (over 5 million) and refugees from the 1967 Six Day War have a right to return to Israel proper to live and to reclaim property lost in 1948 or 1967. Some Palestinians still have the keys to the houses they left, and the keys are a symbol of the will to return. In registering as refugees not only "persons whose normal place of residence was Palestine during the period 1 June 1946 to 15 May 1948, and who lost both home and means of livelihood as a result of the 1948 conflict," but also their millions of descendants, however, the United Nations Relief and Works Agency for Palestinian Refugees in the Near East (UNRWA) takes a unique approach not applied to other refugees. The demand for a comprehensive right of return for both refugees and their descendants has been a key area of contention in negotiations for a settlement of the Israeli–Palestinian conflict. Many both in Israel and internationally regard this as a strategy to undermine or eliminate the Jewish majority in Israel by flooding the country with Palestinians. Of course no one knows how many Palestinians would actually opt to return, though some at least are Palestinian Christians or others who do not seek Israel's dissolution. At Camp David, one Palestinian negotiator suggested that only 10-20 percent of those outside Palestine would seek to return; an Israeli pointed out that represented 400,000 to 800,000 people (Tessler 804). Israel thus cannot take the risk of agreeing to an unqualified right of return. A comprehensive, unqualified Palestinian right of return, which is what BDS advocates, is a deal breaker. Support for financial compensation for Palestinian property lost, however, is widespread, and support for a limited return of Palestinian refugees with family members who are Israeli citizens is common. It is also generally assumed that a Palestinian state would include a right of return for refugees and their descendants to the portion of the West Bank encompassed by the Palestinian state, as opposed to a right of return to Israel. The hope is that the Palestinian Authority would in the end accept such a package, along with a formal recognition of responsibility from Israel, thereby acknowledging the core of the Palestinian narrative. But so far we do not know. While it is unrealistic to expect any people to understand its history or its tragedies comparatively, it is important to remember that some 700,000 Jews also fled from or voluntarily left Arab countries from 1948-1951 and later, many impelled by threats from Arab leaders. Both those events took place in the shadow of the millions of European refugees, including those forced to relocate permanently to other countries, produced in the wake of World War II.

—CN

## EMILY BUDICK

The BDS Movement offers as one of its principles "Respecting, protecting, and promoting the rights of Palestinian refugees to return to their homes and properties as stipulated in UN Resolution 194." This is a resolution that goes back to 1948 and therefore has to do, not with boundaries post-1967, but with the more fundamental issue of whether or not a Jewish state has the right to exist.

The 1948 U.N. Resolution, which calls for "respecting, protecting, and promoting the rights of Palestinian refugees to return to their homes and properties," was passed as part of an attempt to reach a peace agreement between or among the parties—a peace agreement that was not then and still has not been achieved between Israelis and Palestinians. This is so despite the peace treaties finally reached between Israel and Jordan and between Israel and Egypt after 1967 (the post-'67 territories, we need to keep in mind, were seized from Jordan, not Palestine; the Gaza Strip, now returned by Israel to the Palestinian Authority, was taken from Egypt). One of the several planks of Resolution 194 was the right of return for Palestinian refugees, which was conditional on the Arabs'/Palestinians' agreement to live in peace with their neighbors, a commitment hardly borne out by subsequent wars and acts of aggressions against Israel, including the closing of the Suez Canal in 1956, the war of attrition in the 1960s, and the subsequent acts of hostility that resulted in the 1967 War and the Yom Kippur War. That the resolution was vetoed by all of the Arab states who were party to the conflict in 1948 suggests how citing this resolution today is a way of ignoring the historical events that culminated in 1967 and in the plight of the Palestinians from 1948 on, which was as much determined by the Palestinians' Arab allies as by their Israeli enemies. It also lays bare the real agenda behind the call for the return of Palestinian refugees to their homes and properties. The right of return is about the dissolution of the State of Israel as a homeland for the Jewish people. Establishing a Jewish homeland (alongside a Palestinian homeland) was the original intention of the Partition Plan (MAP 1), which the Jews accepted and the Arab nations, including the Palestinians, rejected, and which they still reject.

The BDS movement's call for the return of refugees, which seems on the surface little more than a defense of human rights, serves to eradicate all the history that has intervened between 1948 and now. It abolishes the rights of Jews to live in their national homeland, endorsing instead only the right for the Palestinian people to have a homeland of their own. It is also an historical misrepresentation that falsely accuses Israel's founding as a state of being in violation of international law. ▧

*Adapted from Emily Budick, "When a Boycott is Not Moral Action but Social Conformity and 'The Affectation of Love.'"*

Also see BDS: A BRIEF HISTORY, COORDINATED UNILATERAL WITHDRAWAL, THE NAKBA, and THE ISRAELI-PALESTINIAN PEACE PROCESS.

# PALESTINIAN THEOLOGY OF LIBERATION

TODD STAVRAKOS

## INTRODUCTION

Liberation Theology began as a movement among Latin Americans seeking a religious response to oppressive conditions in their communities. Theologians like Jon Sobrino, Oscar Friere, and Gustavo Gutierrez took to heart Jesus' message in Luke 4: 18, in which he quotes the Prophet Isaiah, "The Spirit of the Lord is upon me, because he has anointed me to preach good news to the poor. He has sent me to proclaim release to the captives and recovering of sight to the blind, to set at liberty those who are oppressed, to proclaim the acceptable year of the Lord." Friere points out that "God is engaged in the liberating and recreating enterprise in this world, particularly by enabling human beings to participate in the struggle for liberation from oppression" (Schipani 26-27).

In Latin America, the church was allied with the status quo; it supported undemocratic governments that served as proxies in the Cold War confrontation between the US and the USSR. The church shunned efforts to speak for the poor, frequently partnering with right wing forces to undermine movements for social change. Sobrino believed liberation theology had a mission to confront this manipulation of Christ's word (Sobrino *Jesus* 12). The Gospel of Luke, the preferred gospel of liberation theologians, offers this version of the Beatitudes: "Blessed are the poor, for theirs is the kingdom."

The church historically translated this to mean that the poor are blessed because they automatically enter into the Kingdom of God upon their death. It is the reward for their travails. Yet the poor also give the rich a way to gain the kingdom—by offering them alms, or gifts. But the poor must exist to give the rich this opportunity. Thus church policy felt justified in keeping the poor in their place.

Liberation theologians suggested that, if the poor are blessed, God must be with them now; if God is with them, then God must be working on their behalf. Thus the church must also act on the poor's behalf. The theologians came to this conclusion by considering the relationship between right words (orthodoxy) and right acts (orthopraxis) (Gutierrez). The right words should spur the right acts, and the right acts in turn should lead to the right words about faith. If the church says it is the champion of the poor, it must act accordingly— proclaiming God's liberating power and acting in solidarity with the poor against the status quo.

This dialectic between orthodoxy and orthopraxis can liberate one from limits derived from other contexts and imposed by other belief systems, thus freeing Latin Americans from European theologies (Sobrino *True Church* 10-38). The process challenges the faithful with continual self-reflection and self-correction. It also placed Liberation Theologians in conflict with the status quo to the point that placed their lives at risk. Archbishop Romero confronted the church and its allied right wing government in El Salvador and paid with his life.

# PALESTINIAN THEOLOGY OF LIBERATION

As Liberation Theology spread from Latin American to other oppressed lands it underwent local modification. In the 1990's a version called the Palestinian Theology of Liberation developed. As formulated by such theologians as Naim Ateek, Johannes Katanacho and Mitre Raheb, Palestinian Theology of Liberation is sometimes referred to as Contextual Theology, since it takes the position that context gives rise to theology.

These theologians sought a new theology to guide both Christian and non-Christian Palestinians in their quest for liberation from the occupation of the West Bank and Gaza. As in Latin America, Palestinian Theology of Liberation begins with an oppressed community and seeks to find inspiration in the Gospel. Whereas Latin American oppression came from the nation and from within the church itself, however, Palestinian Theology of Liberation credits its oppression to external forces—Israel and those Christian theologies that support the Jewish state: "the reality is one of Israeli occupation of

Palestinian territories, deprivation of our freedom and all that results from this situation" (Kairos Palestine).

As Katancho argues, "theology is context" (1), a position relevant to Latin America as well, but Palestinian Theology of Liberation embraces no corrective dialectic. There is neither mention of nor commitment to a dialectic between praxis and doxy that might elevate theology above its context. A theology that speaks only to its context also becomes trapped by it, which is the problem Palestinian Theology of Liberation faces. Christianity's fundamental power is its ability to help us transcend history and culture. Recall Jesus' exchange with Pilate: "My kingdom is not of this world." Is this not a challenge from Jesus about the limits of Pilate's Roman context? When Jesus in the Sermon on the Mount tells us not only not to commit murder but also to avoid anger, he is urging distance from our context. Jesus tells us that we can be blinded by our context, which seems to be the story of John 9, the healing of the blind man. In John 9 Jesus challenges the religious authorities of his day to open their eyes and see the work before them. But they failed to see beyond their context and so were "blind." If I were to pursue the same kind of contextual theology as Ateek, Katanacho, and Raheb, then my context—that of a relatively affluent, white, male Protestant pastor in the United States—would create its own truth. But in Christ I realize that my context, while providing a basis for my theology, can also be a prison that traps me from seeing Christ's work elsewhere in the world. Theology's challenge is to help us address our context and then to help us transcend its limits. If we do not transcend it, we are left trapped in our own creations, instead of being able to glimpse God's.

# THE REAL TRAGEDY OF A PALESTINAN THEOLOGY OF LIBERATION

Why is this dangerous? Latin American liberation theology sought to change its context from inside, from within the Church's understanding of the poor. While many in the church continue to struggle with Liberation Theology, it has left an indelible mark on Christian theology overall. Its challenge to the Western church to match actions to words has forced the church to correct past excesses. It did so through the Word of God. Palestinian Theology of Liberation, to the contrary, seeks to change the external church and our context instead of first looking at its own. In its founding statements, the Sabeel Center states that "Palestinian theologians needed to make a larger contribution to the ongoing ecumenical and inter-religious dialogue. From this perspective, which is rarely fully understood by the dominant Christian

Churches, Palestinians had to face the formidable task of formulating and disseminating their understanding of Christianity" ("What Is" 3).

Naim Ateek and the founders of the Sabeel Center have admirably undertaken to share the Palestinian context. But they do not fully represent its nature. They fail to recognize the Palestinians' role in the oppression of their own people. One strong Palestinian voice, no friend of Israel, who seems able to understand the issue is Rashid Khalidi. In *The Iron Cage* he shows that Palestinians have been ill served by their own leaders to the present day. But Palestinian Theology of Liberation does not address this reality. Bassem Eid, the founder and director of the Palestinian Human Rights Monitoring Group, is one of the few Palestinians who has courageously spoken out against this (Eid "We"). He believes that Palestine's future requires democracy, yet Palestinian institutions are anything but democratic. Sabeel does not confront the undemocratic tendencies within the Palestinian Authority or its human rights violations, nor does it address the failure of Hamas in Gaza to lead the Palestinians into anything but warfare and bloodshed. The Palestinian people are unfortunately oppressed by two entities, the Israeli government and their own. Palestinian theologians do not address the corruption and oppression of their own undemocratic representatives. Furthermore, it is not Christianity or the church that give rise to such persecution. Ateek and his peers point to the West's history of anti-Semitism and its consequent guilt over it as the reason for Israel's founding, then claim Israel is the sole cause of the Palestinian's plight (Jerusalem Sabeel). When one cannot expand upon one's context, one is trapped by it.

Sabeel acknowledges the West's anti-Semitism. But do Palestinians recognize their own role in spreading anti-Semitism? Ateek likes to point out how Palestinian Christians have faithfully followed Christ, remaining in the land from the beginning of the church. But if this is the case, how do they explain John Chrysostom of Syria? John lived in the 4th century and is considered one of the great preachers of the early church, but he also preached anti-Semitism and his work became part of the *Adversus Judaeos* ("Against the Jews") (James Carroll). His reasoning led the church to believe that the Jews were exiled because they failed to accept Jesus Christ. Israel disappeared because Jews had been unfaithful to God. Most churches—Catholic, Protestant, Orthodox and all other variants—have recognized this is an error. The Roman Catholic document *Nostra Aetate* addresses it. But Ateek and Katanacho, in particular, do not seem to accept that conclusion and continue to pursue theologies that question the definition of who is a Jew, or even the Jewish understanding of the land (Kantchanko 7-43). Instead of seeking a dialogue with Judaism, they seek to discredit it and call it a primitive religion (Ateek 102). Adam Gregerman tracks how Palestine theology of liberation puts a new spin on anti-Semitism of old. Its anti-Semitic messages embrace a new form of Replacement Theology or supercessionism, one of the more insidious forms of anti-Semitism, which holds that the Jews have lost their place in God's grace and have been replaced by the church.

This is the key weakness of Palestine theology of liberation: while it gives voice to the plight of the oppression of Palestinians, a voice we desperately need to hear, it fails to engage the greater church in dialogue. Instead the church is given an ultimatum: either except this theology of liberation, or we will equate you with evil. A case in point is the 2004 Sabeel Conference when Christian Zionism was labeled "heretical" (Solheim). Christian Zionism is a minority perspective within the broader church, one many do not view favorably, yet it is a voice *within* the church. It is no more appropriate to label it as heresy than it would be to so label Palestinian theology of liberation, even though both have many detractors.

Perhaps if the Palestinian liberation theologians had engaged the wider church instead of taking an adversarial approach to it, the wider church might have helped produce a theology that speaks to the experience of the Palestinians without resorting to anti-Semitic rhetoric. As Christians we are very concerned about the plight of our brothers and sisters in Palestine, but the answer is not contextual; it must come from the Christ of John 9, who enables us to understand our context yet to expand upon it to see something greater.

# THE PROBLEM WITH BDS

In documents like Kairos Palestine (15) and Sabeel's own statements, Palestinian theologians have offered support to the Boycott, Divestment, and Sanctions movement. The two share core context-based values: a belief that the source of evil and the reason for the violence in Israel/Palestine is the State of Israel and its occupation. You will never hear a word from BDS or Sabeel about the human rights violations of the PA or Hamas' stated objective of destroying Israel.

Mainline denominations like the Presbyterian Church USA have been increasingly infiltrated by Sabeel and FOSNA supporters and have attacked Zionism itself in such publications as *Zionism Unsettled*. These attacks are not nuanced so as to focus on the radical agenda of extreme right wing religious Zionists, but instead condemn all Zionists, anyone who supports a homeland for Jews in Israel. Furthermore, BDS proponents and Sabeel supporters themselves are not interested in dialogue, much like Ateek and Katanacho will not rise out of their own context. Theirs is the only vision that is acceptable, all others are wrong. In a demonstration of this type of vision, Bassem Eid was threatened, and his appearance at a South African university had to be canceled when BDS proponents violently disrupted his speech ("BDS activists").

This violence, from the so-called non-violent BDS movement and Sabeel supporters, is also apparent in their anti-normalization agenda, as the Alliance for Middle East Peace points out (Abuarqoub). The Alliance for Middle East Peace is a group of over 70 organizations, Jewish and Palestinian, that seek to bring the two communities together to understand each other. The BDS movement and Sabeel oppose such connections, believing that any attempt to bring people together only serves the status quo.

Is the BDS movement Christian? Is Sabeel? Is it possible to serve Jesus Christ by pursuing an anti-normalization agenda? If Christians recognize that Christ's work in the world is reconciliation, it would seem our purpose is reconciliation as well. How can reconciliation proceed if two peoples are kept apart? BDS and Sabeel act as if the dividing wall of hostility noted in Ephesians is still in existence. Remarkably, BDS and Sabeel, whether intentionally or not, are fanning the flames of this hostility and making the situation on the ground worse.

Both sides in the conflict suffer from a victim mentality. The only way to free people from their sense of victimhood is to remove them from it; the last thing you want to do is feed that mentality. This is what happens when we fail to see beyond our context. This is also why Palestinian Theology of Liberation, while understandable, is inadequate and why the BDS movement is not helpful. Neither separates its constituents from victimhood. Neither accepts responsibility for its actions and lays claims to the future.

## THE WAY FORWARD FOR CHURCHES

As followers of Christ, we must speak to liberation, we must speak to justice, we must speak to reconciliation, but we must do so not from our own context but from Christ's. There is plenty of guilt on both sides; it is time we stop assessing it. It is time that we speak of love to both sides, perhaps even tough love. Churches must hold the government of Israel accountable for its rightward direction and its failure to engage the Palestinians in a just way. And churches must also hold the Palestinians accountable for their continued violence and their rejection of the State of Israel as the Jewish homeland.

Many churches feel they are not advancing the cause of peace and have turned to the BDS movement out of frustration. But BDS actually moves us away from the goal of two peoples living side by side in peace. So what are the alternatives? One is to support the work of the Alliance for Middle East Peace. Churches can work with one of eighty organizations seeking to build peace between Israelis and Palestinians. As understanding increases between the two peoples they will be able to see beyond their own contexts and create their own future. Another way is help build up the infrastructure of Palestine. Support organizations seeking to improve the quality of life of Palestinians in the West Bank and Gaza, whether by investing in schools or medical facilities. Palestinians must continue to build their nation and national identity and the church can help in these activities.

Perhaps the most significant step the church can take to improve the lives of Palestinians and to increase the chances for a peaceful resolution to the conflict is to invest money in the West Bank and Gaza. Bashar Masri, the man behind Rawabi, was born in Nablus and he deplores the occupation, but he understands that Palestinians are one of the least invested in peoples in the world. As Bassem Eid, Bashar Masri, and others have pointed out, boycotts and other economic actions only harm Palestinians by decreasing the resources flowing into the region (Eid "Boycott"). The church can encourage businesses to invest in Palestine, creating more opportunities for peace and prosperity.

More importantly, we must learn from Christ and bring the two peoples together in all possible arenas, so that Jews and Palestinians can stop seeing each other as devils and realize that they are each beloved children of God. This action models Christ seeking to address our own context to see something greater. For only in seeing God in one another will we be able to envision the peace that God wants for all of us. ■

---

Also see ANTI-NORMALIZATION, BDS: A BRIEF HISTORY, and BDS AND CHRISTIAN CHURCHES.

# PINKWASHING (LGBTQ)

## CARY NELSON

G ay activists recovered the color pink as a symbol of gay pride in the 1970s by reversing the pink triangle used by the Nazis as a concentration camp badge for homosexuals. In the 1980s, the AIDS activist group ACT UP used a pink triangle on a black background as its logo. The use of the word "whitewash" to describe an effort to cover up a political or economic scandal or a crime dates to the nineteenth century. The term "pinkwashing" came into contemporary usage to describe the corporate practice of linking products to breast cancer awareness, while hiding the ways they are actually contributing to cancer through their manufacturing processes.

More recently, the accusation of "pinkwashing" has been adopted as part of an effort to discount Israel's progress in recognizing gay rights and establishing a vibrant gay culture, most notably in Tel Aviv, the country's second largest city. The claim is that Israel promotes its progressive gay culture to distract attention from its mistreatment of Palestinians in the West Bank and its military actions in Gaza. Israel's fundamental commitment to liberal Western values like sexual freedom is thereby discredited as nothing more than a propaganda effort. As Sara Schulman put it in an influential 2011 *New York Times* column, "pinkwashing" is a public relations tool, "a deliberate strategy to conceal the continuing violations of Palestinians' human rights behind an image of modernity signified by Israeli gay life." Some trivialize public pride in Israel's support for its gay community as nothing more than an effort to attract gay tourists to the country. Worse still, some castigate support for Israel's LGBTQ community as nothing more than "homonationalism," despite the fact that Israeli gays often oppose government policy and the military occupation of the West Bank. Such arguments undermine the principle that a country's pro-gay legislation and LGBTQ visibility are an important barometer of social change (Lopez).

Israel inherited anti-sodomy laws from the British Mandate's legal code, but the laws were not enforced against acts performed by consenting adults. The Israeli Supreme Court formally endorsed that principle in 1963 and the old law was officially repealed by the Knesset in 1988. Israel also recognizes same-sex marriages performed in other countries, and gays have been able to serve openly in the Israeli military since 1993. The IDF offers special services to help transgender recruits feel welcome. Gay pride marches and other events are held in many Israeli cities, including Haifa, Jerusalem, and Tel Aviv. The age of consent in Israel is 16.

By contrast, Christian, Muslim, and dominant secular traditions in Palestinian society condemn homosexuality and practice harsh forms of intolerance ranging from disownment to physical assault and murder. Some non-Israeli Palestinian gays have lived secretly in Israel to avoid persecution in their West Bank communities. Israel now helps facilitate their entry into the country.

Persecution of homosexuals is widespread in Middle Eastern countries. Egypt has consistently opposed gay rights and actively pursued criminal charges against homosexual men. Same-sex activity is illegal in Iran, with homosexuals subject to beatings, imprisonment, or execution. In Saudi Arabia, homosexuals can be imprisoned, flogged, or executed. In Algeria, homosexuality is illegal; harassment and violence, even murder, by religious fundamentalists or family members who characterize them as "honor killings" is tolerated. Lebanon and Jordan are the partial exceptions. Although a strong majority of Lebanese oppose homosexuality, laws prohibiting sexual practices "contradicting the laws of nature" are not consistently enforced. In Jordan, same-sex activity is legal, but gays face widespread discrimination. With the rise of ISIS in Syria the world now witnesses the wanton mass murder of homosexuals as public policy. This does not mean, however, that everyone in Arab countries shares homophobic convictions. A number of Arab artists, journalists, and people in the film industry, especially in Egypt and Lebanon, showed personal courage by expressing support for the US Supreme Court decision legalizing same-sex marriage.

As the only fully functioning democracy in the region—contrary to Lebanon's fragile democracy, Jordan's constitutional monarchy and parliament, and the series of nations ruled by tyranny or chaos—Israel and its supporters take justifiable pride in all the ways its society differs from its neighbors. The Israeli LGBTQ communities are also proud of the gains they have made through political action and struggle, struggle that is not a form of "pinkwashing." Like all countries, Israel has characteristics both to admire and to criticize. Paired lists of national virtues and failings cannot compensate for one another, but neither do they cancel each other out. Not in the US nor in Israel nor anywhere else, for that matter, does a country's commitment to gay rights stand in for its entire human rights record. Politicians who single out one arena of equality and claim it proves a comprehensive commitment to fairness and justice are engaged in little more than bombast. But neither is it fair to discount everything progressive about a country unless it resolves all problems, even if some loom larger than others. Israel's strengths and achievements justify advocating for progress in arenas where progress is inadequate. The lack of discrimination against gays is encouragement to end discrimination against Israel's Arab citizens.

Among gay advocates for the elimination of the Jewish state, leveling the charge of "pinkwashing" against Israel gives them license to condemn Israel without reservation, whereas otherwise they might have to join in solidarity with the gay community in Tel Aviv and acknowledge there are things about Israel they admire. The pinkwashing accusation gives license to discount all of Israel's achievements—whether its high tech innovations, its leadership in desalinization and drip irrigation, its medical research and inventions, or its vibrant arts communities—as mere covers for the country's sins. It pits gay human rights causes against Palestinian rights in a divisive strategy that consistently minimizes the importance of the former. The BDS movement as a consequence tends to demonize legitimate gay rights advances as part of a broader anti-Israel stance (Lopez).

A notably different approach is taken by the organization A Wider Bridge, which endorses both pluralism and engagement, seeking increased exchanges and information between Israelis and LGBTQ North Americans and their allies. As their executive director Arthur Slepian writes, "While our work is focused on building connections with, and support for, Israel's LGBT communities, we are acutely aware that other human rights struggles exist, both within Israel and in the Palestinian territories. Our pride and celebration of Israel's progress in LGBT rights does not mean that we endorse all the policies of its government. We hope for a time when Palestinians will live in dignity, free from occupation, and Israelis will no longer live with the daily threat of rocket fire or terrorist attack, or the fear of nuclear war" (http://awiderbridge.org/about/). In January 2016 a protest was mounted over the National LGBTQ Task Force's inclusion of A Wider Bridge in a Creating Change Conference in Chicago. Protestors disrupted a reception and prevented two Israelis from speaking. The protestors carried signs protesting pinkwashing. ▨

Also see ANTI-NORMALIZATION, BDS: A BRIEF HISTORY and CULTURAL BOYCOTTS.

# PROPORTIONALITY AND ASYMMETRIC WAR

## CARY NELSON

Traditional norms governing just conduct in war deal with conflicts in which armies deployed by states are generally separate from their civilian environments and oppose one another on a defined battlefront. Today Israel faces adversaries, especially Hamas and Hezbollah, which engage in asymmetric warfare, operating without uniforms inside densely populated areas and using civilians as human shields. In Gaza combatants, unlike civilians, had a concrete reinforced tunnel system as protection. This does not mean that Hamas and Hezbollah, or any adversary using civilians in this manner (a war crime and crime against humanity), are immune from attack. Israel is entitled by the Laws of War to strike at these adversaries as long as it follows four fundamental principles: 1) Necessity: The use of force must be used exclusively for the military mission. 2) Distinction: Only the enemy combatant can be targeted. 3) Responsibility: All reasonable efforts must be made to limit collateral harm to noncombatants. 4) Proportionality: The collateral harm to non-combatants has to be proportionate to the military gain achieved in the strike. The IDF is committed to pursuing warfare against its adversaries based on these principles and to punishing violations of them.

For at least a decade, a debate has raged—in the media, among politicians and scholars, and in the UN and other international bodies—about whether Israel's military actions have been proportionate to the acts of war and terrorism the country has faced. By one moral calculus, comparing the number of casualties in Israel and the IDF with those among Israel's opponents and in the civilian populations in Lebanon and Gaza is sufficient proof that Israel's actions have been "disproportionate." As Keith Pavlischek writes, "In everyday usage, the word 'proportional' implies numerical comparability, and that seems to be what most of Israel's critics have in mind: the ethics of war, they suggest, requires something like a tit-for-tat response. So if the number of losses suffered by Hezbollah or Hamas greatly exceeds the number of casualties among the Israeli Defense Forces (IDF), then Israel is morally and perhaps legally culpable for the 'disproportionate' casualties." As Alan Johnson puts it, "We look for things to be 'even-Steven'; they are not, and our British sense of fair play is offended." "'Disproportionate' violence" for many members of the press and the public, as Michael Walzer writes, "is simply violence they don't like, or it is violence committed by people they don't like." But proportionality in warfare has a different meaning. Walzer, the author of *Just and Unjust Wars* (2006), adds: "Proportionality doesn't mean 'tit for tat,' as in the family feud. The Hatfields kill three McCoys, so the McCoys must kill three Hatfields. More than three, and they are breaking the rules of the feud, where proportionality means symmetry. The use of the term is different with regard to war, because war isn't an act of retribution ...the law of even-Steven doesn't apply."

In the conduct of war, "proportionality" refers to the question of whether the harm caused to noncombatants is proportional to the goals the military action is designed to achieve. As Laurie R. Blank, the author of *International Law and Armed Conflict* (2013), writes, "Proportionality as a *principle* is a manifestation of the law of war's delicate balance between the military imperative of defeating the enemy as quickly as possible and the humanitarian imperative of mitigating suffering during war as much as possible . . . Like the law of war overall, proportionality seeks to minimize civilian harm, not eliminate it altogether (an eminently laudable, although wholly unrealistic goal)." Proportionality represents both a guiding principle and an operative analytic process. "Once a lawful target is identified," she continues, "implementing proportionality requires an understanding of why a target is militarily valuable. How will destroying, capturing, or neutralizing the target contribute to the tactical and operational goals?" Sometimes there are hours and days or more to consider these questions; sometimes there are only minutes or seconds. On the ground, officers with different levels of experience and different levels of confidence may come to different conclusions about what actions are appropriate and acceptable.

Moreover, as Janina Dill argued in a 2010 policy briefing for the Oxford Institute for Ethics, Law, and Armed Conflict, proportionality "fails to set an absolute standard for results of combat operations and instead prescribes how an actor should intend to employ means with regard to ends." It "does not specify how exactly two dissimilar values, human life and military advantage, should be weighed against each other." Indeed Dill suggests that the very indeterminacy of proportionality has helped escalate international disputes over the conduct of war. In any case, contrary to popular opinion, "rather than the actual collateral damage of an air strike, it is the anticipated damage of a military action that must be proportionate to the expected military advantage." In the end, "professional experience and personal morality rather than a transparent and stable set of criteria determine what is considered proportionate." The effort to specify those criteria, however, is inherently comparative. Scholars and military authorities compare practices and results in different conflicts in different countries in different periods. Standards for proportionality based exclusively on moral and political understanding of one conflict alone, such as the Israel-Palestinian conflict, are likely to be flawed.

Some issues are irrelevant. If only military personnel, arms, or equipment are within the target zone, the amount of force applied is irrelevant. One can drop a large bomb to destroy a small target. Nor is it relevant how many of the enemy are killed. If the number of enemy combatants killed or wounded is much larger, that has no bearing on issues of proportionality. The goal in battle is victory. If one side loses far more people and materials than the other, that counts as winning while playing by the rules. There also is no required symmetry in the force used to repel an attack; the tactical goal may not only be to foil the present attack but also to deter future ones.

The standard in adjudicating proportionality in battle is "reasonableness"— "whether a reasonable commander in the same position would determine, based on the information available at the time, that the expected civilian casualties would be excessive in light of the anticipated military advantage." People considering the number of casualties later might view them as excessive; they might well be. But that is not pertinent. The question is whether the commander's determination that the likely number of civilian casualties would not be excessive was reasonable based on what was known at the time of the attack. A battlefield, moreover, is not a courtroom where evidence can be reviewed in hindsight and over time.

An equally complex issue is deciding how much additional risk troops themselves should take on so as to minimize the possibility of civilian casualties. For example: suppose an Israeli platoon crossing a plaza in a city in Gaza during the July 2014 war comes under fire from neighboring buildings. The

Israelis are receiving fire from all sides. Warnings had been issued to civilians to evacuate. The IDF had leafleted the area urging civilians to leave, had made warning phone calls, sent text messages, and dropped small non-destructive explosive devices on rooftops, but the Israelis nonetheless cannot be certain whether any civilians remain. They are worried that Hamas may have followed its frequent practice of pressuring residents to ignore the IDF warnings, thereby turning them into human shields. The fact that Hamas fighters do not wear uniforms does not make distinguishing between civilians and combatants easier. Do the IDF soldiers try to fight their way out on their own, risking more platoon casualties or do they call in an air strike or artillery to reduce enemy fire? In this case only the officer on the ground can make the decision. Some decisions can be pushed up the chain of command, but the evaluation of risk to the troops in this case has to be made on the spot. Not all officers will assess the relative risks in the same way. Authorities writing about the ethics of a decision like this vary about how much added risk soldiers should take on to reduce the risk of civilian casualties.

Proportionality is largely future oriented. It entails evaluating the consequences of a given action in relation to a war's overall aims. Those aims can evolve as new information emerges during combat action. In Operation Protective Edge the aims included eliminating rocket launchers, assault tunnels reaching into Israel itself, weapons caches, and Hamas command posts and bunkers. The overall aim was to degrade Hamas' capacity to launch rockets into Israel from Gaza and to deter those actions by exacting a cost in men, materials, and leadership. Eliminating the tunnels became a higher priority once their number and branching complexity was discovered. Hamas has since claimed that it only sought to use the tunnels against military targets, but Israel would have been foolish to accept such a claim either then or now. That is a case where past behavior bears on the assessment of the future. The Hamas and Hezbollah record for targeting civilians—whether through rocket barrages aimed at cities, suicide bombings in buses and restaurants, armed commando assaults on schools, hostage taking, and other activities—make it necessary to assume Hamas would have used the tunnels in much the same way. That argument stands even though some commentators let their political bias block rational analysis. For example, the American philosopher Jeff McMahan, an authority on just war theory, unreasonably advised in August 2014 that "the tunnels are nothing more than means of individual entry into Israeli territory—an instance of the sort of physical vulnerability shared by every state that borders on another."

The difficulties of evaluating civilian risk in mid-operation can be clarified with another example, one drawn from a 2015 group conversation with Michael Walzer. An Israeli central command post is using a drone to track three armed Hamas fighters traveling through city streets on motorcycles. Wanting to degrade Hamas's offensive capacity, the IDF wants to target these combatants, so it assesses the changing proportionality issues moment by moment, trying to pick an opportunity for action when the risk to civilians is minimal. The IDF picks its moment, missing the presence of a school nearby, and six children are killed. In retrospect, judgment suggests they should not have taken the shot, but the IDF did not intentionally or knowingly target the children. The tragedy is a powerful lesson for the future, but it is not self-evidently a war crime.

During a November, 2014, presentation at New York's Jewish Theological Seminary, Moshe Halbertal, a medievalist and coauthor of the Israeli Defense Force rules of engagement, addressed the issue of Palestinian deaths during 2014's Operation Protective Edge, the subject of widespread international debate and anger. He pointed out that the ratio of combatants (approximately 30,000) to noncombatants (1.8 million) in Gaza is about 1 to 60. Of the 2,000 people killed in Gaza, about 700 to 900 were combatants. Thus the ratio of Hamas fighters to civilians killed is about 1 to 2, despite the war being conducted in densely populated civilian areas. If Israel had bombed Gaza the way the allies bombed some German cities or the way the US bombed Tokyo, one would expect that only 20 people of the 2,000 who died in Gaza would have been combatants. For the IDF to go from a combatant/population ration of 1 to 60 to a wartime ratio of 1 to 2 killed is contextual evidence that the IDF exercised considerable restraint and sought to honor its rules of engagement.

Assessing proportionality in Gaza was made substantially more difficult by Hamas' decision to place rocket launchers in the midst of the civilian population and weapons caches in schools and mosques. Gaza is not so crowded that there is no open farmland where launchers could have been placed without endangering civilians, but Hamas personnel would have been much more vulnerable then. Maximizing the cost in civilian lives also gave Hamas its major propaganda weapon on the world stage, but the decision to endanger its own people makes Hamas at least partially responsible for Palestinian casualty figures. Indeed Hamas repeatedly discouraged civilians from evacuating buildings that Israel had warned would be struck and occasionally sent civilians to the rooftops of buildings at risk. These are war crimes. So too is the Hamas decision to fire rockets at Israeli civilian population centers. Hamas would later claim it lacks more precise rocket guidance systems, but that is no excuse. In any case, Hamas bragged about its ability to reach Tel Aviv. Even with Iron Dome at its disposal, Israel could not tolerate thousands of rockets falling on its territory. But the future portends still more powerful and longer-range rocket fire from Gaza and Lebanon. Establishing a pattern of Israeli tolerance for rocket barrages would be more than unwise. Meanwhile, international misrepresentation of the issue of proportionality and the accompanying accusations about Israeli war crimes clearly incentivizes Hamas to maximize its civilian casualties. ■

---

Also see GAZA, HAMAS, and IRON DOME.

# THE SECURITY BARRIER

CARY NELSON

A fter decades of cross-border incursions by Arab militants intent on killing or kidnapping Israeli citizens—including years of suicide bombings that killed over a thousand people—Israel built a fence to control the situation and save lives (MAP 3). In 2002, the year before the first continuous segment of the fence was constructed, 293 Israelis were killed and 1950 wounded; in the year following the summer of 2003 only a handful of attacks were successful. By 2010, with more of the barrier complete, only nine terrorist attacks took place. Islamic Jihad acknowledged that the barrier had thwarted the suicide bombings it had wished to carry out. The fence is designed to incorporate the major settlement blocs to the east of the 1949 Jordanian-Israeli armistice line (or "Green Line") that effectively defined Israel's border, so it encompasses only a small percentage of the West Bank (MAPS 2, 3, & 4). The fence is not the only factor eliminating most terrorist attacks, but it has made a major contribution.

Critics of Israeli policy typically characterize the fence as a "wall," but in fact less than 10 percent has been constructed in the form of a 30-foot high concrete wall. Of course one can use the term "wall" metaphorically, to refer to any barrier, but the BDS movement confusedly conflates the two uses and promotes the confusion by distributing photos of the high wall as if they are characteristic of the whole barrier. In urban areas where an actual wall predominates, it prevents random and targeted sniper fire from West Bank locations that endanger motorists and others. The Israeli Defense Forces actually prefer a fence to a wall because people approaching a fence are more visible. The wall requires periodic manned outposts atop towers to achieve the same end. The fence generally takes the form of a two-layer chain-link fence with electronic sensors embedded in the land between them. Surveillance cameras help monitor the area, and sand between the layers of fence registers the imprint of footsteps. In some areas a ditch impedes vehicle access to the fence. Barbed wire discourages approaches to the fence.

More than twenty-five other nations have constructed barriers to protect their borders or reduce violence between opposing groups. The barrier separating Catholic and Protestant neighborhoods in Belfast is popularly known as a peace wall. India has a barrier nearly 500 miles long in Kashmir designed to bar cross-border infiltrations. The United States has erected a fence along portions of its border with Mexico. One may reasonably dispute the placement of some areas of Israel's security barrier, but the effort to demonize the entire project as an "Apartheid Wall" is a hostile political campaign that disregards the many lives the fence has saved. The wall has certainly caused hardships to Palestinians, hardships that should be reduced or eliminated where possible and compensated when not.

It has been made easier for the BDS movement and others to castigate Israel for the construction of the barrier because it functions as part of an interlocking system of control that includes road blocks, checkpoints, and the fragmentation of areas under Palestinian control. If the other elements were to be removed either unilaterally or as part of a peace agreement, the wall could be seen as facilitating a two-state solution.

Although the Israeli government rejects the claim that the barrier constitutes an international border, the security barrier nonetheless constitutes a potential border with a Palestinian state. It offers a prospective point of withdrawal for Israel even if that withdrawal is, at first, unilateral. The barrier unquestionably has been beneficial in helping to eliminate suicide bombings, but it also offers Palestinians a rough potential boundary for their own independent state. It is difficult to imagine a two-state solution without such a barrier. Many on the international left now regard the wall as an unqualified obscenity. But as a potential international boundary it helps sustain the possibility of Palestinian statehood. Certainly Jewish settlers to the east of the wall recognize that, which is why many opposed the wall's construction and still see it as a threat. With the exception of Jerusalem, where drawing permanent borders presents special challenges and where an eventual two-state solution will require continuing co-operation, the construction of new housing units west of the wall or the fence should not be the focus of controversy or political posturing. Far better to concentrate on opposing construction east of the barrier, which really does endanger the two-state solution.

In any case, the exact route the fence takes can and should be adjusted. Under a final status agreement it likely would be. Where it separates people from their farms, divides communities, or causes other hardships without a strong security justification, it should be relocated. Under Aharon Barak, who served as President of the Israeli Supreme Court between 1995 and 2006, Palestinian efforts to reroute the security fence, block house demolitions, or win habeas corpus suits were more likely to receive sympathetic hearings. Barak, a thoughtful jurist of international stature, struggled continually with ways to grant justice to Palestinians within the legal system, but he is now often demonized by the Israeli far right. Unlike the federal courts in the United States, the Israeli Supreme Court is set up to hear individual complaints at a reasonable cost. Legal support provided by NGO's is also sometimes available to those who need it. Progressive observers worldwide could collaborate with sympathetic Israelis and local NGOs like ACRI (The Association for Civil Rights in Israel) to select individual cases to publicize and promote so that the court's decision making becomes more visible worldwide. People can also help fund groups that bring appropriate cases before the court. Specific cases might benefit from international visibility, scrutiny, and debate before they are decided, and good and bad decisions could be evaluated and publicized. The Israeli Supreme Court in, other words, could have the same international visibility that the US Supreme Court has. The goals might include encouraging the court to revive its willingness to reroute the security barrier where appropriate and, alternatively, to mandate compensation to Palestinians who have suffered losses due to its location. International visibility for court deliberations is also critical because there are ongoing assaults on the Israeli judiciary's independence. ■

---

Also see COORDINATED UNILATERAL WITHDRAWAL, THE ISRAELI RIGHT AND RELIGIOUS SETTLER POLITICS, THE ISRAELI-PALESTINIAN PEACE PROCESS, SETTLEMENTS, and THE WEST BANK.

# SETTLEMENTS

## CARY NELSON

In 1975 there were a few thousand settlers in Judea and Samaria [the Israeli government's official designation for the West Bank, echoing the ancient names for the Jewish kingdoms]. In 1995 there were around 120,000. Today there are 400,000. Over the past four decades, the Gush Emunim settlement movement has achieved a complete and total victory over Israeli officialdom. First it established facts on the ground, then it got those facts officially recognized, and then it tripled, quadrupled, and quintupled them using state resources. The result is a toxic demographic-political omelet which will be very hard to turn back into the egg mix from which it came. If the number of residents in Judea and Samaria reaches 600,000, 700,000 or 800,000 by 2025, it will no longer be possible to divide the land, and Israel will become a binational state. Whether this binational state is no longer Jewish or no longer a democracy, the Zionist enterprise will have met its end.
　　　　　—Ari Shavit "We've Entered the Final Decade to Save Israel"

The civilian communities that comprise the Israeli settlements were an outgrowth of Israel's territorial gains during the 1967 Six Day War. Some were first established as military outposts, only later attracting civilians. As of 2016, the settlements included about 400,000 Israelis living in the West Bank and about 375,000 living in East Jerusalem. After the Six Day War, when Israel also captured the Gaza Strip and the Sinai Peninsula from Egypt, settlements were established in those two areas as well, but they have since been evacuated. Israel left the Sinai as part of a 1979 peace agreement with Egypt and made a unilateral decision to leave Gaza in 2005. About 20,000 Israelis live in the Golan Heights, once part of Syria; unlike the West Bank, Israel effectively annexed the Golan Heights in 1981, after having captured the area in the Six Day War.

The first settlement established in the West Bank after the war was Kfar Etzion, just under 3 miles east of the pre-1967 border, in the hills between Jerusalem and Hebron, in 1967. Kfar Etzion is on the site of a small Jewish farming community, Migdal Eder, founded in 1927 but attacked and destroyed during the Arab riots two years later. Early in the next decade, the land was purchased and a village now named Kfar Etzion formed. It was destroyed during the 1936-39 Arab revolt. In the years leading up to the founding of the Jewish state, Kfar Etzion was recreated as a kibbutz, but it was attacked during the 1948 war and 157 of its 161 residents were massacred by the Arab Legion and irregular forces. Few current settlements other than Kfar Etzion and Hebron have such long and painful histories, but all can be cast by some on the Israeli right as part of the ancient heritage of the Jewish people. Yet the settlements are not uniform, nor are their historic, geographical, and symbolic links to the land and to contemporary political realities.

Prime Minister Menachem Begin's government as of 1977 adopted a more aggressive settlement expansion policy. As the number and size of the settlements were expanded, the international community repeatedly reinforced its view that they are illegal. The United Nations considers them a violation of the Fourth Geneva Convention, and the International Court of Justice confirmed their illegality in a 2004 ruling. The very largest settlements have witnessed dramatic growth over the last generation. Established in 1996, Modi'in Illit went from a population of 13,000 in 1999 to over 63,000 in 2014. Established in 1985, Beitar Illit went from 12,700 to nearly 47,000 in the same period. Established by 23 families in 1975, Ma'ale Adumim already had nearly 24,000 residents by 1999; it is now home to over 40,000 people. These large settlements remain exceptions. At the other end of the spectrum are many settlements— nearly 70 such as of 2013—with fewer than 1,000 residents.

About 80 percent of Israeli settlers live in settlement blocs close to the pre-1967 borders (MAP 4). Many were motivated to settle there not only because housing costs are significantly lower than in Israel's major cities but also because other social services, including education, are subsidized. Substantial government subsidies make that possible, and it is easy to commute from there to jobs in Tel Aviv or Jerusalem. The route from Ma'ale Adumim to Jerusalem travels 1.8 miles. The one relatively large Israeli city deeper into the West Bank, some twelve miles east of the pre-1967 border, is

Ariel, with a stable population of 18,000 and a controversial Israeli university. Some Israelis, especially those in settlements deeper into the West Bank, believe they are fulfilling a historic mission to resettle the ancient Jewish kingdoms of Judah and Samaria, the former later Hellenized to Judea. Shortly after the Six Day War the Israeli right began to call the West Bank Judea and Samaria, thereby invoking an aura of destiny to add to other reasons to reclaim the territory. In 1947 United Nations General Assembly Resolution 181 designated "Judea and Samaria" as the area for a future Palestinian state, although at the time it was not limited to the West Bank. Now the Israeli government's official designation for the West Bank, the name Judea and Samaria remains provocative.

Since 2004, Hebrew University historian Danny Gutwein has been pointing out that neoliberal Israeli politicians have gradually dismantled the welfare state and privatized its social services, turning them into commodities only the upper classes can afford to purchase. But Israel has offered those services to the poor and the lower middle classes on the West Bank, so you move there not lured by the ideology of a Greater Israel but to get the education and housing you cannot get on sovereign Israel. Journalist Amira Hass has echoed the argument: "settlements flourish as the welfare state contracts. They offer ordinary people what their salaries would not allow them in sovereign Israel, within the borders of June 4, 1967: cheap land, large homes, benefits, subsidies, wide-open spaces, a view, a superior road network and quality education. Even for those Israeli Jews who have not moved there, the settlements illuminate their horizon as an option for a social and economic upgrade." In order to promote a two-state solution and build a winning coalition, therefore, the left must offer a new version of the welfare state within Israel proper.

Israel has had multiple reasons to promote West Bank settlement, among them to provide "strategic depth" better to protect Israel proper from invasion. But an impulse to create facts on the ground making the establishment of a contiguous Palestinian state difficult or impossible has certainly been the primary motivation for more than one Israeli government. It has also motivated those US foundations, nongovernmental organizations, and private donors who continue to fund the settlement movement. In 2015 Uri Blau wrote a series of articles in *Haaretz* detailing fifty tax-free US foundations—among them the Brooklyn-based Hebron fund and the Manhattan-based Central Fund of Israel—that donated 220 million to West Bank settlements between 2009 and 2013. In doing so they undercut the cause of peace. The Israeli government contributes considerable resources to settler defense, but US donor funding helps expand existing settlements and establish new ones. To that trend may be added the many small illegal outposts created on the West Bank. If many Israelis move to the West Bank to take advantage of much cheaper housing, those who participate in establishing illegal settlements—typically very small groups living in rough accommodations on hilltops—have a more aggressive motivation: to claim land for Israel and bar Palestinians from living there.

Some observers believe settlement expansion has already killed the two-state solution. Arguing against that conclusion, first of all, is the geographical concentration of settlements near the pre-1967 border; the prospective maps for a two-state solution developed over decades envision land swaps with the Palestinians as a means to incorporate those settlements into Israel proper while compensating the Palestinians with equivalent territory. As the important 2013 survey conducted by the Israeli organization Blue White Future demonstrated (http://bluewhitefuture.org/bwf-work/voluntary-evacuation-survey/), many other settlers would willingly leave their homes given fair compensation if an agreement with the Palestinians were to be reached.

Settlement expansion east of the security barrier (MAPS 3 & 4) denies Palestinians much hope in a negotiated agreement that would grant them their own state. That sense of hopelessness maximizes despair and hostility and creates fertile ground for the promotion of violence. And it increases Israel's isolation in the international community. Moreover, there is no route to permanent Israeli control over the West Bank and its Palestinian population that would preserve both Israel's democratic and Jewish character. To be democratic, Israel must give all under its authority full citizenship, which it cannot do in the West Bank without losing or seriously undermining its character as a Jewish state. The only route to preserve Israel's combined democratic and Jewish character is to gradually free itself of most of the West Bank. ▮

Also see COORDINATED UNILATERAL WITHDRAWAL, THE INTIFADAS, THE ISRAELI RIGHT AND RELIGIOUS SETTLER POLITICS, THE PALESTINIAN AUTHORITY, THE ISRAELI-PALESTINIAN PEACE PROCESS, THE SECURITY BARRIER, SETTLER COLONIALISM, and THE WEST BANK.

# SETTLER COLONIALISM

CARY NELSON

The dominant model for a colonial settlement describes it as an extension of the mother country, ordinarily at a distance from it. The founding country may seek to extract the colonized area's resources and exploit its labor or may want to displace the local population and take over the land. An imperial power typically continues to govern or retain authority over its colony, at least for a time, as England did for its colonies in North America and as France did for Algeria. Colonies given qualified self-governing powers may nonetheless continue to rely on the mother country for economic and military support. Often enough the settlers borrow names from the source country for towns and cities, and more broadly they try to transplant or recreate the culture they came from in a new place. None of this applies to Israel. Jews represented no imperial foreign power or metropolitan center. Moreover, the standard settler-colonialism model is inappropriate in the light of the unbroken Jewish presence in the area and Israel's founding in the wake of the Holocaust. As David Hirsh has written, "In the middle of the 20th century Israel was not imagined as a European colony. It is strained, to say the least, to believe that Jews in the refugee camps in Europe and in British Cyprus, recovering from starvation and from existences as non-humans, were thinking of themselves as standard bearers of 'the European idea.' The seamless insertion of the history of 'Zionism' into a schematic history of colonialism casts Jews as going to Palestine in order to get rich on the back of the people who lived there. Jews, who are said to embody some European idea of whiteness, also embodied a European idea of rats and cockroaches, which was held to constitute an existential threat to Europe."

In the 19th century, under the banner of Zionism Jews created a national liberation movement for a people then dispersed to the periphery of several European continental empires, often as a minority people confined to the poorest areas. Far from being agents of imperial power, the Jews were themselves victims of power in the Hapsburg, German, and Russian empires. In many respects, the Jews of Europe were themselves a colonial people. They sought to escape existing anti-Semitism and brutal forms of discrimination, persecution, and violence. They were fleeing empire, not carrying it with them. Instead of trying to recreate the norms of the societies in which they suffered, they sought to create something new. The Israeli kibbutz is the most famous example. As Derek Penslar has written, "the motives behind the Zionist project had little in common with those of Western settlement colonialism" ("Zionism" 93). Indeed one may define "Zionism as an act of resistance by a colonized people" (85).

And the land itself was not new. In settling in Palestine they were returning to *Eretz Yisrael*, their ancestral home where Jews had an unbroken history since antiquity. In that context, the construction of the Jewish state after 1948 may be understood partly as a postcolonial enterprise, with "the Zionist project as akin to state-building projects throughout twentieth-century Asia and Africa" (85). "Before 1948, the *Yishuv* and its Zionist sponsors abroad could not be considered a colonizing state, in that it exercised highly limited authority over small portions of Palestine" (85). The Jewish presence in the Middle East had never been entirely eradicated from the time the Romans expelled the Jews from Jerusalem and renamed the land Palestine. Jews thus have reason to see themselves as an indigenous people, though many BDS advocates reject that argument. Prior to the founding of the State of Israel, the Jewish presence in the Middle East included Jewish communities in Arab countries across North Africa and West Asia that were founded as much as a thousand to two thousand years earlier. Pushed by persecution and violence and attracted by the Zionist idea, most of those Jews—numbering 700,000 people—fled those ancient Jewish communities in Arab countries and made Israel their home after it was created in 1948. Along with later immigration from Ethiopia and elsewhere, these Jews and their descendants comprise a majority of the current population of Israel. To state this differently, just under half of the current Jewish population in Israel is of European origin. Describing Israel as a whole as a European colony is thus historically and demographically inaccurate.

Israel is a remarkable multicultural, multiracial society, with all the richness, complication, and tension such societies can exhibit—a true ingathering of exiles together with many others. Arabs make up twenty percent of its population. Black Jews from Africa are a significant minority group. Other Jews have dark complexions that could qualify them as "people of color," as least as plausibly as Palestinians can claim the designation.

When the *Yishuv*, the Jewish community in Palestine that preceded the state of Israel, was taking form, some Jews sought to integrate the resident Arabs with their new society. Others believed that in a truly Jewish community Jews would need to be the majority population. Some certainly exhibited one attitude typical of many colonial enterprises: they saw themselves as bringing benefits like modern medicine to an underdeveloped rural Arab population. When the Jews drained malarial coastal swamps and made them livable, they were also in fact improving what they found. Yet Zionism's effort at cultural transformation overall was "directed primarily at Jews, not the indigenous Arabs of Palestine. It was not primarily a manifestation of a colonial will to power" (Penslar "Zionism" 94):

> Zionism sought to realize itself in the Middle East, in an area chosen not for its strategic value, natural resources, or productive capabilities, but solely because of the Jews' historic, religious, and cultural ties to the area known to them as the Land of Israel. Because Zionism's *mission civilisatrice* was directed almost entirely inward, to the Jews themselves, Zionism lacked the evangelical qualities of European colonialism in North America, Asia, and Africa, where conversion of the heathen to Christianity served as a justification, consequence, and at times a partial cause of colonial expansion" (Penslar 96).

In contrast to common BDS accounts, moreover, the Zionist movement did not steal the land or take it by force. When the Zionist movement began to bring large numbers of Jews to Palestine in the latter part of the nineteenth century, they purchased land legally from its owners, often absentee Arab landlords living elsewhere. The *Yishuv* was not an imperial force and could not even influence immigration in the period leading up to and through World War Two. The British were the colonizing power; they controlled and severely restricted immigration, exercising a power that left thousands of Jews to die under Nazism. The World Zionist Organization "tried to assume the [economic] role of a colonizing state," but it failed, "primarily due to a lack of means," though it was not in any case "wont to conceive of the Arab as an enemy to be expelled or a body to be enslaved for profit" (86). When the new State of Israel was founded, it also encompassed land once belonging to the Ottoman Empire that had been defeated and dissolved during World War One. Israel, however, did take possession of villages from which Arabs fled or were expelled from during the 1948 war. Some critics of the Jewish state claim that such examples constitute the whole of Israel's story, but that is not true.

Underlying the accusation that Israel is a settler-colonialist state is the conviction that Israelis are white and Palestinians are people of color. As pointed out earlier, it certainly helps the left's settler-colonialist mantra if one opportunistically racializes the Israeli-Palestinian conflict, but the conflict itself historically has not been about race, but rather about how nationalism, religion, ethnicity, and history create peoplehood. If Palestinians are people of color, then surely Egyptian, Ethiopian, Iraqi, Moroccan, and Yemini Jews, among others, are as well. Less than half of Israelis are of European origin, but ignorance and opportunism permits people to think otherwise. In the US, of course, Arabs long identified themselves as white, and some still do. If skin color, a minor genetic feature, is to be the guide, then many Palestinians and Israelis appear equivalently white or brown. Using race to essentialize the parties to the conflict is an invidious political decision. Racializing the conflict makes it more difficult both to understand its complexity and to devise solutions to solve it, but it does facilitate BDS's depiction of it as a Manichean struggle between good and evil, between justice and injustice.

Moreover it eroticizes the conflict in a way that meets the needs of white BDS activists on the left. Following a pattern Gayatri Spivak noted decades ago, it allows anti-colonialist whites to see themselves as rescuing helpless brown victims, a dynamic enhanced by treating Palestinians as blameless victims without agency. The eroticism meanwhile is at once masked and indulged in by being displaced onto a heroic pursuit of justice. This covert eroticism is then freed up to take increasingly degraded forms, as in a presentation, "Inhumanist Biopolitics: How Palestine Matters," that Rutgers University Women's Studies and Gender faculty member Jasbir Puar delivered at Vassar College in 2016. She repeated without criticizing it the blood libel-style slander, summarized by Nathalie Rothschild in 2012, that Israelis are currently harvesting organs from Palestinian bodies, adding to it an echo of Nazi concentration camp medical experimentation, referring to Israel presently "needing body parts, not even whole bodies, for research and experimentation." Her audiences could then participate in voyeuristic fantasy contemplation of dismembered Palestinian bodies under the guise of outraged protest. One might note that there is one area group that has declared itself willing to harvest organs from *live* captives—ISIS (Reuters).

The claim that Israel is a settler colonial society clearly does not represent a neutral, objective description. It is instead a hostile political designation used by those who misrepresent Israel's history and deny its right to exist. Indeed it mounts an essentialist version of both Israeli and Palestinian history. The assertion that Israel is a settler colonialist state, repeatedly advanced by BDS advocates, provides a strategic narrative designed to obscure or deny the anti-colonial nationalism embodied in the story of the Jewish people returning to their homeland. Israeli Jews in this narrative remain settler-colonialists no matter how many generations pass. Although BDS's major spokespeople argue that Israel in its entirety is a settler colonialist state, the claim gained prominence only in the late 1960s as a consequence of Israel's acquisition of Gaza, the Golan Heights, and the West Bank. Israel voluntarily left Gaza in 2005 and could still now agree to the creation of an independent Palestinian state on the West Bank. When the United Nations voted to establish Israel in 1947, the aim was not to eradicate local Arab culture in Palestine but rather to provide for two states for two peoples in which each people could pursue its own destiny. Except for those who demand the expulsion of the Jews from Israel proper—rallying behind a now familiar chant, "From the River to the Sea, Palestine Will Be Free"—the creation of a Palestinian state on the West Bank should end the debate about whether Israel is a settler colonialist nation.

Until and unless Palestinians gain a state, however, Israel is vulnerable to the settler-colonialist critique, especially when no official model exists for what the West Bank will look like in a decade should the status quo be maintained. A colonialist project may aim for permanence, whereas an occupation should be time limited. With the West Bank occupation having lasted half a century and many settlements meant to be anything but temporary, people both within and outside Israel are concerned that current arrangements will be permanent. In any case, analyses of Israel's relation to colonialism need to be comparative, with the histories of all colonialist countries, including the US, taken into account. All settler-colonial histories, moreover, can be ameliorated by present and future actions.

# ILAN TROEN

A widespread, if not dominant, analysis of sociologists, historical geographers, and political scientists construes the Jewish state as founded on the injustices of a "colonial-settler society." While Zionist settlement was supported and even celebrated by an earlier generation of social scientists, it is now viewed as a destructive phenomenon whose negative consequences demand correction. In large measure this view is a product of choosing a radically different historical paradigm (Troen, *Imagining Zion*, ch. 3).

Probably the best known though not the first such analysis is found in Gershon Shafir's *Land, labor, and the origins of the Israeli-Palestinian conflict, 1882-1914*. Shafir's approach is comparative and he begins by identifying multiple types of settler societies in the 400 years of colonialism that began with Columbus and ended with Zionism. Relying on the insights of historians of western imperialism, he and his colleagues review Jewish settlement to determine which of the various colonial models fits Zionism best. The comparative framework based on European colonialism as the sole explanatory instrument inevitably faults Zionism by definition. That is, since he compares the Jews to the Portuguese, Spanish, Dutch, French, and the English and views them exclusively in the European historical framework, Zionist settlement may be more or less benign, but it is always guilty of being colonialist. To borrow a phrase: one cannot be a little pregnant. Shafir posits no additional or alternative model and ignores the possibility that the Jewish case is an anomaly. [Unlike some others who have explored a colonialist analogy for Zionism, however, Shafir has not endorsed BDS—CN.]

The universal reference point for all of such critical or revisionist scholarship is the seminal work of D. K. Fieldhouse, a British scholar whose writings continue to influence generations of researchers. Written during the heyday of de-colonization, with which he identifies, and on the eve of one of the great flashpoints of the Arab/Israeli conflict, the 1967 Six Day War, Fieldhouse's 1966 *The Colonial Empires: a comparative survey from the eighteenth century* is a magisterial and comprehensive work that contains no mention of Zionism. Except for a passing reference to the Balfour Declaration of 1917, Jews and Zionists are totally absent from his work.

Fieldhouse concentrates on an economic and materialistic approach to colonialism derived from the early twentieth century work of J. A. Hobson and V. I. Lenin, even though his conclusions are markedly different. Zionism plays no role in this far-reaching account of European colonial expansion and in the world where empires establish colonies. Contemporary critics, who consistently reference Fieldhouse to support their claim that Zionism is an outrageous and vexing form of colonialism willfully or carelessly distort his definition of "settler society" when they apply it to the Zionist case.

Why did Fieldhouse exclude Jewish settlement that had already been in process for more than 80 years from his research on "settler society" and colonialism? A likely explanation is that it did not fit his definition based on the rubric he established for the Dutch, British, French, Spaniards, Portuguese, Germans, and Italians. Jewish colonization during its first forty years took place in the Ottoman Empire; it was certainly not part of the process of imperial expansion in search of power and markets. It was also not a consequence of industrialization and financial interests. Indeed, as numerous scholars, including Ran Aaronsohn, Baruch Kimmerling, and Simon Schama have noted, Jewish settlement was so unprofitable that it has been pronounced economically irrational. In sum, Fieldhouse's exactingly developed analysis does not fit the Zionist case. Revisionist scholars have wrenched it out of context to describe an entirely distinct historical experience to serve their own ideological purposes. At the same time, their interpretations served pro-Palestinian apologists.

Zionism did not establish plantations or other large units of capitalistic agriculture. Instead, Jews created small truck farms or modest-sized collective colonies. These were more naturally suited for homogeneous communities and totally unlike the large plantations managed by European settlers operating with a significant force of native labor. Small landholders and collective communities did not need native labor. For ideological as well as practical reasons, Jews worked the land themselves.

Ironically, this self-reliance and determination to engage personally in hard work have provided yet another reason to blame the Zionist enterprise in its entirety. The economic and cultural separation between Jews and Arabs is decried as the sole responsibility of Zionist ideology and praxis. The contemporary indictment of Israel as an "apartheid state" is a natural albeit absurd outgrowth of this charge.

A contextualized and more nuanced analysis would note that for centuries Muslims had separated themselves from Jews who they defined as *dhimmis*, tolerated but second-class members of the community. Moreover, separation between Jews and Muslims was the norm throughout the Arab Muslim world and imposed by the Moslem Turks and their predecessors since the rise of Islam in the seventh century. Is it reasonable to castigate a handful of Jews living in remote agricultural colonies under Turkish rule because they failed to overturn such deeply engrained and accepted practices? Faulting them for not implementing the kind of egalitarian and integrated civil society that had yet to be actualized even in the United States is an exercise of imagination that borders on fantasy. Yet, that has become this generation's operative paradigm. Worse, Israel is blamed for instituting this system that is maliciously defined with the epithet "apartheid."

The misuse and abuse of Fieldhouse's "settler society" distorts in another crucial way. Fieldhouse viewed British "settler societies" as intended "replicas" of the home society and "true reproductions of European society" (Fieldhouse 239, 250). The same was true of French colonies: "The French imperial mission was to mold their colonies into replicas of France and eventually to incorporate them into the metropolis." In the case of Algeria, the French even tried to incorporate the colony into the home country (Fieldhouse 318). In marked contrast, as we saw above, Zionist settlements were at once deliberately distinct from Europe and different from Arab society. This was at the core of the idea of "reconstitution." European and American technology, political ideas, and other aspects of modern culture were transferred to Palestine and also transformed; Zionist society was consciously recast into a unique mold dedicated to creating the "new Jew."

Thus, there is a pernicious use of rhetoric that underlies this discourse. Casting Zionists as colonizers represents them as usurpers who occupy a land in which, by definition, they do not belong. Palestine is the home to the one and only indigenous people; there cannot be two. In what must be an extreme anomaly in the history of colonialism, this new scholarship posits Palestine as occupied by two imperial powers—the British and the Jews. In view of the multitudes who desperately sought entry into Palestine prior to independence, this characterization of Jewish imperial power appears as a cruel joke at best. ■

*Adapted from Ilan Troen, "The Campaign to Boycott Israeli Universities: Historical and Ideological Sources," with introductory material added.*

Also see BDS: A BRIEF HISTORY, THE ISRAELI RIGHT AND RELIGIOUS SETTLER POLITICS, THE WEST BANK, WORLD WAR II AND THE FOUNDING OF ISRAEL, ZIONISM AS PHILOSOPHY AND PRACTICE, and ZIONISM: ITS EARLY HISTORY.

# THE SIX DAY WAR (1967)

CARY NELSON, RACHEL S. HARRIS,
AND KENNETH W. STEIN

he Six Day War, which proved a catalyst for Palestinian
political mobilization, took place from June 5 to 10, 1967.
When the Soviets erroneously informed Syria and Egypt
that Israel was amassing troops for an attack in the north,
Egyptian president Gamel Abdel Nasser (1918–1970)
demanded that the UN withdraw from Gaza, Sinai, and the
Straits of Tiran. The UN complied and Nasser blocked the Straits, preventing
Israel's access through the Red Sea to the Gulf of Aqaba, a major trade route.
It amounted to an act of war. The public rhetoric that followed—which
included calls on Nasser to drive the Jews out of Israel and PLO chairman
Ahmad Shukeiri's (1908–1980) boast that "no Jew whatsoever will survive"
in the event of war—evoked memories of the Holocaust for Israelis. When
Jordan's King Hussein then flew to Egypt to sign a mutual defense pact,
Israel reacted to the threat implied in the military alliance and launched a
preemptive strike. Within three hours, the Israeli Defense Force had destroyed
the entire Egyptian air force on the ground. The felling of Syrian and
Jordanian air forces followed swiftly. Over land, IDF forces reached the banks
of the Suez Canal and took possession of the Sinai Peninsula, chasing out
the Egyptian army. Though Israel had hoped to avoid conflict with Jordan,
Jordanian shelling of West Jerusalem and the Ramat David air base led Israel
to respond, eventually taking East Jerusalem and the West Bank, which had
been under Jordanian control since 1948. The resulting Israeli reunification

of Jerusalem, including its old city, gave Jews and other religious groups access to key holy sites, including the Temple Mount. Israel also occupied the Golan Heights, taking this strategic military site from Syria, while capturing the Gaza Strip from Egypt.

But with these new territories came a million Palestinians. Unlike the Arab residents of Israel, who were full citizens, Palestinian residents in these new territories would be governed under martial law and Israel would become an occupying power. It would not be long before the spoils of war became a burden. Meanwhile, the early dream of a Greater Israel—a Jewish state occupying all of Palestine—had long lain dormant, but now it rose again to play a significant role in the Israeli polity for the first time since independence.

The Six Day War was a huge victory whose scale was unpredicted and also unplanned for; no plan for how to govern territory, which Israel did not anticipate winning, was in place, and no advance decisions were made about what the status of its Palestinian residents would be. The ecstasy of victory largely covered the lack of leadership courageous and insightful enough to address the problem in a timely manner. Nonetheless, the press coverage of Israel's victory was extremely positive. *Life* magazine devoted a special commemorative issue to the war that could not have been more enraptured had it been an American victory. But the seeds were sown of a fundamental change in Israel's international status. ▪

*Adapted from Cary Nelson, Rachel S. Harris, and Kenneth W. Stein, "The History of Israel," with additional material added.*

Also see COORDINATED UNILATERAL WITHDRAWAL, FATAH, THE PALESTINIAN AUTHORITY, THE ISRAELI-PALESTINIAN PEACE PROCESS, THE TEMPLE MOUNT / HARAM AL-SHARIF, and THE WEST BANK.

# THE SOCIAL JUSTICE
# MANDATE IN HIGHER
# EDUCATION

CARY NELSON

The concept of social justice embodies the notion that everyone deserves equal legal, economic, political, and social rights and opportunities. Put into practice, it seeks to promote justice by redistributing wealth, opportunities, and privileges within a society, addressing injustice and seeking to correct it, and reforming institutions and their practices as appropriate. John Rawls' 1971 *A Theory of Justice* promoted the idea that the principle is central to the social contract.

Academic fields that train students to work with clients in the public realm often include a social justice mandate as a commitment and perhaps a requirement for the field. Thus the National Association of Social Workers declares that "Social work is a practical profession aimed at helping people address their problems and matching them with the resources they need to lead healthy and productive lives . . . . Social workers aim to open the doors of access and opportunity for everyone, particularly those in greatest need." Students in social work are expected to learn how to meet these goals.

As a social justice perspective has spread to academic disciplines that are more abstract and not client-oriented, including a number of humanities and social science fields, it began to include an expectation of critical self-analysis and interrogation. Students would be asked to examine how they are themselves embedded in social relationships and institutions that undermine social justice. In some cases they would be asked to participate in (and get academic credit for) participation in social justice activism off campus. The participation itself can help empower students to contribute later as adults, but academic credit must be strictly protected from instructor political bias. Some fields offer training in participant observation or other appropriate academic methodologies for students working for academic credit. But many humanities and social science fields have no such traditions, making them vulnerable to instructor bias, in which some social justice organizations and commitments are preferred above others and in which the pressure for self-interrogation has expected outcomes and faculty-approved conclusions and thus becomes coercive. Humanities disciplines can, however, encourage critical analysis of political positions and beliefs; instructors need to encourage, not discourage, student critique of deeply held faculty beliefs. Students also have to feel welcome to participate in organizations devoted to both sides of controversial political issues, including the Arab-Israeli conflict. Not all social and political commitments are controversial, to be sure, at least on many US campuses. A faculty member could endorse student participation in a campaign to give a college education to prisoners, and a university should be ready to defend faculty and student advocacy of local voting rights regardless of the surrounding political climate. But students even in these cases have a right to a different opinion, and the freedom to express that opinion might enhance classroom debates.

## NANCY KOPPELMAN

The social justice mandate holds that higher education should both foster humanist values and support students' efforts to put those values into practice. Initiatives include community-based learning, volunteer work, and internships. A mandate is an official order or commission to perform an ongoing action or work toward a goal. Mandates enact conclusions. They cause people to do things. "When you get tired of just reading and thinking" the logic goes, "and you want to *do* something, join us!"

This formulation of the link between reading and thinking on the one hand, and "doing" on the other, suggests that social justice efforts can bypass or even supersede thoughtful judgment. They can't. Thinking is a kind of doing, and all other kinds of doing, especially in college, ought to be based on it. Nevertheless, many colleges and universities have made "doing" as distinct from reading and thinking into a necessary feature of education by implementing a social justice mandate.

Higher education is supposed to be in the business of questioning, disrupting, and sometimes defeating conclusions, as well as shaping new ones that will also be tested. The solutions of one era become the problems of the next; today's expert knowledge is moot tomorrow. This dynamic of intellectual renewal is the very essence of higher education. When colleges enact the social justice mandate, they must guard against mobilizing conclusions and implicitly condoning political actions that take place under their auspices.

Some social justice efforts enact conclusions that enjoy a broad consensus. For example, initiatives to alleviate hunger, provide literacy services, protect natural resources, assist the homeless, and support at-risk youth contribute to the public good. They link theory to practice and create bridges to students' post-graduate ambitions. They are valuable opportunities for students to experience responsible citizenship by contributing to their communities. They feed and water habits of service that foster a thriving democracy. American higher education has long promoted social change efforts such as these, but today's activities are much more popular than they used to be. Undergraduate programs informed by the social justice mandate are embraced nationwide as fully in keeping with the goals and commitments of higher learning. They enjoy the stamp of approval from accrediting bodies that certify that curricula meet widely shared institutional standards.

In contrast, some academics claim that direct political activism—the kind that citizens do on their own time—can also be legitimate expressions of the social justice mandate. In so doing, they reach well beyond the standards that make higher education what it is and use their institutions as weapons to fight for their own hotly contested causes. This is precisely the case with the Boycott, Divest, and Sanctions movement (BDS). Some faculty who are critical of Israeli policy weigh in on the Israel/Palestine conflict by mobilizing BDS, not in their own names or on their own time, but under the broad banners of higher education and the fields of study in which they claim expertise. Hence the boycott initiatives that have been proposed or adopted by disciplinary organizations. When academics work to get their disciplines to boycott Israel, they reveal that their allegiance to firm conclusions that they share with political allies is stronger than their commitment to cultivate their students' skills and critical capacities. They blur activism and inquiry, thus erasing what W.E.B. DuBois took to be the university's purpose: "above all, to be the organ of that fine adjustment between real life and the growing knowledge of life, an adjustment which forms the secret of civilization" (52-53). They attempt to deploy education and critical thinking on behalf of a highly controversial political orthodoxy. They undermine the aims of education by shutting down discussion and thought and turning inquiry into moral one-upmanship. The message to students is that they need not bother with the difficult intellectual work of understanding culture and history for themselves. They can join a movement instead. Academics who champion BDS are not concerned about distorting genuine inquiry in this manner. To the best of their ability, they proudly captain their institutions and professional organizations to sail with the current of BDS.

The reason for this moral certainty is not that they are right. Their activism is based on two conclusions that have come to undergird scholarship in the humanities and social sciences: a commitment to human rights, and anti-colonialism. On the face of it, this seems as uncontroversial as feeding the hungry. Who in American academia, or nearly anywhere else, would fail either to condemn colonialism or to value human rights? Here is where the social justice mandate rubs against the grain of the well-worn post-modern groove from which conclusions about human rights and colonialism have issued. Concepts of truth, fact, and certainty have been eclipsed by theories of social constructionism and contingency. Some who embrace the social construction of reality resist the notion that there are facts and truths to be adjudicated. Yet in spite of embracing contingency and constructionism as guiding principles, some of the very same academic activists make rather bold certainty claims about the Israel/Palestine conflict. These certainties are quite dissonant with, indeed contradictory to, what appears to be a stalwart skepticism fundamental to their intellectual culture. The BDS enclave is an outcome of this development and embodies these contradictions.

Given the way the idea of human rights informs the social justice mandate, what kind of knowledge do academics who advocate boycotting Israeli higher education institutions rely on to undergird their certainties about colonialism and human rights? Can they be trusted to make sound judgments and enact conclusions about the Israel/Palestine conflict that are in keeping with the mission of higher education?

The answer to the latter question is "no." The knowledge—or more properly the lack of it—that academics in the BDS movement rely on to justify their activism reveals an ignorance of the history of human rights, and a failure to engage deeply with the disturbing insights that a historical understanding of colonialism yields. Due to how they frame their scholarly interests, they do not know how ideas in history intersect with post-Enlightenment institutions and social formations, and why this knowledge matters to social justice efforts. More disturbing still, they keep their students away from this kind of understanding by tightly controlling the discourse about the Israel/Palestine conflict.

BDS principles aim toward an outcome that is already known by its adherents, based on an analysis of causes that they do not think they ever need to question again. This conclusion-driven approach threatens the wide range of emergent work by Israelis and Palestinians alike who are collaborating, often against terrible odds, to address the decades-long conflict plaguing their people even as geography undeniably ties their fates, like their histories, tightly to one another. Questioning certainties takes time, patience, commitment, and trust that is deserved: a more demanding set of factors than it takes to recruit political allies and maintain their loyalty. For all these reasons, academic boycotts corrupt higher education's *raison d'être*, which is not primarily to enact the social justice mandate, but to promote careful thinking and a continual exploration and revision of what justice is and might be in the future. If higher education is to participate in aiming effectively for social justice, the structures and institutions that nurture the habits of mind through which the very outlines of justice can be debated, developed, revised, and ultimately mobilized must be protected even from within. ■

*Adapted from Nancy Koppelman, "'When you want to do something, join us!': The Limits of the Social Justice Mandate in American Higher Education," with introductory material added.*

---

Also see ACADEMIC BOYCOTTS, BDS AND CHRISTIAN CHURCHS, BDS AND THE AMERICAN ANTHROPOLOGICAL ASSOCIATION, and ORIENTALISM AND THE ATTACK ON ENLIGHTENMENT VALUES.

# SOCIALLY RESPONSIBLE INVESTING (SRI)

## CARY NELSON

The acronym SRI refers to two interrelated and partly interchangeable investment strategies—"Socially Responsible Investing" and "Sustainable, Responsible, and Impact Investing." Overall, as of 2016, about 20% of US investments are in some version of SRI. That percentage is expected to grow, especially as the millennial generation matures and acquires resources to invest. From 2012 to 2014, SRI investing grew at a rate of more than 75 percent. There were estimated to be 167 SRI mutual funds in 2001 and 415 in 2014. These investment strategies aim to combine competitive financial returns with positive social impact. In addition to the terms above, some investors describe the goal as ethical, values-based, mission-related, community-based, or green investing. SRI investors include individuals, credit unions, medical facilities, foundations, religious organizations, pension plans, corporations, unions, and mutual funds. SRI investing ranges across a series of different products and asset classes, from stocks to private equity to real estate to venture capital. It can promote human rights, social justice, equality, racial or ethnic diversity, environmental stewardship, consumer protection, and ethical corporate governance. It is a way of driving change through investment. Some SRI agendas avoid investing in weapons development and manufacture, tobacco, fossil fuels, pornography, or other products. Some SRI protocols seek mainly to avoid doing harm, while others have more proactive social agendas. Negative screening enables funds to avoid practices of which they disapprove. Some of these concerns and strategies have been widely employed in the debates over the status of companies doing business in Israel.

Socially responsible investing has a long history, arguably dating to a 1758 decision by the Religious Society of Friends to prohibit members from participating in the slave trade. The Methodist leader John Wesley (1703–1791) urged his followers not to invest in tanning and chemical production that could damage workers' health. This inaugurated the commitment to avoid investment in "sin stocks." Given this history, it is not surprising that these same religious groups are among those involved in SRI debates over investment in Israel. An August 10, 2015, letter from the president of the United Church of Christ's United Church Funds operation gives one model of how SRI can frame anti-Israel resolutions. The first three paragraphs tell Church members "you can be proud that you are already part of the growing trend of investors that consider environmental, social, and governance factors when deciding how to be responsible stewards of their assets," then detail the Church's divestment from fossil fuel companies. Only in the fourth paragraph does the letter report the Church is urging support for the BDS movement. By then, presumably Israel can seem little more than another enterprise extracting "thermal coal or oil in tar sands." The letter closes by reiterating the fund's "continued pleasure to serve our investors in aligning values and mission with finances" (Hart). So critique of Israel is surrounded by self-congratulatory affirmations of moral righteousness.

Since the 1950s, labor unions have done targeted investing with their pension funds. In the 1970s investors targeted companies manufacturing napalm and other Vietnam war weapons, and many institutions began divesting from companies doing business in South Africa, a movement that gained force in the following decade. In 2007 the SRI in the Rockies Conference scheduled a pre-conference to address the needs of indigenous peoples. Shareholder activism is increasing as a way to promote SRI investment and divestment.

Perhaps the most widely publicized shareholder actions have been those directed at the pension fund giant Teachers Insurance and Annuity Association—College Retirement Equities Fund (TIAA-CREF), a Fortune 100 financial services organization that is the leading retirement provider for people who work in the academic, research, medical, and cultural fields. In 2011 Jewish Voice for Peace began a campaign to get TIAA-CREF to divest from Caterpillar and other companies they accused of profiting from Israel's military occupation of the West Bank. Two years later a coalition of BDS groups submitted another divestment resolution before the TIAA-CREF board. There were organized protests in several cities objecting to TIAA-CREF's failure to divest from companies that "profit from segregated services, home demolitions, militarized violence, and other human rights abuses." TIAA-CREF officials resisted taking a vote at its annual shareholder meetings because it preferred to remain apolitical. Nonetheless, it dropped Caterpillar from one fund obligated to comply with a list maintained by an external investment ratings group.

Shareholder resolutions can be submitted for a vote at annual meetings, but the results are advisory, not binding on corporate boards. The courts have been reluctant to give resolutions more authority because shareholders who object to management policy can easily sell their stock and move on. They are not bound to a company to the degree an employee might be.

In 2012 Holy Land Principles was launched to provide an opening for a less antagonistic shareholder process aimed at delegitimizing and destabilizing Israel. Nine Holy Land Principles resolutions have been filed for votes at shareholder meetings in 2016. Targeted in 2015, the Silicon Valley technology company Cisco Corporation in 2016 will be asked to end claimed employment discrimination against Palestinians. The 2016 resolution demands an ethnic breakdown of Cisco officials and managers, professionals, technicians, sales personnel, office and clerical workers, skilled craft workers, semiskilled operatives, unskilled laborers, and service workers, not that Cisco on its own can create the educational opportunities necessary to guarantee ethnic parity in all these job categories. Intel, Coca Cola, Pepsi, FedEx, UPS, GE, GM, and McDonalds are asked to sign the Holy Land Principles. Management is likely to recommend voting against the resolutions, but they will be included in the packets for the meetings. The American Friends Service Committee has condemned the Holy Land Principles for not explicitly calling for divestment from companies doing business on the West Bank.

BDS activists have adopted a strategy of buying single shares in publicly held companies so they can gain entrance to and speak at shareholder meetings in favor of anti-Israel resolutions. At Boeing Corporation for several years those inside interventions against the sale of Boeing products to Israel's military have been coordinated with demonstrations outside shareholder meetings. While the probability of Boeing complying with these demands is exactly nil, the protests help create an atmosphere than can lead other companies to avoid investment in Israel to escape comparable controversy.

As reported in the entry on Divestment Campaigns, these strategies are increasingly being supplemented by the use of SRI investment vehicles that simply quietly omit companies doing business in Israel from their funds. That way disinvestment from Israel can be unremarked and instead the moral virtues of a mutual fund can be touted without any overt antagonism toward the Jewish state. Although there are many existing ways to invest in Israel, there is also a clear need for pro-Israel options in SRI investing. The Jlens Investor Network was founded in 2012 to fill that need, and other pro-Israel SRI investing options may materialize as well. Overall, SRI funds have five available strategies, all of which are being directed against Israel:

1.  Engaging in advocacy and dialogue with corporate management.
2.  Filing shareholder resolutions to force companies to address their concerns.
3.  Voting proxy statements in favor of SRI shareholder resolutions.
4.  Divesting company stock, so a company is no longer included in a fund.
5.  Investing in top companies on the basis of environmental, social, and governance (ESG) factors.

These tactics can embody either overt or covert hostility toward the Jewish State. Israel's supporters need both defensive and offensive options in response. The risk to Israel's economy is real, both from those companies that withdraw and those that quietly decline to participate in Israel in the first place. ■

Also see BDS: A BRIEF HISTORY, DIVESTMENT CAMPAIGNS, and ECONOMIC BOYCOTTS

# TEACHING ARABS
# AND JEWS IN ISRAEL

T oo many in the West assume Israeli students are virtually all Jewish and thus have no sense of what a multi-ethnic Israeli classroom might actually be like. Ignorance about daily life in such a classroom makes it easier to endorse academic boycotts. Even some who are committed to the rise of feminism and feminist theory over nearly fifty years in the West are willing to condemn the Israeli university without knowing how their own cultural commitments play out there.

—CN

SHIRA WOLOSKY

Among those who initiate, those who support, and those who are concerned about the issues raised by the academic boycott initiatives against Israel, few, I suspect, have a very vivid picture of what academic life in Israel is like. Since I am among the ones who would be boycotted, I would like to share my experience there.

About one third of the students in the classes I teach in the English Department of the Hebrew University of Jerusalem are Arab Israelis, mainly women: Christian and Muslim and secular, studying with other Israelis who are Russian, American, British, French, Ethiopian, and/or whose parents arrived from European and Arab countries at various times and in various ways, including expulsion or flight.

My own teaching has centered mainly in courses on American literature and culture; on feminist theory; and also on religion and theory. Each of these topics opens to cultural adventure, as the diverse students of my classes encounter each other. In my experience, the Israeli university should be especially supported and praised as a public sphere in which different sectors who otherwise have few social spaces for doing so can meet each other, all pursuing a common project of education in whatever different fields and ways, and before or outside the structure of lives that will soon be separated by work, family, locality, and sectorial pressures.

Certainly that is how I view my own classroom: as a civic scene, beyond whatever material is under discussion. I see student engagement in the class as civic training to democratic participation and cultural activism. Critical analysis of texts, however canonical; considered debate of positions, however apparently authoritative; perhaps above all, the ability and the desire to address each other in ways that respect difference but also explore terms and seek accommodation: these are the educational opportunities I see the classroom offer. Class discussions become intense scenes of exchange and debate, where persons from and within very distinct contexts are invited and goaded to address and attend to each other.

My class on Feminist Theory is an extraordinary experience. Together my students and I discover a language that names and places our own lives, revealing issues and situations we did not even know were there. It is especially challenging for women to learn to use their voices, to project their voices into the public sphere, to participate in discussion and debate. Doing critical thinking and bringing it to expression run counter to women's social roles, often working against religious norms, although not—as we also explore—necessarily dictated by religious texts themselves. Religious traditions can acquire new meanings when examined through different modes of interpretation and different (women) interpreters. Such questions of speaking and being heard, of resisting silencing both external and internal, are core concerns throughout feminist theory. In the classroom there are women with covered hair and without covered hair, Muslim and Jewish, Christian and many sorts of transnational Israelis, traditional to varying degrees. My goal is to create the classroom itself as a public sphere. It is the chance for women to develop analytical and critical skills for interpreting texts and claims, however sacred or standard, for examining and becoming conscious of their own narratives, and to learn that there are different ones. The class is driven by the attempt to open speaking space to those unfamiliar to it. I try to slow discussion down, to open time for each person to speak despite often deeply ingrained hesitation. I try to ask questions that will invite other questions. I try to create an atmosphere and ethos in which students will speak to each other.

Topics in my feminism course include body image and comportment as forms of social coercion; the political theories of liberalism and communitarianism, weighing how selves conceived through private self-determination compare with selves conceived as embedded in culture. Women's history provides a powerful entry into old recognitions, revealing ways in which one's own experience is not one's own only, not limited to the specific contexts which each woman herself inhabits. Legal, economic, and social histories and constraints are examined, most crucially the very lack of access to public discourse denying women the possibility of shaping the laws under which they live. Women's invisible work in the home, the continued inequalities of work opportunities and conditions, but also continued commitments to family and community, are discussed, as is how to balance them. Not least, histories of religious institutions in America, of access to sacred texts, of debates about how these are interpreted and perhaps most urgently by whom—with women's emergence as interpreters of their own religious traditions and claims to religious authority—have special resonance in this Middle Eastern classroom.

Some texts open extraordinary scenes of cultural encounter and confrontation. The portrait of a young girl in Henry James' *Daisy Miller*, who, defiant of social convention, dies from the malaria she contracts when she visits the Roman Forum unchaperoned at night with an Italian man, splits the class among those who sympathize with her independence and those who see her end to be a fit warning against wildness. Most women in the classes, however, are riveted by the women's points of view we uncover, the social, political, historical, and psychological attempts to bring the hidden, which is to say publicly and privately ignored, lives of women into the light of record and recognition. Yet most women in my classes, Jewish and Arab, Christian and Muslim, identify themselves closely with the tradition(s) and communities they see themselves to be part of. Theirs is not a performative individualism, answerable only to themselves. There is no "identity" apart from their memberships, to which on the whole they remain deeply attached. To address them and to listen to them is to respect these community memberships, while also developing critical perspectives on them, and discovering the terms and norms of other communities in which other students are members in ways that are both critical and respectful. This means exploring the resources within the cultures themselves for recognizing and respecting other cultures, for upholding one's own particularity while also upholding the Other's.

This is the university world that is now under attack and threat of boycott. From a feminist stance I wonder: in these discussions of human rights, are women human? The many places in which women are in fact severely constrained do not occasion calls for boycotts and are not condemned by resolutions. Instead it is the academy in Israel which boycotts denounce, where women have what for many is their most dramatic and self-conscious opportunity to emerge into voice and participation. ■

*Adapted from Shira Wolosky, "Teaching in Transnational Israel: An Ethics of Difference."*

Also see ACADEMIC BOYCOTTS, BDS: A BRIEF HISTORY, and ISRAELI-PALESTINIAN UNIVERSITY COOPERATION.

# THE TEMPLE MOUNT / HARAM AL-SHARIF

## CARY NELSON

## THREE RELIGIONS, ONE SYMBOL

The Temple Mount is a raised rectangular platform covering 35 acres in the Old City of Jerusalem. The site itself may well have been sacred in various belief systems for 4,000 years, but its present shape dates from the first century B.C.E., when the Roman King Herod the Great expanded the site and enclosed it in a 100-foot-high retaining wall made of limestone blocks quarried from the Jerusalem Hills. The structure itself is imposing and unforgettable, enhanced by the fact it comes to us from the ancient world, and it includes what is arguably the city's most iconic landmark: the Dome of the Rock, an Islamic shrine whose dome atop an elaborate octagonal base is covered in 24-carat gold leaf that gleams in the sun. The site also includes the large but architecturally less dramatic al-Aqsa mosque, located along the platform's southern edge. The Temple Mount has been called the most contested piece of real estate on earth, and it is located in the most sacred and conflicted of cities. It is sacred to three monotheistic religions, here listed chronologically:

- In Jewish tradition the Temple Mount is taken to be built on the place where God gathered the dust from which he created Adam.

There too Abraham, the founding father of Judaism, is said to have faced the ultimate test of his faith, when he was commanded to bind his son Isaac and prepare to sacrifice him. Moving closer to historical time, the Temple Mount is the place where Solomon built the First Temple about 1000 B.C. It was destroyed by the Babylonians and replaced by the Second Temple in 516 B.C. before it too was destroyed, this time by the Romans in 70 A.D, though the lower portions of the wall remain. A tiny minority of Jews obsessively believe a Third Temple must be built on the raised platform if the messiah is to come, whereas others believe that will not be possible until after a messiah ushers in the era in which the Temple can be revived.

- Christians consider it the place where Jesus was blessed and returned to teach. It is where he chased the money-lenders from the Temple. They locate his crucifixion a few hundred yards away and historically prayed there. Some evangelical Christians share a belief that the Temple must be rebuilt and destroyed to herald the second coming of Christ.

- For Muslims, who call it Haram al-Sharif (the Noble Sanctuary), it is Islam's third-holiest site after Mecca and Medina. There they believe Muhammad took the Miraculous Night Journey on the back of a winged horse to receive from God the principles and practices of Muslim prayer. It is thus the place where the ultimate religious figure underwent the ultimate religious experience. Because this holy place stands above other places in the city, Muslims often consider it a symbol of Islam's supersession over Judaism and Christianity.

All three religions invest end-of-days narratives either in the Temple Mount itself or in the City of Jerusalem. These narratives all project the image of a distant idealized past, testify to a ruptured present, and imagine their return to a glorious future.

As Gershom Gorenberg has pointed out, it is a very dangerous thing for a place loaded with this much myth to be real. Yet the stories the three religions tell about the Temple Mount could coexist. As the three religions are all monotheistic, they could treat the Temple Mount as a symbol of the one God they all worship. But physical control over the site suggests to some they possess its central truth, that it is their God's home above all others.

# INTERSECTIONS OF POLITICS AND FAITH

Ideas and feelings leak back and forth across the uncertain border between religion and modern political ideologies. Today's far-right

Israeli activists concerned with the Mount are mostly religious. But they represent the stream of Israeli Judaism that has most thoroughly absorbed radical nationalism's concern with power, glory, and territory .... On the Palestinian side, [Amin] Al-Husseini's (1897-1974) contemporary successor is Sheikh Raed Salah (1958-), who has built his hardline faction of the Islamic Movement in Israel on the slogan, "Al-Aqsa Is in Danger." ... Holy places are symbols, and symbols act like parabolic mirrors: They reflect energy and focus it on a single overheated spot. On the Israeli right, the Temple Mount has become a symbol of the gap between what it thought that possession of the homeland would mean and the reality of dealing with another people. For Palestinians, Al-Aqsa is a symbol of Palestine under occupation and threat. These are nationalist sentiments. When re-absorbed into religion, they produce harsher religions. To describe the conflict around the contested holy site, and the contested country, as a battle of religions is to miss much of what is happening and to make it seem much more comfortably distant from modern Western ideologies than it is.

—Gershom Gorenberg "Sacred to the Nation"

The Temple Mount has been a flashpoint in the Israeli-Palestinian conflict and a microcosm of its defining tensions. The 1929 Arab riots in Palestine began at the Western Wall, the western border of the Temple Mount. Over centuries, Jews had established the right to pray there, but both Arabs and Jews amidst rising tensions were willing to use the Wall and the Mount as combined religious and political symbols. In 1929 Haj Amin al Husseini, the Mufti of Jerusalem, distributed leaflets to Arabs claiming that the Jews were planning to take over the al-Aqsa mosque atop the Mount, a claim that has often been heard since. It was then that some Jews called for the building of a Third Temple on the site, making matters worse, and that too has remained a minority ambition.

When Israel captured the rest of Jerusalem in the Six Day War in 1967 Jews and other non-Muslim faiths regained the access to the Western Wall that been denied them for the nineteen years of Jordanian control. Despite its victory, Israel chose to leave the Temple Mount itself to be administered by the Islamic trust, or *Waqf*, with the proviso that Jews could visit the site but not pray there. But Arabs remained sensitive to any change in procedures that could be taken as a sign Israel was changing its policies and might have the ambition to take over the site. In the 1980s Israelis discovered an extremist right-wing Jewish plot to dynamite the Dome of the Rock as way to provoke hostilities with the surrounding Muslim countries and make withdrawal from the Sinai impossible. In 1996 the Tunnel Riots broke out in protest of nearby Israeli archeological research beneath the surface.

Almost all parties to the 2000 peace negotiations at Camp David near Washington, DC, agree that the status of Jerusalem in general and Temple Mount in particular proved deal breakers. For Yasser Arafat (1929-2004), the status of Haram al-Sharif was the highest priority in the negotiations over Jerusalem (Tessler 803). Ehud Barak (1942-), then Israeli Prime Minister, offered Arafat some form of "custodianship" or "functional sovereignty" over the elevated platform of Temple Mount/Haram al-Sharif, but under overall actual Israeli political sovereignty. Neither Barak nor Arafat, however, was willing to concede actual sovereignty, in part because both were convinced their respective publics would not accept that result. Neither had the political capital to win popular support over such a volatile issue. Barak also insisted on the Jewish right to pray on the Mount, though Israel had banned the practice since the 1967 war, motivated both by religion and security. All this was taken as a move to cement Israeli power over the site, and Arafat responded by declaring that there never had been a Jewish presence or Jewish temples on Haram al-Sharif; the Temple had really been in Nablus (Golan 142-165). When Ariel Sharon (1928-2014) visited the Temple Mount in 2000, it confirmed the fears of the Palestinian public that Israel sought full sovereignty over this Muslim holy site and helped trigger the Second, or Al-Aqsa, Intifada.

Recent developments combine a repetition of past confrontations and the invention of new ones. Most surreal among such events have been the November 2015 war games held by the Iranian Revolutionary Guards. On a hilltop in the holy city of Qom in central Iran a life-size plastic replica of the Dome of the Rock was erected so a ground troop and helicopter assault, preceded by aerial bombing runs against hypothetical enemy targets, could liberate it. Iranian news releases revealed they had confused the Dome with the al-Aqsa mosque. By setting the war games in Qom Iranians insured a religious dimension to a military exercise.

Shortly before this, a far more serious conflict developed. Once again rumors of an Israeli takeover of the Mount circulated, this time helping to produce a new and uniquely desperate form of protest: random stabbing attacks carried out by Palestinian teenagers and others against Israeli soldiers and civilians in Jerusalem, Hebron, and elsewhere. Real-time incitement and the spread of rumors about the Mount on social media added to the difficulty of defusing the situation. Both Israelis and Palestinians died in the process, victims of a politico-religious mix of manipulated passion, cynicism, and authentic despair. Statements from the Israeli prime minister's office assur-ing Palestinians that no changes were planned in Temple Mount policies had little effect, not only because people are now highly skeptical about anything that anyone in authority on either side of the Green Line says but also because other members of the government issued provocative messages suggesting more aggressive Israeli ambitions for Temple Mount. Meanwhile, Palestinian Authority president Mahmoud Abbas played a comparable double game, simultaneously warning about Israeli intentions toward the Mount and directing his security services to contain the violence.

A December, 2015, report by Eran Tzidkiyahu summarizes other developments over the last decade and currently that have redefined the political and religious dynamic:

"Since late 2005, the sight of yeshiva students, police officers, and Waqf staff following each other around and scrutinizing each other's moves has become common at the sacred site. Since 2010, this tragi-comic scenario has been accompanied by raging masses of hundreds of Muslim men, women, and children of all ages, who spend time studying the Quran in groups, and whose function is to bellow 'Allahu Akbar' (in English: 'God is the greatest') every time a visibly religious Jew passes. Lately, as tensions increased, these calls have expanded to target all Jews and tourists on the Temple Mount (p. 4)." The Northern and Southern Factions of the Islamic Movement in Israel, the former outlawed late in 2015, for two years have been sponsoring free bus service to bring tens of thousands of worshippers from Israeli towns and cities to Temple Mount to resist "the Israeli siege on the al-Aqsa Mosque." Meanwhile Israelis on the far right have increasingly been demanding the right to pray on the Mount, a movement facilitated by a gradual erosion of the rabbinic prohibition against entering there for fear of breaching the location of the Second Temple holy of holies. Once again, the demand for the right to pray combines religious and political strategy, mixing a religious impulse with an assertion of sovereignty. ■

Also see THE INTIFADAS, THE ISRAELI RIGHT AND RELIGIOUS SETTLER POLITICS, THE OSLO ACCORDS, THE PALESTINIAN AUTHORITY, THE ISRAELI-PALESTINIAN PEACE PROCESS, and THE SIX DAY WAR.

# THE TWO-STATE SOLUTION

## CARY NELSON

onceptually, the two-state solution to the Israeli-Palestinian conflict is relatively straightforward. It proposes that Israelis and Palestinians occupy separate but contiguous sovereign states, with borders roughly based on the 1949 armistice lines that gave relative closure to formal 1948 hostilities (MAP 2). The two-state solution is designed to give a reasonable measure of justice to both peoples. As such, it is based on compromise. Neither Israelis nor Palestinians would get everything they want, but both peoples could ideally thereafter live in peace and pursue their economic, political, and social destinies in freedom from the unremitting antagonism and violence that define so much of their lives now.

As a significant political proposal, the two-state solution dates from the July 7, 1937, report of the Peel Commission. Following World War I and the dissolution of the Ottoman Empire, the League of Nations in 1922 granted Britain power over the area roughly designated as Palestine. The British Mandate came into effect the following year. It included responsibility for establishing a national home for the Jewish people, built on the principles of the Balfour Declaration of 1917, itself confirmed by the victorious allied powers in 1920. The mandate text, however, also specified that "nothing should be done which might prejudice the civil and religious rights of existing non-Jewish communities in Palestine." Suffice it to say that maintaining that balancing act proved an impossible challenge; the effort played out in a series of contradictory policies, themselves put forward in the context of rising nationalism, political unrest, and periods of violence. The Peel Commission (headed by Lord Peel), officially the Palestine Royal Commission, was appointed in 1936 to study the causes of the conflict and recommend solutions. The 440-page report concluded that the only way to bring an end to Arab-Jewish unrest was to partition Palestine into separate Arab and Jewish nations. Most Jews accepted the recommendation, however reluctantly. The Arabs rejected it. The plan included a recommendation to transfer as many as 225,000 Arabs and 1,250 Jews to create coherent Arab and Jewish territories. In effect, the 1948 war produced a version of that population transfer.

The two-state solution is opposed by various constituencies on both sides—by Arabs mortally offended by the presence of a Jewish homeland in what they consider Muslim land; by Jews who believe God gave them all of Palestine, including Judea and Samaria (the West Bank); and by idealists who believe Jews and Arabs should live together peacefully in one bi-national country. Meanwhile, repeated efforts to negotiate an agreement have failed, though some have come close. Yet no viable alternative to the two-state solution exists. As journalist Jeffrey Goldberg has written, "The choice is difficult: create conditions on the West Bank for the emergence of a Palestinian state, or give the Palestinians the vote in Israel. The third option—the permanent disenfranchisement of the West Bank Palestinians—is not an acceptable option, practically or morally. It is certainly not a legitimate option in the eyes of the international community, and such an option would be rejected by millions of Jews in the United States and elsewhere." Many of those who continue to work for a two-state solution believe it is the only way for Israel to "remain a Jewish-majority democracy and a safe haven for the Jewish people."

Jewish settlements close to the 1949 armistice line (MAP 2, known as the "Green Line" because that was the color of the line drawn on a map) would likely stay in Israel in any final agreement, with land adjacent to Gaza and south of the West Bank swapped in exchange (MAP 4). Perhaps 80 percent of West Bank Jews live in those nearby settlements, most of which do not actually present insurmountable barriers to an agreement. Settlements deeper into the West Bank, however, represent serious impediments; they are likely to have to be abandoned, contrary to the fanciful proposal some advance that Jews could safely live as citizens of a Palestinian state. Some Israelis reject the need to divide Jerusalem into Jewish and Palestinian capitals, though distinct Jewish versus Arab neighborhoods already exist and suggest a basis for apportioning sections of the city to each people. The considerable hostility between Hamas and the Palestinian Authority, the groups respectively controlling Gaza and designated sections of the West Bank, present an obstacle to what had for long been hoped to be one Palestinian nation composed of both areas. But a two-state solution could be realized in stages, so that all these problems would not have to be solved at once.

One may summarize the major concessions each side would have to make before a final status agreement could be reached. Israel would (1) explicitly abandon all ambitions to establish a Greater Israel encompassing the West Bank; (2) commit itself to accepting a modified version of the pre-1967 borders; and (3) agree to the division of Jerusalem with East Jerusalem as the capital of a Palestinian state. The Palestinians would (1) specify that a final status agreement would settle all issues and end the conflict; (2) recognize Israel as a homeland for the Jewish people, and agree that the right of return for Palestinian refugees would be limited to returning to a Palestinian state, except for those who have family members who are Israeli citizens; and (3) accept a form of national sovereignty consistent with restrictions to guarantee Israel's security. The Palestinian state would thus have to be demilitarized, with no offensive military capacities.

One might clarify the Palestinian concessions by pointing out, first, that acknowledgement of Israel as a homeland of the Jews is not the same as declaring Israel to be a theocracy or possessing a state religion. It simply recognizes a historical fact. Combined with recognition of Israel's borders and the country's democratic status, it effectively concedes that the Jewish majority has the key role in shaping the country's future. It is also important that Israel acknowledge the catastrophic character of the Nakba (the Palestinian flight from Israel in 1948) and support the principle of financial compensation for those who lost property as a result. Palestinians have to date often insisted that the millions of descendants of the 700,000 Palestinians who left be allowed to return to Israel if they chose, but that could create a Palestinian majority and eliminate Israel as a Jewish state. Of the Palestinians who fled, it is likely that fewer than 50,000 remain alive.

At the same time, Israel's military occupation of the West Bank threatens its character as a democratic country. Israel cannot indefinitely contain a second-class group of Palestinian non-citizens and sustain its core values. The two-state solution remains the only route past these problems. ■

Also see BI-NATIONALISM, COORDINATED UNILATERAL WITHDRAWAL, GAZA, HAMAS, THE ONE-STATE SOLUTION, THE OSLO ACCORDS, THE PALESTINIAN AUTHORITY, THE ISRAELI-PALESTINIAN PEACE PROCESS, THE SECURITY BARRIER, THE TEMPLE MOUNT / HARAM AL-SHARIF, and THE WEST BANK.

# THE WEST BANK

CARY NELSON

The West Bank is an area of about 2,178 square miles (5,640 km) bounded on the north, west, and south by Israel, with Israel's eastern border defined by the 1949 Jordanian-Israeli armistice (MAP 2). The West Bank is bordered on the East by the Jordan River and the Dead Sea, boundaries shared with Jordan. The term West Bank was adopted to distinguish it from the East Bank of the Jordan River, which is part of Jordan itself. The West Bank population includes about half a million Israelis and 2.8 million Palestinian Arabs. The Jewish population of the West Bank has grown from 12,000 in 1980, but about 80 percent of the Jewish population is concentrated in settlement blocs near the Green Line marking the boundary of Israel after the 1948 war (MAPS 2 & 4). Most plans for the creation of a Palestinian state envisage Israel incorporating those settlement blocs in exchange for some of its own territory. In 2014, over 90,000 West Bank Palestinians regularly entered Israel to work; that remains an important part of the local economy.

For four centuries the area was controlled by the Ottoman Empire, but after World War I Britain gained power over it through the September 1922 Trans-Jordan Memorandum that supplemented the July 1922 League of Nations Mandate for Palestine. The United Nations partition plan for Palestine (MAP 1) envisioned that the West Bank would be part of a future Arab state, but that plan failed when Jordan captured the area in the 1948 war. Jordan made an effort to annex the West Bank two years later, but only the United Kingdom and Pakistan recognized the action. Several facts are essential to keep in mind when reflecting on the history of the area. Though Jordan controlled the West Bank for twenty years, from 1948 through the 1967 war (MAP 2), it was not referred to as an "occupied territory"; indeed it had no clear national status to warrant the term. One may argue that it hadn't been a sovereign territory for two thousand years. Nor was there an internationally recognized movement to create an independent Palestinian state during the time Jordan controlled the West Bank. That movement took form only after the 1967 Six Day War when Israel captured the area. Jordan formally relinquished its legal and administrative authority over the West Bank on July 31, 1988.

Except for the period when Jordan controlled the area, there has been a Jewish presence on the West Bank for centuries. That underwrote the conviction that Jews were returning to Hebron and other places when they resettled them after the 1967 war. But that does not mean it makes sense for Jews to remain in those communities as part of a two-state solution. Hebron is the extreme case, a fragmented collection of about 800 Jews in the middle of a Palestinian city of 250,000. A large IDF presence is required to guarantee their safety. Although some have suggested West Bank Jewish communities could remain part of a Palestinian state, it is difficult to see how Israelis could rest easy with Palestinian security forces as their sole source of protection, and it is equally difficult to see how Palestinians could accept Israeli soldiers embedded throughout their country. Despite their deep religious significance, abandonment of such settlements is likely to be a necessary part of any final peace agreement.

West Bank violence substantially predates 1967, mainly in the form of armed Palestinians infiltrating from the Jordanian-controlled West Bank into Israel. These included the Palestinian Fedayeen, nationalist guerillas or terrorists (depending on your point of view) who operated not only from Jordan but also from Egypt and Syria. Immediately after the 1948 war, infiltrations from the West Bank were often innocent, as Palestinians sought to recover property lost when they abandoned their homes and farms, but within a few years the infiltrations turned violent and by the mid-1950s the Fedayeen were crossing the border with the aim of killing Jews. Perhaps 400 Israelis were killed and 900 wounded in such attacks between 1951 and 1956. Counterattacks by Israeli forces targeted Palestinian villages in a strategy that tended to intensify the cycle of violence. In many ways that dynamic continues to the present day.

Both because it misrepresents the historical status of the West Bank—and because an internationally recognized "occupied territory" brings with it legal requirements that the occupying power is expected to observe—the

Israeli government and many of its allies worldwide object to that designation. Nevertheless, Israel's own High Court recognizes that the West Bank is overseen by a military occupation. Recognizing that fact, however, does not concede a history of sovereignty that would justify the "occupied territory" designation. Whatever the legal arguments, to be sure, there is a history of political efficacy behind the "occupied territories" designation; it dramatizes the fundamentally opposed interests of the settlers and the Palestinians and lends political force to opposition to the occupation. Thus the terminological battle is more political than legal; I raise these issues here in part to reach out to those who object fiercely to any reference to "the occupation." To claim that there is actually no military occupation itself would be irrational and contrary to reality. Even if one accepts the Israeli contention that these are "disputed," rather than occupied, territories, they are still being subjected to a military occupation. Military occupations can, however, be beneficial. Japan's occupation of Manchuria was brutal and inhumane. China's occupation of Tibet led to a million Tibetan deaths. But the American occupation of Germany and Japan enabled those countries to transition to democracy. The Israeli occupation of the West Bank denies Palestinians full citizenship and the right to political self-determination. The development of universities and some of the political institutions necessary to self-government, few of which existed in 1967, however, could facilitate the occupation's end. A peaceful transition to a nonmilitarized Palestinian state with a modified form of sovereignty remains possible. Were that to happen, attitudes toward the occupation would eventually evolve. Our understanding of the past can be altered by future events. The present system—in which West Bank Palestinians are condemned to second-class status—is politically unsustainable and ethically unacceptable. And it undermines the viability of a majority Jewish state that can remain the homeland of the Jewish people. One overdue change would be to guarantee West Bank Israelis and Palestinians equal protection under the law. As it stands, there is one legal system for West Bank Jews, which enables them as much as possible to feel like they are living in Israel proper, and quite another legal system for Palestinians. ■

Also see COORDINATED UNILATERAL WITHDRAWAL, THE ISRAELI RIGHT AND RELIGIOUS SETTLER POLITICS, THE OSLO ACCORDS, THE PALESTINIAN AUTHORITY, THE ISRAELI-PALESTINIAN PEACE PROCESS, SETTLEMENTS, SETTLER COLONIALISM, THE SIX DAY WAR, and THE TWO-STATE SOLUTION.

# WORLD WAR II AND
# THE FOUNDING OF ISRAEL

CARY NELSON, RACHEL S. HARRIS,
AND KENNETH W. STEIN

World War II and the Holocaust, along with the development of well-established Jewish institutions in Palestine, were the pivotal events and conditions that made it possible for the Zionist movement to realize its long-pursued dream of founding a nation in the ancient homeland of the Jewish people. Without that stimulus, it is doubtful the United Nations would have authorized the creation of a Jewish state in 1947.

While most of Europe and North Africa was in armed conflict during the war period, life in many ways continued as normal in Palestine; though geographically strategic, the region was out of the line of fire. The Arab leadership, divided and living mostly in exile, used this time to ingratiate themselves with British officials, often under the direction of Haj Amin al-Husseini (1897-1974), even though he was barred from attending the conferences convened to discuss the Palestine Question. Simultaneously some Arab leaders worked with the Nazis, particularly al-Husseini, who promised Arabs independence when the Germans defeated Britain and even went so far as to recruit Muslims for the Waffen-SS to hasten this end. As Avraham Sela summarizes it, "As of late 1943, [al-Husseini] became increasingly linked to the S.S. and attempts to prevent deals to exchange Jews from the

German-occupied Central European countries for lorries and other material resources" (66). There were also Arab leaders in Egypt and Transjordan aligned with the allies, and al-Husseini's personal influence faded rapidly after the war ended.

Zionists focused on bringing Jews to Palestine, legally when possible and illegally when immigration quotas were so limited that it was impossible to gain access by other means. In prewar Palestine (1934-1939), 50,000 Jews had entered illegally, but during the war Britain adopted a brutal policy of capturing and deporting Jewish immigrants. During 1939, the Haganah formed a small offshoot to smuggle Jews out of Europe, but these efforts were increasingly restricted as the war spread. In Palestine, the Haganah developed the Palmach, an elite military strike force with a subdivision, the Palyam, responsible for preparing potential Jewish refugees in areas of crisis to emigrate, arranging for their transport and initial settlement in Palestine.

As early as 1941, the West received news of large-scale Jewish killings by the Nazis. In 1942, the Polish government in exile in London reported that 700,000 Polish Jews had already been murdered by the Germans and, in December of that year, the Allies formally announced that Hitler had embarked on the mass murder of Jews. But immigration quotas to Palestine held, and, with most international borders closed to Jews, the progress of the "final solution" through which Jews would be rounded up and sent to camps "in the East" for extermination continued unabated. In 1943, amidst mass extermination of Jews, representatives of the US and Great Britain concluded a meeting in Bermuda where the issue of the disastrous European Jewish condition was debated, but neither country was willing to open its doors to Jewish refugee settlement.

Jews were vulnerable not only in Europe. As a 1941 anti-Semitic outburst in Baghdad showed, when 200 Jews were killed and homes and businesses destroyed, Jews could have no security within other nations. Using the partition plan (MAP 1) as a template, David Ben Gurion, head of the Jewish Agency, used the war years to build support among American Jews and the Zionists for the establishment of a Jewish state in Palestine. But in Palestine Zionists were less patient and military activities continued. In 1944, five years after the war had started, Menachem Begin (1913-1992) assumed command of the Irgun (a militant underground Zionist group founded in 1931); concluding that Germany's defeat was imminent, the group returned to the earlier priority of driving the British from Palestine. The Irgun began attacking British targets, activities which the Haganah and Palmach opposed. But by war's end, the Haganah would side with the Irgun to launch the Hebrew Rebellion Movement and attack British targets. In that effort, the Irgun followed the same policy as LHI, a paramilitary group that had split with the Irgun in 1940 so as to begin assaults on British targets then. LHI (or Lehi) was also known as the Stern Gang, after its founder Abraham Stern (1907-1942). Simultaneously, the Haganah stepped up its illegal immigration activities, assisting nearly 71,000 Jews to settle in Palestine between August 1945 and May 1948. Mostly war refugees and Holocaust survivors, many of these Jews were now trapped in internment camps in Germany and Eastern Europe, where they continued to face murder by the local population. In response to the illegal immigrations, the British began a campaign to destroy Haganah ships in European harbors, and from 1946 on forcibly detained the passengers of ships they intercepted in holding camps in Cyprus. Famously, passengers of the Exodus were returned to a British-controlled area of Germany and then removed to displaced persons camps, making the Jewish refugees return to the source of their persecution. Despite US president Harry Truman's (1884-1972) support for increased Jewish immigration, which became public knowledge in 1945, international borders remained closed to Jews, and Arabs rejected proposals for a single binational state that would be jointly governed by Arabs and Jews.

In 1944, after repeated pressure from the more moderate Jewish leaders who wished to support the British in their fight against the Axis powers, British prime minister Winston Churchill established the Jewish Brigade. Some 25,000 to 28,000 Palestinian Jews volunteered to serve in the British army, and the Jewish Brigade with its distinctive blue-and-white flag saw action in Italy. After the war, this military training would help Jewish immigration activities, and later would furnish military leaders in the battle for Israel's independence in 1948.

After repeated attempts by Britain to find a compromise for the two warring factions, the British proposed the Morrison-Grady (or Provincial Autonomy) Plan for a binational state in 1946. It was the product of an Anglo-American Committee of Inquiry tasked with studying the problem. The twelve Committee members toured the Middle East in February-March 1946. Documents were submitted from both sides, a three-volume survey (*The Problem of Palestine*) from the Arabs and a 1,000-page report (*The Jewish Case Before the ACC of Inquiry on Palestine*) from the Jewish Agency. (Founded in 1908, the Jewish Agency for Israel evolved through various names to become the primary organization responsible for bringing immigrants to Israel and aiding their absorption into the Jewish state.) The Committee also toured Displaced Persons centers, especially in Poland, where over 1,000 Jews had been murdered since the war's end. The refugees in the DP centers made it clear they wanted to live in Palestine. In May 1946 the Committee recommended that immigration be increased but rejected partition. Both Arabs and Jews rejected the report, and Truman announced US support for the partition of Palestine into two states (MAP 1), thereby further undermining a one-state (binational) solution. By then, Britain concluded it could no longer manage the situation in Palestine. In May 1946, Transjordan, previously part of the British Mandate, was recognized as an independent sovereign kingdom, constituting 75 percent of the territory for which Britain was responsible. The following year, in the wake of devastating losses to British military and administrative personnel when the King David Hotel was blown up by Irgun forces—killing 91 people, including Britons, Arabs, and Jews, and destroying the southern wing of the hotel, where the British administration was based—Britain turned over the Palestine problem to the United Nations. Britain had certainly wanted out long before the hotel bombing, but that settled matters.

In response, the UN General Assembly established the UN Special Committee on Palestine (UNSCOP) to study the matter and make recommendations. The Arabs demanded a state that would expel the illegal immigrants and grant no political rights to the remaining Jews. In 1947, as David Horowitz reports, Azzam Pasha (1893-1976), the head of the Arab League, told three Jewish Agency representatives that "the Arab world is not in a compromising mood. You won't get anything by peaceful means or compromise. You can perhaps get something, but only by force of arms. We shall try to defeat you. I'm not sure we'll succeed, but we will try. The Arab world regards you as invaders. It may be that we shall lose Palestine. But it's too late to talk of peaceful solutions." Jews, by contrast, welcomed UNSCOP and led the delegations on tours of energetic settlements. In comparison, the Arab villages seemed backward, and the Arab leadership and local economic development offered little to recommend itself to governance of the entire remaining area of the Mandate. A majority of eight of the eleven UNSCOP members endorsed a September 1, 1947, report recommending partition of Palestine into an Arab and a Jewish state (MAP 1), with an economic union and independent regime for the Jerusalem/Bethlehem areas. But the Arab states were unwilling to compromise with a Jewish state. The local Arab leadership in Palestine was more open to avenues for compromise, willing to cooperate and even work with the Zionists, though the Mufti, in exile, adamantly opposed Zionism and Jews. Local collaborations with Jews occurred in many ways: Palestinians provided key information to Zionists about Arab strengths, aided in the acquisition of military supplies, sold land to the Zionists, and cooperated on commerce and trade.

On November 29, 1947, the UN adopted a Partition Resolution sanctioning the creation of a Jewish state (MAP 1). The Soviets supported it, briefly reversing their long-standing anti-Zionism with the goal of diminishing British influence in the region. Pressure from Jewish Agency lobbyists at the United Nations significantly contributed to the vote for partition;

American Jews thus helped keep the US aboard. The voting at the UN was broadcast live on radio worldwide. Listeners were tense in Palestine, as the UN charter required a two-thirds majority for passage. Thirty-three nations voted yes, thirteen voted no, and ten (including Britain) abstained. As Anita Shapira writes:

> What appeared to the Jews as a divine miracle, a sign that a global system of justice existed, was perceived by the Arabs as a flagrant wrong, a miscarriage of justice and an act of coercion. They were being called upon to consent to the partitioning of a country that only 30 years earlier had been considered Arab, and to the establishment of a Jewish state in it. To them recognition of the Jews' national rights in Palestine was insufferable, and the only possible response was armed resistance (156). ■

*Adapted from Cary Nelson, Rachel S. Harris, and Kenneth W. Stein, "The History of Israel."*

Also see ISRAEL: DEMOCRATIC AND JEWISH, JEWISH HISTORY BEFORE ZIONISM, THE 1948 WAR OF INDEPENDENCE, ZIONISM AS PHILOSOPHY AND PRACTICE, and ZIONISM: ITS EARLY HISTORY.

# THE YOM KIPPUR WAR (1973)

## CARY NELSON, RACHEL S. HARRIS, AND KENNETH W. STEIN

D espite the resounding defeat of the Arab countries during the 1967 war, hostilities continued, culminating in the 1969-1970 War of Attrition, an escalating series of border clashes with Egypt. The IDF reduced cities along the Suez Canal to rubble and Egyptian refugees flooded into Cairo. US interventions set in place a ceasefire when in 1970 Egyptian president Nasser died suddenly, to be succeeded by Anwar Sadat (1918-1981).

In 1973, The Yom Kippur War (the October War) took place from October 6-24. The conduct of the war was initially shaped by the failure of Israeli intelligence to recognize the extent of Egypt's humiliation in the 1967 war, the political pressure for revenge it created, and the ongoing violence that followed. As a consequence of that failure of understanding, they did not pay attention to the heavy buildup of Egyptian troops along the Suez Canal, the massing of Syrian troops at the border, and even disregarded a September 25 warning from King Hussein to Prime Minister Golda Meir (1898-1978) that a coordinated Egyptian-Syrian attack was forthcoming. Meir had become Prime Minister in 1969 upon the sudden death of Levi Eshkol (1895-1969). Complacency about the condition of the Egyptian army, given their easy thrashing in 1967, lessened the motivation of the intelligence services to react. In consequence, the Israeli air force took heavy losses from SAM missiles, while Russian anti-tank missiles destroyed a number of Israeli tanks on the Egyptian front. In the first two days of the attack, top Israeli officials believed the entire country could be lost. The Israelis counterattacked in the Golan Heights on October 11 and within days advanced toward Damascus. Meanwhile, US President Richard Nixon (1913-1994) agreed to an emergency airlift of military equipment to Israel, beginning October 14. That same day the Egyptian army launched a disastrous assault that cost it 250 tanks, compared to an Israeli loss of 20. Soon the IDF crossed the canal and encircled Egypt's Third Army. What began as a rout of Israeli forces ended in a major victory for them, but 2,500 Israeli soldiers died, the highest toll since the 1948 war. Moreover, the country's confidence was shaken by its intelligence failures and lack of preparation. Then, too, the recent introduction of television in 1969 meant that the Yom Kippur War was the first war to be televised and to appear in people's homes. The sight of bound and blindfolded soldiers being led across the screen reinforced the Israeli public's sense of existential threat.

The Yom Kippur War shook confidence in the government. In the 1960s and 1970s, the citizenry was also rocked by a series of public scandals, including the revelation of Leah Rabin's illegal bank account in the US and Moshe Dayan's sexual escapades and personal possession of national archeological treasures. Political infighting in the Labor party and the demographic rise of the Mizrachi voting bloc then combined to put an end to 30 years of Labor dominance of Israeli political institutions. In the spectacular election of 1977, in an upset that Israeli television anchor Haim Yavin spontaneously called a *ma'apach* ("political revolution"), Menachem Begin (1913-1992) and the right-wing Likud party came to power. The election permanently changed the landscape of Israeli politics.

In November 1977, Anwar Sadat flew to Israel and spoke before the Israeli Knesset. His visit revealed the ongoing secret international efforts to lead Israel and Egypt into an agreement offering principles for managing the autonomy of the Palestinians and negotiating a peace treaty between the two warring countries. In 1979, Sadat and Begin signed an agreement at the White House following the Camp David Accords (1978), a series of meetings between Egypt and Israel facilitated by US President Jimmy Carter. Sadat and Begin shared the Nobel Peace Prize that year. Though Israel withdrew from the Sinai, returning the territory to Egypt and dismantling eighteen settlements in the process, Egypt was barred from the Arab League for ten years for signing the peace agreement. That was part of an effort to persuade other Arab countries not to make similar agreements. In 1981 Sadat was assassinated during an annual Egyptian victory parade by an Egyptian military officer who was a member of a Jihadist cell. ■

*Adapted from Cary Nelson, Rachel S. Harris, and Kenneth W. Stein, "The History of Israel."*

Also see THE SIX DAY WAR.

# ZIONISM: ITS EARLY HISTORY

CARY NELSON, RACHEL S. HARRIS,
AND KENNETH W. STEIN

## FIRST STIRRINGS

The first traces of modern Zionism emerged among British Protestant supporters of Judaism in the first half of the 19th century. After the establishment of a British Consulate in Palestine in 1838, the Church of Scotland commissioned a report on the condition of the Jews; widely disseminated, it was followed by *Memorandum to Protestant Monarchs of Europe for the Restoration of the Jews to Palestine*. Moses Montefiore (1784–1885), in his role as President of the Board of Deputies of British Jews, entered into a correspondence with Charles Henry Churchill (1807–1869), then British consul in Damascus in 1841–42; that correspondence produced the first recorded proposal for political Zionism. The British, particularly under Prime Minister Benjamin Disraeli (1804–1881), imagined a Jewish country that would operate as a British Protectorate, much like Egypt, which accorded with their larger plans for wresting control of the region from the Ottomans. In 1891, American Protestant William Eugene Blackstone (1841–1935) presented US President Harrison with a petition signed by political, business, and religious leaders calling for the return of Palestine to the Jews, echoing a sentiment expressed by the Mormon Church in 1842.

These events, though momentous in their way, were distinct from the grassroots activism taking place among Jews in central and Eastern Europe. In 1834, Rabbi Judah Alkali (1798-1878) of Sarajevo called for Jews to return to the Land of Israel and to establish Jewish organizations to oversee national activities there, including a fund to purchase land for settlement. In 1862, in Prussia, Avi Hirsch Kalischer (1795-1874) published "Seeking Zion" and Moses Hess (1812-1875) published *Rome and Jerusalem*, both urging Jews to move to the land of Israel, buy property, and settle there. These calls heralded the rise of many small Zionist organizations that began to consider a return to Zion as a political option for Jews. According to Kalischer, "the redemption of Israel, for which we long, is not to be imagined as a sudden miracle . . . [that redemption] will begin by awakening support among the philanthropists and by gaining the consent of the nations to the gathering of some of the scattered of Israel into the Holy Land" (Hertzberg 111). These political murmurings reflected the increasing concern that Jews would never be free of the anti-Semitism that continued to thrive in Europe. As Hess observed, "we shall always remain strangers among the nations." "My nationality," he declared, is "inseparably connected with my ancestral heritage, with the Holy Land." Reflecting on the paradoxes of nationalism, he warned that "anti-national universalism is just as unfruitful as the anti-universalist nationalism of medieval reaction" (Herzberg 121, 119, 129). When Dr. Yehuda Leib Pinsker (1821-1891), a Russian physician who founded the Hovevei Zion (Lovers of Zion) movement, published *Auto-Emancipation: A Warning to His Kinsfolk by a Russian Jew*, a pamphlet analyzing anti-Semitism in the wake of a series of pogroms in Russia in 1881, his call for the establishment of a Jewish homeland found an audience receptive to a new solution to European intolerance.

The 1881-1884 wave of pogroms (riots against Jews) that swept across southwestern Russia's "Pale of Settlement," the area where Jews were forced to live, came at the end of a century of anti-Semitic government policies that had isolated Jews. Russia forced Jews into military conscription, often for long periods and from an early age. It controlled all aspects of Jewish dress, education, and the ritual slaughtering of meat, and it demonstrated that Russian Jews could not depend on the protection of the Russian government or police forces in the face of local violence. In response, Jews emigrated West to the New World, including the United States, Canada, and South America, as well as to agricultural settlements in North and South America and Palestine, where Jewish benefactors created new opportunities for the destitute refugees, funded by the

Jewish Colonization Association (JCA) established by Baron Maurice de Hirsch (1831–1896).

# THE DREYFUS AFFAIR AND THEODOR HERZL

During 1894–95, a scandal erupted in France whose repercussions were to shape the future of the Zionist movement. Alfred Dreyfus (1859–1935), a Jewish artillery captain on the French general staff, was wrongly convicted of treason and sentenced to Devil's Island. Though the military was relatively open to Jews, Dreyfus had repeatedly experienced anti-Semitism and, when he reported it, was judged to be "unlikeable," which limited his professional advancement. Evidence identifying the real traitor came to light but was suppressed; when it was leaked to the press, Dreyfus' supporters, including French novelist and journalist Emile Zola (1840–1902), cried out against the endemic anti-Semitism in the country. Though these efforts led to Dreyfus receiving a pardon in 1899, he was not exonerated until 1906. The trial, and the virulent anti-Semitism which accompanied it, showed that even France, the very incubator for the belief that all men were equal, was subject to unremitting prejudice toward Jews.

Among the crowd of journalists who reported on the event was an assimilated Jew who would become the figurehead for the coalescence of the disparate Zionist groups under a single umbrella. Arguing that Zionism offered the only real political solution for a Jewish people who would forever be considered pariahs within other nations' states, Theodor Herzl (1860–1904), convened The First Zionist Congress in Basel, Switzerland, in 1897. His 30,000-word pamphlet *Der Judenstaat: Versuch einer modernen Lösung der Judenfrage* ("The Jewish State: Proposal of a Modern Solution to the Jewish Question") offered a concrete consideration of Zionist aspirations, and the Congress issued a call to establish a Jewish homeland in Palestine.

With Herzl's guidance, Zionism became an internationally recognized political movement. But among its detractors were "ultra-Orthodox and assimilationists, revolutionaries and capitalists, dreamers and pragmatists" (Shapira 5). Some traditionalists considered Zionism a threatening secular movement seeking to supplant God's role in bringing about the redemption of the Jews, though a minority of Orthodox communities did support the movement. Some assimilated Jews felt Jewish nationalism would threaten their status in the countries in which they lived. As Benny Morris writes in *Righteous Victims*, "A central aspiration of Zionist ideology was the attainment of honor and respect in place of the shame and contempt that were the hall-marks of Jewish life in the Diaspora, especially in the Czarist Empire" (21). "No longer abject victims, middlemen, peddlers, protected moneylenders, rootless, soft-skinned intellectuals," he adds, "the Jews were to change into hardy, no-nonsense farmers, who would take abuse from no one" (45). The possibility of establishing a Jewish homeland somewhere else was considered, but nowhere else had the historic resonance that Palestine did; a 1903 British proposal to give Jews a high plateau in Uganda was deemed unrealistic for many reasons.

# THE FIRST ZIONIST IMMIGRANTS

The ancient term for going up to the Temple in Jerusalem and for the honor of being called upon to read from the Torah on the Sabbath, aliyah ("ascent"), has come to refer to the Jewish immigration from the Diaspora to the land of Israel. The Jews who migrated to agricultural colonies in the late 19th century are described as the First Aliyah of Zionist immigration. In contradistinction to those Jews who had moved to the Old *Yishuv* (the Jewish community in Palestine prior to the rise of Zionism) over the centuries, the migration that took place in the wake of the Russian pogroms brought young ideologues to Palestine, and that impulse intensified as persecution increased. The 1903–1906 pogroms were more lethal than those of the 1880s. The 1903 pogrom in Kishinev was publicized in dramatic terms by the international press, including the *New York Times*: "There was a well laid-out plan for the general massacre of Jews on the day following the Orthodox Easter. The mob was led by priests, and the general cry, 'Kill the Jews,' was taken up all over the city. The Jews were taken wholly unaware and were slaughtered like sheep . . . . The scenes of horror attending this massacre are beyond description. Babies were literally torn to pieces" (*NYT*, April 2).

Interested in agricultural endeavors, members of Hovevei Zion (Lovers of Zion) groups and BILU (an acronym based on a verse from the Book of Isaiah 2:5, "House of Jacob, Let us ascend") were supported in their pioneering endeavors by the Odessa Committee; officially known as "the Society for the Support of Jewish Farmers and Artisans in Syria and Palestine," this was a charitable organization with roots in Europe and the United States which helped organize immigration to Palestine. With little to no experience of working the land, many enrolled in Mikveh Yisrael, an agricultural school established outside Jaffa in 1870, which equipped the new inhabitants with some of the basic skills they would need to survive. But they remained dependent on the largess of rich benefactors to make the pioneering projects succeed, and Montefiore, Baron Edmond de Rothschild (1845-1934), and

Baron Hirsch were key figures in facilitating these dreams. Rothschild would fund settlements and their key needs, from land purchases to well drilling and seed acquisition—often from wealthy Arabs who functioned as absentee landlords. Zionist land purchases from 1880-1914 were concentrated in the coastal plain south of Haifa and in the Jezreel and Jordan valleys, areas largely swampy, uncultivated, and sparsely inhabited. Between 1878 and 1908, Jews purchased about 400,000 dunams, or 100,000 acres. Land purchases often resulted in the dispossession of the tenant farmers, though they received monetary compensation and usually resettled in the immediate environs. Though substantially more land was available for sale, funds were limited and land speculation soon drove up prices significantly.

The Eastern Europeans built early settlements in Rishon le-Tzion (1882), Rosh Pinna (1882), Zikhron Ya'akov (1882), and Gedera (1884)—agricultural farm holder villages (moshavot) that relied on Rothschild's patronage. Yet the inclement climate, disease, and prohibitive Ottoman taxation soon alienated many of the young Zionists. At the same time, Jewish migrants from Yemen arrived in the country, spurred by the messianic promise of a return to the ancestral homeland; they moved mainly to the cities or worked as laborers on the newly created citrus groves of the subsidized farms. Of the 35,000 Jews who arrived with the First Aliyah, 15,000 would leave or die. By 1903, the Jewish population in Palestine numbered 55,000.

But Palestine was not operating in a vacuum. For the Ottoman Turkish authorities who had been at war with the Russian Empire for two hundred years, the sudden influx of Russian immigrants in the late 19th century appeared as a new tactic for Russian authorities to use in seizing control of the dying empire. But with additional and increasingly violent pogroms erupting (1903-6), the tide of Jewish migration from Russia would continue to burden the concerned Ottoman authorities, and when World War I broke out, with Russia and Turkey on opposing sides, entry permits for Russian Jews were stopped. Taher al-Husseini (1842-1908), the Mufti of Jerusalem, urged in 1899 that Jews who had recently settled in the area since 1891 be pressed into leaving or be expelled, and he awakened concerns among the authorities that stretched beyond the new inhabitants' Zionist aims, back to their land of origin.

Meanwhile Arabs were also becoming aware of the national aspirations that had rocked the stability of the Ottoman Empire since Greece first sought independence (1821-32). Egypt's attempts to gain sovereignty from the British had failed, but Arab nationalism spread as a movement from Egypt throughout the Levant and Iraq, and raised new fears for the Ottomans. In 1904-1905, Najib Azouri (c. 1873-1916), a Maronite Christian, published two pamphlets denouncing the Ottoman Empire and calling for an independent Arab state from the Euphrates to the Suez Canal. Though his call met with little enthusiasm, the end of the Ottoman Empire in 1922 created new opportunities for Arab nationalists. ▪

*Adapted from Cary Nelson, Rachel S. Harris, and Kenneth W. Stein, "The History of Israel."*

Also see JEWISH HISTORY BEFORE ZIONISM, WORLD WAR II AND THE FOUNDING OF ISRAEL, and ZIONISM AS PHILOSOPHY AND PRACTICE.

# ZIONISM AS PHILOSOPHY AND PRACTICE

Zionism was founded as the national liberation movement of the Jewish people. Israel is the fulfillment of the Jewish people's right to national self-determination in its historic homeland. Israel's identity as the nation state of the Jewish people and its obligation as a democracy to afford all of its citizens equal rights under law are not mutually exclusive; in fact, they are complementary.

RACHEL FISH, ILAN TROEN, CARY NELSON,
RACHEL S. HARRIS, & KENNETH W. STEIN

## INTRODUCTION

Zionism was a nineteenth-century European project; it encouraged a transformation of the Jewish people from objects of history to subjects. Zionism reflected a realization that emancipation in Europe was inherently flawed, indeed in many ways was a failure. Emancipation did not overcome all individual limitations placed upon Jews and often required Jews to relinquish their distinctive collective identity. Zionism as a form of Jewish activism called for Jews returning as agents to their own history and narrative. It was a revolt against past Jewish passivity, inspiring many to begin imagining what it would mean to chart their own future. Many early immigrants to Israel saw themselves as rebels, for they were unwilling to remain passive during waves of pogroms and increased anti-Semitism and discrimination. Many of the early pioneers harbored anger at Jewish passivity, along with the Jewish leadership and religious institutions that accepted the realities of the European context. And some saw the return as a messianic issue. Many Zionists felt Jewish values ought to be expressed in collective action, rather than on reliance on either divine intervention or the host societies. Indeed Zionism preached rebellion as much against the shackling of Jews by the agents of Jewish religion as by alien rulers. Independence meant Jews would be liberated from the rule of rabbis no less than from that of the Czars.

Yet there was no one unified or homogenous Zionist vision. Rather, competing visions of Zionism were expressed in terms of secularism, politics, religion, socialism, and spiritualism. Each of the Zionist camps revitalized a particular mythical past and applied it to the present with the purpose of refashioning Jewish history and identity for the sake of cultivating a new reality expressed in a shared narrative, history, culture, tradition, government, and language. The Zionist leadership was thus challenged to make this plural kaleidoscope functional. This diversity was inherent in Jewry's varied European experience. So it was no surprise to have this cacophony transplanted to the Yishuv, the Jewish community in Palestine prior to the creation of the Jewish state. The Zionist movement, *Yishuv* politics, and Israeli governments have all been governed by coalition politics. Divisions within the strains of Zionism are rooted in ideology and belief. All the Zionist perspectives sought to influence the shape of the movement, the driving forces that compelled the nation, and the principles to be articulated as motives for a functioning sovereignty. The process of navigating between ideas, ideals, and realities determined the success or failure of each Zionist stream.

Zionists who made *aliyah*—or immigrated into Palestine—from the end of the 19th century yearned for a natural and direct connection with the country. The phrase employed in the 1922 League of Nations Mandate for Palestine and repeated throughout the discourse on the relationship of Jews to the country reflects what once had been common wisdom. The Mandate's preamble thus asserted that "recognition has thereby been given to the historical connection of the Jewish people with Palestine and to the grounds for reconstituting their national home in that country." "**Re**-constitution" had a shared meaning found in other key concepts widely employed in describing Zionism: **re**-turn, **re**-claim, **re**-build, **re**-store. The reiterated "**re**", or "again" was crucial. It reiterated that the relationship between Eretz Israel and Jews had never been lost and that it was now being renewed. The sense of recapturing identity with the Land of Israel has been brilliantly detailed in Boaz

Neumann's *Land and Desire in Early Zionism*. Pioneers were at one with a land where they had come to invest their sweat, tears, joy, and blood. Termed "sabras"[the cactus fruit found in much of the countryside] by the 1930s, their offspring were natives, the natural realization of the longing to return to build and be rebuilt in their historic homeland. In this view, Jews were a people, entitled to a state located in the land where they had originated, where they had been resident continuously for millennia and in the region where they still constituted a vital presence in proximate areas of North Africa or throughout the Middle East.

# CULTURAL ZIONISM

The Zionist ideas vying for traction were all involved in the early stages of Israel's inception. Prior to the establishment of the Israeli state, Zionist leaders engaged and debated one another to advance their particular visions for the future. One camp within the movement was that of the cultural/spiritual Zionists. They were interested in recovering and renewing Judaism's spiritual character, but anti-Semitism did not play a role in their perspective. Indeed, the cultural/spiritual Zionists were not interested in Herzl's articulation of political Zionism and sought to counter his vision of creating a sovereign nation-state without particular Jewish content.

Spiritual Zionist Ahad Ha'am, (1856-1927) was interested in accommodating the Diasporic existence and not relegating Jews in exile to a subordinate position. For Ahad Ha'am there was no comparability between Palestine and Diaspora. Palestine was considered the geographical and spiritual center, for only in Palestine could Judaism radiate its vitality by developing a rejuvenated religion and culture. The purpose of the state, according to Ahad Ha'am, was to help facilitate a cultural and linguistic renaissance. Cultural Zionists were interested in reviving Hebrew culture and language and these efforts should spread from Palestine throughout the Jewish Diaspora. Their central focus was not the mere creation of a political entity but the spiritual growth of individuals and the development of Jewish content and literacy. Spirituality, however, did not necessarily refer to God; rather belief in God was replaced with an emphasis on peoplehood.

For cultural Zionists the models for ethical behavior were based on the Biblical prophets and the ethical mandates of Deuteronomy. The prophets evoked notions of equality and justice and emphasized these values as prerequisites for creating community. The cultural Zionists appropriated these ideas as the defining qualities of a nation-state. Their litmus test was to judge how equality and justice would be realized in interaction between the Jewish and Arab peoples in the land of Palestine. Thus cultural Zionist warnings about

Arab-Jewish relations in Palestine were recognized as issues Zionism had to confront. The manner in which Jewish nationalists approached the Arabs would determine the fate and success of the Jewish community in Palestine. Prior to the establishment of the state of Israel, many cultural Zionists advocated the formation of a bi-national state in which there would be cooperation and coexistence between Jewish and Arab populations throughout Mandatory Palestine.

# ZIONISM IN PRACTICE: 1904–1923

The Second Aliyah (1904–1914), or major wave of immigration from the Diaspora to Israel, embraced a new Hebrew ideology that moved beyond the purely agricultural aspirations of their predecessors. Building on the work of Eliezer Ben Yehuda (1858–1922), who had arrived with the First Aliyah and was the guiding spirit behind the revival of the Hebrew language, members of the Second Aliyah rejected Yiddish and the Diasporic languages of their countries of emigration. They embraced the Hebrew language and Hebrew culture, which they saw as powerful manifestations of their connection to the historic homeland. As Anita Shapira writes, "Converting Hebrew from the language of prayer and sacred texts into the language of Hebrew culture, and beyond that into the language of the street and home, was one of the Zionist movement's most magnificent achievements" (57).

Zionist economic development in the first years of the 20th century continued to focus on agriculture and the building of new communities. In 1907–1908, the Palestine Office, headed by Arthur Ruppin (1876–1943), was established in Jaffa to coordinate Zionist activity in Palestine. In 1909, the same year that Tel Aviv was founded as a suburb of Jaffa and lauded as the first Jewish city built in 2000 years, Degania was established—offering a new kind of collective agricultural settlement built on socialist values. This was the kibbutz:

> From the 1880s until the First World War, Jewish settlement was concentrated almost exclusively in the *moshava*, a traditional kind of colony whose members farmed their land independently. The early moshavoth (plural of *moshava*) failed to achieve economic independence and did not develop quickly enough to enable large-scale colonization within a reasonable time. Attempts at reform and experimentation led to the design of the *kibbutz*, or *kvutza* (collective settlements), and the moshav (cooperative farming village)." (Troen *Imagining Zion* 4)

But these agricultural settlements were often victims of theft and sometimes local violence. In response, *HaShomer* ("the watchman") was created as a defense system with guards who drew on the customs and dress of local Bedouins, Druze, and Circassians. The Second Aliyah's focus on using only Jewish laborers and guards led to ongoing conflict with private plantation owners who often preferred the cheaper and more experienced labor of local Arabs. Hiring *HaShomer* led to repeated conflict where "mixed" Arab and Jewish employment occurred. By the end of the first decade, signs of Arab discomfort with the Jewish settlements were increasingly apparent. In 1911, Najib al-Khuri Nassar, who had been a land purchasing agent for the Jewish Colonization Association, published a critique of Jewish ambitions in the region; *al-Sihyuniyaa* (Zionism), was the first Arab book to examine the new forms of Jewish immigration.

On the eve of World War I, the Jewish community in Palestine numbered 85,000, more than half living in Jerusalem, though there were also 45 agricultural settlements whose total population exceeded 12,000. But the war was to have a devastating effect on the *Yishuv's* economy, enough in fact to threaten famine. The community only survived with the arrival of money and supplies donated by American Jews and delivered on American warships. Hundreds of Arabs drafted into the Ottoman Turkish army died in battle or from disease, along with thousands more who were non-combatants. After repeatedly appealing to the British to serve in the army in order to liberate Palestine from the Ottomans, 650 Jews were at first recruited into the Zion Mule Corps and served in the Gallipoli campaign; later five battalions of Jewish volunteers became the Jewish Legion (1917-1921). Around 91 died in action, but among the survivors were future Israeli members of Knesset, prime ministers and presidents, leading thinkers, artists and writers, and several pioneers from the First Aliyah.

On June 4, 1917, Jules Cambon (1845-1935), director general of the French Foreign Ministry, issued a statement declaring that "it would be a deed of justice and reparation to assist, by the protection of the Allied Powers, in the renaissance of the Jewish nationality in that land from which the people of Israel were exiled so many centuries ago." His comments followed from member of Parliament Winston Churchill's claims in 1908 that Jews must have their own homeland in Palestine. On November 2, 1917, British foreign secretary Arthur Balfour (1848-1930) issued a Declaration on behalf of the government, with strong concurrence of prime minister Lloyd George (1863-1945), stating that "His Majesty's Government view with favour the establishment in Palestine of a national home for the Jewish people, and will use their best endeavours to facilitate the achievement of this object, it being clearly understood that nothing shall be done which may prejudice the civil and religious rights of existing non-Jewish communities in Palestine, or the rights and political status enjoyed by Jews in any other country." Britain thereby strengthened its own interests, for, as Benny Morris writes, "by endorsing Zionism, Britain was legitimizing its own presence there as the protector of Jewish self-determination" (73). The British were also influenced by Chaim Weizmann (1874-1952), a University of Manchester chemist who helped encourage what amounted to a pro-Zionist lobby among British leaders. Weizmann would become president of the Zionist Organization and later the first President of Israel.

The issuing of the Balfour Declaration helped consolidate and solidify Arab nationalism around the rejection of Zionism. From the Arab perspective, the world powers had no right to award territory that was not theirs to give. As a matter of principle, therefore, the promise to the Jews was without validity. The Jews, on the other hand, maintained that they had a historical right to the land of their ancestors, that they were righting a two thousand-year injustice, and that Palestine already had a Jewish community residing on legally purchased property.

In December 1917, British General Sir Edmund Allenby (1861-1936) entered Jerusalem with his army and ended four centuries of Ottoman rule. Palestine had been left in ruins, with crops destroyed, trees uprooted, and village life economically devastated. Zionist anticipation that British rule would lead to Jewish self-governance met with disappointment when the military administration revealed a distinctly anti-Zionist outlook. Yet the Zionists continued to invest and in 1918 laid the cornerstone of the Hebrew University in Jerusalem that would open in 1925. At the San Remo conference in 1920 World War I's victorious powers formally adopted the Balfour Declaration with its commitment to a Jewish home in Palestine. Three years later, with League of Nations support, the British Mandate for Palestine commenced. The transition to the full Zionist dream would take until 1948, but the process had begun. ■

*Adapted from Rachel Fish, "The Bi-nationalist Fantasy within Academia," Ilan Troen, "The Campaign to Boycott Israeli Universities," and Cary Nelson, Rachel S. Harris, and Kenneth W. Stein, "The History of Israel."*

Also see JEWISH HISTORY BEFORE ZIONISM, WORLD WAR II AND THE FOUNDING OF ISRAEL and ZIONISM: ITS EARLY HISTORY.

# CONCLUSION: ZIONISM TODAY

## CARY NELSON

Much of this book, in one way or another, has been about Zionism today. Beginning with the Durban conference in 2001, when the slander that Zionism is racism was first promoted, and moving through its evolution as a BDS slogan more than a decade later, we have reached its present, demonized status on the international left: as an epithet. In many purportedly progressive quarters, labeling someone a Zionist burdens them with a series of assumptions that bear no necessary relationship to their actual beliefs: that they see Palestinians as less than human or as an invented and dismissible people, that they lust after the whole of Palestine from the Mediterranean Sea to the Jordan River, that they reject the Palestinian right to national self-determination and oppose the creation of a Palestinian state.

*Dreams Deferred* has tracked the relationship between Zionism and Anti-Semitism in a separate entry. It has thought through the distinctive phenomenon of Jewish anti-Zionism. It has accounted for the anti-Zionist element in the BDS movement and its projects of anti-normalization and the economic, cultural, and academic boycotts of Israel. The anti-Zionism and anti-Semitism of Hamas and Islamic Jihad are recognized and analyzed. The book has sought as well to account for the dangerous Zionism that prevails on the religious and political right in Israel and the US.

Yet the book as a whole has also sought to define the terms of an alternative—a progressive Zionism for our own time. This is a Zionism that honors the reality of the Nakba and its place in the Palestinian narrative. It looks for ways to promote a two-state solution despite all the forces aligned against it. Its critique of Israeli government policy is unstinting, while it embraces the right of the Jews to a nation in their ancient homeland. It treasures Israel's myriad achievements, while recognizing the country's limitations, complications, paradoxes, and contradictions. It also addresses the Palestinians' role in sabotaging their own cause.

Honoring both Israeli and Palestinian humanity is not (or should not be) a major challenge. It is also relatively easy to validate their separate national narratives, however difficult integrating them has proven to be. Negotiating the two people's divergent and multiple political agendas is obviously far more difficult. The tensions that accompany that effort still traverse this book; they cannot be easily overcome. Yet the ongoing project is essential; we cannot abandon it either in despair or in irrational proposals.

To reclaim a progressive Zionism requires us not only to claim the Zionist label despite its demonization, but also to escape the counter-productive and crippling debate that consumes campuses worldwide—a debate alternating between attacks on and defenses of the Jewish state—and instead marshal the analytic and inspirational strengths of the academy and deploy them in the cause of peace. That will be very difficult, because it will require students, faculty, and community members to think in terms fundamentally different from those that currently preoccupy them. But otherwise the academy shows little hope of contributing anything better than incivility, fear, conformity, and hatred to the public sphere. *Dreams Deferred* attempts to provide some of the resources needed to help make that progressive Zionism possible. ∎

# SOURCES

Aaronsohn, Ran. "Settlement in Eretz Israel—A Colonialist Enterprise? 'Critical' Scholarship and Historical Geography," *Israel Studies* 1:2 (Fall 1996), 214-229.

Abowd, Thomas. "The Boycott, Divestment, ad Sanctions Movement and Violations of Academic Freedom at Wayne State University." In Chatterjee and Maira, eds. *The Imperial University*, 169-185.

AbuKhalil, As'ad. "A Critique of Norman Finkelstein on BDS." *alakhbar English* (February 17, 2012), available online at http://english.al-akhbar. com/node/4289.

Abunimah, Ali. "ICAHD endorses one-state solution, warns against 'warehousing' of Palestinians," *The Electronic Intifada* (blog), September 14 2012, available online at http://electronicintifada.net/blogs/ali-abunimah/ icahd-endorses-one-state-solution-warns-against-warehousing-palestinians.

_____. *The Battle for Justice in Palestine.* Chicago: Haymarket Books, 2114.

Abuarqoub, Huda and Joel Braunold. "A Bigger Threat Than BDS: Anti-Normalization." *Haaretz* (July 2, 2015), available online at http://www. haaretz.com/jewish/the-jewish-thinker/.premium-1.664018.

Adwan, Sami, Dan Bar-On, and Eyal Naveh, eds. *Side by Side: Parallel Histories of Israel-Palestine.* NY: New Press, 2012.

Ali, Ayaan Hirsi. *Nomad: From Islam to America.* New York: Free Press, 2010.

Ali, Lorraine. "A Bomb Thrower's Life." Newsweek.com. *Newsweek*, February 26, 2007. Web. Nov. 10, 2013.

Allport, Gordon. *The Nature of Prejudice*. NY: Doubleday, 1958.

al-Omari, Ghaith. "Ills of Anti-Normalization." *Fikra Forum* (June 19, 2015), available online at http://fikraforum.org/?p=7021#.VjDarNBZFtc.

Althusser, Louis. *Philosophy of the Encounter: Later Writings*, 1978-1987. London: Verso, 2006.

Althusser, Louis and Etienne Balibar, *Reading Capital*. London: Verso, 1970.

Amis, Martin. "You Ask the Question." Independent.com. *Independent*, January 15
2007. Web. February 27, 2014.

Amnesty International. "Palestine (State of): 'Strangling Necks,' Abductions, Torture and Summary Killings of Palestinians by Hamas Forces During the 2014 Gaza/Israel Conflict" MDE 21/1643/2015 (May 26, 2015), available online at https://www.amnesty.org/en/documents/mde21/1643/2015/en/.

"An Assessment of The 2014 Gaza Conflict" (High Level Military Group) Friends of Israel Initiative: October 2015, available online at http://www.high-level-military-group.org/pdf/hlmg-assessment-2014-gaza-conflict.pdf.

Anderson, Benedict. *Imagined Communities: Reflections on the Origins and Spread of Nationalism*. Verso: New York, 1991.

Antonius, George. *The Arab Awakening: The Story of the Arab National Movement*. Simon Publications: New York: 1939.

Arendt, Hannah. *The Origins of Totalitarianism*. NY: Schocken, 2004.

Arnold, Sina. "Antisemitism and the Contemporary American Left: An Uneasy Relationship." Paper presented at "Deciphering the 'New' Antisemitism." Bloomington: Institute for Contemporary Antisemitism, Indiana University, April 2014.

Ateek, Naim. *Justice and Only Justice: A Palestinian Theology of Liberation*. Maryknoll, NY: Orbis Books, 1989.

Azoulay, Ariella and Adi Ophir. *The One-State Condition: Occupation and Democracy in Israel/Palestine*. Translated by Tal Haran. Stanford: Stanford University Press, 2013.

Baker, Alan and Adam Shay, "Manipulation and Deception: The Anti-Israel 'BDS' Campaign (Boycott, Divestment, and Sanctions), *Jerusalem Issue Briefs*, Vol. 12, No. 2 (2012), available online at http://jcpa.org/article/manipulation-and-deception-the-anti-israel-bds-campaign-boycott-divestment-and-sanctions/#sthash.y5wtaqkC.dpuf.

Bard, Mitchell. "Arab League Boycott: Background & Overview," *Jewish Virtual Library*, last modified September 2007, available online at http://www.jewishvirtuallibrary.org/jsource/History/Arab_boycott.html.

Bard, Mitchell G. and Jeff Dawson. *Israel and the Campus: The Real Story*. Chevy Chase, MD: The American-Israeli Cooperative Enterprise, 2012.

Barghouti, Omar. *BDS—Boycott, Divestment, Sanctions: The Global Struggle for Palestinian Rights*. Chicago: Haymarket Books, 2011.

_____. "A Secular Democratic State in Historic Palestine: Self-Determination through Ethical Decolonization." In Anthony Loewenstein and Ahmed Moor, eds., *After Zionism: One State for Israel and Palestine*. London: Saqi Books, 2012.

Bartram, David B. "Foreign Workers in Israel: History and Theory." *International Migration Review* 32: 2 (Summer, 1998), pp. 303-325.

Bauerlein, Mark. "Social Constructionism: Philosophy for the Academic Workplace," in *Theory's Empire: An Anthology of Dissent*, ed. Daphne Patai and Will H. Corral (New York, NY: Columbia University Press, 1995), 341-353.

Baum, Steven K. *Antisemitism Explained*. Lanham, MD: University Press of America, 2012.

_____. "Christian and Muslim Antisemitism." *Journal of Contemporary Religion* 23 (2009): 77-86.

Baum, Steven K and Masato Nakazaw. "Antisemitism and Anti-Israeli Sentiment." *Journal of Religion & Society* 9 (2007) 1:9.

"BDS activists interrupt Palestinian speaker in South Africa" *The Times of Israel* (March 4, 2015), available online at http://www.timesofisrael.com/bds-activists-interrupt-palestinian-speaker-in-south-africa/.

Becker, Ulricke. "Post War Antisemitism: Germany's Foreign Policy Toward Egypt," in *Global Antisemitism: A Crisis of Modernity* ed. Charles Asher Small. Leiden, The Netherlands: Brill, 2013, 283-296.

Bedein, David. "Trauma: the unreported casualty of war." *Therapy Today* (June 2009), available online at http://www.therapytoday.net/article/show/449/trauma-the-unreported-casualty-of-war/.

Ben-Gurion, David. *My Talks with Arab Leaders*, trans. Areyh Rubinstein and Misha Louvish. Jerusalem: Keter Books, 1972.

Benvenisti, Meron. *Sacred Landscape: The Buried History of the Holy Land Since 1948*. Berkeley, CA: University of California Press, 2000.

Berman, Lazar. "Presbyterian Church Group: Zionism is the Problem," *Times of Israel*, February 11, 2014.

Berman, Paul, "Preface," in Nelson and Brahm, eds., *The Case Against Academic Boycotts of Israel*, pp. 4-11.

_____. *The Flight of the Intellectuals*. Brooklyn, NY: Melvillehouse, 2010.

_____. *Terror and Liberalism*. New York: Norton, 2004.

_____. "Who's Afraid of Tariq Ramadan? tnr.com. *The New Republic*, May 29, 2007. Web. February 24, 2014.

Berman, Russell, "The Boycott as an Infringement on Academic Culture," in Nelson and Brahm, eds., *The Case Against Academic Boycotts of Israel*, pp. 49-59.

Bernstein, David. "BDS and the Rising Danger of 'Intersectionality.'" *Forward* (January 4, 2016), available online.

Blau, Uri. "Does Your Jewish Charity Donate to the Settlements?" *Haaretz* (December 8, 2015), available online at http://www.haaretz.com/settlementdollars/1.690056.

Blau, Uri. "Haaretz Investigation: U.S. Donors Gave Settlements More Than $220 Million in Tax-exempt Funds Over Five Years." *Haaretz* (December 19, 2015), available online at http://www.haaretz.com/settlementdollars/1.689683.

Bledstein, Burton. *The Culture of Professionalism: The Middle Class and the Development of Higher Education in America* (New York, NY: W.W. Norton, 1978).

Booth, William. "While Israel held its fire, the militant group Hamas did not." *The Washington Post* (July 15, 2014), available online at https://www.washingtonpost.com/world/middle_east/while-israel-held-its-fire-the-militant-group-hamas-did-not/2014/07/15/116fd3d7-3c0f-4413-94a9-2ab16af1445d_story.html.

"Boycott of Jewish Businesses," *Holocaust Encyclopedia*, available online at http://www.ushmm.org/wlc/en/article.php?ModuleId=10005678.

Brackman, Harold. *Boycott Divestment Sanctions (BDS) Against Israel: An Anti-Semitic, Anti-Peace Poison Pill*. Los Angeles: Simon Wiesenthal Center, 2013, available online at http://www.wiesenthal.com/atf/cf/%7B54d385e6-f1b9-4e9f-8e94-890c3e6dd277%7D/REPORT_313.PDF

Brahm, Gabriel Noah and Asaf Romirowsky, "In Intent, If Not in Effect: The Failure of BDS," in Nelson and Brahm, eds., *The Case Against Academic Boycotts of Israel*, pp. 75-84.

Braunold, Joel & Huda Abuarquob. "A Bigger Threat Than BDS: Anti-normalization." *Haaretz* (July 2, 2015), available online at http://www.haaretz.com/jewish/the-jewish-thinker/.premium-1.664018.

Braverman, Mark. *Fatal Embrace: Christians, Jews, and the Search for Peace in the Holy Land*. Austin, TX: Synergy Books, 1010.

Bregman, Ahron. *Israel's Wars: A History Since 1947*. New York: Routledge, 2010.

Brettler, Marc. "The Copenhagen School: The Historiographical Issues," *Association for Jewish Studies Review* 27 (2003): 1-21.

Bruckner, Pascal. *The Tyranny of Guilt: An Essay on Western Masochism.* Princeton: Princeton University Press, 2010.

_____. "Antisemitism and Islamophobia: The Inversion of the Debt." In Rosenfeld, ed. *Deciphering the New Antisemitism*, pp. 7-20.

Buber, Martin. *A Land of Two Peoples: Martin Buber on Jews and Arabs*, ed. Paul Mendes-Flohr. Gloucester, MA: Peter Smith, 1994.

Budick, Emily, "When a Boycott is Not Moral Action but Social Conformity and the 'Affectation of Love,'" in Nelson and Brahm, eds., *The Case Against Academic Boycotts of Israel*, pp. 85-103.

Butler, Judith. *Parting Ways: Jewishness and the Critique of Zionism.* New York: Columbia University Press, 2012.

_____. "The End of Oslo." LRB Blog (September 25, 2011), available online at http://www.lrb.co.uk/blog/2011/09/25/judith-butler/the-end-of-oslo/.

_____. "Remarks to Brooklyn College on BDS," *The Nation*, Feb. 7, 2013.

_____. "Academic Freedom and the ASA's Boycott of Israel: A Response to Michelle Goldberg," The Nation, December 8, 2013, available online at http://www.thenation.com/article/177512/academic -freedom-and-asas-boycott-israel-response-michelle-goldberg#

Bytwerk, Randall L. *Julius Streicher: The Man Who Persuaded a Nation to Hate Jews.* NY: Stein and Day, 1983.

Cambanis, Thanassis. "Hamas U." *The Boston Globe* (February 28, 2010), available online at http://www.boston.com/bostonglobe/ideas/ articles/2010/02/28/hamas_u/?page=full.

Carroll, James. *Constantine's Sword.* Boston, MA: Houghton Mifflin, 2001.

Caspit, Ben. "Who are Israel's hilltop youth?" *Al Monitor* (December 9, 2015), available online at http://www.al-monitor.com/pulse/originals/2015/12/ hilltop-youth-douma-murder-dawabsha.html.

Cattori, Silvia. "Omar Barghouti: 'No State Has the Right to Exist as a Racist State.'" Voltairenet.org (December 7, 2007), available online at http://www.voltairenet.org/article153536.html.

Chandler, Doug. "'Struggling' With IDF Proportionality." *The Jewish Week* (December 2, 2014), available online at http://www.thejewishweek.com/news/new-york/struggling-idf-proportionality-issue.

Chatterjee, Piya, and Sunaina Maira, eds. *The Imperial University: Academic Repression and Scholarly Dissent*. Minneapolis: University of Minnesota Press, 2014.

Chomsky, Noam. "On Israel-Palestine and BDS." *The Nation* (July 2, 2014), available online at http://www.thenation.com/article/israel-palestine-and-bds/.

_____. "On Israel-Palestine and BDS: Chomsky Replies." *The Nation* (July 22, 2014), available online at http://www.thenation.com/article/israel-palestine-and-bds-chomsky-replies/.

Chomsky, Noam and Ilan Pappe. *Gaza in Crisis: Reflections on Israel's War Against the Palestinians*. London: Penguin, 2010.

Clark, Harry. "Noam Chomsky and BDS." *Dissident Voice* (February 11, 2015), available online at http://dissidentvoice.org/2015/02/noam-chomsky-and-bds/.

Cohen, Debra. "The Year BDS Became the Number One Concern for American Jews." *Haaretz* (December 27, 2014), available online at www.haaretz.com/jewish/features/.premium-1.633972.

Cohen, Florette, Lee Jussim, Gautam Bhasin, and Elizabeth Salib. "The Modern Anti-Semitism Israel Model: An Empirical Relationship Between Modern Anti-Semitism and Opposition to Israel." *Conflict & Communication Online* 10 (2011):1.

Cohen, Florette, Lee Jussim, Kent D. Harber, and Gautam Bhasin, "Modern Anti-Semitism and Anti-Israel Attitudes." *Journal of Personality and Social Psychology* 97 (2009): 290-306.

Cohen, Hillel. *Army of Shadows: Palestinian Collaboration with Zionism, 1917-1949*. Berkeley: University of California Press, 2008.

Cohen, Mitchell, "Anti-Semitism and the Left That Doesn't Learn," in Nelson and Brahm, eds., *The Case Against Academic Boycotts of Israel*, pp. 156-163.

Cohen, Nick. *What's Left?* London: Harper Perennial, 2007.

Cohen, Roger. "The B.D.S. Threat." *New York Times* (Feb 10 2014).

Cohen, Steve. *That's Funny, You Don't Look Antisemitic. An Anti-Racist Analysis of Left Antisemitism*. Manchester: Beyond the Pale Collective, 1987.

Cohn, Norman. *Warrant for Genocide: The Myth of the Jewish World Conspiracy and the Protocols of the Elders of Zion*. Oxford: Oxford University Press, 1970.

Cook, David. *Contemporary Muslim Apocalyptic Literature*. Syracuse: Syracuse University Press, 2008.

Dajani, Khuloud K. and Rafael S. Carel, "Neighbors and Enemies: Lessons to Be Learned from the Palestinian-Israeli Conflict Regarding Cooperation in Public Health," *Croatian Medical Journal* 43, no. 2 (2002): 138-140.

Davis, Angela Y. *Freedom Is a Constant Struggle: Ferguson, Palestine, and the Foundations of a Movement*. Chicago: Haymarket Books, 2016.

Davis, Douglas. "The BBC is quickly becoming one of the world's 'kosher' purveyors of hate," *Jewish World Review* (July 24, 2002), availaable online at http://www.jewishworldreview.com/0702/davis_bbc.html.

Davies, Philip. *In Search of Ancient Israel*. Sheffield: T&T Clark, 1992.

Dawidowicz, Lucy S. *The War Against the Jews*. NY: Bantam, 1986.

Dennoune, Karima. *Your Fatwa Does Not Apply Here: Untold Stories from the Fight Against Muslim Fundamentalism*. New York: W. W. Norton, 2013.

Deutscher, Isaac. *The Non-Jewish Jew and other essays*. London: Merlin Press, 1981.

DuBois, W.E.B. *The Souls of Black Folk*. Mineola, NY: Dover, 1994; rpt of 1903 edition.

Dyer, J. E. "Anti-Israel BDS nuttery at the port of Oakland." *Liberty Unyielding* (August 19, 2014), available online at http://libertyunyielding .com/2014/08/19/anti-israel-nuttery-port-oakland/#UyzQeqpizEksj RwR.99.

Eagleton, Terry. *The Idea of Culture*. Oxford: Blackwell, 2000.

Edelman, Samuel M. and Carol F S. Edelman, "When Failure Succeeds": Divestment as Delegitimation," in Nelson and Brahm, eds., *The Case Against Academic Boycotts of Israel*, pp. 235-242.

Eid, Bassem. "We Palestinians hold the key to a better future." *The Times of Israel* (February 12, 2015), available online at http://blogs.timesofisrael.com/ we-palestinians-hold-the-key-to-a-better-future/.

_____. "Boycott the Israel Boycott." *The Spectator* (August 29, 2015), available online at http://www.spectator.co.uk/2015/08/boycott-the-boycott/.

Eligon, John. "Black Lives Matter Seeks Political Voice From the Din of Protest." *The New York Times* (November 19, 2015), pp. 1, 12.

Elliot, Gregory. *Althusser: The Detour of Theory*. London: Verso, 1987.

Elshtain, Jean Bethke. *Just War Against Terror: The Burden of American Power in a Violent World*. New York: Basic Books, 2004.

Endelman, Todd M. "Antisemitism in Western Europe Today." in Penslar, ed. *Contemporary Antisemitism*, pp. 64-79.

European Commission. Higher Education in the Occupied Palestinian Territory. Ramallah: 2012, available online at http://eacea.ec.europa.eu/ tempus../participating_countries/overview/oPt.pdf.

European Union Monitoring Center, "Manifestations of Antisemitism in the EU 2002–2003" (Vienna: European Union Agency for Fundamental Rights, 2004), available online at http://fra.europa.eu/sites/default/files/ fra_uploads/184-AS-Main-report.pdf

"Ex-Cambridge professor boycotts 13-year-old Israeli girl over Palestinian issue" *The Jerusalem Post* (December 1, 2015), available online at http://

www.jpost.com/Diaspora/Cambridge-professor-to-Israeli-Ill-answer-your-questions-when-there-is-peace-in-Palestine-435935.

Farsoun, Samih K., with Christina E. Zacharia. *Palestine and the Palestinians*. Boulder, Colorado: Westview Press, 1997.

Feige, Michael. *Settling in the Hearts: Jewish Fundamentalism in The Occupied Territories*. Detroit: Wayne State University Press, 2009.

Feldman, Kiera, "BDS and the Park Slope Food Coop: Why the Vote Against Was a Win for the Boycott," *The Nation* (March 29, 2012), available online at http://www.thenation.com/article/bds-and-park-slope-food-coop-why-vote-against-was-win-boycott/.

Ferguson, Niall. *Civilization: the West and the Rest*. New York: Penguin, 2011.

Fieldhouse, Dennis K. *The Colonial Empires: A Comparative Survey from the Eighteenth Century*. London: Weidenfeld and Nicolson, 1966.

Filiu, Jean Pierre. *Apocalypse in Islam*. Los Angeles: University of California Press, 2011.

Fisk, Robert. "My Beating by Refugees Is a Symbol of the Hatred and Fury of This Filthy War." Independent.com. *Independent*, 8 Dec. 2001. Web. 1 February 2014.

Fine, Robert, "Speaking in Opposition," in Nelson and Brahm, eds., *The Case Against Academic Boycotts of Israel*, pp. 465-470.

_____. "The Lobby: Mearsheimer and Walt's conspiracy theory." *Engage* (blog), March 21, 2006, available online at http://www.engageonline.org.uk/blog/article.php?id=310

Finkelstein, Norman. *Image and Reality of the Israel-Palestine Conflict*. London: Verso, 1995.

Fish, Rachel, "The Bi-nationalist Fantasy within Academia," in Nelson and Brahm, eds., *The Case Against Academic Boycotts of Israel*, pp. 365-374.

Foxman, Abraham H. "An Open Letter on Academic Freedom and University Responsibility," *Commentary*, February 2013, available online at http://www.commentarymagazine.com/wp-content/uploads/2013/02/adlletterbds.pdf

Frantzman, Seth. "The Politicization of History and the Negev Land Claims; A Review Essay on Indigenous (In)justice," *Israel Studies* 19, no. 1 (2014): 48-74.

Furnish, Timothy. *Holiest Wars: Islamic Mahdis, Their Jihads, and Osama bin Laden*. NY: Praeger, 2005.

*The Future Vision of the Palestinian Arabs in Israel*. Nazareth: National Committee for the Heads of the Arab Local Authorities in Israel, 2006, available online at http://www.adalah.org/newsletter/eng/dec06/tasawor-mostaqbali.pdf

Geras, Norman. "Alibi Antisemitism." *Fathom* 2 (2013), available online at http://www.fathomjournal.org/policy-politics/alibi-antisemitism/.

Gershuni, Hillel. "A Jewish ISIS Rises in the West Bank." *Tablet* (January 11, 2016), available online at http://www.tabletmag.com/jewish-news-and-politics/196516/jewish-isis-in-the-west-bank.

Ghermezian, Shiryn. "Activists Say Historical Black Struggle 'Hijacked' After 'Black Lives Matter' Leaders Endorse BDS." *The Algemeiner* (August 19, 2015), available online at http://www.algemeiner.com/2015/08/19/activist-says-historical-black-struggle-hijacked-after-blacks-lives-matter-activists-endorse-bds/.

Gilbert, Martin. *The Routledge Historical Atlas of Jerusalem*. NY: Routledge, 2008.

Gilligan, Carole. *In a Different Voice*. Cambridge: Harvard University Press, 1984.

Gillman, Sander. *Jewish Self-Hatred: Anti-Semitism and the Hidden Language of the Jews*. Baltimore: Johns Hopkins University Press, 1986.

GISHA. *Rafah Crossing: Who Holds the Keys?* (March 2009), available online at http://www.gisha.org/UserFiles/File/publications/Rafah_Report_Eng.pdf.

Glazov, Jamie. *United in Hate: The Left's Romance with Tyranny and Terror.* NY: WND Books, 2009.

Glock, Charles Y. and Rodney Stark. *Christian Beliefs and Anti-Semitism.* NY: Harper & Row, 1966.

Golan, Galia. *Israeli Peacemaking Since 1967: Factors Behind the Breakthroughs and Failures.* NY: Routledge, 2015.

Goldberg, Jeffrey, "Obama, Netanyahu, and the Future of the Jewish State," *The Atlantic* (September 15, 2015).

Gorenberg, Gershom. *The Unmaking of Israel.* NY: HarperCollins, 2011.

_____. "Sacred to the Nation." *The American Prospect* (November 12, 2015), available online at http://prospect.org/article/how -far-right-nationalism-fuels-jerusalems-temple-mount-controversy.

Gregerman, Adam. "Old Wine in New Bottles; Liberation Theology and the Israeli-Palestinian Conflict." *Journal of Ecumenical Studies* 41:34 (Summer/Fall 2004), 313-340.

Gutierrez, Gustavo. *The Truth Shall Make You Free.* Maryknoll, NY: Orbis Books, 1990.

Gutman, Stephanie. *The Other War: Israelis, Palestinians and the Struggle for Media Supremacy.* NY: Encounter Books, 2005.

Guttman, Nathah and Britta Lokting. "Can Jews Back #BlackLivesMatter and Be Pro-Israel?" *Forward* (December 21, 2015), available online.

Gutwein, Danny. "Some Comments on the Class Foundations of the Occupation." *Monthly Review* (June 16, 2006), available online at http://mrzine.monthlyreview.org/2006/gutwein160606.html.

Halbertal, Moshe. "Moral Challenges in Asymmetric War." Berlin: Berlin Social Science Center (January 2014), available online at https://www.wzb.eu/sites/default/files/u32/paper_moshe_halbertal_moral_challenges_in_asymmetric_warfare.pdf.

Halbertal, Moshe and Arnold M. Eisen. "Gaza, the IDF Code of Ethics, and the Morality of War" NY: Jewish Theological Seminary, November 24, 2014, available online at https://www.youtube.com/watch?v=6jnnMeBZT9E.

Hallward, Maia Carter. *Transnational Activism and the Israeli-Palestinian Conflict*. NY: Palgrave Macmillan, 2013.

Hanieh, Adam. "The Oslo Illusion," *Jacobin* (April 2013), available online at https://www.jacobinmag.com/2013/04/the-oslo-illusion/.

Hareuveni, Immanuel. *Yiśra'el: ha-yishuvim ye-atare 'ati otehem*. [The Settlements of Israel and Their Archaeological Sites](Givatayim-Ramat Gan: Masadeh, 1979) (Hebrew).

Harris, Sam. *The End of Faith*. New York: W.W. Norton, 2005.

Harrison, Bernard. *The Resurgence of Antisemitism*. Lanham, MD: Rowman & Littlefield, 2006.

_____. "The Uniqueness Debate Revisited." In Rosenfeld, ed. *Deciphering the New Antisemitism*, pp. 289-325.

Hart, Don. "Update on General Synod Policy Changes and Socially Responsible Investing." United Church Funds (August 10, 2015), available online at http://ucfunds.org/2015/08/update-on-general-synod-policy-changes-and-sri/.

Hass, Amira. "Israel Knows hat Peace Just Doesn't Pay." *Haaretz* (November 5, 2009), available online at read more: http://www.haaretz.com/amira-hass-israel-knows-that-peace-just-doesn-t-pay-1.275795.

Hayden, Tom. "The Port Huron Statement." *The American Reader: Words that Moved a Nation*. Ed. Diane Ravitch. New York: Harper Perennial, 2000.

Helm, Sara. "ISIS in Gaza." *The New York Review of Books* LXII: 1 (January 14, 2016), 18-20.

Hellman, Ziv, "Why the Oslo Accords Failed," *MyJewishLearning* (2003), available online at http://www.myjewishlearning.com/article/why-the-oslo-accords-failed/.

Herf, Jeffrey. *Nazi Propaganda for the Arab World*. New Haven: Yale University Press, 2009.

Hermann, Tamar. "The Bi-National Idea in Israel/Palestine: Past and Present," *Nations and Nationalism* 11, no. 3 (2005).

Herzberg, Arthur. *The Zionist Idea: A Historical Analysis and Reader.* Philadelphia: The Jewish Publication Society, 1997.

Herzl, Theodor. *Der Judenstaat*, trans. Sylvie d'Avigdor. NY: Dover Publications, 1982.

Herzog, Chaim. *The Arab-Israeli Wars: War and Peace in the Middle East from the 1948 War of Independence to the Present*. Updated by Shlomo Gazit. New York: Vintage Books, 2010.

Hillman, Arye L. "Economic and Behavioral Foundations of Prejudice," in *Global Antisemitism: A Crisis of Modernity* ed. Charles Asher Small. Leiden, The Netherlands: Brill, 2013.

Hirsh, David, "The American Studies Association Boycott Resolution, Academic Freedom, and the Myth of the Institutional Boycott," in Nelson and Brahm, eds., *The Case Against Academic Boycotts of Israel*, pp. 119-127.

_____. "Rebels Against Zion." *Fathom Journal* 5 (2014), available online at http://www.fathomjournal.org/reviews-culture/rebels-against-zion/.

_____. "Antisemitism, not the accusation of antisemitism, is the dirty trick," *Engage* (September 3, 2015).

_____. "Accusations of Malicious Intent in Debates about the Palestine-Israel Conflict and about Antisemitism: The Livingstone Formulation, 'Playing the Antisemitism Card' and Contesting the Boundaries of Antiracist Discourse," *Transversal* 1 (2010): 47-76.

Hirschorn, Sara. "Ultra-nationalism, settlements and Jewish extremism: an interview with Sara Hirschorn." *Fathom* (Autumn 2015), available online at http://fathomjournal.org/ultra-nationalism-settlements-and-jewish-extremism-an-interview-with-sara-hirschhorn/.

Hitchens, Christopher. *Arguably: Essays by Christopher Hitchens*. New York: Twelve, 2011.

_____. *Hitch-22: A Memoir*. New York: Twelve, 2010.

_____. "Assassins of the Mind." Vanityfair.com. *Vanity Fair*, February 2009. Web. March 5, 2014.

Hobson, John A. *Imperialism; A Study*. London: J. Nisbet, 1902.

Honig-Parnass, Tivka. *False Prophets of Peace: Liberal Zionism and the Struggle for Palestine*. Chicago: Haymarket Books, 2011.

Horowitz, David. *State in the Making*. New York: Knopf, 1953.

Horowitz, Richard. "U.S. Church Puts 5 Banks From Israel on a Blacklist." *Jewish Business News* (January 14, 2016), available online at http://jewishbusinessnews. com/2016/01/14/u-s-church-puts-5-banks-from-israel-on-a-blacklist/.

Irwin, Robert. *For the Lust of Knowledge: the Orientalists and their Enemies*. London: Allen Lane, 2006.

Israel Today Staff. "International Expert: Children in Southern Israel Suffer PTSD." *Israel Today* (November 2, 2014), available online at http://www. israeltoday.co.il/NewsItem/tabid/178/nid/25475/Default.aspx.

Jacobson, Howard. "Let's see the 'criticism' of Israel for what it really is." *Independent* (July 10, 2014), available online at http://www.independent. co.uk/voices/commentators/howard-jacobson/howard-jacobson-letrsquos-see-the-criticism-of-israel-for-what-it-really-is-1624827.html.

Jacobson, William A. "List of Universities rejecting academic boycott of Israel." *Legal Insurrection*. (December 22, 2013), available online at http://legalinsurrection.com/2013/12/list-of-universities-rejecting-academic-boycott-of-israel/.

James, Clive. *Cultural Amnesia: Necessary Memories from History and the Arts*. New York: W. W. Norton, 2007.

"Jerusalem Sabeel Document: Principles for a Just Peace in Palestine Israel." Sabeel Ecumenical Liberation Theology Center (2010), available online at http://sabeel.org/statements.php?eventid=14.

Jewish Labor Committee. *Introduction to Labor: The U.S. Trade Union Movement and the Organized Jewish Community.* NY: JLC, 2008.

"Jews in the American Labor Movement." Ohio: Congress of Secular Jewish Organizations, 2015, available online at http://www.csjo.org/resources/essays/jews-in-the-american-labor-movement/.

Jikeli, Gunther. "A Framework for Assessing Antisemitism." In Rosenfeld, ed. *Deciphering the New Antisemitism*, pp. 43-76.

Johnson, Alan. "The Ugly History of the Apartheid Smear," *The Telegraph* (February 18, 2014), available online at http://blogs.telegraph.co.uk/news/alanjohnson/100259951/the-ugly-history-of-the-apartheid-smear/.

_____. "Intellectual Incitement: The Anti-Zionist Ideology and the Anti-Zionist Subject," in Nelson and Brahm, eds., *The Case Against Academic Boycotts of Israel*, pp. 259-281.

_____. "Parting Ways" *Fathom* 2, (2013), available online at http://www.fathomjournal.org/reviews-culture/parting-ways/

_____. "This barrier stops fascists: A response to Bethlehem unwrapped," *The Times of Israel* (blog), January 8, 2014, available online at http://blogs.timesofisrael.com/this-barrier-stops-fascists-a-response-to-bethlehem-unwrapped/.

_____. "More Palestinian than the Palestinians," *World Affairs* (blog) October 16, 2012, available online at http://www.worldaffairsjournal.org/blog/alan-johnson/judith-butler-more-palestinian-palestinians.

_____. "What a one-state solution really means." *The Jewish Chronicle*, October 17, 2012, available online at http://www.thejc.com/comment-and-debate/comment/86919/what-a-one-state-solution-really-means

Julius, Anthony. *Trials of the Diaspora: A History of Antisemitism in England.* Oxford: Oxford University Press, 2010.

"Kairos Palestine: A Moment of Truth." Bethlehem, available online at http://www.kairospalestine.ps/content/kairos-document.

Kalmar, Ivan Davidson and Derek J. Penslar, eds., *Orientalism and the Jews*. Hanover, NH: University Press of New England:, 2005.

Kaplan, Edward H. and Charles A. Small, "Anti-Israel Sentiment Predicts Anti-Semitism in Europe." *Journal of Conflict Resolution* 50 (2006): 548-561.

Karsh, Efraim. *Palestine Betrayed*. New Haven: Yale University Press, 2010.

Katanacho, Yohanna. *The Land of Christ*. Eugene OR: Wipf and Stock Publishers, 2013.

Kayyali, A. W., Ed. *Zionism, Imperialism, and Racism*. London: Croom Helm, 1979.

Kershner, Isabel. "Israel: Hawking Joins Academic Boycott," *New York Times*, May 9, 2013.

Khalaf, Issa. *Politics in Palestine: Arab Factionalism and Social Disintegration 1939-1948*. Albany: State University Press of New York, 1991.

Khalek, Rania. "Does the Nation have a problem with Palestinians?" *The Electronic Intifada* (December 19, 2013), available online at http://electronicintifada.net/content/does-nation-have-problem-palestinians/13022.

_____. From Ferguson to Palestine: Israeli Apartheid and the New Jim Crow." We Are Many (July 2, 2015), available online at http://wearemany.org/a/2015/07/from-ferguson-to-palestine.

Khalidi, Rashid. *The Iron Cage: The Story of the Palestinian Struggle for Statehood*. Boston: Beacon Press, 2006.

Kimmerling, Barch. *Zionism and Territory: The Socio-Territorial Dimensions of Zionist Politics*. Berkeley, CA: University of California Press, 1983.

Klaff, Lesley. "Holocaust Inversion." *Fathom* 5, 2014, available online at http://www.fathomjournal.org/policy-politics/holocaust-inversion/

_____. "Political and Legal Judgment: Misuses of the Holocaust in the UK." Social Science Research Network (May 8, 2013), available online at http://papers.ssrn.com/sol3/papers.cfm?abstract_id=2284423

Klein, Naomi. "Israel: Boycott, Divest, Sanction," *The Nation* (January 26, 2009), available online at http://www.thenation.com/article/israel-boycott-divest-sanction.

Koppelman, Nancy. "'When you want to *do* something, join us!':The Limits of the Social Justice Mandate in American Higher Education," in Nelson and Brahm, eds., *The Case Against Academic Boycotts of Israel*, pp. 202-217.

Küntzel, Matthias. *Jihad and Jew-Hatred: Islamism, Nazism, and the Roots of 9/11*, trans. Colin Meade. NY:Telos, 2009.

Landes, Richard, "Fatal Attraction: The Shared Antichrist of the Global Progressive Left and Jihad," in Nelson and Brahm, eds., *The Case Against Academic Boycotts of Israel*, pp. 293-310.

_____. *Heaven on Earth: The Varieties of the Millennial Experience*. New York: Oxford, 2011.

_____. "Jews as Contested Ground in Post-Modern Conspiracy Theory," *Jewish Political Studies Review*,Vol. 19:3-4 (2007): 9-34.

_____. "Does Burston really think it's legitimate to view BDS as Tikkun Olam?" Augan Stables (Decembr 18, 2010), available online at http://www.theaugeanstables.com/2010/12/18does-burston-really-think-its-legitimate-to-view-bds-as-tikkum-olam/.

Landes, Richard and Steven Katz, eds. *Paranoid Apocalypse: A Hundred Year Retrospective on The Protocols of the Elders of Zion*. NY: NYU Press, 2011.

Laqueur,Walter. *The Changing Face of Anti-Semitism: From Ancient Times to the Present Day*. Oxford, U.K.: Oxford University Press, 2006.

Laor,Yitzhak. *The Myths of Liberal Zionism*. London:Verso, 2009.

Latour, Bruno. "Why Has Critique Run out of Steam? From Matters of Fact to Matters of Concern," *Critical Inquiry* 30 (Winter 2004): 225-248.

Lenin, V.I. *Imperialism, the Highest Stage of Capitalism: A Popular Outline*. NY: International Publisher, trans., 1939.

Lewis, Bernard. *Semites & Anti-Semites*. NY: W.W. Norton, 1986.

Lewis, Bernard. *Semites & Anti-Semites*. NY: W.W. Norton, 1986.

Lim, Audrea, ed. *The Case for Sanctions Against Israel*. New York: Verso, 2012.

Loewenstein, Anthony and Ahmed Moor, eds. *After Zionism: One State for Israel and Palestine*. London: Saqi Books, 2012.

Lopez, Tyler. "Why #Pinkwashing Insults Gays and Hurts Palestinians." *Slate* (June 17, 2014), available online at http://www.slate.com/blogs/outward/2014/06/17/pinkwashing_and_homonationalism_discouraging_gay_travel_to_israel_hurts.html.

Makdisi, Saree. "The Power of Narrative: Reimagining the Palestinian Struggle." In Loewenstein and Moor, ed. *After Zionism: One State for Israel and Palestine*.

Makiya, Kanan. *Cruelty and Silence: War, Tyranny, Uprising, and the Arab World*. New York: W.W. Norton, 2007.

Mallmann, Klaus-Michael and Martin Cüppers. *Nazi Palestine: The Plans for the Extermination of the Jews in Palestine*, trans. Krista Smith. NY: Enigma Books, 2005.

Marcus, Kenneth L. "Is the Boycott, Divestment and Sanctions Movement Anti-Semitic?" in Nelson and Brahm, eds., *The Case Against Academic Boycotts of Israel*, pp. 243-258.

_____. "Anti-Zionism as Racism: Campus Anti-Semitism and the Civil Rights Act of 1964," *William and Mary Bill of Rights* 15, no. 3 (February 2007): 837-891.

_____. *Jewish Identity and Civil Rights in America*. (NY: Cambridge University Press, 2010).

_____. *The Definition of Anti-Semitism*. NY: Oxford, 2015.

Marcus, Sharon. "Surface Reading: An Introduction," *Representations* 108, no. 1 (Fall 2009): 1-21.

Marks, Jonathan. "'Zionist Attack Dogs'? The MLA's Debate on Israel Might Go Viral." *Chronicle of Higher Education*. May 21, 2014. Available at http://chronicle.com/blogs/conversation/2014/05/21/zionist-attack-dogs-the-mlas-debate-on-israel-might-go-viral/.

Marshall, Paul and Nina Shea. *Silenced: How Apostasy and Blasphemy Codes Are Choking Freedom Worldwide*. New York: Oxford UP, 2011.

Masri, Bassem. "The Fascinating Story of How the Ferguson-Palestine Solidarity Movement Came Together." *AlterNet* (February 18, 2015), available online at http://www.alternet.org/activism/frontline-ferguson-protester-and-palestinian-american-bassem-masri-how-ferguson2palestine.

Mead, Walter Russel. "Jerusalem Syndrome: Decoding The Israel Lobby", *Foreign Affairs* (November/December 2007), available online at http://www.foreignaffairs.com/articles/63029/walter-russell-mead/jerusalem-syndrome.

Mearsheimer, John J. and Stephen M. Walt. *The Israel Lobby and US Foreign Policy*. London, Penguin, 2007.

Mendelson, Edward. Ed. "Preface." *The English Auden: Poems, Essays, and Dramatic Writings 1927-1939*. London: Faber & Faber, 1977. xiii-xxiii.

Mendes, Philip and Nick Dyrenfurth. *Boycotting Israel is Wrong*. Sydney: NewSouth Publishing, 2015.

Michaels, Sean. "Paul McCartney promises Israel gig will go ahead despite death threats." *The Guardian* (September 16, 2008), available online at http://www.theguardian.com/music/2008/sep/16/mccartney.refuses.to.cancel.gig.

Miller, Arthur. *Timebends: A Life*. New York: Grove Press, 1987.

Moor, Ahmed. "BDS is a long term project with radically transformative potential." *Mondoweiss* (April 22, 2010), available online at http://mondoweiss.net/2010/04/bds-is-a-long-term-project-with-radically-transformative-potential/.

Morris, Benny. *Righteous Victims: A History of the Zionist-Arab Conflict, 1881-2001*. New York: Random House, 2001.

_____. "The Liar as Hero," *The New Republic* (March 17, 2011), available online at http://www.newrepublic.com/article/books/magazine/85344/ilan-pappe-sloppy-dishonest-historian.

_____, *One State, Two States: Resolving the Israel/Palestine Conflict*. New Haven, CT: Yale University Press, 2010.

Mirawiec, Laurent. *The Mind of Jihad*. NY: Oxford, 2006.

Nafisi, Azar. *Reading Lolita in Tehran: A Memoir in Books*. New York: Random House, 2004.

Nathan-Kazis, Josh. "Survey of Campus BDS Finds Few Serious Cases," *The Forward*, May 4, 2011, available online at http://forward.com/articles/137518/survey-of-campus-bds-finds-few-serious-cases/#ixzz30EMT88hi.

Nelson, Cary, "Introduction." in Nelson and Brahm, eds., *The Case Against Academic Boycotts of Israel*, pp. 12-29.

_____ "The Problem With Judith Butler," in Nelson and Brahm, eds., *The Case Against Academic Boycotts of Israel*, pp. 164-201.

_____. "The New Assault on Israeli Academia (and us). *Fathom* (Spring 2014), available online at http://fathomjournal.org/the-new-assault-on-israeli-academia-and-us/.

_____. "Multi-stage Coordinated Unilateralism: A Proposal to Rescue the Two-State Paradigm," *Fathom* (July 1, 2015).

Nelson, Cary, Rachel S. Harris, and Kenneth W. Stein, "The History of Israel," in Nelson and Brahm, eds., *The Case Against Academic Boycotts of Israel*, pp. 385-440.

Nelson, Cary, and Gabriel Noah Brahm, eds., *The Case Against Academic Boycotts of Israel* (Chicago and New York: MLA Members for Scholars' Rights/Distributed by Wayne State University Press, 2015).

Neumann, Boaz. *Land and Desire in Early Zionism*. University Press of New England: Waltham, MA, 2011.

Nirenberg, David. *Anti-Judaism: The Western Tradition*. New York: Norton, 2013.

Oliver, Anne-Marie and Paul Steinberg. *The Road to Martyr's Square: A Journey into the World of the Suicide Bomber*. NY: Oxford, 2005.
Ottolenghi, Emanuele. "Present-day Antisemitism and the Centrality of the Jewish Alibi." in Alvin H. Rosenfeld, *Resurgent Antisemitism: Global Perspectives*.

"Palestinian Authority, The." Jewish Virtual Library, available online at http://www.jewishvirtuallibrary.org/jsource/Peace/PalAuthority.html.

Palestinian Campaign for the Academic and Cultural Boycott of Israel (PACBI). "Israel's Exceptionalism: Normalizing the Abnormal." PACBI website (October 31, 2011), available online at http://www.pacbi.org/etemplate.php?id=1749.

Palumbo-Liu, David. "Why an Academic Boycott?" *Los Angeles Review of Books*. March 16, 2014. Available at https://lareviewofbooks.org/essay/why-an-academic-boycott.

Pappé, Ilan. T*he Idea of Israel: A History of Power and Knowledge*. London: Verso, 2014.

Patterson, David. "Denial, Evasion, and Antihistorical Antisemitism: The Continuing Assault on Memory." In Rosenfeld, ed. *Deciphering the New Antisemitism*, pp. 326–349.

Penslar, Derek J. "Zionism, Colonialism and Postcolonialism." *The Journal of Israeli History* 20: 2-3 (2001), 84-98.

_____. "Anti-Semites on Zionism: From Indifference to Obsession." *The Journal of Israeli History* 25:1 (March 2006), 13-31.

Penslar, Derek J., Michael R. Marrus, and Janice Gross Stein, eds. *Contemporary Antisemitism: Canada and the World*. Toronto: University of Toronto Press, 2005.

Pinker, Steven. *The Black Slate: The Modern Denial of Human Nature*. New York: Penguin, 2003.

Pogrund, Benjamin, "Israel has many injustices. But it is not an apartheid state," *The Guardian* (May 22, 2015).

Poliakov, Léon. *The History of Anti-Semitism*, vol. 1, *From the Time of Christ to the Court Jews*, trans. Richard Howard. NY: Vanguard, 1974.

Poller, Nidra. *Al Dura: Long Range Ballistic Myth*. Paris: authorship international, 2014.

Postone, Moishe. "Zionism, anti-semitism and the left: an interview with Moishe Postone," *Workers' Liberty*, February 5, 2010, available online at http://www.workersliberty.org/story/2010/02/05/zionism-anti-semitism-and-left

Prashad, Vijay. "Understanding the Boycott of Israel's Universities." washingtonpost.com. *Washington Post*, January 25, 2014. Web. March 2014.

Puar, Jasbir. "Citation and Censure: Pinkwashing and the Sexual Politics of Talking about Israel." In Chatterjee and Maira, eds. *The Imperial University*, 281-297.

_____. "Inhumanist Biopolitics: How Palestine Matters." Unpublished transcript (2016).

Ravitch, Diane. "Multiculturalism: E Pluribus Plures." *Debating P.C.: The Controversy Over Political Correctness on College Campuses*. Ed. Paul Berman. New York: Laurel Trade Paperbacks, 1992. 271-98.

Ra'ad, Basem. *Hidden Histories: Palestine And The Eastern Mediterranean*. London: Pluto Press, 2010.

"Report of the Secretary-General's Panel of Inquiry on the 31 May 2010 Flotilla Incident," available online at http://www.un.org/News/dh/infocus/middle_east/Gaza_Flotilla_Panel_Report.pdf.

Reuters. "Islamic State Sanctioned Organ Harvesting from Captives in Document Taken in US Raid." Vice News (December 25, 2015), available online at https://news.vice.com/article/islamic-state-sanctioned-organ-harvesting-from-captives-in-document-taken-in-us-raid.

Richter, Elihu D. "How to (not) defeat the lies of BDS." *The Times of Israel* (December 6, 2015), available online at http://blogs.timesofisrael.com/how-to-not-defeat-the-lies-of-bds/.

Robbins, Bruce. "The Logic of the Beneficiary." *n+1 Issue* 24 (Winter 2016), available online at https://nplusonemag.com/issue-24/politics/the-logic-of-the-beneficiary/.

Robinson, David. *The Status of Higher Education Teaching Personnel in Israel, the West Bank and Gaza*. Ottawa: Canadian Association of University Teachers, 2010.
Rose, Jacqueline. *The Last Resistance*. London: Verso, 2007.

Rosen, David M. "Isaiah Silver and the Strange Crimes of Israeli Anthropologists." *Anthro-Dialogue* (October 28, 2015), available online at https://anthrodialogue.wordpress.com/2015/10/28/isaiah-silver-and-the-strange-crimes-of-israeli-anthropologists/.

Rosenberg, Yair. "American Historical Association Decisively Rejects Anti-Israel Resolution, 111-51." *Tablet* (January 11, 2016), available online at http://www.tabletmag.com/scroll/196523/american-historical-association-decisively-rejects-anti-israel-resolution-111-51.

Rosenfeld, Alvin H., ed. *Resurgent Antisemitism: Global Perspectives*. Bloomington, IN: Indiana University Press, 2013.

_____. ed. *Deciphering the New Antisemitism*. Bloomington, IN: Indiana University Press, 2015.

Rossman-Benjamin, Tammi. "Interrogating the Academic Boycotters of Israel on American Campuses," in Nelson and Brahm, eds., *The Case Against Academic Boycotts of Israel*, pp. 218-234.

Rotenstreich, Nathan. "The Revival of the Fossil Remnant: Or Toynbee and Jewish Nationalism," *Jewish Social Studies* 24, no. 3 (July 1962): 131-143.

Rothschild, Nathalie. "The Blood Libel That Won't Quit." *Tablet* (December 3, 2012), available online at http://www.tabletmag.com/jewish-news-and-politics/118035/the-blood-libel-that-wont-quit.

Rubin, Barry. *Assimilation and Its Discontents*. NY: Times Books, 1995.

Rubin, Barry and Wolfgang G. Schwanitz. *Nazis, Islamists, and the Making of the Modern Middle East*. New Haven: Yale University Press, 2014.

Rynhold, Jonathan, and Dov Waxman. "Ideological Change and Israel's Disengagement from Gaza." *Political Science Quarterly* 123:1 (Spring 2008), available online at http://www.baruch.cuny.edu/wsas/academics/political_science/documents/IdeologicalChangeandIsrael.pdf.

Sachar, Howard M. *A History of Israel: From the Rise of Zionism to Our Time*. 3rd Edition. New York: Alfred A. Knopf, 2010.
Sacramento BDS, "Products." Available online at http://sacbds.org/products/.

Saghiyeh, Hazem and Saleh Bashir. "Universalizing the Holocaust: How Arabs and Palestinians relate to the Holocaust and how the Jews relate to the Palestinian victim," *Palestine-Israel Journal*, Vol.5 Nos. 3 & 4, 1998.

Said, Edward. *Orientalism*. New York: Vintage Books, 1979.

_____. *Culture and Imperialism*. Vintage: New York, 1993.

_____. "The Morning After," *London Review of Books* (October 21, 1993), available online at http://www.lrb.co.uk/v15/n20/edward-said/the-morning-after.

_____. *After the Last Sky: Palestinian Lives*, 2nd edition. NY: Columbia University Press, 1999.

_____. *Blaming the Victims: Spurious Scholarship and the Palestine Question*. Verso: New York, 2001.

Salaita, Steven. *Israel's Dead Soul*. Philadelphia: Temple University Press, 2100.

_____. "How to Practice BDS in Academe." *The Electronic Intifada*. May 27, 2014. Available at http://electronicintifada.net/blogs/steven-salaita/how-practice-bds-academe.

Salih, Sabah A. "Islamism, BDS, and the West," in Nelson and Brahm, eds., *The Case Against Academic Boycotts of Israel*, pp. 141–155.

Sand, Shlomo. *The Words and the Land: Israeli Intellectuals and the Nationalist Myth*. Los Angeles: Semiotext(e), 2011.

Santis, Yitzak and Gerald M. Steinberg. "On 'Jew-Washing' and BDS: How Jewish anti-Israel activists are gaining influence among Christian groups." *The Jewish Week*, July 24, 2012, available online at http://www.thejewish-week.com/editorial-opinion/opinion/jew-washing-and-bds.

Sasson, Talia. *Havat Da'at (Beina'im) Benose Ma'ahazin Bilti Murshim* (Opinion Concrning Unauthorized Outposts). Jerualem, 2005.

Scham, Paul, Walid Salem, and Benjamin Pogrund, eds. *Shared Histories: A Palestinian-Israeli Dialogue*. Walnut Creek, CA: Left Coast, 2005.

Scham, Paul, Benjamin Pogrund, and As'ad Ghanem, eds., special issue, *Shared Narratives—A Palestinian-Israeli Dialogue*, Israel Studies 18, no. 2 (Summer 2013).

Schama, Simon. *Two Rothschilds and the Land of Israel*. NY: Knopf, 1978.

Scheindlin, Dahlia. "The quieter, more dangerous boycott." +972 (September 3, 2015), available online at http://972mag.com/the-quieter-more-dangerous-boycott/111353/.

Schiff, Ze'ev and Ehud Ya'ari. *Israel's Lebanon War*. New York: Simon and Schuster, 1984.

Schipani, Daniel. *Conscientization and Creativity*. Lanham, MD: University Press of America, 1984.

Schreck, Adam. "Qatar criticized as Gaza ceasefire talks collapse." *The Globe and Mail* (August 21, 2014), available online at http://www.theglobeand-mail.com/news/world/qatar-criticized-as-gaza-ceasefire-talks-collapse/article20148907/.

Schulman, Sara. "Israel and 'Pinkwashing.'" *The New York Times* (November 22, 2011), available online at http://www.nytimes.com/2011/11/23/opinion/pinkwashing-and-israels-use-of-gays-as-a-messaging-tool.html?_r=0.

Schwartz, Yardena. "In Palestinian city of the future, few residents and charges of collusion with Israel." *Jewish Telegraphic Agency* (January 21, 2016), available online.

Sela, Avraham. Ed. *The Continuum Political Encyclopedia of the Middle East.* New York: Continuum, 2002.

Shafir, Gershon. *Land, Labor, and the Origins of the Israeli-Palestinian Conflict, 1882-1914.* Berkeley, CA: University of California Press, 1989.

Shahak, Israel. *Jewish History, Jewish Religion: The Weight of Three Thousand Years.* London: Pluto Press, 2008.

Shapira, Anita. *Israel: A History.* Waltham, MA: Brandeis University Press, 2012.

Sharansky, Natan. "3D Test of Anti-Semitism: Demonization, Double Standards, Delegitimization." *Jewish Political Studies Review,* 16 (Fall 2004): 3-4, available online at http://jcpa.org/phas/phas-sharansky-f04.htm.

Shatz, Adam. "Is Palestine Next?" *The London Review of Books,* July 14, 2011, available online at http://www.lrb.co.uk/v33/n14/adam-shatz/is-palestine-next.

Shavit, Ari. *My Promised Land: The Triumph and Tragedy of Israel.* NY: Random House, 2013.

_____. "We've Entered the Final Decade to Save Israel." *Haaretz* (December 24, 2015), available online at http://www.haaretz.com/opinion/. premium-1.693502.

Shenhav, Yehouda. *Beyond the Two State Solution: A Jewish Political Essay.* Cambridge: Polity Press, 2012.

Shepherd, Robin. *A State Beyond the Pale: Europe's Problem With Israel.* London: Orion, 2009.

Smith, Barbara. *The Roots of Separatism in Palestine: British Economic Policy, 1920-29.* Syracuse: Syracuse University Press, 1993.

Smith, Jordan Michael. "An Unpopular Man." *New Republic* (July7, 2015), available online at https://newrepublic.com/article/122257/unpopular-man-norman-finkelstein-comes-out-against-bds-movement.

Smith, Ted A., and Amy-Jill Levine. "Habits of Anti-Judaism: Critiquing a PCUSA report on Israel/Palestine." *The Christian Century* (June 29, 2010), available online at http://middle-east-analysis.blogspot.com/2010/06/habits-of-anti-judaism-critiquing-pcusa.html.

Sobrino, Jon. *The True Church and the Poor*, trans. Matthew O'Connell. Maryknoll, NY: Orbis Books, 1984.

_____. *Jesus in Latin American*, trans. Robert R. Barr. Maryknoll, NY: Orbis Books, 1987.

Solheim, James. "Jerusalem Conference Calls Christian Zionism a 'heresy.'" *Worldwide Faith News* (April 28, 2004).

Spivak, Gayatri Chakravorty. "Can the Subaltern Speak?" In *Marxism and the Interpretation of Culture*, ed. Cary Nelson and Lawrence Grossberg. Urbana: University of Illinois Press, 1988, pp. 271-316.

Stein, Kenneth. *The Land Question in Palestine, 1917-1939.* Durham: University of North Carolina Press, 1984.

_____. "Palestine's Rural Economy, 1917-1939." *Studies in Zionism* 8:13 (1987), 25-49.

_____. *Heroic Diplomacy: Sadat, Kissinger, Carter, Begin and the Quest for Arab-Israeli Peace.* New York: Routledge, 1999.

_____. *History, Politics, and Diplomacy of the Arab-Israeli Conflict: A Source Document Reader for College Courses and Adult Education.* E-book: www.israel.org, 2013.

Steinberg. Gerald M. "On Europe, terrorism and demonizing Israel: Time for a reset." *The Times of Israel*. October 19, 2015, available online at http://blogs.timesofisrael.com/on-europe-terrorism-and-demonizing-israel-time-for-a-reset/.

Steinberg, Gerald and Yitzak Santis, "On Jew-Washing and BDS," *The Jewish Week*, (July 24, 2012), available online at http://www.thejewishweek.com/editorial-opinion/opinion/jew-washing-and-bds.

Stern, Kenneth S. *Antisemitism Today: How It is Different and How to Fight It.* NY: American Jewish Committee, 2006.

Sternhell, Zeev. "In Defense of Liberal Zionism." *New Left Review* 62 (March-April 2010).

Strenger, Carlo. "Judith Butler: Zionism is Opposed to Jewish Values." *Huffington Post* (January 14, 2003).

Susser, Asher. "The Two-State Solution: Getting From Here to There." *Foreign Policy Research Institute E-Notes* (October 2012), available online at http://www.fpri.org/docs/media/Susser_-_Two_State_Solution.pdf.

Sydie, Rosalin. *Natural Women / Cultured Men: A Feminist Perspective on Sociological Theory.* New York: NYU Press, 1994.

Taguieff, Pierre Andre. *Rising from the Muck: The New Anti-Semitism in Europe.* Chicago: Ivan Dee, 2004.

Tamari, Sandra, and Tara Ferguson. "From Ferguson to Palestine, We See Us." *Huffington Post Blog* (October 16, 2015), available online at http://www.huffingtonpost.com/tara-thompson/from-ferguson-to-palestine_b_8307832.html.

Teoh, Siew Hong, Ivo Welch, and C. Paul Wazzan, "The Effect of Socially Activist Investment Policies on the Financial Markets: Evidence from the South African Boycott," *Journal of Business* 72:1 (January 1999).

Tessler, Mark. *A History of the Israeli-Palestinian Conflict*, 2nd edition. Bloomington: Indiana University Press, 2009.

Thompson, Thomas L. *Early History of the Israelite People from the Written and Archaeological Sources.* Leiden: Brill Academic Publishers, 1992.

Trigano, Shmuel. "Les juifs de France visés par l'Intifada?" *Observatoire du monde juif*, 1 (November 2000), available online at http://obs.monde.juif.free.fr/pdf/omj01.pdf.

Troen, Ilan S. *Imagining Zion: Dreams, Designs, and Realities in a Century of Jewish Settlement*. New Haven: Yale University Press, 2003.

_____. "The Campaign to Boycott Israeli Universities: Historical and Ideological Sources," in Nelson and Brahm, eds., *The Case Against Academic Boycotts of Israel*, pp. 312-326.

_____. "The Israeli-Palestinian Relationship in Higher Education: Evidence from the Field," in Nelson and Brahm, eds., *The Case Against Academic Boycotts of Israel*, pp. 375-383.

Troy, Gil. *Moynihan's Moment; America's Fight Against Zionism as Racism*. Oxford University Press: New York, 2013.

Troy, Gil and Martin J. Raffel. "Israel: Jewish and Democratic." NY: Israel Action Network, 2013, available online at http://israelactionnetwork.org/wp-content/uploads/2013/08/Israel-Jewish-and-Democratic-.pdf.

Turck, Nancy. "Arab Boycott of Israel," *Foreign Affairs* 55, no. 3 (April 1977): 472-493.

Turki, Fawaz. *The Disinherited: Journal of a Palestinian Exile*. New York: Monthly Review Press, 1972.

"Two States for Two Peoples." Presbyterians for Middle East Peace, 2016, available online at http://www.pfmep.org/images/stories/PDFs/TwoStatesforTwoPeoples.pdf.

Tzidkiyahu, Eran. "'Whose surroundings we have blessed': The Islamic Movement in Israel Unites around the Al-Aqsa Mosque." *Bayan* No. 6 (December 2015), available online at https://www.academia.edu/19801738/Bayan_The_Arabs_in_Israel_No._6_Recent_Crisis_English_.

Vattimo, Gianni, and Michael Marder, eds. *Deconstructing Zionism: A Critique of Political Metaphysics*. New York: Bloomsbury, 2013.

Victory for Israel at APHA. *Jerusalem: Hebrew University of Israel Faculty of Medicine*, 2013, available online ar httos://medicine.ekmd.huji.ac.il/schools/publichealth/En/newsandEvents/news/Pages/APHA.aspx.

Vilnay Ze'ev., *ha-Yishuvim be-Yiśrael : 'arukhim be-seder alef-bet be-li yat tsiyurim e-tarshimim*. [The Settlements in Israel] (Hebrew) (Tel-Aviv, 1951).

Volkov, Shulamit. "Readjusting Cultural Codes: Reflections on Anti-Semitism and Anti-Zionism." *Journal of Israeli History: Politics, Society, Culture* 25, no. 1 (2006): 51-62.

Walzer, Michael. "On Proportionality." *The New Republic* (January 7, 2009), available online at https://newrepublic.com/article/64580/proportionality.

Weisfeld, Hannah. "When BDS And Anti-Semitism Meet," *The Daily Beast*, December 14, 2012, available online at http://www.thedailybeast.com/articles/2012/12/14/when-bds-and-anti-semitism-meet.html.

Weiss, Martin A. *Arab League Boycott of Israel*. Washington, D.C.: Congressional Research Service, (June 10, 2015), available online at http://www.fas.org/sgp/crs/mideast/RL33961.pdf.

Weiss, Phillip. "Ululating at Vassar: the Israel/Palestine conflict comes to America," *Mondoweiss* (March 20, 2014), available online at http://mondo-weiss.net/2014/03/ululating-israelpalestine-conflict.html.

Weiss, Phillip and Adam Horowitz, "'The Nation' and the privileging of Jewish voices on Israel/Palestine." *Mondoweiss*, December 23, 2013, http://mondoweiss.net/2013/12/privileging-voices-israelpalestine.html.

"What is Palestinian Liberation Theology." *Cornerstone* 1 (Spring 1994), Sabeel Liberation Theology Center, available online at http://sabeel.org/datadir/en-events/ev19/files/Issue%201.pdf.

Whitlam, Keith. *The Invention of Ancient Israel: The Silencing of Palestinian History*. Routledge: London, 1996.

Wieseltier, Leon. "The Academic Boycott of Israel is a Travesty," *New Republic*. (Dec 17, 2013).

Williams, Joanna. "BDS: censorship disguised as justice." *Spiked* (February 3, 2016), available online at http://www.spiked-online.com/newsite/article/bds-censorship-disguised-as-justice/17995#.VrJZ5FJZFUM.

Willis, Ellen. "Is There Still a Jewish Question? Why I'm an Anti-Anti-Zionist." In Tony Kushner and Alisa Solomon, eds. *Wresting with Zion: Progressive Jewish-American Responses to the Israeli-Palestine Conflict.* New York: Grove Press, 2003, pp. 226- 232. Available at http://web.archive.org/web/20130618070828/http://contested-terrain.net/willis.

Winkett, Lucy. "Bethlehem Unwrapped is about 'beautiful resistance' not taking sides," *Guardian Comment is Free*, January 2, 2014, available online at http://www.theguardian.com/commentisfree/2014/jan/02/bethlehem-unwrapped-not-taking-sides-israel-security-wall.

Wistrich, Robert S. *A Lethal Obsession: Anti-Semitism from Antiquity to the Global Jihad.* NY: Random House, 2010.

_____. *From Ambivalence to Betrayal: The Left, the Jews, and Israel.* Lincoln: University of Nebraska Press, 2013.

_____. "Anti-Zionism and Anti-Semitism in the 21st Century." *Jewish Virtual Library*, available online at http://www.jewishvirtuallibrary.org/jsource/isdf/text/wistrich.html.

Wittenberg, Ed. "Oberlin College Rabbi Downplays Impact of Divestment Resolution," *Cleveland Jewish News*, May 7, 2013, availaable online at http://www.clevelandjewishnews.com/news/local/article_5e71bbc0-b777-11e2-b41b-0019bb2963f4.html.

Wolosky, Shira, "Teaching in Transnational Israel: An Ethics of Difference," in Nelson and Brahm, eds., *The Case Against Academic Boycotts of Israel*, pp. 352-364.

_____. *Feminist Theory across Disciplines: Feminist Community and American Women's Poetry.* NY: Routledge, 2013.

_____. "Cosmopolitanism vs. Normative Difference: From Habermas to Levinas," *The Israeli Nation State: Political, Constitutional and Cultural Changes* ed. Yedidya Stern and Fania-Oz Salzberger. Brighton, MA: Academic Studies Press, forthcoming.

Yahel, Havatzelet, Ruth Kark, and Seth J. Frantzman. "Are the Negev Bedouin an Indigenous People?" Middle East Quarterly (Summer 2012): 3-14.

Yakobson, Alexander and Amnon Rubenstein. *Israel and the Family of Nations: The Jewish nation-state and human rights*. Trans. by Ruth Morris and Ruchie Avital. NY: Routledge, 2009.

Zakim, Michael, and Feisal G. Mohamed. "The Best of Intentions: Debating the ASA Boycott." *Dissent* (November 5, 2014), available online at http://www.dissentmagazine.org/online_articles/best-of-intentions-asa -boycott-bds-debate.

# NOTES ON CONTRIBUTORS

**Paul Berman**, a senior editor of *The New Republic*, writes widely about politics and literature. His books include *Terror and Liberalism*, *The Flight of the Intellectuals*, *A Tale of Two Utopias*, and *Power and the Idealists*.

**Russell A. Berman**, Walter A. Haas Professor in the Humanities at Stanford University and Professor of Comparative Literature and German Studies, is the author of *The Rise of the Modern German Novel: Crisis and Charisma*; *Modern Culture and Critical Theory: Art, Politics and the Legacy of the Frankfurt School*; *Enlightenment of Empire: Colonial Discourse in German Culture*; *Anti-Americanism in Europe: A Cultural Problem*; *Fiction Sets You Free: Literature, Liberty and Western Culture* and other books. He is a former president of the Modern Language Association.

**Gabriel Noah Brahm**, Associate Professor of English at Northern Michigan University, is coauthor of *The Jester and the Sages: Mark Twain in Conversation with Nietzsche, Freud and Marx* and coeditor of *Prosthetic Territories: Politics and Hypertechnologies*.

**Emily Budick**, Ann and Joseph Edelman Professor of American Studies and Director of the Center for Literary Studies at the Hebrew University of Jerusalem, is the author of the forthcoming *The Subject of Holocaust Fiction* and eleven other books.

**Mitchell Cohen** teaches political theory and contemporary politics at Baruch College. His books include *The Wager of Lucien Goldmann and Zion and State*.

**Donna Divine**, Morningstar Professor of Government at Smith College, is the author of *Politics and Society in Ottoman Palestine: The Arab Struggle for*

*Survival and Power; Postcolonial Theory and The Arab-Israeli Conflict;* and *Exiled in the Homeland: Zionism and the Return to Mandate Palestine.*

**Carol F. S. Edelman** is CSU Chico Emerita Professor of Sociology and former Associate Dean of Behavioral and Social Sciences.

**Samuel M. Edelman** is CSU Chico Emeritus Professor and former Dean of Undergraduate Education at the American Jewish University.

**Rachel Fish** is associate director of the Shusterman Center for Israel Studies at Brandeis University.

**Harvey E. Goldberg** is professor emeritus in the Sarah Allen Shaine Chair in Sociology and Anthropology at the Hebrew University of Jerusalem. Currently he serves as President of the Israeli Anthropological Association. His work has sought to combine anthropology and Jewish Studies, including a translation from Hebrew of an indigenous account of the Jews of Libya, *The Book of Mordechai* by Mordecai HaCohen. Goldberg has authored *Cave Dwellers and Citrus Growers; Jewish Life in Muslim Libya; Jewish Passages: Cycles of Jewish Life,* edited *Sephardi* and *Middle Eastern Jewries,* and co-edited *Perspectives on Israeli Anthropology* with Esther Hertzog, Orit Abuhav, and Emanuel Marx.

**Rachel S. Harris** teaches Israeli and comparative literature at the University of Illinois at Urbana-Champaign. She is the author of *An Ideological Death: Suicide in Israeli Literature* and the coeditor of *War: Dissent and Narrative in Israeli Culture and Society.*

**David Hirsh**, Lecturer in Sociology at Goldsmiths College, University of London, is the founder of Engage, a campaign against academic boycotts of Israel. He is the author of *Law Against Genocide: Cosmopolitan Trials.*

**Alan Johnson** is the Editor of *Fathom: for a deeper understanding of Israel and the region.* A professor of democratic theory and politics, he is a Senior Research Associate at the Foreign Policy Centre, an editorial board member at Dissent, and co-author of the 2006 "Euston Manifesto," a modern statement of social democratic antitotalitarianism. He blogs at *World Affairs.*

**Nancy Koppelman** is professor of American Studies and Humanities at Evergreen State College. She creates and team-teaches full time inter-disciplinary undergraduate academic programs with colleagues from the humanities, the sciences, and the social sciences, all based on the pedagogy of learning communities. For four years, she was the Lead Faculty for the Teaching American History Project serving school districts in South Puget Sound, WA.

**Richard Landes**, Professor of History at Boston University, is the author of *Relics, Apocalypse, and the Deceits of History*; *Heaven on Earth: The Varieties of the Millennial Experience*, and other books.

**Kenneth L. Marcus** is President and General Counsel of the Brandeis University's Louis D. Brandeis Center for Human Rights Under Law and author of *Jewish Identity and Civil Rights in America and The Definition of Anti-Semitism*.

**Sharon Ann Musher**, Associate Professor of History at Richard Stockton University of New Jersey, is the author of *Democratic Art: The New Deal's Influence on American Culture*.

**Cary Nelson**, Jubilee Professor of Liberal Arts and Sciences and Professor of English at the University of Illinois at Urbana-Champaign is the author or editor of 30 books, including *Manifesto of a Tenured Radical*; *No University is an Island: Saving Academic Freedom*; and *Revolutionary Memory: Recovering the Poetry of the American Left*. He was president of the American Association of University Professors from 2006-2012 and is currently co-chair of The Third Narrative's Advisory Council. His work and career are the subject of the edited collection *Cary Nelson and the Struggle for the University*.

**Asaf Romirowsky** is a fellow at the Middle East Forum and coauthor of *Religion, Politics, and the Origins of Palestine Refugee Relief*.

**Sabah A. Salih**, professor of English at Bloomsburg University, is the author of *Modernism or Art Under the Watchful Eyes of Art*.

**Todd Stavrakos** is Pastor of the Gladwyne Presbyterian Church in Montgomery County, Pennsylvania, near Philadelphia.

**Kenneth W. Stein**, Professor of Contemporary Middle Eastern History, Political Science and Israeli Studies at Emory University, is the author of *Heroic Diplomacy: Sadat, Kissinger, Carter, Begin, and the Quest for Arab-Israeli Peace*; *Making Peace Among Arabs and Israelis: Lessons from Fifty Years of Negotiating Experience*; and *The Land Question in Palestine, 1917-1939*. He is the president of the Atlanta based Center for Israel Education.

**Kenneth S. Stern** is executive director of the Justus and Karin Rosenberg Foundation. His books include *Loud Hawk: The United States Versus the American Indian Movement and Antisemitism Today: How It is Different and How to Fight It.*

**Ilan Troen**, Stoll Family Chair in Israel Studies and Director of the Schusterman Center for Israel Studies at Brandeis University, is also Lopin Professor of Modern History, emeritus, Ben-Gurion University of the Negev. He is the author or editor of eleven books, including *Imagining Zion: Dreams, Designs and Realities in a Century of Jewish Settlement*; and, with Jacob Lassner, *Jews and Muslims in the Arab World; Haunted by Pasts Real and Imagined.*

**Shira Wolosky**, professor of American Studies and English at Hebrew University, has written *Poetry and Public Discourse in Nineteenth Century America; Language Mysticism: The Negative Way of Language in Eliot, Beckett, and Cela; Feminist Theory across Disciplines: Feminist Community and American Women's Poetry* and other books.

# INDEX